WRONGS

OF

PASSAGE

WRONGS OF PASSAGE

Fraternities, Sororities, Hazing, and Binge Drinking

HANK NUWER

*Indiana
University
Press*

BLOOMINGTON & INDIANAPOLIS

This book is a publication of

Indiana University Press
601 North Morton Street
Bloomington, IN 47404-3797 USA

http://www.indiana.edu/~iupress

Telephone orders 800-842-6796
Fax orders 812-855-7931
Orders by e-mail iuporder@indiana.edu.

The paper used in this publication meets the minimum requirements
of American National Standard for Information Sciences—Perma-
nence of Paper for Printed Library Materials, ANSI Z39.48-1984.

MANUFACTURED IN THE UNITED STATES OF AMERICA

Library of Congress Cataloging-in-Publication Data

Nuwer, Hank.
Wrongs of passage : fraternities, sororities, hazing, and binge
drinking / by Hank Nuwer.
p.   cm.
Includes bibliographical references (p.   ) and index.
ISBN 0-253-33596-5 (alk. paper)
1. Greek letter societies—United States. 2. Hazing—United States.
3. College Students—Alcohol use—United States. 4. College
students—United States—Conduct of life. I. Title.
LJ51.N89 1999
378.1'98'55—dc21   99-14864

1   2   3   4   5   04   03   02   01   00   99

For Jenine Nuwer, Frederick D. Kershner, Fraser Drew,
and the Rev. Msgr. Cyril Trevett,
and in memoriam,
Frank J. Ruck, Ray Ballou, and Charles Wright.

The cold passion for truth hunts in no pack.

—Robinson Jeffers

CONTENTS

PROLOGUE

My research on hazing began in 1978 when I wrote "The Dead Souls of Hell Week" for *Human Behavior* magazine. *Broken Pledges: The Deadly Rite of Hazing,* my first book on the subject, came out in 1990. That book focused on the alcohol-related death of fraternity pledge Chuck Stenzel at Alfred University following a hazing incident, and the subsequent crusade of his mother, Eileen Stevens, to obtain answers about his death that she had not been able to get from the college and local authorities.

I had hoped *Broken Pledges* would eliminate hazing occurrences the way Upton Sinclair's *The Jungle* reduced abuses in the meat-packing industry. It did not. Too many members of collegiate social clubs—encouraged by alumni and insufficiently discouraged by parents and educators—continue to haze, convinced that making pledges earn membership by displaying submission ensures fraternal group stability and their high status on campus. Moreover, some college administrators who were in fraternities themselves maintain alliances with their own national (or international) fraternal organizations. These administrators may be unable to recognize the importance of expelling misfit Greek chapters, or may reject damaging information about a fraternity and place too much faith in its empty promises to reform. Also problematic are some administrators' attempts to protect their institution's reputation by blocking the disclosure of particulars to the press when members of student organizations commit offenses such as criminal hazing. On the other side of the issue, many fraternity leaders maintain that school officials at Bowdoin and other colleges who are biased against Greek organizations have discriminated against young citizens by banning national Greek groups, thus taking away these citizens' first-amendment right to "protected association." Some of the leaders also

charge that anti-alcohol advocates were overzealous and overly concerned with political correctness when they convinced individual states
to raise the drinking age to twenty-one.

I wrote this second book on collegiate hazing because sweeping
developments in fraternal affairs dictated that I cover the topic more
broadly than I did in *Broken Pledges*. In addition, after completing a
computer-assisted list of fraternity-related deaths, I concluded that the
high number of deaths among members of campus social, athletic, and
spirit clubs made it essential that hazing be studied as it relates to alcohol health and safety risks that not only the fraternal world but also
the public and higher education must confront. Therefore this book
examines alcohol misuse as well as hazing, because drinking is often a
factor when collegians die as a result of roof falls, vehicular accidents,
and fraternal rituals (such as bottle exchanges). Finally, I saw a need
for a volume that parents, educators, and Greek leaders could use, either individually or collectively, as a basis upon which to form a plan
of action for reducing the risks associated with belonging to a social
club.

On the positive side, since the publication of my last book a growing number of national fraternity and sorority headquarters and university Greek-life offices not only have joined the families of deceased
pledges in expressing abhorrence for fraternal abuses but have admitted to former shortcomings and have instituted top-to-bottom plans
for reform meant to eradicate hazing, alcohol abuse, sexual assaults,
and racism. A political controversy has arisen as to whether such reforms should be carried out by independent and insular individual
national fraternities or by cooperative fraternal umbrella groups (such
as the National Interfraternity Conference and the National Panhellenic Conference) in conjunction with a nationwide group of Greek
advisers, the Association of Fraternity Advisors.

Some fraternal leaders, both black and white, have stressed that in
order for these reforms to succeed, a substantial change in undergraduate student culture must first occur. One irony of today's massive fraternal reform movement is that a chasm separates reformist fraternal
headquarters from their undergraduate members and younger alumni
who came of age in the post–*Animal House* era, while the more permis-
sive national fraternity executives claim or actually have complete solidarity with their member chapters.

To take another point of view, hazing activists and fraternity critics
considering pledging reforms such as alcohol-free housing and zero
tolerance for hazing are wondering whether they will succeed or rather
will wither away, as the once highly touted "Greek Week" and "Help
Week," programs, and the abolition of pledging in some groups, all
did. If the new programs turn out to be mere palliatives and not solu-

tions, the U.S. educational and fraternal communities will be forced to come to grips with the ethical and legal questions that arise when the constitutional right to free association clashes with the realities associated with maintaining a Greek system tainted by wrongful deaths.

In addition to dealing with contemporary issues, *Wrongs of Passage* also examines hazing from an historical viewpoint, exploring the reasons that this social problem has, throughout history, demeaned and occasionally killed young people. The book also examines legal issues and issues of behavior in an attempt to illuminate the fraternities' and sororities' apparent need to haze and submit to hazing, or to drink and make others drink.

Appendix A, titled "A Chronology of Deaths among College Students as a Result of Hazing, Fraternal Alcohol Syndrome, Pledging, Fraternity-Related Accidents, and Other Miscellaneous Occurrences," serves as evidence that too many college students have died ignobly.

Wrongs of Passage demonstrates that more student deaths, injuries, and post-traumatic stress disorder cases will occur unless internal and external pressures, the execution of well-intended organizational reforms, and educational awareness programs can change today's collegiate environment by creating taboos against hazing and alcohol abuse. The book also offers a number of anecdotal cautionary tales involving hazing and binge drinking during pre-initiation rites. These stories reveal the destructive patterns of organizational life and the hefty price that must be paid when groups make poor decisions about how they socialize new members. Such stories do more than thousands of pages of psychological theory to show that hazing destroys lives, interferes with the educational process, and perpetuates barbaric acts similar to student deeds that outraged educators in the Middle Ages. The endings of these paradigmatic cases are also important, because they demonstrate that while some fraternal groups and schools have begun stepping in promptly to punish individuals and chapters whose behavior is egregious, others seem to stonewall and to deny reality, thereby losing an opportunity to use each student death as a springboard for encouraging students to change their dangerous ways.

Given the collegiate environment in which many fraternal groups that haze and swill liquor enjoy elevated status in the eyes of many undergraduates, only large-scale, directed strategies can cause social change. To alter the reprehensible behavior that has claimed the lives of at least one sorority or fraternity member or pledge every year since 1970 will take the directed actions of legislators, educators, sociologists, psychologists, anti-hazing activists, law-enforcement officers, counselors, journalists, researchers, leaders of Greek national and local organizations, parents, undergraduates, former hazers, and survivors of hazing.

Also needed are attitude changes on the part of college presidents, deans, lawmakers, judges, district attorneys, and Greek advisers who appear to be on the side of reform and the law but who have not sufficiently distanced themselves from their own undergraduate experiences with fraternities and sororities to deal objectively with the new realities of life in today's party-animal Greek system. If the full picture is to be seen, the public also has to stop looking at African American and white fraternities and sororities as one homogeneous group. The Greek world consists of well over one hundred national organizations that range from insular, self-appointed battlers of political correctness (who believe that their members as adults are meant to rule U.S. politics) to missionary-like champions of character and values who view themselves as social activists as well as social beings.

The book's final chapter, entitled "Strategies: What Can Be Done?" notes the reforms that administrators, Greek leaders, parents, and police forces are already trying to implement. The chapter ends by offering solutions that may help end or reduce the carnage, and it presents a list of source materials to which readers can turn for additional help.

My hope is that this book will inspire educators, parents, and fraternal leaders to escalate the search for ways to end the twin evils of hazing and collegiate alcohol abuse. In particular, it is my fervent wish that the book will serve to encourage undergraduate fraternal members to display civil behavior toward newcomers in their groups, and that it will help to make mutual respect and responsible drinking the new social norms on campus.

Hank Nuwer

SELECTED LISTING OF KEY PERSONS AND FRATERNAL ORGANIZATIONS

James "Jim" Arnold: Arnold is an Oregon-based alcohol researcher who observed alcohol misuse and hazing activities firsthand in a fraternity house as part of the research he did while working toward a doctorate in higher education at Indiana University.

Ray Ballou and Maisie Ballou: The Ballous won a precedent-setting lawsuit against Sigma Nu fraternity after the 1980 alcohol-related hazing death of their younger son, L. Barry Ballou, at the University of South Carolina.

Donna Bedinger: An Alpha Gamma Delta sister at Eastern Illinois University, Bedinger was probably the first sorority member to die in a pledging-related incident and was also the first Greek member to perish during "kidnapping" activities conducted by pledges. Alpha Gamma Delta has since adopted stringent anti-hazing guidelines.

Robert A. Biggs: The executive vice president of one of the largest international fraternities, Phi Delta Theta, Biggs has vowed to put an end to death and injury in the organization he heads by pushing to end or at least reduce the role alcohol plays in the socialization of new members. Biggs is looked upon by many as an advocate within the Greek system who is working to end hazing and alcohol misuse.

Jonathan J. Brant: The long-time executive vice president of the National Interfraternity Conference, and its most visible spokesman, Brant became increasingly involved in the fight against hazing and alcohol misuse in Greek student organizations in the 1990s. He resigned his post unexpectedly effective August 27, 1999.

Marilyn Bullock: The national vice president of Kappa Kappa Gamma, an international female fraternity based in Columbus, Ohio, Bullock found herself addressing the problem of physical hazing after three pledges at the DePauw University chapter in Indiana were burned with cigarettes as part of an initiation stunt that had been taking place annually for about four years. Kappa Kappa Gamma's in-house publications had often condemned hazing and alcohol misuse.

Michael Carlone: Before his decision to leave Greek life for a job in the private sector in 1999, Carlone headed and developed Sigma Phi Epsilon's "Balanced Man Program." The program de-emphasized pledging in favor of developing individual members over four years through mentoring and community-service programs. During the mid-'90s, Carlone professed a no-tolerance attitude toward behaviors that had led to serious injuries in some Sig Ep chapters.

Howard Clery and Constance "Connie" Clery: The parents of Jeanne Clery, who was raped and murdered at Lehigh University in Pennsylvania in 1986, began Security on Campus with the aims of making campuses violence free and of pressuring universities to disclose accurate campus crime statistics.

C. Grant Davis Jr.: Davis, director of student life at Auburn University (AU), and AU President William Van Muse found themselves in the national spotlight after the death of a community college student who had been pledging the AU chapter of Phi Delta Theta. The pledge had been acting in violation of school rules, which dictate that only students enrolled at the university may pledge an AU fraternity or sorority. The high-profile role was unfamiliar to the two administrators, since AU had previously been known for its anti-hazing programs and for strongly advocating risk management in Greek houses.

Jason DeSousa: An educator from Alabama, DeSousa is an alumnus of a historically African American fraternity. He conducts research in the area of black Greek issues.

David K. Easlick, Jr.: The executive director of Delta Kappa Epsilon, the largest international fraternity to break with the National Interfraternity Conference, Easlick cites free association as he battles universities that have ended or threatened to end their association with fraternities. Delta Kappa Epsilon was formed as a junior class society at Yale University in 1844. While the fraternity is known for its alumni's impressive political achievements, over the years the press has scathingly criticized some chapters for hazing, alcohol problems, and other transgressions.

Douglas Fierberg: A trial attorney and a partner with the Washington, D.C., law firm of Sherman, Meehan, Curtin, & Ain, Fierberg represents a number of young people in claims against fraternal organizations, but also speaks knowledgeably about liability and damage issues with regard to fraternities.

Mark Freeman: Freeman, the director of police and security at DePauw University during the investigation of the DePauw branding incident involving Kappa Kappa Gamma pledges, resigned in December 1998. He was one of seven staffers to leave DePauw who were associated closely with students at the Greencastle, Indiana, campus. He became project coordinator for the Governor's Commission for a Drug-Free Indiana.

Michael V. W. Gordon: Once a dean at Indiana University who took a hard line against hazing and alcohol violations in Greek groups, Gordon is now executive director of the National Pan-Hellenic Council, Inc. (NPHC). The NPHC is an umbrella group for the largest historically African American fraternities and sororities. Gordon is a member of Kappa Alpha Psi.

Alice Haben: The death of Haben's son Nicholas propelled the former Illinois church secretary to become an activist against hazing and alcohol abuse by Greek-letter group members, high school students, and collegiate athletic clubs and teams.

Ruth Harten: The mother of Gabriel "Gabe" Higgins, a University of Texas student who drowned while participating in alcohol-centered ceremonies near the Colorado River, campaigns for the abolition of fraternities and sororities.

Gabriel "Gabe" Higgins: Higgins was a University of Texas (UT) fraternity member who hoped to become a member of the UT Texas Cowboys, a prestigious spirit club known for its presence on campus, its alums in high places, and its fundraising on behalf of charitable organizations. He died during a Cowboys initiation event.

Julie L. Joynt: Joynt, an anti-hazing activist from Maryland, began speaking out after her brother died following strenuous pledging activities conducted by a Frostburg State University fraternity.

Chris Karamesines: After the branding of Jessica Zimmerman and Damara Karamesines in a Kappa Kappa Gamma sorority initiation at DePauw University, Karamesines, along with Jessica's mother Cindie Zimmerman, condemned sorority hazing. Some parents of chapter members directly and indirectly involved in the branding also criticized DePauw for its handling of the case. Although evidence that similar brandings had taken place over the past four years was uncovered, only members involved in the latest branding were punished and named publicly in media accounts.

Frederick Doyle Kershner: As the historian of Delta Tau Delta, one of the oldest and larger international fraternities, in the late '70s Kershner not only researched the history of fraternity hazing for the NIC but also became an unflinching critic of those who wanted hazing to remain unchanged as part of tradition.

Lambda Chi Alpha: One of the larger international fraternities, Lambda Chi Alpha tried to reform pledging in 1972, when it began referring to pledges as associate members. It also prohibited chapters from buying alcohol in 1988.

Mortimer N. Leggett: A Cornell University student and Kappa Alpha Society pledge, Leggett was probably the first Greek to die during a pledging activity. He died in 1873.

Maurice "Mo" Littlefield: During the 1980s, as the executive director of Sigma Nu international fraternity, Littlefield found himself under attack in a civil suit brought by the parents of a University of South Carolina pledge who died after ingesting a lethal quantity of alcohol during a chapter ritual. Afterwards, Littlefield strongly stressed a return to the anti-hazing stand taken by the fraternity's founders, and he promoted internal reforms, a move toward dry fraternity houses, and improved leadership programs to help shape the character of members and to help them resist group pressures to haze and to abuse alcohol.

Teresa Loser: The associate dean of students at DePauw, a university with one of the stronger fraternity systems, Loser and President Robert G. Bottoms became embroiled in a hazing scandal following a burning ritual conducted in secret by some members of the Kappa Kappa Gamma chapter.

Phi Gamma Delta: The international fraternity instituted a number of innovative alcohol-risk-reduction programs after its image was tarnished by the alcohol-related coma and subsequent death of pledge Scott Krueger at Massachusetts Institute of Technology in 1997. Frank Norris, a well-known author, was an influential member of the fraternity, and he started several traditions still observed by chapter houses.

Pi Kappa Alpha: A secret society begun at the University of Virginia in 1868, the large international fraternity is best known for its leadership academy and its recruitment successes. Undergraduate rushees, pledges, and members of the fraternity have died as a result of drinking, hazing, and pledging incidents at Indiana University, Georgetown College, Texas Tech University, Mississippi State University (two deaths), the University of Arkansas, the University of Richmond, and Southwestern University.

Brian Rahill and Elizabeth Allan: The married co-founders of The StopHazing.org web site (http://www.stophazing.org/) serve as advocates for anti-hazing legislation and programs. Allan, a former University of New Hampshire Greek Affairs head, provides an administrative perspective. Rahill, whose undergraduate fraternity was closed because of hazing, handles research and development of the site.

Frank J. Ruck, Jr.: Ruck, a past grand president of Sigma Phi Epsilon and one-time NIC president, raised eyebrows and some hackles with his demand that those who hazed or otherwise embarrassed their fraternities be held strictly accountable. His death on August 2, 1998, silenced a strong advocate for fraternal reform.

Chad Saucier: A community college student who loved Auburn University, which he hoped to someday attend, Saucier pledged Auburn's Phi Delta Theta chapter and died during a traditional Christmas pledge party at the fraternity.

Rita Saucier, K. Scott Saucier: The parents of Chad Saucier, a Phi Delta Theta pledge who died at Auburn University, the Sauciers have been highly critical of national fraternities that haze and of college presidents who tolerate hazing and alcohol misuse. Rita Saucier is nationally known for her criticism of hazing in Greek organizations in general and at Auburn specifically. Nonetheless, she returned to Auburn by invitation to speak about hazing.

Richard Sigal: a New Jersey sociologist, Sigal writes and speaks about fraternity hazing. As an undergraduate he was a member of Klan Alpine at Alfred University, but he has since questioned the value of Greek systems.

Sigma Alpha Epsilon: SAE is known for a leadership school founded in 1930, its stone lions in front of chapter houses, and its influence (it has 250,000 initiated members). The death of pledge Ben Wynne at its Louisiana State University chapter was a crushing setback for the fraternity's decades-long campaign against hazing and alcohol misuse.

Sigma Chi: One of the largest and oldest international fraternities (it was founded in 1855), Sigma Chi is known for its anti-alcohol abuse and anti-hazing messages sent to alums and undergraduates in fraternity publications. The fraternity has a comparatively good house safety record. However, the suicide of a pledge at the University of Mississippi in 1998 uncovered evidence of hazing and pointed out that the actions of a single chapter can cast a pall over the larger organization.

Amanda Lynn Smith: Smith, a former Phi Mu female fraternity pledge who (together with Judy Smith, her mother) speaks about the psychic trauma she says some Greek groups inflict on pledges as a result of mental though often noncriminal hazing. Phi Mu is one of the oldest female fraternities and is known for its philanthropic activities.

Walt Smith: The director of security services at Anderson University in Indiana, Smith advocates the training of campus police as emergency medical technicians to enable them to respond more effectively to a variety of emergency situations (see cover simulation). Anderson University, which officially bans alcohol, has not had to use its police to save lives in drinking incidents. However, campus police elsewhere who arrived in a timely fashion at the scene of an emergency lacked the skills that might have kept severely intoxicated youths alive until trained personnel could take over.

Chuck Stenzel: Stenzel, a fraternity pledge, died after participating in the intense drinking required by Klan Alpine fraternity at Alfred University during the university's traditional first night of pledging.

Eileen Stevens: The founder of the Committee to Halt Useless College Killings (CHUCK), Stevens lost her son, Chuck Stenzel, because of alcohol-related hazing at Klan Alpine fraternity at Alfred University in New York State. In 1999 Stevens announced her decision to accept an honorary doctorate from Alfred (offered to her in a letter dated November 18, 1998, written by President Edward G. Coll Jr.) to honor her volunteer work. In 1999 Alfred University, in cooperation with the National Collegiate Athletic Association (NCAA), launched the first-ever comprehensive study of hazing among U.S. collegiate athletes.

Maureen Syring: One of several no-nonsense leaders in the National Panhellenic Conference (NPC), Syring is a strong opponent of hazing and binge drinking.

Lionel Tiger: A Rutgers University professor, Tiger writes about male behavior and other subjects in anthropology and sociology. He is the author of *Men in Groups* and *The Decline of Males*. He also wrote a commentary on hazing for the February 17, 1997, issue of *The New Yorker*.

Jacques L. Vauclain III: Vauclain, Sigma Phi Epsilon executive director, has yanked numerous charters of chapters whose members' behavior fell below standards set by the international's headquarters. During the 1990s the number of press reports of hazing incidents associated with this large national fraternity fell significantly. Under Vauclain's direction, Sigma Phi Epsilon developed an extensive steward program that was better able to serve and supervise undergraduate members.

Henry Wechsler: The director of the College Alcohol Studies Program at the Harvard University School of Public Health, Wechsler has brought the term "binge drinking" into the public's consciousness with his numerous studies of college-student drinking. In addition, Wechsler has written opinion pieces for the *Chronicle of Higher Education* criticizing universities for continuing their association with fraternities, saying that members tend to be binge drinkers, to engage in risky sexual behavior, and to let drinking interfere with their studies.

Dave Westol: The executive director of Theta Chi, an international fraternity, Westol travels the country to present his anti-hazing program, "Hazing on Trial," at universities. Westol faced one of the greatest challenges of his career in 1997 after a seventeen-year-old Theta Chi pledge, Binaya "Bini" Oja, perished in an alcohol-related incident at Clarkson University in New York.

John A. "Tony" Williams: A Tennessee State University educator, member of Alpha Phi Alpha, and executive director of the Center for the Study of Pan-Hellenic Issues, Williams states that the ever-swelling numbers of black fraternities and sororities is a visible sign of students' sense of racism and tension on predominantly white campuses. In his words, the belonging that African American students hope to achieve is not tied to the campus or to white culture, but to groups that reflect their heritage and culture, such as historically black fraternities and student unions.

Cindie Zimmerman: Along with Chris Karamesines (mentioned in more detail above): the mother of Jessica Zimmerman condemned sorority hazing after her daughter and Damara Karamesines were involved in a hazing incident at a Kappa Kappa Gamma sorority initiation at DePauw University.

GLOSSARY

active member: a member who has been initiated into a social club.

adviser: a university staff member who advises fraternities and/or sororities; also an individual who advises a single chapter.

alcohol-free housing: a joint National Interfraternity Conference (NIC) and National Panhellenic Conference (NPC) initiative to remove alcohol from chapter properties to turn houses into learning centers providing members and guests with a safer living environment. The pioneer NIC fraternities committed to alcohol-free housing are Alpha Kappa Lambda, Delta Sigma Phi, FarmHouse Fraternity (which has always advocated alcohol-free houses), Phi Delta Theta, Phi Gamma Delta, Phi Kappa Sigma, Sigma Nu, and Theta Chi.

alumni member: a member of an African American fraternal organization who pledges as an adult after graduating from college.

alumnus: a member of a fraternity who was initiated as an undergraduate and continues his or her lifelong involvement in a group.

Association of Fraternity Advisors, Inc. (AFA): a national professional organization made up mainly of Greek advisers working in colleges.

bid: an invitation to a nonmember (rushee) with an interest in Greek life to join a fraternity or sorority to be considered for membership.

big brother: an active male fraternity member who agrees to look out for a specific male pledge (known as a little brother) or female pledge (known as a little sister) belonging to a sorority closely aligned with his fraternity.

big sister: an active female fraternity member who agrees to look out for a specific female pledge (known as a little sister) in her sorority.

binge drinking: controversial term used by many alcohol researchers to refer to the consumption of five or more drinks at one sitting by males or four or more drinks at one sitting by females. Some researchers say the term misleads the public, which is unaware that according to one study, fraternity males are more likely than are non-Greek male students to drink thirteen or more drinks in one session (the corresponding number for sorority females is seven to twelve drinks). Other researchers complain that the term misleads the public into thinking that all college students misuse alcohol.

blackball: a vote taken to deny membership in a group to a pledge deemed undesirable by a member or members of the group.

broken pledges: a term coined by the author in 1990 to describe victims of hazing.

chapter: a group at a particular institution affiliated with a national (or international) fraternity or sorority.

depledging: quitting pledging, on the part of a pledge.

dry: An adjective used to describe events, campuses, or houses that do not allow alcohol on the premises.

field officers/representatives: staff members (usually entry-level) hired by national fraternities or sororities who visit chapter houses across the country to spread goodwill and to try to ascertain whether or not the national's procedures and policies are being carried out.

founders: the young men or women who as undergraduates began what later turned into a national fraternity or sorority. All Greek groups were founded upon certain principles that the founders held sacred.

fraternity: a male Greek organization, or an active female Greek organization that uses that legal name instead of calling itself a "sorority."

fraternity executives: The paid career overseers of fraternities and sororities. They may have titles such as executive director, executive vice president, general secretary, and so forth, depending upon the organization. For example, while David L. Westol is executive director of Theta Chi and Robert "Bob" Biggs is executive vice president of Phi Delta Theta, their duties are quite similar, and both usually serve as spokesmen for their national fraternities.

Fraternity Executives Association: an organization of national fraternity heads.

Greek: a member of a fraternity or sorority; also a fraternal organization.

Greekthink: this author's adaptation of Irving L. Janis's term "groupthink"; it refers to fraternal groups that indulge in reckless behaviors and pre-initiation rituals, display near-delusional feelings of invincibility, fail to heed an individual member's (or their national executive's) moral qualms in the interest of group unanimity, put a newcomer in harm's way with seeming disregard for his stress and safety, and demonstrate post-incident denial in the face of clear-cut evidence that they have erred. Janis found that the more "esprit de corps" a group has, the less likely it is to engage in critical thinking. Instead, the group's loyalty prompts a need for "agreement" and inhibits problem solving.[1]

hazing: an activity that a high-status member orders other members to engage in or suggests that they engage in that in some way humbles a newcomer who lacks the power to resist, because he or she wants to gain admission into a group. Hazing can be noncriminal, but it is nearly always against the rules of an institution, team, or Greek group. It can be criminal, which means that a state statute has been violated. This usually occurs when a pledging-related activity results in gross physical injury or death.

hell week: traditionally the most demanding period (it can last more or less than a week) of pledgeship, during which pledges are subjected to a final round of indignities and ordeals before gaining admission to the group.

historian: a volunteer who serves as an official source of information on the founders, past events, constitution, prominent members, minutiae, and other items of interest to a fraternity or sorority. Often, although not always, the historians are university faculty or administrators. Delta Tau Delta historian Frederick D. Kershner, for example, taught at Columbia until his retirement. Pi Kappa Alpha historian Jerome Reel is a Clemson University administrator.

initiation: the ceremony involving agreed-upon rituals that are performed when pledges become members of fraternities and sororities.

intake: the process by which African American fraternities take new members into fraternities and sororities.

leadership seminars: Many fraternities and sororities put on a yearly seminar treating different aspects of chapter life and management. Essentially alumnae and collegians work together during an intensive weekend of training. For example, Delta Gamma (female) fraternity puts on seminars that stress finance, leadership, and community service and programming.

legacy: a member of a fraternity or sorority whose relative or relatives belong to the organization, or belonged to it in the past.

lineup: a term describing a common hazing infraction. During a line-up, male or female pledges form a line and are then subjected to verbal or physical abuse (such as forced calisthenics, beatings, and forced consumption of unpleasant foods or beverages) as punishment for real or imagined lapses.

local fraternity/sorority: a fraternity or sorority based at a single campus.

mental hazing: any activity or verbal abuse intended to put a pledge under stress or to demean that person.

national fraternity/sorority: a fraternity that is a member of the historically white NIC or a sorority/female fraternity belonging to the NPC. Also a fraternity or sorority belonging to the historically African American National Panhellenic Council (NPHC). Those with chapters in Canada and elsewhere term themselves international fraternities or sororities.

National Interfraternity Conference (NIC): an Indianapolis-based umbrella group historically made up of national white fraternities. All fraternities now are integrated, although some have had few minority members. Some sixty-plus fraternities belong to the NIC.

National Panhellenic Conference (NPC): an Indianapolis-based umbrella group of historically white (now integrated) sororities and female fraternities.

National Panhellenic Council (NPHC): an umbrella organization of nine integrated fraternities and sororities that have a common historically black culture; it is currently based in Bloomington, Indiana.

peer pressure: in the context of this book, this terms refers to a group whose members are roughly equals and that has the power to influence the behavior of peers or newcomers.

physical hazing (sometimes called rough hazing): hazing in which members exert themselves by doing exercises, or are manhandled, paddled, beaten, encouraged to drink alcohol or to drink or eat concoctions, and so forth.

pledgemaster: A fully initiated member who is put in charge of pledge "training."

pledges: nonmembers of fraternities and sororities who are doing what is required of them to gain full admission to those organizations. In African American fraternities and sororities, pledges are expected to be like "dots on a line." Hence to pledge is to go "online."

pledge sneaks: when the pressure on pledges builds, members encourage newcomers to get a limited amount of revenge, taking brothers into the country for a "ride," for example. Several members have been killed or injured as a result of such activities. Today most Greek organizations consider these events hazing incidents, although schools regarded a small number of pledge sneaks that ended in death during the '70s and '80s as non-hazing events.

president (chapter): individual, usually serving for a one-year term, elected by the members to be the head of a fraternity/sorority chapter.

risk management: the function of keeping legal liability problems to a minimum, or eliminating them. Fraternal areas of risk include hazing, alcohol misuse, illegal-substance use, sexual assault, and house safety and maintenance.

roof deaths: the deaths of fraternity and sorority members who die in falls from house roofs, windows, and ladders—usually while intoxicated.

rush: a specific time period during which fraternity and sorority chapters can choose new members. Many Greek reformers wish to do away with rush, which has led to abuses and even deaths; according to the NIC, the alternative is year-round recruitment.

rushee: a college student who attends Greek recruiting events with an interest in joining a fraternity or sorority.

Select 2000: An NIC initiative to change student behaviors by empowering members of individual fraternities to find workable solutions to problems involving alcohol, ethics, substance abuse, and safety. The new NIC emphasis is on developing value-centered leaders, scholars, alumni role models, and alcohol-free house learning centers.

spirit club: an often prestigious campus organization that invites members of various social clubs to join in order to boost school spirit, perform charitable services, and enjoy social occasions.

sub-rosa, renegade, or underground groups: fraternities (usually) and sororities that operate without the approval of a school or fraternal group.

tapping night: a celebration in some groups that takes place on the night rushees are "tapped" for membership.

wet: an adjective describing events or houses that permit people legally entitled to drink to be served alcohol on the premises.

ACKNOWLEDGMENTS

I wish to acknowledge the assistance of the following persons, some of whom are now deceased, who have helped me with my work on hazing since 1978: Marshall Lumsden, Irving L. Janis, Eileen Stevens, Roy Stevens, John Gallman, Ruth Barzel, Rita Saucier, K. Scott Saucier, Richard Sigal, Erikka Bettis, D. Jason DeSousa, Sue Havlish, Larry Bolles, Joseph Snell, Ronald J. Fosnaugh, Max Aguilera-Hellweg, Joe Nikiel, Joseph and Rosemary Englehardt, Jim Hardin, C. Grant Davis Jr., Lissa Bradford, Robert Biggs, Rich Zeoli, Louis Ingelhart, John "Tony" Williams, Joe Jansen, Walt Smith, Maureen Syring, Lewis Eigen, Howard and Connie Clery, Myra R. H. Kodner, Layne Cameron, James "Jim" Arnold, Charles Eberly, Steve Nash, Jessica Zimmerman, Cindie Zimmerman, Bob Waite, Thomas Hayes, Teresa Loser, Julie Joynt, Gary Eller, Michael Spear, Dave Easlick, Michael Carlone, Frank Ruck, Brian Rahill, Kent C. Owen, Jacques Vauclain III, Matt Chittum, Jonathan Brant, Charles Moskos, Stanton Dodson, Marilyn Bullock, Michael Emmerling, Dave Massey, Jane Lyle, Roy Reid, Maisie Ballou, Buddy Litchfield, Anne Kenne, Alice Haben, Daria D'Arienzo, Robert McNamara, Rob McNamara, Roger Harrold, Nancy Hayes, James Brown, Frank Lorenz, Elaine Engst, Richard Sigal, Darron E. Franta, Mike Moskos, Roy Stevens, Gary Horowitz, Lionel Tiger, Mark Taff, Joan Cerra, Ray Ballou, Mary Lenaghan, Dorothy Flowers, Ed Gabe, Adrienne Harris, Elizabeth Allan, Gerald Shoultz, Debbie Conner, Ryan Johnson, Bev Pitts, William Van Muse, Steve Rogers, and Mary Ann Roser.

The National Panhellenic Conference archives at the University of Illinois at Champaign–Urbana were valuable for research. Larry Lockridge of New York University provided me with valuable correspondence pertaining to his pledgeship to Phi Gamma Delta and also gave me permission to quote from *Shade of the Raintree* (Viking, 1994), his biography of his father, Ross Lockridge Jr. My writing about hazing was aided by a 1988 Gannett Foundation grant. I am grateful for support from librarians at the New York Public Library, the Anderson (Indiana) Public Library, the Indianapolis Public Library, the Library of Congress, and the following college and university libraries: Anderson University, Ball State University, Miami University of Ohio, Cornell University, Muhlenberg College, Cedar Crest College, the University of Illinois, Harvard University, Indiana University, and Purdue University.

WRONGS

OF

PASSAGE

CHAPTER

1

The Tradition

THE "DEAD-DAY" PARTY AT SWEET AUBURN

Chad Saucier was "raised right," as his neighbors in Mobile, Alabama, liked to say. Bright and articulate, he warmed friends, teachers, and others with a smile that years of braces had aligned. In some ways Chad was a contradiction. He hung out in high school with the in crowd, but he stood up for unattractive classmates. His sisters Jacy and Kori regarded him an affectionate, protective big brother. He was truly a good kid, his parents assured one another.

Chad acted as if a spotlight were following him. Handsome and funny, on occasion he substituted charm for rigor in school, relying on his "cuteness" to convince teachers to pass him to the next grade, according to his father, K. Scott Saucier. Chad's dad, a doctor but no ballplayer, admired his boy's athletic ability. From a bleacher seat Dr. Saucier watched his son hit five home runs—two game winners—in one Little League season. During Chad's teen years at St. Paul's Episcopal [High] School, he was a spark plug and a workhorse, whether he was playing football or basketball. Although he lacked the superior skills needed to attract recruiters from Division I college sports powers, Chad occasionally played well enough to get his name on the local sports pages. Once, while St. Paul's was losing a football game, Chad stood on the sidelines and waved his helmet until he persuaded fans to stomp and cheer. Then he went into the game on offense, delivering a well-timed block that helped spring a teammate to score the winning touchdown.

Sometimes Chad's father and mother worried that he cared too much about what his friends thought of him. The sons of community-oriented people, such pals were hardly delinquents, but they had a taste for partying. "In Mobile there's a lot of drinking," said Rita Saucier, Chad's mother.[1]

Chad sometimes failed to show common sense and to leave when his high school friends indulged in underage drinking. Because he was not one to defy or hurt his parents, the Sauciers never saw him consume alcohol, though he drank even in high school. Haunted by sour memories of an uncle with a drinking problem, Rita Saucier made her aversion to alcohol clear to Chad, as she had to Scott Saucier when she was dating him. "When I was setting ideal qualities in a husband, I said I would not marry a man who drank," said Mrs. Saucier.[2]

When Chad applied to Auburn University (AU) for admission, he was refused on the basis of his so-so scholastic record. Crushed, he settled for acceptance to Southern Union Community College, a two-year school a few minutes from AU. Confident that AU would admit him as a transfer student after he had pulled up his grades, which he was determined to do, he rented an apartment near campus with Hays Waller and Mark Mostellar, first-year AU students from Mobile. He confided in his father his dream of becoming a veterinarian, and the two talked about buying a hobby farm to satisfy their mutual love for dogs and horses. "He became focused and serious about his future," said Dr. Saucier.[3]

But Chad also wanted a social life. Before fall semester started he accepted a bid from Phi Delta Theta, an AU fraternity favored by many young men from Mobile. Chad connected with the Phis partially through a Mobile pal, Joseph Strada, who even in high school occasionally drove to the fraternity house to party with older fellows from his hometown. Waller and Mostellar also decided to pledge the Phis. When Chad told his father and mother that he intended to join the house, they were against it. Rita Saucier worried that Chad's grades might suffer, killing his chances of getting into a veterinary program. He might get paddled too, she knew, but he had endured a paddling to get into his high school fraternity, and it hadn't seemed to upset him that much.

Mrs. Saucier knew little about Greek organizations. She had attended the University of Southern Mississippi for two years and had decided not to pledge a sorority. Her thoughts then were fixed on Scott, her sweetheart since high school. They wed in college, and soon she quit her studies to work for a telephone company to help him pay for medical school. But the romantic dream winked out in 1991. After the divorce, Mrs. Saucier commuted to Mississippi to take care of her gravely ill parents.

Chad enjoyed the fraternity house's atmosphere during his frequent visits. Like the members of other social fraternities, the Phi Delts displayed a readiness to accept a member so long as he did whatever was required to get into the group. The fact that Chad was a community college outsider seemed to bother no one at the house. Cheating the system to pledge without AU administrators catching on wasn't hard. At the Phi Delt house Chad's pledgeship was kept secret because the school's written policy stated that "a rushee may not be formally pledged until enrolled at Auburn University."[4]

It was AU's policy to ask fraternities to comply voluntarily with eligibility regulations. Fraternities signed a policy agreement contract promising not to haze. The school's student affairs staff insisted that members abide by a policy on hazing published in the *Tiger Cub* student handbook, but the Phi Delt chapter signed off in pro forma fashion, said AU Director of Student Activities C. Grant Davis Jr. in a 1998 telephone interview with the author.

Fraternity houses at AU are not under direct university control, as dormitories are. They are regarded as private homes. AU advises Greeks and sets rules, but to avoid legal entanglements the administration chooses not to control Greek organizations absolutely. If the director of student affairs receives a complaint about minors hazing, he or she, or a staff member, goes to a fraternity house to investigate. If denied access, the director or staff member leaves and asks the national fraternity to join AU in taking disciplinary action. AU campus police trying to enforce state laws must usually directly witness an act of hazing, or there is little chance that serious charges will stick.

Hazing and underage drinking in fraternity houses are forbidden by the state and by the university. AU regards student pre-initiation rituals and alcohol swilling as persistent problems that the school actively opposes, according to Davis, who was interviewed by phone in 1998. Although alcohol is not permitted in dormitories, it is permitted on university land that AU leases to fraternities for houses, as well as on property owned by fraternities. One package store sells liquor on property adjacent to a fraternity house, and the windows of town bars boast various low-cost drink specials week in, week out.

AU's campus is considered "dry," a confusing term for outsiders given the visible role of alcohol in the college's social life. Wednesday through Sunday can seem like one extended weekend in Auburn, a town of 34,000 in which high-spirited, enthusiastic students put on athletic pep rallies and parades that make the university seem a throw-back to pre-1960 America. At the center of much of this exuberant activity are the fraternities and sororities that dominate AU's party and social scene.

AU, like many U.S. colleges, is examining its recruitment proce-dures in an attempt to build a more diverse student body. Many schools have recently reported Greek membership drops of up to 25 percent from peak years in the early '90s. Some individual chapters across the country say their memberships have dropped more than 50 percent from their highest enrollments. A few universities show no drop at all.

Fraternity houses and "dry" dormitories at AU are alike in that each has resident advisers on the premises. In 1993 the Phi Delt house's resident adviser was a house mother. She was not a university em-ployee, like a dormitory resident assistant, but was employed by the fraternity. The university and national Phi Delt headquarters required certain things of house mothers. One of those was that she report un-derage drinking. The performance of house mothers varies with the individual and with the attitude of the members, according to Execu-tive Vice President Robert A. Biggs of Phi Delta Theta headquarters in Oxford, Ohio, who was interviewed by phone in 1998.

Chad enjoyed many things about fraternity life. He enjoyed the company of other pledges, and he liked playing sports, attending AU football games, revving up a barbecue grill, and confiding his dreams to males who didn't mock his plans. The fraternity connected Chad to social life at AU. He also loved the campus, which was always green and rich with the aromatic scents of southern pine, dogwood, and crepe myrtle. Although he enjoyed his Southern Union classes and found his professors competent, he wanted more than a two-year degree. The Phi Delt pledgeship reassured him that some day he would belong at "Sweet Auburn," which was nationally known for its programs in aero-space engineering, agriculture, physics, physiology, and the liberal arts. Alums include Henry "Hank" Hartsfield, '58, a Delta Chi brother; and Ken Mattingly, '54, of Delta Tau Delta. Both had been astronauts on America's fourth *Columbia* space shuttle mission. More important to Chad, a perpetual sports fan, the school was famous for turning out football stars such as kicker Al Del Greco, Fob James (former Alabama governor), and Heisman Trophy winners Pat Sullivan and Bo Jackson; legendary John W. Heisman himself coached AU football from 1895 to 1899.[5] Although the school is located in a remote locale, thousands of loyal alums stop by their old fraternity houses on the day of big home games. The Phi Delt alumni were as fanatical as any other alums about AU football and the joys of Saturday tailgate parties with cold chicken and beer.

"In a world that changes so rapidly—on every front—people need anchors," said Richard Sigal, a sociology professor who has written op-ed pieces for the *New York Times* and other publications. For Chad and his friends from Mobile, the fraternity served as an anchor to Auburn's glorious past and present. Studies have shown that the values of students who belong to Greek groups differ from those of nonjoiners, said Sigal. He said that fraternity members particularly seem to need such anchors to keep their bit of turf from revolving as fast as the rest of the world seems to be.[6]

The year before Chad pledged the university, Phi Delt headquarters had learned that Phi pledges at AU were involved in hazing. Pledges were made to perform rigorous exercises, to sleep crammed into a bathroom like packaged shrimp, to eat and drink unpleasant concoctions, and to drink alcohol. The university learned all this because the father of a Phi pledge complained that some activities had required pledges to line up for verbal abuse and, in one instance, for a hard shove. Responding to pressure from AU officials, Phi Delta Theta headquarters asked alumni to assume responsibility for day-to-day house affairs. The house hired an adult adviser to maintain order. Because he lived across the state line in Georgia, the adviser was sometimes unaware that the chapter had ignored his orders. When he confronted the members he was told that pledging was neither violent nor dangerous. The adviser informed pledges that they were to phone him if they were hazed. Neither Chad nor his pledgemates called him when they were required to clean the house and run errands. Ignoring the pleas and rules of their national headquarters, many members view housecleaning and errand-running not as hazing but as positive exercises that build a pledge's pride in the organization. Such a viewpoint overlooks the fact that pledges are frequently made to work like serfs, that members often trash a house just to watch pledges work, and that the grades of young men often fall drastically while they pledge houses that haze.

During Chad's pledge semester, some Phi Delt members, such as Doug Ray, the chapter president, abhorred hazing—or at least the things they considered to be hazing. "[They] didn't want to see it and I mean, made their best attempt to try to not have it go on of any kind," said Strada.[7] Nonetheless, the fraternity's officers never confided in the adviser when the national's prohibitions against hazing were ignored.

John H. "Bo" Bowen III, province president for Phi Delta Theta, visited the AU house three months before Chad accepted a bid. He saw evidence that led him to believe hazing and underage drinking were problematic in the chapter. The deeply religious Bowen tried to impart his view that drinking was destructive and that young men needed to live a moral life, but he made no attempt to crack down hard on the men; nor did he send either AU or Phi headquarters a detailed report describing his reservations. Other evidence that not all was well with the AU chapter existed for anyone who cared to investigate. Complaints against the Phis littered the desks of Auburn police officers and of Greek affairs office personnel. In one three-day period, police responded to three calls about the Phi Delt house. The Auburn Rugby Club claimed that the fraternity had damaged its goal posts. A partygoer at the house was injured by a thrown beer bottle. Bands played loud music after hours while neighbors fumed. Members fought with fraternity males from rival houses.

Unknown to Bowen or the police, Chad continued to pledge even after he had incurred a back injury. When his parents asked about his back, Chad said he might have hurt it moving furniture for brothers. The Sauciers sensed a fib and confronted him. He confessed that a shove had caused the injury. His parents were under the impression that he felt intimidated by the hazing. Rita Saucier said,

> Chad was always big for his age, but he was fearful. Some kids, they'll do whatever even if they get kicked in the head or hurt. Chad was not like that. He didn't like being hit or hurt. That's why he was so scared in that fraternity. He was also fearful for what was happening to the other [pledges]. Every time he came home we'd talk about him getting out of it. He said they would hide under the table in someone's apartment so they [the members] couldn't make them run errands. It was like they sort of controlled their lives. But in the meantime he bonded with the other pledges, and I guess that's what [the fraternity] wanted.[8]

Chad sat out during pledge calisthenics sessions, though he feared that one of his brothers would have to do his exercises to take up the slack for him. In spite of the rest, by Thanksgiving he was in so much pain that he sought medical treatment in Mobile. Upset by this development, Dr. Saucier grilled his son. Chad said that he had been blindfolded and forced to eat unpleasant substances. "Chad agreed to tell me about the hazing he was experiencing only if I promised not to tell anyone; he was very scared that he would be punished if they found out he was telling," said Dr. Saucier.[9]

After hearing the story, Dr. Saucier felt ethically obliged to renege on his promise. Hoping to spare Chad, the doctor wrote an anonymous letter to the Auburn Interfraternity Council (IFC). He charged that a Phi Delt pledge had been blindfolded, stripped to his drawers, and shoved during a lineup. Dr. Saucier might as well have kept his letter in a drawer. Auburn's interfraternity body failed to conduct a house inspection, perhaps because the complaint lacked a signature.

Chad Saucier had a way of making his mother, Rita Saucier, laugh. His death following an Auburn University Phi Delta Theta traditional party devastated her, and it prompted her to found a largely one-woman anti-hazing group called CHAD (Cease Hazing Activities and Deaths). *Photo courtesy of Rita Saucier*

In spite of the sore back, Chad continued pledging, driven by pride, susceptibility to peer pressure, and inertia. He hated to think that the hard work he had put into pledging would be wasted. Chad followed a sort of eleventh commandment—*thou shalt not quit*—that, ever the athlete, he refused to break.

In early December Chad came home from AU to serve as a pall-bearer for his maternal grandfather. He helped his mother deal with her loss, seemingly without regard for his own. After the funeral, Chad hugged his mother and drove back to Auburn. One of his fraternal obligations was to purchase a silly costume for the Phi Delt Christmas Party. The traditional chapter party was scheduled for the Thursday evening before "Dead Day," which marked the end of AU classes and the beginning of exams.

Pledges were in a celebratory mood on the day of the party. Big brothers let it slip that this was the last night of pledging. Whether the pledges were actually to be inducted, only the members knew. One common form of mental hazing is for members to tell initiates they are one step from induction, and then—after putting them through a physical ordeal—to yank the carrot away under the pretext that the pledges are undeserving. "Hi, Mom," Chad said in a message he left on Rita Saucier's answering machine. "I'm dressed like an elf going to the Christmas party. [I'm] getting up early tomorrow morning to come home."[10]

Chad met fellow pledges at an appointed apartment. A friend snapped a photograph of them wearing grins and green hats. They passed each other Jagermeister, selected not for its cloying minty taste, but because it had a reputation for getting collegians drunk fast. Growing more boisterous with each swallow they took, the pledges scrambled into cars for the drive to the fraternity house. Only one of the drivers had drunk nothing.

No AU police were at the house to supervise activities. Police were not mandated to attend private fraternity parties unless there was live music, and they worked parties only when a band played. Not only was the adviser absent, but the house mother went to her room to turn in early.

The pledge brothers arrived at the rambling Delta Phi house, showing their lowly place by climbing through an open window on the first floor. Most of the pledges brought unopened bottles. The Phi tradition at AU was for little and big brothers to swap liquor. Another pledge had bought Chad's bottle for him using a fake ID card.[11]

Chad swapped bottles with his big brother, John M. Lamberth, who was twenty-one.[12] Members expected that pledges would gulp their bottle's contents—if they dared. Growing uneasy as the alcohol level on Chad's bottle sank rapidly, Lamberth suggested that Chad switch from booze to soda pop. Chad retorted that if he had to drink it, he might as well drink it fast.[13]

Bottle exchanges are prohibited by AU and Phi Delt headquarters. The National Interfraternity Conference (NIC) has found this custom one of the hardest traditions to change. Traditions provide new members with a sense of connection to past and present members, said Sigal, who was an undergraduate in Klan Alpine at Alfred University (but who stressed that he would no longer join a fraternity today) some years before Chuck Stenzel died during a Klan pledging activity involving heavy drinking. "It is these traditions, whether rites of passage or a family party at Thanksgiving, that keep us from getting lost, give life meaning and maintain our sanity to the extent they can," he said.

In addition to finishing off the bottles they had exchanged, pledges, exuberant about being treated as near-equals, drank when brothers called their names and bade them drink. Members ordered pledges Hays Waller and Timothy DeLong to "shoot" shots as soon as they walked into the house.[14]

America fell in love with Charles (Chuck) Stenzel when he starred as "Chucky" with his grandmother, Doreen Stenzel, in a 1971 Geritol commercial. After his death at Alfred University while he was a Klan Alpine pledge, his mother fought for tough hazing laws in New York and other states.
Photograph courtesy of Eileen Stevens and CHUCK

As the liquor took effect, bedlam swept the enormous Phi house. People threw bottles against walls, smashed them on steps. Spilt alcohol permeated every crevice. Vomit lay where it fell. The Phi Delts egged on the swillers, razzed those who spilled whiskey. If pledges killed a bottle, members cheered. If pledges motioned "no mas," members hooted. "I wanted to do it. Everybody that was there was doing it. Nobody was specifically yelling at my face or anything, you know, 'turn that bottle up,' or anything," said Strada. "It was just—I mean, it was just understood, that you were there, you were going to drink."

Not all the members liked the frenzied drinking. Doug Ray threw Strada's bottle in the trash. Other brothers tried to get the pledges to slow down. But the members who wanted the drinking to continue prevailed. Members stationed in various rooms encouraged the pledge class to shoot more whiskey, ignoring a sign that said no one under twenty-one was allowed to drink. Chad began dancing by himself. When he talked, his speech was loud and slurred. Although he was able to stand, he staggered when he tried to walk. Nor was he alone in this behavior. A pledge who wasn't drinking would have stood out like a sore thumb, Strada said. "When you are an eighteen-year-old college freshman, that's not what you want to be."[15]

"There was definitely pressure," said Strada. "Pretty much everybody there was drinking. And I mean you got a bottle of liquor—so you could . . . go along with the crowd."

Shortly after 9:00 P.M. the members gathered for the traditional skit. A brother in a Santa Claus suit roasted the brothers to the elves. Lamberth attended the spoof. Chad failed to show.

The alcohol started hitting other pledges hard. Waller began to stagger. A brother locked him upstairs in a room, saying it was for Waller's safety. Strada, too, was having trouble navigating. He and a second pledge accepted a set of car keys from a Phi Delt, went to a car in the house's parking lot, and fell asleep out of everyone's sight. Mark Mostellar left the scene early. He went back to the apartment without Waller and Chad.

At 10:50 P.M. about two dozen Phis swapped fists with neighboring Pi Kappa Phi members. A police cruiser pulled up, and everyone scattered. Back in the Phi house pumped-up fighters sang the praises of the best fighters and jeered those who had been knocked down.

Just before or after the squabble, Lamberth went outside and located Chad snoring near some bushes next to an air-conditioning unit. A light rain was falling. Chad's elf suit was torn. Other members came by. One turned him over to clear his air passage. Chad showed no sign of awakening. Vomit freckled his mouth.

Members had trouble carrying Chad up the steps. Broken glass cut into his skin as he bounced on the stairs and floor. Lamberth wanted to give Chad his room, but a member who lived in Room 107 was insistent. "Let's just put him in mine," he said.

Members removed the befouled elf suit. Chad wore only briefs. They put a pillow under his head and covered him with a comforter. Blood from his gashes stained the floor. Chad's snoring was loud. Members took this for a reassuring sign that he was sleeping off the booze. They put him face down. A cooler of beer sat a few feet away from where he slept. The members intended to check on Chad when they came in to get a new bottle. But there were other places in the house where they could grab a beer, and consequently half an hour or an hour passed during which no one checked. Some members continued to ask pledges to drink. Others left the house to eat, or played pool. When at last a young man entered the room where Chad lay, he recognized that Chad's breathing was shallow. Vomit coated the pillow and comforter. Instead of phoning 911, the young man asked fraternity brothers to help.[16]

Members turned Chad this way, then that way. They were shocked when he wheezed and began writhing on the floor. Insufficient aeration of the blood had turned the surface of his skin a sickly blue. Alarmed, the young men debated what to do. Lamberth sat on the couch, petrified. Jeff Foster patted Chad's back. "Come on, Chad," he said. "Come on."

"Who knows CPR?" someone demanded. One member knew a little. In a panic he tried to revive Chad. Chris Roberts pounded the pledge's chest. Every now and then the young men cursed and blamed one another for not keeping an eye on him. Denying the reality in front of them, the members hoped Chad would sit up so they all could laugh with relief. Perhaps a few recalled Phi Delta Theta and AU warnings about the dangers of hazing and alcohol.

At 11:45 P.M. a police dispatcher took a call. The young men with Chad had called 911 at last. "Someone is choking in the Phi Delt house," the caller said.

Police arrived to not one but two emergencies. Hays Waller was on the ground outside the house. He had fallen through the window of the room in which he had been locked. He was dazed and bleeding from facial cuts but had survived the fall, which could have snapped his neck. Not only was he intoxicated, but his mobility was impaired because he had pulled his stretch tights down around his ankles, for whatever reason.[17] The thump of Waller's body meeting the earth had awakened the Phi Delt house mother, and she approached an officer who was assisting the pledge. An emergency unit whisked Waller to East Alabama Medical Center.

Inside the house, fraternity member Brett S. Sheedy was trying to get air into Chad as police and then paramedics arrived. Although Chad was still, the fraternity men standing watch outside Room 107 took comfort from Sheedy. He was sure Chad had a pulse.

Evidence of a bacchanal was everywhere. Broken glass and rubble crunched under the rescuers' shoes. In other places they walked through pools of liquid. Bottles littered the stairs and hallways. Cups covered the floor like shells on a battlefield. The stench of stale beer permeated everything. Some people told the police that Chad had consumed a quart of liquor; some said it had been a fifth.

Paramedics ranked Chad's condition as "unresponsive," the lowest value on a four-point scale. He didn't respond to sounds or to pain. He had no heartbeat. His respiratory system had shut down.

The rescue team cleared his airway, hooked him up to an oxygen tank, and administered epinephrine and atropine. When he failed to respond, they put him inside a second ambulance that took off with its red light flashing. In the vehicle a paramedic and a police officer took turns attempting to revive Chad with chest compressions. For thirty seconds his pulse flickered. The shrieking ambulance reached East Alabama Medical Center. It was now Friday, December 10, 1993.

Dead Day at AU had begun.

ALTERED LIVES

A phone call awakened Dr. Saucier. The Center's emergency room physician tersely rattled off the facts. Chad had passed out at "a party." Rescuers had been unable to bring him back. He had pronounced Chad dead at 1:20 A.M. So very sorry for your loss.

Dr. Saucier thought he was hearing words in a nightmare. He told himself to stand on the cold hardwood floor, and he would wake up.

He stood. Heard the caller still talking. Knew he was awake.

"As a physician I have always been struck by how senseless the death of a young person seemed to be," said Dr. Saucier. "Frequently I wondered how the family would cope, how their lives would be altered forever. Now I know."

At 3:00 A.M. Rita Saucier heard knocking, first in a dream, then in reality. She slipped into a robe. Saw her ex-husband through double glass doors.

"What is it?" She beheld the horror in his eyes, saw him fight for composure. "Is it my mom?"

He shook his head.

"It's *not* Chad."

She screamed and screamed. The two Saucier daughters ran into the room.

"He's not dead. *No, he's not dead!*" she told Saucier. She ran into Chad's room. Looked for things important to him. Found his baseball cap and a favorite picture of his. *If I hold onto these*, she thought, *he won't be dead*.

Dr. Saucier was firm. "You've got to call your family."

"No, if I don't call them he won't be dead."

He helped her to the phone, and she called her sister. Chad *was* gone.

The phone rang. A neighbor offered Rita Saucier her condolences. The shattered Phi Delt pledges and members had called their parents, their friends at the University of Alabama, their siblings in Mobile.

Had Dr. Saucier arrived minutes later, he would have been too late to break the news to his ex-wife.

Back at AU, Mostellar awoke to find his fraternity big brother in the apartment he shared with Waller and Chad Saucier. The big brother shook Mostellar. "Get out of here," Mostellar said.

"Wake up. Chad is dead, and Hays is in the hospital."

Even in the earliest fraternities, hard-drinking members clashed with fraternity leaders who thought drunkenness tarnished the fraternity's image. As the leader of the Old Miami of Ohio chapter of Phi Delta Theta, future U.S. president Benjamin Harrison kicked out several brothers who had embarrassed the fraternity while drinking. *Photo courtesy of Benjamin Harrison Home*

Mostellar groped for words. "When is [Chad] going to be back?"

"Chad is dead."

"Okay," said Mostellar. He sat up.

REFORMERS V. HEDONISTS IN BENJAMIN HARRISON'S FRATERNITY

Phi Delta Theta was founded by six students at Miami of Ohio in 1848. It operated as a sub-rosa organization until it gained the approval of a college president at Old Miami who at first opposed collegiate secret societies. The six founders saw their organization as a fraternity based on strong moral principles. They outlined the group's values in a declaration they called "The Bond of the Phi Delta Theta."

One of the first to join Old Miami's Phi Delt chapter after its founding was a transfer student named Benjamin Harrison. An orator in an age when smooth talkers were campus icons, Harrison became the Phi's chapter president in 1851. The Miami chapter had problems caused by alcohol, as did nineteenth-century adult secret societies such as the "merry" Masons, and U.S. society as a whole. The Old Miami chapter of Phi Delta Theta was chaotic with dissension between fraternal idealists and hedonists. Harrison, an idealist, believed alcohol needed to be consumed either not at all or in moderation. In chapter meetings he stressed that members' individual conduct reflected on the entire fraternity.[18]

Eventually some fraternity members' drinking reached a crisis point. Two fun-loving, hail-fellow-well-met Phi Delts embarrassed their chapter by becoming intoxicated at an out-of-town reception for Pierson Sayre, the last living Revolutionary War soldier. Some citizens had to dump the bodies of the two Phi Delts aboard a stage to get them back to the campus. Harrison, furious and shamed, warned the two to stay sober. They promised. But their thirst soon got them in trouble again. This time Harrison expelled them. Some other members quit the fraternity to support their ousted brothers, leaving only seven Phi Delts in the chapter. Determined to see the fraternity succeed, Harrison recruited replacements. Phi Delta Theta endured. And many years later, on the night that Benjamin Harrison was inaugurated as president of the United States, Phi Delt chapters and alums celebrated a brother's accomplishment.

At first the Phi Delts had little impact on the fraternal world outside Oxford, Ohio. But over time the international fraternity grew. It now has 180 undergraduate chapters, 100 alumni clubs, and 150,000 living alumni, making it one of the larger fraternities nationally and internationally (it has twelve chapters in Canada). Young men who joined the Phis in college include Neil Armstrong, Roger Ebert, Dabney Coleman, Lou Gehrig, Sam Nunn Jr., and college football legends Tom Harmon and Al Wistert. The national headquarters was particularly successful at creating new chapters in the South from 1873 to 1883. The Phi Delts were one of the three original fraternities founded at AU (then known by a different name) in the late 1870s. Fraternities came late to many southern schools, but once they arrived they were embraced by undergraduates struggling to figure out what it meant to be male in the defeated, post-Confederacy culture.

GOOD INTENTIONS AND PATTERNS OF MISBEHAVIOR

Before Chad's death, the international Phi Delta Theta organization had seen other young men perish or suffer injury as a result of alcohol abuse, hazing, and violent confrontations. Mike Spagoletti, eighteen, died of multiple stab wounds in a fight at Valparaiso University in Indiana after fraternity members tried to kick him out of the house. Dennis Redenbeck, a first-year student, died in his sleep after a long night of drinking beer, vodka, tequila, and brandy in bars and at the Iowa State University Phi house. University of Texas Phis transported pledges in a rental truck, stunned them with a cattle prod, and coated them with unappetizing foods and hot sauce. Paul Hayward, a visitor, died in an accidental fall at the Virginia Tech Phi Delt house after drinking beer he had brought with him. Jeff Nolting fell from the roof of the Kansas State University house during an annual chapter ritual that consisted of throwing televisions, stereos, and furniture off the roof. He died.

Though these losses may not suggest it, the Phi Delta Theta headquarters was one of the fraternities trying to end hazing in the late '70s. "The exception that has resulted in injury or death has become so common that fraternities can no longer permit any form of a hazing—period," noted Glen Cary, president of the Phi Delt General Council, in a confidential memorandum of February 15, 1979, that was sent to all chapter presidents. The memorandum continues:

> The risk is too great! The odds are against us. Hazing does not serve any constructive purpose we can identify. The purpose of a fraternity is the encouragement of the growth and development of the individual student. Hazing is detrimental to their growth and possibly harmful to health. Therefore, all hazing shall be eliminated. . . . Inspiring, motivating and leading pledges is hard work. Many do not now have that ability. So you must recognize that as your initial problem.
>
> We love each of you. We want to be as positive as possible. We want you to have a good time and enjoy your fraternal association. We want everything great and good to come your way. We want to honor and commend you for top performance and for being a credit and example to the Fraternity. But if we have no other alternative and if we must, we are prepared to be as tough as we have to be to stop hazing. We are committed to this objective and we hope that you will join us in our endeavor to make Phi Delta Theta a safe Fraternity to pledge, where all men are treated with respect!

JUSTICE OR INJUSTICE?

The day Chad died, the high school friends he had promised to meet at the St. Paul–Colbert County football game in Mobile stood with bowed heads after the public address announcer requested a minute of prayer. Coach Bob Rutledge announced that he had dedicated the game to Chad's memory. Chad's funeral attracted everyone from Mobile who knew him, and many who did not. Phi Delta Theta brothers and pledges attended. In spite of the circumstances, Rita Saucier appreciated their presence. She found herself ill equipped to bear another funeral so soon after the death of her father. Her grief overcame her. For nearly a year, she fought to talk about Chad without breaking down.

After the funeral, a dam of silence separated the Phi Delt pledges from the Saucier family, said Mrs. Saucier. Investigators of hazing deaths and injuries are often stymied in their attempt to get facts because members of secret societies believe that breaking their code of silence is disloyal, and insurance carriers instruct fraternities never to admit liability when faced with a potential claim. For some, loyalty is the same as integrity, to borrow a phrase from the movie *L.A. Confidential*. Rita Saucier said she learned that the Phi Delt attorney had advised the pledges not to talk to the media. "Here they are having lost one of their almost brothers, and you'd think [headquarters] would be sending someone to help these boys with their grief, and [instead] they send someone to tell them not to talk to anybody," said Mrs. Saucier in a 1998 telephone interview for this book. "Then they say nothing they did was wrong."

The Phi Delt members quickly initiated the pledges. AU had suspended Delta Phi, but the chapter conducted initiation ceremonies at Georgia Southern. One of Chad's pledgemates declined to be initiated.

Strada accepted. "I feel the fraternity was responsible for what happened, but I think that if it had been a year later, I would have been participating in the exact same events and would have been just as much the blame for it," Strada later said. "[Phi] was responsible [because] if we wouldn't have done it that night, he would probably still be alive."[19]

In time the Sauciers received the autopsy report. Chad's blood-alcohol level was 0.353 at the time of his death. He had swallowed enough alcohol to make four men his size drunk.

AU clamped a lid on all but essential facts, said Rita Saucier. University President William Van Muse told the *Mobile Register* that all questions would need to be answered by Pat Barnes, vice president for student affairs. Barnes in turn declined to comment.[20]

Nonetheless, newspaper reporters and the Sauciers began collecting information about the evening. Mrs. Saucier heard with disbelief that Chad's snoring had reassured the members that her son was all right and had contributed to the brothers' decision to delay calling 911 until Chad's system had all but shut down. "Snoring means people are dying and trying to breathe," she said. "The thing is that it would have been *so* simple to save him."

She phoned President Muse. "He was sorry and said, 'accidents happen,'" said Mrs. Saucier in a 1998 interview for this book. "He said if there was anything he could do, let him know."

She did let him and the student affairs staff know, and some of her requests were heeded. In time, AU advertised a phone number so students could report hazing, for example. But the administration refused her request that they dissolve the chapter and end its charter. "Grant [Davis] and Muse called Chad's death an 'isolated incident,'" she said. "They considered Chad's death an accident."[21] No member of the Phi Delt chapter was ever prosecuted for criminal hazing.

As is true of many university presidents today, the sixty-year-old William Van Muse's vita lists more impressive fiscal and leadership accomplishments than it does noteworthy scholarly achievements. He has shown himself willing to make unpopular decisions; he eliminated 350 jobs at AU shortly after coming to the institution from the University of Akron presidency in 1992. He has tried to raise faculty salaries and has quieted grumblings over academic freedom of expression that sprang up during the previous president's tenure.

Muse has a strong backer in the NIC. Executive Vice President Jonathan J. Brant offers compelling anecdotal evidence that undergraduate Greeks need positive role models such as Muse in their lives. In an age during which research-oriented university professors often distance themselves from students, fraternal leaders stress that involved college administrators such as Muse should be praised, not condemned, for their concern about and willingness to devote time to students.

The son of a Mississippi Church of God pastor, Muse has been a successful chief operating officer leading a university known in the '80s and '90s for respectable academic offerings and a generally strong sports programs in spite of modest state appropriations. In addition, his experience with Greek life on the national level has given him a positive perspective on fraternities and sororities. Muse has been a long-time NIC director, and his Marquis *Who's Who in the South and Southwest* listing notes not only that he is a current member and past national president of Tau Kappa Epsilon fraternity, and that he once worked for TKE as a field supervisor, but that he maintains his memberships in Blue Key, Omicron Delta Kappa, Phi Kappa Phi, Delta Sigma Pi, Beta Gamma Sigma, and Pi Omega Pi. One of the two books he has written is titled *Management Practices in Fraternities*. During the mid- to late 1960s, before the rash of pledging-related deaths occurred and while he held the chair in the College of Business Administration at Ohio University, Muse called upon national fraternities to make sweeping changes in pledging programs. Muse's background would have rankled Upton Sinclair, an author known for his savage attacks on academics who supported their fraternities, gave the Greeks privileges and status, and sometimes even sold them campus land at giveaway prices to build houses. In *The Goose-Step: A Study of American Education*, Sinclair pricked what he viewed as the blind cronyism of "academic bigwigs" whose *Who's Who* biographies listed "their Kappa-Gamma-Gobbles and their Alpha-apple-pies."

On the other hand, is such a dismissal actually fair in the case of Muse, who continues to address Greek fraternities and sororities nationally, imploring young people to change their ways and encouraging Greek organizations to maintain a strong presence in their college and larger communities? Even Muse, who said he had the best possible undergraduate chapter experience as a TEKE, has grown discouraged by the failure of fraternities in particular, and sororities to a far lesser extent, to learn from past failures or to take advice from fraternal elders such as himself. "Absolutely, the Greeks are making the same mistakes over and over again on the same issues," said Muse. "My own gut feeling from being on the international fraternal scene is that there is a growing intolerance and weariness about fraternities, even among those who are generally supportive of fraternities."

Dr. and Mrs. Saucier strongly maintain that at some level political considerations influenced the almost total absence of punitive actions taken on the part of AU in the aftermath of Chad's death. Douglas Fierberg, an attorney who has handled a number of cases involving hazing incidents, said that his decision whether or not to sue a school or fraternal group is based on the appropriateness of the authorities' response once they have determined that hazing or some other fraternal misbehavior has occurred. On one hand, a check of AU policies showed that steps taken by the school following Chad's death were in line with established procedure for student judicial cases. On the other, Fierberg certainly would have questioned the school's punishment of fraternity members, had the case been his. Just one member of Phi Delta Theta was found guilty of furnishing a minor with alcohol; he was given fifty hours of community service and a paper to write. The punishment fell short of what the Sauciers expected. "Oh, he wrote a paper!" snapped Mrs. Saucier when she was asked if she was satisfied that justice had been done.[22] The police cited only one person attending the party for underage drinking.

Rita Saucier wanted Muse and Davis to slap the 114-year-old Phi Delt chapter with the stigma of being hazers and recommend expulsion. But after examining all the evidence, AU decided that suspension was the appropriate punishment. A council tried twenty-seven Phi Delta Theta members for hazing and found all not guilty. "How on earth can they say there was no hazing?" asked Mrs. Saucier.[23]

Dr. and Mrs. Saucier maintain that the AU administration turned a blind eye to dysfunctional aspects of the Greek system. The fact that the Christmas party took place year after year at the Phi house made it no "isolated" instance, in her view. She saw the actions of members who encouraged the chugging as either negligent or something more serious, charging that they should have been aware of the possible consequences of their actions.

President Muse certainly has not forgotten the incident, and he does ponder whether today's rampant alcohol problems in Greek affairs and in society at large merit more drastic punishments. "Maybe we should have been tougher; maybe we should have said [to such chapters as Phi Delta Theta], 'You're gone forever,'" he said in February 1999.

For President Muse, the decision to punish the chapter for three years and to ban the perpetrators from all Greek involvement as undergraduates seemed the right one at the time. He said that Phi Delta Theta and other fraternal organizations involved in serious incidents are punished with an eye toward educating the individuals involved. But with deaths escalating and his own best efforts too often ignored by students in Greek groups, he does say that he now sometimes considers taking more forceful action in the future based upon what has happened in the past. "From our perspective on campus we had to take quick, decisive action, as we did . . . , against both the organization and the individuals who are directly involved. There should not be any equivocation in doing so," said Muse in an interview with the author on February 18, 1999. "It's intended to be a learning experience. You hope that when young people encounter these kinds of situations that they will learn from it. . . . There certainly have to be lessons. You hope that all the young men involved or women who are present on such occasions learned a great deal from the [hazing and binge drinking deaths and injuries]. You hope they learn very clearly and sadly some of the consequences of behavior of this sort."

Eileen Stevens, who began the Committee to Halt Useless College Killings (CHUCK) after her son, Chuck Stenzel, died at Alfred, befriended Mrs. Saucier after Chad's death. She said that when a group has engaged in a systematic pattern of hazing and someone is seriously hurt or killed, a crime, not an accident, has occurred. To Stevens, hazing over time means that the odds will eventually catch up with the hazers, making these injuries or deaths almost inevitable, and not "isolated."

Days after Rita Saucier buried her son, she went to the Phi Delt house. She was taken aback by the immensity of the gray stucco mansion. She had been unaware that some houses at AU are valued at more than one million dollars. "Looking at it from the outside, you imagine that the inside is beautiful, but it wasn't," said Rita Saucier. "It was destroyed."

The Phi Delts had been suspended and were moving out. She said hello to a young member packing boxes. He and she looked uneasily at the ruined interior. "It's like they tried to tear it up," she said. The pledge educator—a fraternity member chosen by the brothers to oversee pledging—showed her Room 107. Although someone had scrubbed the floor, Chad's blood (and that of a rescue worker cut by glass) remained.

A BAND-AID ON A HEART WOUND

Dr. Saucier sued Phi Delta Theta and the AU Beta chapter of Phi Delta Theta, the fraternity's adviser, and several individual members of the AU chapter. Under state law, AU and its officials could not be sued, although some had to testify.

"The administrative officials from Auburn were smug. Some were products of Auburn University and had been active in fraternities themselves," Dr. Saucier said. His impression was that the immunity gave some AU officials confidence almost to the point of arrogance. "They had the appearance of politicians adept at dodging issues, and [they] had come up through the ranks being politically correct. Their message was that the fraternity house was a private home and they had no jurisdiction over [it], although it was located on campus and did have to follow other rules and regulations of the university. It became obvious that this was posturing which had been used before."

In contrast, the students talked freely about their alcohol consumption, balking only when asked to point fingers at their peers. Dr. Saucier anticipated that the students would be nervous. Instead, with one exception, they were poised. "John Lambert was visibly remorseful," said Dr. Saucier. "John took Chad's death hard."[24]

He said that some of the members and former pledges who shared Chad's final minutes may not realize the full impact of their actions until they have sons and daughters of their own. "They will someday learn that their lives have been unfairly changed," he said. "Most of these young men were very bright and articulate who came from very loving and caring families. Unfortunately, these young men were recruited into [a fraternity] and placed their trust in an organization that had lost its focus and perspective."[25]

When members of the Auburn police force testified in the case, their depositions gave Dr. Saucier the impression that AU had tied their hands with regard to enforcing alcohol regulations. The police "had seen it all, and you could get the feeling that if they had their way, without administrative interference, things would be different on campus," said Dr. Saucier. "They knew the magnitude of the problem and knew that the administration would just as soon not know [about violations of the law]."[26]

During the depositions taken by Saucier's attorney, the disclosures most damaging to the defendants came from Bo Bowen, who had been the province president for Phi Delta Theta. He was a nondrinker whose own drinking had accelerated as a fraternity member and star football player at Ole Miss. He testified that he quit "because drinking would have killed me if I hadn't." Bowen's responses to attorney questions illustrate the gap between the Phi headquarters' hazing/alcohol policies and the day-to-day activities of undergraduates. He admitted that he had been aware that hazing and underage drinking occurred at the chapter house, but that he had failed to expose the practices. "I think . . . anyone that has gone to college in America . . . knows what the practice is in fraternity houses . . . that, generally speaking, . . . there is much drinking at fraternity parties across the board with all ages," he said.[27]

Dr. Saucier's attorneys experienced delay after delay before they could get Bowen to give his deposition. "Once we were able to depose him, it became obvious as to why they had tried to stall," said Dr. Saucier. "He was one of the administrative officials who was honest to admit and recognize that Phi Delta Theta had a problem within its organization and had failed to act in a responsible manner. He came up to me after his deposition and apologized for his organization's action or the lack of. He indicated to me that he had been telling his superiors for a long time that they were trying to place a Band-Aid on something that needed heart surgery."

Phi Delta Theta settled with Dr. Saucier in January 1996. Court documents were blacked out in the area specifying a settlement. But the *Mobile Register* cited a source close to the case, Dr. Saucier's attorney, who claimed that the settlement was in the amount of "several million dollars."

WHEN BAD THINGS HAPPEN TO GOOD PROGRAMS

Unlike much larger schools where multiple hazing deaths have occurred, AU is not nationally regarded as a hotbed of hazing. In fact, several national AU administrators and staff have a good reputation for fighting hazing. Grant Davis and his wife have supported Eileen Stevens's anti-hazing group, as has AU's President Muse. Deborah Shaw Conner of AU's Office of Student Life has published her outspoken views against sorority hazing; she is also a spokesperson against hazing in *Friendly Fire*, an anti-hazing educational film paid for by many NIC and National Panhellenic Conference (NPC) Greek groups.[28] Auburn's IFC publishes a "Parents' Guide to Fraternities."[29] In spite of all this, Chad Saucier died on the AU campus. "There are so many things we have learned from Chad's death, but if I had to state one thing—and that is relevant to AU—it would be that even a conservative, traditional, friendly campus in a small town such as Auburn University is not immune to the dangers of alcohol and hazing," said Conner.[30]

Chad's death made it clear that protections available under Alabama state law for administrators and parents whose child dies while in college are different from those in place in some other states. Given that Chad was an adult capable of making adult choices about drinking, if the death had occurred in a state with a harsher hazing statute, the university could have been brought to court to determine whether school negligence was a factor. In order for the university to have been acquitted, a lawyer for the plaintiff would almost certainly have had to prove that the university had failed in its duty to do everything in its power to quash an extended pattern of dangerous activity at the Phi house. Nationally, outside of a handful of cases, schools tend to escape litigation after a hazing or pledging-related death, particularly if the university maintains a hands-off relationship with Greek groups or if the incident occurred off campus.

What the Sauciers learned as a result of their lawyer's research was that the AU Phi Delta Theta chapter was made up of an odd mixture of people who could act magnanimously one evening and like buccaneers the next. On the one hand, it produced a number of alumni who gave generously to the school and who became useful citizens as adults. On the other, after 1960 the history of the AU Phi Delt chapter includes all the following misdeeds:

◆ The AU Phi chapter was on disciplinary probation in 1961/1962 and on social probation from 1962 to 1964. The Phi Delts were disciplined by the IFC and by the AU administration.

◆ A January 22, 1963, memorandum from an AU dean decried Phi Delta Theta's problems with alcohol.

◆ Alcohol and discipline problems escalated in the two decades following 1960. The Committee on Fraternities and Sororities, made up partially of AU faculty, recommended that AU cease to recognize the Phi Delts. But influential alums helped the chapter evade the death penalty.

◆ In 1982, Grant Davis criticized Phi Delta Theta, saying it had shown "blatant disregard" for the IFC court.

◆ In 1984, members disrupted one pep-rally parade so thoroughly that AU authorities insisted the chapter stay away from the next parade.

◆ Allowed to take part in pep rallies again, Phi Delts exposed their bare behinds to marchers. The chapter was suspended in 1985.

◆ The chapter showed racial insensitivity, propping a demeaning black figurine on the house roof.

◆ The chapter failed to maintain its house. Once a suspicious fire occurred on the premises.

◆ The Phis were cited once after members destroyed the interior of the fraternity house.

◆ Women sometimes charged that the chapter treated them badly.

Police arrested Phi Delts for public intoxication after a female passerby said that members had harassed her. A second woman complained about what she termed a Phi Delt pledge's offensive behavior at an AU football game.

◆ Several years before Chad's death, the house pledged a young man who drank so much alcohol that he lapsed into a coma and would have died had he not received medical intervention. The 1986 AU president wrote a letter to Bob Biggs, who was the director of chapter services at Phi Delta Theta headquarters at the time, saying that the AU chapter had "a long record of irresponsible, unethical and dangerous behavior."[31] AU gave the chapter another chance in spite of AU Committee on Fraternities and Sororities findings concluding that Phi Delt's conduct was "irresponsible," "undesired," and "at times dangerous."[32]

◆ During the early 1990s, sober servers were not in attendance at Phi Delt parties; nor were designated drivers available to drive intoxicated persons home. Underage Phi Delts and visitors drank in the house. Hazing became problematic, too.

After Chad Saucier's death, Jack Walton, who was the AU police chief at that time, informed the *Mobile Register* that he "would not confirm student reports that the fraternity, made up mostly of Mobile residents, had a reputation for being 'rowdy.'"[33] Nonetheless, AU clearly did take notice of the death. It has instituted some changes and has successfully obtained many grants for reducing risks related to alcohol and other dangers on campus. Edward Lee Thomas Jr., AU's former assistant director of student activities, was named CADRE (Creating Alcohol and Drug Resistance through Education) coordinator. AU received a two-year federal grant from the U.S. Department of Education's Fund for the Improvement of Post-Secondary Education, enabling the university to use a community-meeting approach to launch awareness campaigns. The NIC named AU, together with Miami of Ohio and San Diego State University, as one of three model Adopt-a-School programs, an educational initiative designed to put undergraduates in elementary school classrooms to serve as role models for children.

It is significant that in spite of the administration's anti-hazing fervor, the university has had problems controlling hazing and drinking. Greek and university officials find it frustrating that all their hard work and programs are for naught when tragedies occur in Greek houses. Undergraduates seem to defy their leaders' mandates when the young people are asked to institute reforms. Witness the following: No other national fraternity executive spends as much time talking to university students about hazing as does Executive Director Dave Westol of Theta Chi, a national fraternity begun in 1856. But in 1997 and 1998, Theta Chi headquarters revoked at least two charters and put twenty-nine chapters on probation for financial irresponsibility and/or alcohol, drug, and hazing incidents. Two alcohol-related deaths occurred during this period, and just a fifty-minute drive from Theta Chi headquarters, the Indiana University chapter house was raided by campus police for major alcohol violations. Some Greek observers think the crackdown is a good thing, saying that Westol is indicating clearly that he will not tolerate fraternal lapses in individual chapters. Others worry that the work of fraternal reformers has inspired rebellion in their own undergraduates.

Rita Saucier expressed her concern that recent hazing incidents occurring at AU appear particularly odious and may indicate a pattern of misbehavior that will only get worse if those chapters are not rooted out permanently. Sigma Pi pledge Kyle Long complained that he'd been beaten and kicked, and that dog feces had been wiped on him, although criminal charges were dismissed for lack of evidence and because of fraternity claims that he had participated willingly in some hazing events. Kappa Alpha Order members verbally abused pledges and intimidated them with firecrackers, according to the witness accounts of Davis and of Jim Hardin, assistant director of student life. Kappa Alpha members made pledges slide in the intestines of a deer; endure a barrage of raw eggs; and stand in a ditch filled with water, excrement, and vomit, according to charges made by former pledge Jason Jones. At Kappa Sigma, two TV reporters posed as brothers from another school to videotape members encouraging pledges to drink. The *Dateline NBC* tape was never shown nationally by the show's producers because Kappa Sigma and AU officials convincingly argued their belief that unfair tactics had been employed to catch the fraternity in the act. Even AU's honor society, Spades, found itself in trouble. Members tied a newcomer to a tree, brandished a gun, and told him he was going to die. Spades received a two-month suspension.

Davis wants undergraduates to take responsibility for their actions—to see their foolish behaviors for what they really are and to change them. He said that one reason it is so difficult to eliminate hard drinking and hazing is that many collegiate men and women view alcohol-related events "as fun," although he stressed that he himself sees such events as anything but fun. At the time of Chad's death, the AU Phis had survived so many alcohol theme parties, celebrations, and chugging contests, and had seen so many young men pass out without being harmed, that they not only were inured to the dangers of drinking but also regarded risk-taking as a form of entertainment. For AU to modify its students' alcohol use, said Davis, a national shift in students' attitudes toward alcohol and proper pledging activities first has to take place. In a 1998 interview with the author, he emphasized his point with a thick stack of publications that AU puts out in an attempt to change unhealthy student attitudes. Muse was forthright when asked if all the expense and staff time would someday bring about changes in the Greek world in general and in society at large. "Am I optimistic that young people are going to see the error of their ways and change?" pondered Muse in a 1999 interview, shortly after many international fraternity undergraduate delegates had rejected pleas from their adult leaders to get rid of alcohol by 2000. "I really don't know. . . . Something has to turn the attitude of the young people around."

More than three decades after the end of in loco parentis on American university campuses, a growing number of administrators from AU to the University of Washington have been trying to change the attitudes of the estimated eight out of ten undergraduates in Greek groups who regularly drink alcohol to excess. The figures come from a 1998 Harvard School of Public Health study conducted by investigator Henry Wechsler, Ph.D., and from a telephone interview with Wechsler conducted by the author on January 29, 1999.

During that interview, Wechsler said that the evidence compels him to say that alcohol and hazing are so much a part of the very bloodstream of Greek organizations that he can see no outcome other than the gradual dissolution of Greek groups on college campuses. "We've demonstrated that there are problems to the drinker and to the others on campus with drinking at that [high] level," said Wechsler. "I've noted fraternity people telling me they're cleaning up their acts, but I don't see it."

In February 1999, Lincoln University in Pennsylvania announced that it was seriously thinking about dissolving its Greek system because of recurrent problems, while in New Hampshire, Dartmouth's president ordered Greek groups to go coeducational or go away, a decision that sparked immediate campus protests and vigils.

Muse said he is not willing to accept Wechsler's recommendations or to follow Dartmouth's example and shut down AU's still-strong Greek system. For Muse, to do so would be to give up on young people altogether, and that goes against the grain of his impulse to educate young people to see for themselves that hazing and binge drinking are the wrong moral choices to make. Muse said that national awareness of alcohol and hazing problems needs to begin with young people themselves, so that a change in the culture can begin to take place. "The quick solution is to eliminate fraternities, and you eliminate the problem but I don't think that is true," said Muse, adding that he doesn't see anyone eliminating athletic teams because surveys show that athletes are heavier-than-average drinkers. "I think it is a more deep-seated psychological problem in young people that they are acting out now through alcohol abuse. You're not going to eliminate binge drinking at Harvard either by getting rid of fraternities.

"I think the national fraternity leaders and the Greek campus leaders all have to maintain a consistent strong position that the behavior being exhibited by young people both individually and collectively in groups is not acceptable. It's not the kind of thing we endorse or condone. We need to take strong action when we find our policies have been violated—as we have done [at AU] on a number of occasions in alcohol- and hazing-related cases. While we [administrators] suspend operations of organizations, at the same time, for any significant shift in behavior to take place, the undergraduate leaders have to internalize and [change behavior]. [Instead,] the exterior pressure moves underground to a greater level of secrecy, and that's been our greatest problem with hazing. Unless the undergrads accept that hazing is not a good thing, they will simply go underground. It will be a very secret part of their operation, and you simply won't know about it until a pledge gets killed or something [bad] happens that exposes it to view."

Did the AU administration become a media scapegoat when its warnings about the dangers of alcohol consumption, hazing, and underage drinking went unheeded? Chad's tragic death involved young adults who were clearly out to deceive the administration when they pledged an ineligible nonstudent and sanctioned a drinking tradition that was considered hazing under AU and Phi Delta Theta rules. What were Chad's responsibilities? What about his parents'? Rita Saucier said she still blamed Phi Delta's leaders and AU for her son's death. It might have been prevented if the Phi Delt international and university officials had heeded warning signs and expelled the chapter as a repeat offender, she said.

However, Mrs. Saucier said she has also endured the agony of self-blame. In particular, she has hashed over the period following her divorce when she was away from Mobile tending her ill parents in Mississippi. Part of her way of atoning for what she feels is her role in the tragedy and of giving Chad's death some meaning has been to make a dramatic entrance as an anti-hazing activist, overcoming what she says are her woeful inadequacies as a public speaker and her minimal acquaintance with the Greek system to enhance awareness and to inspire pledging and alcohol reforms. Her crusade began when she returned to AU on November 5, 1997, accepting the invitation of AU's Lambda Chi Alpha chapter to speak about hazing. "They listened, and quite a few came up later and really wanted more information on alcohol," said Mrs. Saucier. She also said that a number of Chad's pledgemates came to see her after the talk and admitted to her that hazing went on the semester they pledged.

Stressing in her talks that she was against all Greeks who haze, not all Greeks, Mrs. Saucier expressed her opposition to chapters that view hazing and pledging as one and the same. She has asked fraternity executives to rethink their philosophies about philanthropy, requesting that they put more time into risk issues to protect members and pledges. "The fraternity that does good things can do as many philanthropic activities as it wants, but those don't equal the death of one man killed by that fraternity," said Mrs. Saucier.[34]

Inspired by Eileen Stevens's anti-hazing group CHUCK, Mrs. Saucier began CHAD (Cease Hazing Activities and Deaths). She spoke as an advocate against hazing on TV talk shows and wrote a letter about losing Chad that appeared in the Ann Landers column in 1998. She paid for anti-hazing messages to be published in the AU and University of Alabama student newspapers and approved a billboard reading "Hazing Kills—Break the Silence." In addition, Mrs. Saucier began lobbying to toughen Alabama's statute against hazing. How effective she can be as a public symbol of loss and grief remains to be seen. Her loss has changed her. "Since Chad died, I am not the same person," said Mrs. Saucier. "I try to go on, but nothing is ever the same as it was. That happy person is gone. She died with my son." Does Rita Saucier think fraternities have any redeeming qualities? "I try to look at it that there are some fraternities doing what they're meant to do, but I would say there are very few," said Mrs. Saucier.[35]

Her ex-husband has also tried to go on. Dr. Saucier bought the hobby farm Chad had dreamed of co-owning. "There are times when I sense his presence," he said.

AU welcomed back the Phi Delt chapter as a colony in 1997. Although former brothers were not permitted to be part of the group, many of Chad's pledgemates came to meetings. One stressed that fraternity membership had been a positive experience for him in spite of Chad's death. "You cannot learn in a classroom the important lessons life in a fraternity house teaches you," said John Montgomery, president of the recolonized chapter, in a 1998 telephone interview with the author.

Fraternity headquarters concurred with AU that Phi Delta Theta had completed all the steps required to return to campus. The AU chapter was rehabilitated and deserved a fresh start. "The chapter is now alcohol-free," said Biggs in a 1998 telephone interview, "and accountable." The Phis were fully reinstated in 1998.

Rita Saucier was outraged by the chapter's return. "Accountability? No way," she said in a 1998 telephone interview with the author. "The day a fraternity is closed down, the alumni get together to bring it back to campus. The chapter gets a slap on the hand, and the national looks good [in the eyes of the public]. Then, when the death of a pledge is out of people's minds, they come back."

Harvard's Wechsler tended to agree, saying fraternities are not solving their alcohol problems but are merely swapping the locales where they swill liquor. "I've just given up on them listening to reality. I think colleges have got to get very tough with them," said Wechsler in a 1999 interview for this book. "I see in the reports [from fraternities] that in the year 2000 or 2001 they're going to go alcohol free. What does dry really mean if they just go across the street?"

The degree to which Chad's death has influenced the chapter is unclear. The revamped Phi Delta Theta chapter said in a 1998 rush booklet published by the AU IFC that it is striving to maintain its founders' values of friendship, sound learning, and moral rectitude. But the Phis also reaffirmed the chapter's long commitment to partying, in spite of Chad's ghastly death five years earlier. "A strong social calendar is very prevalent to Phi Delta Theta," noted the fraternity's self-description. "We have many different parties during each quarter. Fall quarter has parties after each football game along with a homecoming party. Winter quarter has the ever famous Winter Whiskey and Bowery Ball. Last comes spring quarter which contains RastaPhi and Roman Party. These are only the big name parties which do not include smaller socials with other fraternities and sororities."[36]

Chad's death continued to haunt Biggs at the Phi headquarters in Ohio. "I didn't devote myself for life to the fraternity in order to attend the funerals of pledges and members," he said in a 1998 telephone interview with the author.

Chad Saucier's death, the attendant bad publicity, and Mrs. Saucier's crusade—combined with other Phi scandals nationally—appear to have had the effect of a sobering wakeup call on Biggs, who was able to use his personal influence as a highly regarded senior Greek administrator to persuade the Phi's General Council to change international headquarters' "talk tough" pose of 1979 to its present "act-tough" policies. Phi Delta Theta has become one of the national leaders of the attempt to make all fraternity houses dry during the twenty-first century, said Biggs in a 1998 telephone interview with the author. The Phi Delta Theta Foundation approved a $469,850 grant to the fraternity. Some of the money was earmarked for training and programs. Some was designated to give to twenty individual chapters for house improvements and other worthy enterprises on the condition that members make a no-return commitment to alcohol-free housing.

Like Sigma Phi Epsilon, Sigma Nu, Theta Chi, and several other fraternities, Phi Delta Theta has taken demonstrable action not just to shut down "animal houses" but also—in spite of the unpopularity of such activities—to educate and discipline bad-actor alumni members and to urge reform-minded alumni to play a larger role in helping undergraduates eliminate safety risks from Phi houses. "We are putting our future on the line for this principle," Biggs said in concluding an interview for this book. "We are determined to make Phi Delta Theta alcohol free."

Yet the road to reform may be blocked by the bad intentions of contumacious undergraduate Phi Delt chapters. In October 1998, Biggs faced three cases of clear undergraduate subordination, two of which had serious consequences. In one, the Stanford chapter, which had been in trouble for disciplinary problems since 1986, served alcohol in spite of a house ban, and resident Michael Howard, twenty-one, fell from a balcony and incurred serious brain and eye injuries. Stanford University immediately booted out the Phi Delta Theta chapter.

In the second case, after a Phi member gave a woman a lavaliere inscribed with Greek letters, Drake University Phis used tape to bind him to a tree on the chapter's property, and then covered him with spittle and spoiled food. He wore only underwear. Although the practice is banned as noncriminal hazing—if it does not cause injury and if it is performed with the consent of the person being taped—by the school and by national headquarters, the chapter was impenitent when police cut the man loose, and members promised to keep the tradition alive.

They may be legally able to do so. Several students at Iowa-based Loras College sued the school in 1997 after they were expelled for a noncriminal initiation involving their sub-rosa fraternity. The school ended up settling with the students in 1999, giving pause to advisers dealing with initiations that fall short of causing physical harm and that initiates or pledges claim they participated in voluntarily.[37]

The Loras initiation for a fraternity (not sanctioned by the school) involved covering newcomers with foodstuffs such as molasses and eggs. At least one serious injury occurred in an initiation in which eggs were used. A pledge at Alpha Tau Omega's University of Texas chapter contracted a severe bacterial infection after being pelted with eggs. He too won a settlement in that case.[38] Iowa's law (like weaker laws in Virginia and other states) does not sufficiently protect school officials trying to halt "voluntary" initiations.

In the third case, in October 1998 new Chi Omega pledges who were visiting the University of Michigan (UM) Phi Delt house, which had pledged to go dry, were given congratulatory bottles of champagne and allowed access to kegs of beer before eighteen-year-old pledge Courtney Cantor fell to her death from a dormitory window. Biggs and the national fraternity took forceful, unpopular action, yanking the UM charter and ordering members to leave the house. "The chapter members broke their commitment to keep their house alcohol-free," Biggs told the *Detroit News*. "The culture of alcohol is destructive to those values and has no place in Phi Delta Theta."[39]

In an October 1998 interview for this book, Lissa Bradford of the NPC called Biggs's decision to commit to alcohol-free houses "courageous." Bradford said that Biggs and other Phi Delt officers were "absolutely committed to an alcohol-free chapter house environment as the way to restore values to the fraternity experience. They are not going to turn back, and they are not scared to do the difficult enforcement, as evidenced by the closing of their Michigan chapter. Fraternities must quit being entertainment centers and return to their organizations the purpose and principles on which they were founded. They must reestablish themselves as places for scholars and leaders, not as a haven for those who are looking for a party house."

But it seems unlikely that fraternities will change in the way Bradford describes any time in the immediate future. Says Deborah Shaw Conner, "I have dealt with five hazing cases in the last three months, all at AU, all with some of our older, traditional chapters. One in particular sounds so similar to what the Phi Delts (Chad's group) were doing the night Chad died. . . . A Christmas party with lots of alcohol, pledges getting drunk, pledges performing for the actives, etcetera. Why are things not different after Chad's death? I wish I had the answer."[40]

2

Greekthink

DEFINING AND DEALING WITH HAZING

Most universities—Auburn among them—accept the definition coined by administrators of college social fraternal organizations belonging to the Fraternity Executives Association (FEA). That trade organization considers hazing to be "any action taken or situation created intentionally, whether on or off fraternity premises, to produce mental or physical discomfort, embarrassment, harassment or ridicule." Student guidelines often maintain that hazing can take place with or without the consent of the hazed. In reality, schools sometimes fail to press charges if pledges appear to have consented to some aspects of hazing and to have then tried to halt the proceedings. Fraternity executives and advisers to Greek groups cannot stress enough to members that no always means no in initiation situations.

Hazing is an extraordinary activity that, when it occurs often enough, becomes perversely ordinary as those who engage in it grow desensitized to its inhumanity. Hazing can lead to death or serious injury in four ways. One, ritual brings out people's innate propensity for violence. Two, members who act aggressively toward pledges may be using them as scapegoats through which to vent their own frustrations. Three, drinking itself has become ritualistic in universities. Shot glasses sport college logos, steins bear fraternal letters, and drinking games have conventional "rules" of play; even talking about drinking becomes habitual in certain circles, as does going out drinking as a form of recreation in itself. Four, rituals may provoke members who have psychological problems to behave violently.

Of course rituals may evoke positive human responses as well; they can be extremely beneficial for individuals who find ceremonies comforting or even life-enhancing.[1]

Fraternity members' group negligence, together with a failure on the parts of individuals to recognize the severity of a hazing situation because others in their company whom they trust seem unconcerned, is a hallmark of all hazing deaths. Students have died in ritualistic kidnappings, baptism-like water immersions, alcohol-chugging cases, and calisthenics in which violent activity was either absent or minimal.[2] Some have died or suffered permanent injuries as a result of brutal beatings administered by other fraternity members.

Although the public and the media view hazing as primarily a college fraternity and sorority problem, it has also been a social problem in the United States on amateur and professional athletic teams and in high schools, spirit clubs, bands, the military (particularly in elite units), some occupations and professions, adult secret societies, and youth groups such as the Boy Scouts and Future Farmers of America. Thus far in the United States, hazing deaths have predominantly occurred in schools of higher education, although activists worry that a fatality soon may occur as the result of a high school hazing during which an older student asks a first-year student to consume large amounts of alcohol. Of the dozens of hazing- and pledging-related deaths that have taken place in U.S. colleges since 1970, all but a handful happened in fraternities or sororities. Even some of those few apparently nonfraternal deaths (for example, those that occurred in a lacrosse club and in spirit clubs) involved young men who were also fraternity members. Athletic and spirit-club hazing differs from semester-long hazing in fraternities because the former generally takes the form of a single frenzied night of drinking or other potentially risky activities. In addition to hazing deaths, many other kinds of deaths occur in fraternities and sororities, as the computer-assisted search of records (Appendix A) in this book demonstrates. These include the deaths of members and guests because of accidental falls from house roofs, vehicular accidents, drinking overdoses, suicides, shootings, stabbings, fires, and pledging-related incidents that college authorities rightly or wrongly say do not involve hazing.[3]

Hazing is not only a campus safety issue; it poses ethical problems, too. It almost always involves rules-breaking and violations of honor codes. Frequently deception occurs before an incident, as when the Auburn Phi Delts pledged a young man who was not a student at the university. It also occurs afterward, as school and law-enforcement officials try to determine the truth about what has happened from pledges and members who maintain a stern silence.

Some hazing experts also regard hazing as a human-rights violation. Hazing victims who live may feel that they have been deprived of their dignity, or they may be traumatized to the point that the quality of their lives is permanently affected. Other victims feel cheated because they risked so much to get into a fraternity or sorority, only to be rebuffed by the group for reporting hazing. While the importance of Greek societies to their members is clear—black Greeks often cheer spontaneously when a past or current chapter president merely walks into a room, for example—it is hard for outsiders to understand why the groups arouse such passion in pledges who seemingly would do anything to belong. Studies indicate that people who place a high value on fraternity and sorority membership tend to be emotionally devastated if they must stop their ritualistic journey before reaching their destination.

All or nearly all schools can suspend or expel students who haze, but judicial groups made up of faculty, staff, and students are often reluctant to term an action hazing, and they thus prevent justice from occurring. While the judicial systems at a few schools—most notably Northern Illinois University—have dealt severely with hazing cases, often what appear to be clear cases of hazing as it is defined by school statutes are dismissed, making some school regulations barely a cut above worthless, according to press law expert Louis Ingelhart. An emeritus journalism educator from Ball State University, Ingelhart said in a telephone interview that he opposes school judicial groups' handling cases that involve apparent criminal hazing. These groups have been formed with good intentions, but they have a vested interest in protecting a school's reputation. On occasion, cases that clearly constituted hazing according to the FEA's definition were ruled nonhazing cases, and punishment was light or nonexistent. In an interview conducted on April 16, 1998, educator John Williams expressed a view similar to Ingelhart's. "Campus officials are 'guilty' of not reporting crime statistics as they are federally mandated to do, by minimizing these incidents," and of claiming that hazing beatings and other crimes committed by students need not be reported by universities if they occur off campus, said Williams, whose doctoral dissertation covered panhellenic issues.

In addition, incidents that are handled entirely by a school and not by criminal courts usually end in punishments that fall far short of jail time. Or, according to Eileen Stevens, the judicial board uses privacy concerns as an excuse for keeping the details of the punishment of student hazers from ever reaching the public. For example, the University of Georgia's judicial panel found members of Phi Beta Sigma fraternity guilty in the hazing of a school football player, Roderick Perrymond, in a secret session, and refused to divulge to the press which individuals were punished. Perrymond, twenty-one, had been hospitalized with bruised buttocks and broken blood vessels. He charged that three fraternity members—one the chapter adviser—had paddled him more than seventy times.

A great deal of evidence points to the conclusion that schools cannot function well in place of judges and courts of law, said Ingelhart during a 1998 telephone interview. Nor should it come as a surprise that universities generally have performed woefully in their attempts to solve social problems. "All America's social problems end up in school," said social critic Neil Postman, deriding the societal assumption that it is "the school's business" to deal with problems such as the moral aspects of sex, drug use, alcohol use, and underage drinking. He didn't mention hazing, but he might have without a stretch. He said,

> There is a reasoned complaint against the schools' trying to do what other social institutions are supposed to do but don't. The principal argument is that teachers are not competent to serve as priests, psychologists, therapists, political reformers, social workers, sex advisers, or parents. That some teachers might wish to do so is understandable, [because] in this way they may elevate their prestige. That some would feel it necessary to do so is also understandable, because many social institutions, including the family and church, have deteriorated in their influence. But unprepared teachers are not an improvement on ineffective social institutions; the plain fact is that there is nothing in the background or education of teachers that qualifies them to do what other institutions are supposed to do.[4]

School administrators also find it hard to halt the actions of alumni who haze (or who encourage undergraduates to haze), because penalties such as school suspension that deter students are no threat to alums. Another problem is the unevenness of enforcement across schools. In particular, many noncriminal pledge activities (wearing "dinks" or beanies, silly clothing, or pledge pins; getting members to sign undergarments; lining up without being subjected to verbal or physical abuse) are considered hazing by authorities at one institution, while the same actions are tolerated at another. Yearbooks at Gallaudet University in the '80s and early '90s carried pictures of student club members being hazed, for example, and these "harmless" initiations were vigorously defended by some Greeks. After the ex-wife of a Kappa Gamma fraternity pledge sent photographs of her ex-husband's bruised buttocks to the author and to CHUCK's Eileen Stevens, Kappa Gamma officers Brian A. Bippus and Paul R. Rutowski defended their hazing activities performed behind closed doors on the Washington, D.C., campus of Gallaudet. "Our paddling was based purely on a voluntary basis, and it was always done with a purpose. Paddling is a common practice among fraternities and sororities, as well as secret societies across the nation. . . . We are not in this alone."[5] Stevens wants all schools to ban "harmless" activities that involve the dominance of a group over nonmembers who wish to belong. If you allow objectionable pre-initiation rituals, you increase the odds that a tragedy will eventually occur, she said. Talking to thousands of students and parents as an activist and speaker on the college circuit has convinced her that all hazing practices enslave the hazed and hazers alike. In a 1997 telephone interview, she said that hazing creates what is tantamount to a caste system at schools dedicated to ensuring equality for all.

Colleges such as Auburn University frequently give Greek groups a list of objectionable behaviors that the student life staff believes constitute hazing practices. Williams said that the danger of circulating such a list is that undergraduates scan it carefully to find loopholes. But without some criteria, said Teresa Loser, a DePauw University administrator who works with Greek groups, undergraduates maintain that they didn't know an action—no matter how outrageous or objectionable—constituted an act of hazing.

Hazing occurs when a group perceived to have power over a newcomer requires someone to do any of the following:

◆ engage in servitude, run errands, and perform so-called favors

◆ participate in intimidation; use derogatory terms to refer to pledges; terrorize; use verbal abuse or create a hostile environment

◆ engage in acts of degradation such as required nudity, partial stripping, rules forbidding bathing, and games played while someone is in a state of undress

◆ engage in rough rituals involving physical force, paddling, electric shocks, beatings, calisthenics, and sexually demeaning behavior

◆ sing explicit songs and perform sexist, racist, or anti-Semitic acts, including denying someone membership in an organization on the basis of religion, skin color, or ancestry

◆ employ deception and deceptive psychological "mind games"

◆ suffer from sleep deprivation (six or fewer hours of sleep a night)

◆ coerce or be coerced by others to consume any substance, concoction, drug, or alcoholic beverage, regardless of whether the person being coerced is of legal drinking age or appears to be participating willingly

◆ keep vile, sexist pledge books, or require alumni or members to sign such books

◆ participate in road trips and in the so-called "kidnapping" of pledges or in their abandonment

◆ require or use peer pressure to get someone to agree to undergo branding, tattooing, chemical burning, burns with cigarettes or cigars, and any mutilation of the skin whatsoever

◆ participate in dousing of initiates involving dangerous or objectionable substances such as chemicals, animal scents used by hunters or anglers, urine, human or animal feces, cleaning fluids, objects to be retrieved from toilets, and spoiled foods capable of causing or transmitting diseases or bacterial infections

◆ make someone eat or drink objectionable, unusual, or spicy concoctions, substances, liquids, and foods

◆ participate in boxing and wrestling matches, unauthorized swimming across lakes, ponds, and rivers, or hold competitions that are demeaning to those who participate

◆ ask pledges to perform daily duties such as phoning members to awaken them

◆ demand that pledges learn trivia about members and about the chapter, perform foolish pranks, and attend all-night pledging-related sessions; ask prospective members to learn chapter history if such a request interferes with academic study

◆ require initiates to wear silly or unusual clothing or objects; require initiates to ask members or alumni to sign articles of clothing or flesh; force initiates to carry objects such as spears, paddles, oars, bricks, concrete blocks, stuffed animals, live animals, and so forth

◆ require initiates to perform calisthenics, jogging, and exercise sessions or to engage in athletic contests such as football games in which members have protective gear and pledges do not

◆ require raids on rival schools, groups, or organizations

◆ require the performance of dangerous stunts or throw out dares that a prospective member feels obligated to take

◆ demand that pledges keep silent or refrain from visiting their parents or nongroup members

◆ hold activities during ordinary class times and study sessions, or that interfere with legitimate extracurricular, school-sponsored activities

◆ extort money or demand fees not approved by the school or by the fraternal organization's headquarters and board of directors

◆ participate in pledge lineups or anything leading to sleep deprivation

◆ engage in harassment or shunning to coerce new individuals into quitting or to punish an initiate who has reported hazing to superiors

◆ participate in illicit scavenger hunts requiring thievery or property destruction

◆ engage in any activity that treats an initiate as a nonperson, an object to make sport of, or a being to be held in low regard because he or she has not yet been accepted as a member

♦ require pledges to sleep in a closet, bathroom, or other unsatisfactory quarters

Hazing involves a group's request (or the request of individuals within that group that the person in a subservient position perceives to be important) that a newcomer take some action in order to be held in esteem by the group and/or to gain entrance into an organization.

Requests defined as hazing can be explicit (e.g., "Pledge, I'd like you to . . .") or implicit (e.g., putting alcohol in front of a newcomer with the unspoken expectation that it will be consumed).

Community standards in the past have determined whether hazing is banned or condoned by authorities. In the United States during much of the nineteenth and twentieth centuries, in order to build school spirit many universities and their surrounding communities tolerated or even encouraged hazing so long as severe injuries or death did not result. Today any institution or organization that encourages or tolerates such activities would be considered derelict in its duty to preserve the peace and to provide a safe environment.

Activists and Greek risk-management experts say that people who haze and expect those who are hazed to behave in a certain way fail to consider the fact that some newcomers are chronic worriers who are deeply distressed by verbal abuse, or that some come to the group with a sad past, have contemplated quitting school, are addicted to alcohol, or perhaps have considered suicide. Even strong and healthy people have limits to which they can be pushed. Add in the fact that many hazing traditions are inherently negligent, and sad consequences such as wrongful deaths become all too likely, particularly when members and pledges drink.

GROUP IDENTITY

Why is hazing so hard to stamp out? Why does it persist or return after it seems to have been eradicated? Modern psychology offers possible explanations. The theory of social exchange put forward by psychologists Harold H. Kelley and John W. Thibaut states that a reciprocal rule guides most human behavior—that is, with regard to behavior, material things, and actions, a person gives, and another then returns something in kind, whether in lesser, equal, or greater measure. Perhaps one reason hazing tends to stick around even when it is prohibited by law or school rules is that participating in such activities may result in the hazed individuals' becoming psychologically unbalanced. The gusto with which some hazers perform activities suggests that hazing satisfies some sort of primitive psychic need to symbolically take revenge for hazing that they themselves once endured. Several writers have compared people who have been hazed and who then haze to those who have been abused and who in turn abuse others.

A related theory proposed by Kelley and Thibaut may offer additional insights into group behavior. To put their theory of equity in somewhat simplified terms, it suggests that groups such as fraternities and cadet corps tend to reward with power and status individuals who are perceived as making the group better.[6] If hazers are perceived to be doing the group a service by teaching newcomers precedence and getting weaklings to "toughen up" or quit, they are rewarded with a kind of status. Why? Because the group likely concluded that the hazers are trying to uphold its quest for higher standards.

Hazers are in effect extremists; they justify actions that are outside the range of normal human behavior. People join extremist groups because they crave relationships and acceptance, not primarily because they respond to the group's particular ideology. People who are friendless, who move to a new locale, who lack focus, or who need a romantic attachment are vulnerable to the recruiting efforts of extremists.[7] Fraternities and sororities "rush" predominantly first-year male and female college students who find themselves in unfamiliar settings, away from family and from childhood friends, and who seek a feeling of belonging. Part of the exhilaration some students experience upon their arrival at college involves their ability to choose a Greek group that offers them friendships, some of which are quite likely to endure for life. To these young people, enduring hazing beats the pain of loneliness.

Not that joining a group is wrong. Students seek membership in a caring primary group as a way to avoid feeling alone for four years in a "holding pen," as James Ridgeway, author of *The Closed Corporation: American Universities in a Crisis,* called undergraduate life. Those willing to undergo harsh mental and/or physical abuse to gain admittance into a group as members may have insecurities that are not all that apparent on the surface. Rather than feeling elated about being accepted into a given university, they may still be smarting from a rejection letter from a more prestigious institution. Large classes at large universities leave many first-year students with a craving for membership in fraternal societies in which spontaneity, intimacy, and individuality are encouraged.[8] Several colleges welcome students as quasi–family members through positive, non-hazing rituals. The Church of God–sponsored Anderson University assigns new students a "family" of "brothers" and "sisters" who answer questions about the school; parents are eased through their own adjustment at a special orientation where they simulate the experiences their children are having. The historically black Morehouse College in Atlanta also has a church-like ceremony that welcomes new students and makes them cognizant of the importance and solemnity of their decision to get an education and to make a difference in the world.

However, such ceremonies have not eradicated hazing. After some acts of noncriminal hazing that administrators found unseemly in view of the college's spiritual mission occurred at Anderson University in 1997, the administration tightened regulations on how student clubs can initiate newcomers. And Joel Harris, who had given up competitive swimming because of a health problem, collapsed and died at Morehouse College during harsh physical hazing required for admission to Alpha Phi Alpha fraternity.

Even though most undergraduates cannot articulate what it is they are seeking when they pledge a fraternity or sorority or try out for an athletic club, such clubs and others like them respond to vulnerable individuals' need for primary group support. Social organizations become even more attractive if they are perceived as providing entrance into a campus group with prestige, a way of meeting attractive members of the opposite sex, an opportunity to belong to a group that values participation in sports or other activities, or something meaningful that can be put on a resume.

Hazing demonstrates a group's power and status; it teaches precedence as a way to subjugate the individual for the perceived good of the group. And in many fraternities whose members believe that their high status has been accorded because of "manly" accomplishments such as drinking, athletic success, sexual "conquests," or even crimes such as gang rape, there is a high degree of what an author of a book on male rituals has termed "macho posing and phallic swagger."[9] Thus the sadomasochistic sexual assaults or threats of such assaults that occur as part of some fraternal hazings may be performed by members to demonstrate male dominance over other males.

Those who are hazed in fraternities, sororities, and military schools are often told that they cannot gain admission to the group until all pledges or plebes demonstrate unity, loyalty to the larger organization, and respect for tradition. Greek-letter society members and military school cadets push the more aggressive members of the pledge or plebe class to pressure their peers to conform. Inevitably, pledges and cadets lose their identities as individuals to take on a collective identity that will likely resurface after initiation, ensuring that the new high-status people in the group will haze the next round of newcomers.[10]

Fraternities put so much emphasis on group identity that even people who have never joined a Greek group have a common perception of them. Too many Greek groups for too long have contributed to their own national stereotype with public displays of drunkenness, boorishness, and hazing activities. Robert Egan's vulgar *From Here to*

Fraternity, written in 1985 and described by Egan as a "Comprehensive Guide to Fraternities and Sororities from Alpha to Omega," contains interviews with hundreds of Greeks at 100 colleges in thirty-five states. The book glorifies hazing, sexism, and alcohol-abuse rituals that are gleefully at odds with what fraternal and university leaders say a collegiate educational experience should be.[11]

For many years a chapter's overall grade-point average (GPA) and member accomplishments helped determine whether that fraternity had high or low status on campus. Today, "high status" fraternities too often rate high in the pecking order because of superficial attributes. "If there is a responsible group on campus with a high GPA, but the physical attractiveness of their members is low or they're regarded as nerds—more the academic type than the jock type—their status is a lot lower than the group that has great parties and rates very highly on the physical appeal of its members," said James "Jim" Arnold, an Oregon counselor who has studied fraternities firsthand. In his experience, what sometimes happens is that a chapter regarded as low-status will over time try to raise its collective self-esteem by emulating the less-admirable aspects of the high-status group, for example by introducing hazing or throwing an unauthorized multikeg party. "We can find fraternities and sororities that are not on the high-risk end of these kinds of groups, but my opinion is if it walks like a duck and quacks like a duck it must be a duck," said Arnold. "If it's called a fraternity, it's going to exhibit fraternity behavior. There seems to be a general knowledge [on campuses] of what being a fraternity member means."[12]

There is also a fraternal consensus on what national Greek leaders want the fraternity of the future to mean to members. The NIC Commission on Values and Ethics has said that fraternity is a belief "in developing the human spirit." The commission statement concludes, "It is through the values expressed in our ritual that we share this belief," and "it is through our actions that we exemplify this belief."[13]

Pledges hungry for group identity may condone attitudes, behaviors, and group mores they would ordinarily find objectionable. In that respect, executives of Greek-letter groups, much like authorities in charge of facilities to train law-enforcement officers, firefighters, attorneys, and doctors, must remain vigilant against hazing outbreaks. What these unlike groups have in common is a profound respect for the traditions of an organization or a profession, a reluctance to follow suggestions for reforms offered by outsiders who lack direct experience as members, a certain amount of secrecy in regard to their rituals, and a belief in systems of order that preserve the status quo and foster fear of change. And whenever there is secrecy in organizations, members of certain groups tend to refrain from reporting the wrongs of other members.[14]

What is true of initiations in police recruit schools, pro football training camps, or oil-rig shower stalls applies equally to hazing in Greek-letter groups. The experience involves a great deal of idealism and personal excitement and is associated with detachment from the old life and immersion in the new. An important part of learning comes from observing veteran members, and members regard their very seniority and the fact that they have survived the rigors of the first days on the job as evidence of their superiority.[15] Newcomers detect subtle and not-so-subtle differences between the done thing and the formal rules, as well as between a culture and its subcultures.[16] Newcomers in groups that haze are also outcasts, in that initiated members call them disparaging names and ridicule them. But what is true of hazed pledges is also true of police academy recruits. After members consider the pledges full-fledged group members, all the hazing stops.[17] What remains are the resentments and the physical or psychological wounds.

All members, and to a lesser degree all pledges, share a common belief that one is either a member of a group or an outsider. Those who drop out of the group may despair because group members view them as misfits. Would-be members who die or are hurt during hazing are viewed by the chapter as people who failed to measure up. Had they been equal to those in the group, they would have survived all the ordeals the members survived when they pledged. The group rarely blames itself for perpetuating collective idiocy unless the entire group becomes traumatized when a death occurs and members see how their actions are perceived by the press, the public, and, in some cases, the lawyers who take them to court in a civil suit. Because those in the group continue to harass dropouts with reproachful looks, threats of violence, or abusive words, many who leave a fraternity also end up leaving school. Auburn's Davis said that he encourages pledges to fight back by staying at the university after reporting hazing. He said that he is trying to empower pledges to end the hazing abuses. "Pledges have a lot more power than they think they do," he said, adding that members know fraternities will die without new recruits. "If they will just stick together and say no to hazing, the fraternities will back down."[18] Rita Saucier disagreed. A whole semester of coercion and intimidation can paralyze anyone's independent spirit, she said.[19] That pledges typically do not report hazing shows that fraternal members who haze have created a true subordinate subclass. In hazing fraternities, pledges must symbolically display a penitent, servile demeanor long enough to gain acceptance by the group. True, rebels exist in every pledge class, but members control them by beating them down or punishing their

J. B. Joynt, a tired and ill pledge at Phi Sigma Kappa at Frostburg State, died following a long night of traditional wrestling with members. His older sister Julie Joynt found a note among his possessions. "I've come too far to quit now," wrote Joynt. "I've done too many dishes, too many pushups, and been bitched at by one too many brothers to quit now. I'm halfway there & I'm ready to do whatever it takes to get Phi Sigma Kappa letters." Julie Joynt disputed school and chapter claims that her brother's death was caused solely by illness, insisting that he would have lived beyond that night had he not pledged.
Photo taken by Nancy Joynt and courtesy of Julie Joynt

fellow pledges until the rebellious behavior ends. Sleep-deprived and frustrated, J. B. Joynt wrote a telling note to himself just before his sudden death in a pledging activity at Frostburg State University in Maryland. "I've come too far to quit now," wrote Joynt. "I've done too many dishes, too many pushups, and been bitched at by one too many brothers to quit now. I'm halfway there & I'm ready to do whatever it takes to get Phi Sigma Kappa letters."[20]

Why don't some people who are hazed fight back? Some are too intoxicated to make reasonable judgments about what is happening to them. Some are sleep-deprived, and some cower after being physically beaten. Other students unlikely to report hazing are men or women who believe the Greek group provides them access to members of the opposite sex that they otherwise would not meet. For example, a shy male pledge might put up with abuse if he is rewarded for doing so by being admitted to the fraternity's regular closed parties with sororities. A student with low self-esteem may feel grateful for any sort of acceptance, particularly if members otherwise tolerate his or her substance addictions, excesses, or personality quirks. Then, too, an impressionable person is unlikely to reject a group by quitting, even if he or she is forced to participate in hazing in order to remain a member. Potential new members who come aboard because someone in the group urged them to give pledging a try will probably not report hazing lest they lose the satisfying feeling that they are a part of something large and worthwhile. Pledges either already share a fraternal organization's system of beliefs before joining, or they accept these beliefs after joining because their need to belong is so great.

Students typically do not report hazing to authorities, although many more are doing so in the '90s as hazing awareness spreads and schools and Greek headquarters encourage people to make such reports. Without a complaint, law enforcement officers are unlikely to intervene until someone has been killed, is injured, or seeks counseling because of hazing. The exception would be those rare instances in which the authorities can charge people with criminal hazing because they come upon a hazing activity in progress or receive a tip from a parent that hazing is to take place. However, a parent who reports hazing may get no thanks from the child—the pledge—who resents the fact that his ritualistic journey has come to an end prematurely.

While Chuck Stenzel at Alfred (Klan Alpine), Scott Krueger at MIT (Phi Gamma Delta), and Nicholas Haben at Western Illinois University (lacrosse club initiation) were light drinkers who ended up dead following initiations involving the swilling of alcohol, some who died during similar incidents had previous brushes with the law for alcohol possession or were called heavy drinkers by their friends or family. The Sauciers first learned that Chad had been experimenting with alcohol in high school when police ticketed him and some friends at a beach party; greatly upset, they punished him by yanking his car insurance. Probably the first student to die in an initiation required for admission into a spirit club was Mike Nisbet, twenty-eight. An alcoholic with one alcohol-related vehicular accident, he died at the University of Missouri, Rolla, in October 1991 after choking on his own vomit during a drinking ritual required of new members being initiated into St. Pat's Board, a spirit group.[21] Sigma Alpha Epsilon pledge and Louisiana State University student Benjamin Wynne, twenty, who died of alcohol poisoning off campus in 1997 after swigging some twenty-four drinks and ingesting a small amount of a date-rape drug, had "three [prior] brushes with the law, including an arrest (blood-alcohol level 0.165) for driving while intoxicated" (his blood-alcohol level measured 0.588 at the time of his death, according to an article in the August 16, 1998, Baton Rouge *Advocate*).

Greek leaders do not want to see pledges punished, and yet they concur that pledges must be held accountable for their actions, said Maureen Syring, a nationally known expert on fraternal risk-management issues and a National Panhellenic Conference (NPC) assistant development director, in a 1998 telephone interview.

Fraternity members have claimed that pledges serve as active participants in the group. Additional research is needed to determine whether this claim is valid. Eileen Stevens has attacked such claims, terming them self-serving justifications made by members after a pledge death. "Stop blaming the victims," she said in a 1997 telephone interview. But in a follow-up interview in 1998, she said that human behavior researchers have an obligation to look into such claims in order to prove or disprove them in the interest of preventing other deaths. Some pledges, to judge from comments they made in depositions, perceive what they go through to be exhilarating. In cases where a few members have sadistic tendencies and some pledges are deeply masochistic, it may be only a matter of time before injuries or embarrassing incidents occur.

Pledges who ask to be hazed should be reprimanded by chapter officers and school authorities; those who turn the tables and haze members, or who break the law by stealing or damaging property and assaulting others, should also be punished, according to the policies of nearly all national Greek organizations.

CULT-LIKE BEHAVIOR

Dr. Scott Saucier has concluded that Greek-letter groups resemble cults. "I, along with other parents, entrusted Phi Delta Theta to create an atmosphere of brotherhood and support, to serve as a role model so that young men entering college can have someone to emulate," said Dr. Saucier, interviewed in May 1998. "Instead, they allowed an atmosphere of abuse and degradation, in some ways creating a cult-like atmosphere."

Greek groups who haze may be cult-like, agreed fraternity executive Michael Carlone, although he does not see them as cults to fear, like those operated by a Jim Jones or Charles Manson. Rather, said Carlone, they are cult-like in the sense that certain business corporations have cult-like aspects. *Built to Last* authors James C. Collins and Jerry I. Porras described such companies as "cult-like" in that they strive to whip up absolute loyalty in all employees, and that they want employee behavior "to be consistent with the company's ideology."[22]

Dr. Saucier said he sees Greek chapters that resemble cults as less admirable than such companies. His view of hazing groups is that they, like cults, employ what psychologist Edgar Schein calls "coercive persuasion," and cult expert Margaret Thaler Singer calls "systematic manipulation of psychological and social influence."[23]

"Cult," of course, is a word that has an unpleasant connotation for many people. Although clinical psychologists tend to use the term in a descriptive sense, few religious groups, Greek-letter organizations, or political organizations want to be labeled by it. Nonetheless, Singer lists many characteristics that are common to cults, and at least nine cult-like similarities can be applied under certain circumstances to fraternities and sororities that haze:[24]

1. Like cults, hazing fraternities and sororities trumpet their exclusivity to potential recruits, promising to solve pressing problems or to meet needs. Just as cult members tend to think they have the one true answer, so too do many hazers arrogantly claim to have special knowledge, telling pledges that the abuse will make sense once they become members.

2. Like cults, hazing fraternity and sorority chapters expect members to be as two-faced as Janus, disclosing all to those in the group and often being less than honest to outsiders (the press, college officials, their own national leaders). There is a presumption that being the one true organization gives members the right to deviate from normal standards of morality for the good of the group. In hazing fraternities and sororities, a pledge educator becomes an ultimate authority to the pledges and may feel little compunction about asking pledges to break school or state laws. Fraternities and sororities often monopolize pledges' time, restrict their movements, strip them of power, introduce fear and a feeling of dependency, and symbolically or actually replace their belief system with new attitudes and values inculcated by members. Pledges find that they are not welcome to criticize or change the system. What was once the unthinkable becomes normal. For example, a white pledge who is not a racist may find himself putting on blackface to attend a racist party. A pledge who has never stolen before may pilfer a Christmas tree and bring it to the house for a party decoration.

Pledges, depending upon the fraternity or sorority to which they wish to gain entrance, sometimes endure activities that are remarkably similar to cult behaviors. They have been forbidden to bathe, ordered to eat only certain foods or food laced with salt, told to talk to no old friends outside the group, made to consume unpleasant substances, forced to wear unusual clothing and to wear their hair a certain way, and in general, to give up their independent lives as they submit to the control and influence of the group they hope to join. Those who disobey orders sometimes are paddled in a way reminiscent of the physical abuse dished out by organizations such as Ecclesia Athletic Association. The goal is to get all members to exclude outsiders, to feel they are part of a noble enterprise, and to go to the group for all their emotional needs.[25]

3. Like cults, hazing fraternities and sororities tend to be obsessed with control. Members dictate when pledges can come and go, study, eat, drink, smoke, or bathe.

4. Like cults, some hazing fraternities and sororities try to isolate recruits, keeping them away from their family, old friends, other student organizations, jobs, and significant others. In this way they achieve "control and enforced dependency," according to Singer. Thus students swept up in the life of such a fraternity tend to avoid immersion in other campus activities, running for student offices, or becoming active in student publications, non-Greek volunteer efforts, and off-campus study.

5. Like cults, hazing fraternities and sororities tend to be authoritarian, refusing to allow pledges to report injustices to a Greek council, a school administrator, or even their own national executives. Many hazers possess overall charisma and/or an unusual ability to dominate others. If the pledge class happens to include masochists, sadistic members can push them to terrifying limits. And groups that haze often have self-appointed sadists or hazing fanatics who are recognized for their zeal by others in the group.[26]

6. Like the members of some cults, members of hazing fraternities and sororities believe that pledges are not one of the group until they have endured an ordeal and/or have successfully made it through an initiation ceremony.

7. Like those of some cults, members of hazing fraternities and sororities emphasize the idea of family, calling one another brothers, sisters, pledge moms, and pledge dads. Once pledges consider themselves to be part of a family of fraternity members, it is highly likely that peer pressure will affect their behavior.

8. Like cults, some hazing fraternities and sororities have a belief system that "ends up being a tool," in Singer's words, to manipulate recruits, to bind members to the organization, and to ultimately satisfy the whims and ambitions of those who haze and encourage others to do the same. Almost always present in Greek groups that haze and in cults is what cult expert Robert Jay Lifton termed a "pattern of manipulation and exploitation from above and idealism from below."[27] The fraternal manipulation and exploitation is conducted by chapter leaders who haze, while pledges who endure hazing can certainly be described as idealistic.

9. Hazing fraternities and sororities, like cults, make it clear to pledges and followers that there is but one path. Cults tend to have

special secrets published in a book that amount to "some revealed 'word,'" according to Singer. While Greek-letter groups hand down secret rituals and documents that originated with the groups' founders, no one claims that these are tantamount to divine revelation. Nonetheless, many fraternities guard their rituals with surprising ferocity. One national fraternity executive who in 1998 recommended that all rituals be made public was overruled by a governing board of directors.

Fraternal newcomers—whether they are labeled neophytes, pledges, associate members, or line brothers—are asked to put trust and blind faith in the group and its members, as if they were suddenly incapable of making important life decisions on their own. Hazers use mental games, verbal abuse, and peer pressure to make newcomers bend to the will of the group. The peer "pressure" referred to here is usually manifested in taunting or disrespectful remarks, although physical pressure caused by pushing, shoving, and beatings sometimes occurs. Only when an individual capitulates to group members' wishes does he or she solidify a connection to those members.

One significant difference distinguishes cults from fraternal groups that haze. A cult looks to its leader as a quasi-deity, but members of a Greek organization that hazes unite as one to sponsor hazing activities they believe will assimilate the newcomers fully into the group. Nonetheless, the role of a leader or leaders in hazing groups is worth further study. Just as a dashing military leader can get soldiers to overcome their fears, rekindle hope, and fight even if the odds of surviving are against them, so too can a convincing pledge-class leader or pledge educator convince pledges to endure abuse, try risky behaviors, and refrain from criticizing those who abuse them. In effect, the fraternal leaders convince pledges that even hazing activities are worth enduring to gain entry into the Greek system. The behavior of a leader who is a role model can cause an effect on a group that students of human behavior call inhibition. To describe the meaning of inhibition in simplified terms, the group takes its collective courage from its leader, and individuals suppress ordinary thoughts, fears, urges, and, in many cases, common sense. Such leaders nonetheless differ from cult leaders. While leaders of cults inevitably focus attention on themselves, those who haze do not.

Undergraduates who haze feel disconnected from their fraternal leaders at national headquarters who tell them not to haze and to obey drinking laws. They view the leaders as authority figures who are out of touch, since these leaders either have never hazed or have repudiated any hazing they did. A few national fraternity reformers, such as Theta Chi executive Dave Westol and former Phi Beta Sigma national president Charles Wright (now deceased), have disclosed to undergraduates their own former involvement in hazing, stressing that it caused people a great deal of pain.

Many Greek leaders, particularly leaders of sororities, were never involved in hazing. Their decision to pursue careers that involve working with fraternities and sororities may be evidence of their satisfaction with Greek life. "I was not hazed," said DePauw Associate Dean/Director of Greek Affairs Teresa Loser during a 1998 interview at her office. Loser was a member of Sigma Kappa sorority as an undergraduate. "I think I would have walked." But Singer said that people who do not belong to cults and who declare that they could never fall prey to the influence of someone else in fact probably could under certain circumstances. "People like to think that their opinions, values, and ideas are inviolate and totally self-regulated," wrote Singer. "They want to preserve the myth that other people are weak-minded and easily influenced while they are strong-minded. . . . There is an almost universal aversion to accepting the idea that we ourselves are vulnerable to persuasion. . . . Neither education, age, nor social class protects a person from this false sense of invulnerability."[28]

The willingness of members of certain groups to endure pain and humiliation seems absurd, even comical, to those who have no desire to participate in that group. Outsiders assume that there must be something strange about anyone who would succumb to the influence of a cult or who would join a student group that hazes, manipulates, and deceives people. That assumption may be unwarranted. "All of us, at various times, can fall into vulnerable states during which another person can wield more influence over us than at other times," wrote Singer in *Cults in Our Midst*. "We are all more vulnerable to flattery, deception, lures, and enticements when we are lonely, sad, and feeling needy. In such periods of transient vulnerability, most of us are more manipulable, more suggestible, and more likely to be deceived by the flattery and inducements of designing persons."[29]

All off us need acceptance, whether we try to fulfill this need by buying some expensive, unessential item because we fell for a sales specialist's pitch, or by becoming involved in a relationship with someone whose charms prove superficial. Those of us who have a "joiner" mentality may find ourselves overcommitted or in league with other group members whom our good sense in retrospect tells us we should have avoided. While the idea of enduring hazing may be foreign to some people, most have done something they later can't believe they did, because they listened to the urgings of others.

Gary Eller, an author and part-time teacher of creative writing at Iowa State University, earned his undergraduate degree at the University of North Dakota and pledged Sigma Chi. Someday, Eller predicts, Greek leaders will be in the spot tobacco magnates once found themselves in, trying to explain away the past, to justify why they didn't or couldn't do more to end hazing. In a 1998 interview Eller said,

> [I have] lots of difficult things to confront and bare. Debt, lies, humiliation, shaming myself and parents—six or seven years to get a bachelor's, and maybe the essence was the realization of what character I lacked. I went along with all that [hazing], because I wanted to be liked and couldn't figure out a way to accomplish that except to be all things to all people. In trying to be something I could not be I prostituted myself. I insisted on such items as a car and clothes that my father could not at that time afford, but in his pride and desire to see me achieve, somehow did. My sense of self loathing became exacerbated with the eventual realization that not only was I trying to be someone I could not be, but indeed someone I really had no desire to be—the type of individual whom I have since come to despise, one whose whole purpose seems to be based on the most shallow of values, one for whom the burden of thought has been removed in deference to the larger group which says in effect, 'Don't worry, we will take over that responsibility for you. In return you abandon your personality, your sense of inquisitiveness, your self-identity, your silly and outdated values, your soul.' Given such an irresistible offer— without the burden of decision making there can be no bad decisions, no miscues. [Because] everything is in another's hands—hazing appeared a small price. So why then did I haze [after getting into the fraternity]? I had to. I'd bought into the system in the same manner that an executive two years from retirement would look the other way upon discovering his company is corrupt.

Just as cults make it hard for their members to leave, fraternities and sororities make quitting pledging difficult. In order to leave, a pledge must be "blackballed" by the group, must quit of his or her own volition, or must be persuaded to stop by a family member or other confidant.

Often, when individuals shake free of a cult or of a Greek-letter group that hazes, they will stress the fact that they were deceived during recruitment or rush. This deception in effect helps the cult leader or Greek pledge educator assume control of each individual who hopes to join the group. Both cults and hazing Greek-letter groups recruit hard lest they eventually wither and die, choosing members who they believe will fit well into the group and who can be transformed over time into people who will then deceive and recruit their own successors.

The pull of the group is particularly exhilarating for young, impressionable pledges and newly initiated members who have probably not thought much about their actions. To be sure, the level of participation in hazing activities differs from one initiated member to another. Some members are particularly gung-ho. Some go along with the group. Some like to make sport of the initiates. And some are enablers, not approving of events and yet never exposing the group's hazing to outsiders.

Until young people gain maturity, if they ever do gain it, loyalty takes precedence over moral qualms.[30] This explains why even young males who were "raised right," like Chad Saucier and Gary Eller (who national Greek-letter groups would like to think can be counted on to stop hazing), end up letting events unfold in ways they later regret—if, that is, they, like Eller, live to do so. It is critical that fraternal reformers hoping to inspire young people to respect values be aware of and understand this tendency. Loyalty is typically considered a value worthy of commendation, but young people who adhere to it above all else may deny a fraternal group's problems with hazing and/or alcohol abuse, uniting in silence or in the sticky web of a made-up story. Those likely to remain loyal to the group rather than to listen to their conscience include members with authoritarian personalities. Sociologist Rupert Wilkinson, author of *The Broken Rebel*, noted that "Authoritarians exhibit a deep wish to yield to strong authority, especially the authority of an 'in-group,' be it family or nation, church or fraternity." In Wilkinson's view, authoritarianism is "a particular ambivalence about authority, involving maladjustments within the personality and unconscious feelings of weakness." He has studied both male and female authoritarian personalities, finding that while gender-based stresses may differ, both exhibit extreme submission at some time in their early lives that "damages self respect," causing the young person to seek a source of strength by aligning with an in-group that seems "a source of power."[31]

Wilkinson's findings should interest educators who wonder why a fraternity member can flout the university administration by hazing and then rabidly support the very same administration at another time, or even become a university administrator later in life. In New York City in the 1920s, for example, Columbia fraternity members backed the school's administration by throwing eggs at non-Greek students protesting the expulsion of the *Spectator* newspaper editor who had written pieces critical of the football team. On another occasion, in the '30s, Greeks bearing bats at the University of Minnesota supported police and went after striking drivers with a fury.[32]

How individuals behave in organizations has come to be termed "Groupthink," a term first used by psychologist Irving L. Janis to explain why human beings react differently in groups than they do as individuals. Merely surviving dangerous or contumelious hazing situations makes members feel invulnerable, particularly when alumni and older undergraduates shrug off these activities that they too endured as part of tradition. "The group itself does not think of these things as impossible demands," said Janis. "They themselves have gone through the initiation rite. The members merely tend to think of what they are doing as simply parallel to what they endured."[33]

For the purposes of this book, I use a modification of Janis's term "groupthink" that I call "Greekthink" as a way of explaining what happens in fraternal groups that engage in negligent and dangerous behaviors during hazing, act as if members and pledges were invincible, value group practices above individual human rights, and deny that there is anything wrong with the uncivil rites they take part in.[34]

An instance of what could probably be characterized as "Greekthink" occurred at Southeast Missouri State University in 1994, when paramedics responded to a call from the Kappa Alpha Psi house. When the paramedics arrived, pledge Michael Davis had stopped breathing. Hazers told the paramedics that Davis had been hurt in a pickup football game, according to a 1998 interview for this book with Edith Davis, his mother. A police investigation showed that he had been savagely beaten by at least seven fraternity members.[35]

Another well-laundered version of events was given by Alpha Tau Omega members at Indiana University in 1992 after pledge Dennis Jay, twenty, went into cardiac arrest when his blood-alcohol level reached 0.48 percent. At first the ATO house director reported that Jay had been casually drinking with his fraternity "dad" and other members while watching an IU–Purdue basketball game on TV. But the story uncovered by the *Indiana Daily Student* was far more sinister. It said that Jay had been encouraged to drink two fifths of whiskey and a mixture of beer and wine in a bong while fraternity members and sorority "moms"—the latter of which are illegal at Indiana—watched him perform. When he was passed out, members scrawled slogans all over his skin. Jay's roommate opined that the ATO members were "totally controlling" Jay, and that they wove a story for him to tell.[36]

Just as cult members must allow themselves to be monopolized by the group when they are not working or attending classes, so too do pledges in a hazing Greek group devote every hour to the group when they aren't attending classes. Even so, there is no pleasing members, who complain without justification that they never see the pledges.[37]

Both cult members and pledges in fraternal groups that haze seem to lose touch with reality, or at least to gain a new perverse sense of what constitutes reality after they have sacrificed their individuality to the group. As Singer has noted about cults, as pressure on the initiate mounts, "powerlessness increases" while "good judgment and understanding of the world" diminish. The same is true of pledges. To ascertain what takes place in the mind of a person who is being hazed, it is useful to examine Singer's views on thought-control programs in cults, remembering that in her view such programs (1) "destabilize a person's sense of self," (2) "get the person to drastically reinterpret his or her life's history and radically alter his or her worldview [to] accept a new version of reality and causality," and (3) "develop in the person a dependence on the organization."[38]

Stated simply, a cultist or a pledge is reduced to little more than an agent in the host group's program.

The only way a hazed pledge class can reclaim a measure of autonomy is if individuals accept their role meekly. If they do so, members will encourage pledge rebellions, also known as pledge sneaks, without making the newcomers aware that they have been manipulated into rebelling. A rebellion may take the form of pranks in which pledges hide members' stereos and TVs, or it could be a kidnapping during which the group's president or senior officers are encouraged to drink and then are taken into the country, dropped off, and left to find their own way back. Pledges may also kidnap a member for their own reasons, for instance to seek revenge for abuses and indignities they have endured, said Maureen Syring in a 1998 telephone interview. Often these sneaks have disastrous consequences. For example, the pledges of Alpha Tau Omega at the University of Central Oklahoma carried out a pledge sneak in 1998, spiriting ATO member Kevin Crowder to an area far from campus and either making him drink or encouraging him to drink. At some point Crowder jumped into a car and sped away, striking and dragging pledge Stacy Aldridge, nineteen, whose pelvis was crushed.[39]

And when pledges in a high-intensity hazing fraternity or sorority depledge to begin their lives anew, they can experience the same type of post-traumatic stress, disconnectedness, and angst that experts have associated with cult members who opt to leave the group. The deadly, demeaning, and insistent hazing practices occurring in a minority of Greek chapters can and do damage the lives of individuals and their families. Singer has written that courts generally need to broaden their definition of who specifically should be entitled to reparations in civil suits, saying that people who have been subjected to "enforced dependency" in cults ought to receive compensation when they are injured as a result of their exposure "to thought-reform processes" and "systematic manipulation." Attorney Douglas Fierberg has taken on at least three cases in which he has cited the long-lasting negative consequences of mental hazing for his clients.

To be hazed in a club, a fraternity, or a high school, one must typically qualify for membership in some group or achieve a certain class standing in school. Thus, hazing thrives in a society that has empowered its education system to create what author Jacques Barzun terms a bureaucratic mandarin system. "I mean by this that in order to achieve any goal, however, modest, one must *qualify*," said Barzun in *The American University*. "Qualifying means: having been trained, passed a course, obtained a certificate. 'Show me your credentials. Where was this work done? What was your score on the S.A.T. . . . ? Any letters of recommendation? Good, but who wrote [the letter]? I mean, was he the man in charge?' The young in college were born into this system which in this country is not much older than they, and they feel, quite rightly, intense claustrophobia. They have been in the groove since the sandbox."[40]

Like fraternal organizations, universities put a special value on loyalty. In the eyes of institutions of higher education, loyalty is not only an admirable quality but a marketable commodity. Millions in the United States—even non-alums who have adopted schools—regard their colleges as treasured institutions. University and national Greek officials have no trouble appreciating the importance of loyalty in people's lives. The loyalty of university and fraternal alums can reward both with cash contributions, scholarship programs, and endowments; a 1998 National Interfraternity Conference (NIC)–funded survey conducted by an independent research team at the University of Missouri provides evidence that fraternity and sorority membership is a predictor of generous financial support when members become alums. Universities and their surrounding communities also benefit economically when alumni return to their Greek houses for sporting events and annual traditions such as Homecoming. In short, the love of Greeks for their fraternal organizations extends to a love of alma mater—another reason administrators are reluctant to permanently ban certain hazing Greek groups and rather give them every opportunity to recolonize.

RITUALS: SEPARATION, LIMINALITY, AND REINCORPORATION

In U.S. culture, few rituals celebrate the crucial awakening of young people upon reaching sexual maturity. This lack is one cause of the violent acts that so occur often on campuses, Barzun has theorized. "Perhaps our lack of proper ceremonies for initiation into the tribe leaves the young to devise their own proof of manhood," he said.[41]

Other than taking part in acts of violence, the only way many young people can acknowledge their longing for a ritual is by becoming sexually active, noted Tom F. Driver, an expert on ritual. People who ignore or dismiss rituals fail to grasp the fact that they are very important for many individuals, he said.[42] Two observers of Greek culture, Frederick Kershner, an emeritus professor from Columbia Teachers College, and Ed King of Bradley University, have often remarked on the importance of ritual for fraternity and sorority members. In fraternities and sororities, many rituals have meaning, and many individuals, including Jonathan Brant of the NIC, stress the importance these rituals had for them as undergraduates and later as adults. After new members undergo what Brant, during a 1998 interview for this book at the NIC offices, called "a church-like initiation" (i.e., a ceremony devoid of hazing), they are permitted to purchase clothing with Greek letters, dress in symbolic fraternal colors, and sing songs, chant sayings, or give handshakes known to members everywhere.

If rituals were limited to a formal reading at initiation ceremonies, society at large would have no serious problem with Greek groups. But some contemporary fraternity men who complain that this ritual has no meaning for them find satisfaction instead in acts of buffoonery and hazing that have been a part of fraternities and sororities since the nineteenth century. Such informal rituals occur, for example, when pledges are asked to perform drinking rites such as swigging wine from loving cups or consuming a specific type of cheap drink, like Mad Dog (MD) 20/20.

People turn to rituals in times of stress and danger.[43] Participation in fraternal rituals has comforted more than one uncertain, stressed-out first-year student. Folklorist Michael Olmert, writing in *Smithsonian* about hazing and initiations, said that ceremonies in themselves are harmless so long as the ordeals remain symbolic. The problem comes when "mean-spirited dolts" dish out ordeals all too liberally.[44]

The Greek system itself demonstrates the power of ritual-based organizations to serve as a benchmark for individuals needing to see themselves moving upward in the social hierarchy of high school or college. "As the initiate symbolically passes through the social hierarchy—to a status that is somehow 'better,' 'higher,' 'nobler,' etc. than the one he presently occupies—he discovers the significance this social transformation has for his personal character," anthropologists Gary Schwartz and Don Merten have said about the meaning of initiation rituals. "[The initiate] sees the kind of person he has become and likes what he sees. At the same time, he perceives some of the less benign implications of what he would have become or remained had he not completed this ritual journey."[45]

Hazing, even if it is banned, is thus likely to go on behind closed curtains as long as newcomers want to be recognized as "transformed" in the eyes of peer members, as Thomas A. Leemon noted in *The Rites of Passage in a Student Culture*. During the pledging process, pledges symbolically leave their families and former lives to enter an entirely different social system inhabited by previously initiated members. Until pledges "forget" their past, they can count on members' browbeating and verbally ripping them until "a qualitative disassociation from their past" occurs, noted Leemon.[46]

Aside from their fear that their son or daughter may die or sustain injury in a hazing incident, many parents object to their child's being transformed by a predominantly social organization whose purpose is to take that child away from them. Too often parents send a child to college and, rather than watching their offspring's intellect blossoming, are faced with a confused individual whose grades are dropping, who lacks self-assurance, whose attitudes have changed, whose mind is being controlled, whose body and soul are being abused, and whose appearance has altered for the worse. Those parents find themselves trying to come to terms with their children, much as the parents whose children become members of cults must. Like the parents of the more than three thousand current and former cult members (many of them University of California, Berkeley students) that Singer has interviewed, the mothers and fathers of severely hazed college students talk about observing in their children "a sudden change in personality, a new way of talking, a restriction of emotions, a splitting from family and the past."[47]

The ritual wherein an "unworthy" initiate becomes a fully initiated member can be broken down into three stages—those of separation, liminality, and reincorporation.[48] The three stages apply whether the initiation takes place among sailors on the sea or in fraternities and sororities.[49] The separation phase is a period during which members and pledges are continually reminded of the differences between the two groups. Lacking seniority, pledges in hazing organizations learn that a day-long Hell Night or week-long Hell Week is going to be the test of endurance they will need to pass before being admitted into the company of their "betters." The ritualistic period of liminality occurs during Hell Night or Hell Week. Pledges experience insecurity, knowing that a significant ritual symbolizing their leaving of pledgeship is about to take place, and realizing that completing the arduous trial will be necessary if they are to become the equal of initiated members who themselves once triumphed by surviving their own Hell Weeks.

Once Hell Night, Hell Week, or the equivalent begins, and pledges enter liminal space, their mood is one of confusion and uncertainty, according to experts on rituals. As bad as pledging was, the pledges had begun to adapt to it. Now it is difficult to go back to that old world where the pledge was likely subservient to his or her parents. A male typically does not pledge twice, and so the only option is to survive the Hell Week ordeal or to drop out of the organization. Often members begin Hell Week with a ceremonial prank. Some members may cut or shave the hair of pledges. Notably, the roughness of the ordeal and the fact that one's near-peers administer the punishment seems significant at this stage of the ritual.

Finally, the third step of the ritual—reincorporation—takes place. Exhausted, battered pledges are welcomed with handshakes, hugs, libations, and often a special meal. A solemn reading occurs, and there may be an awarding of certificates or clothing with the group's letters, or the presentation of a symbolic paddle with the names of the pledge or pledge class painted on it. Folklorist Keith P. Richardson, author Lionel Tiger, and social researcher Elliott Aronson have postulated that initiation ceremonies may serve some useful bonding purpose, meaning, for example, that throughout time such rituals have traditionally brought about a calming of tensions between newcomers and senior members.[50] Richardson has said that ritualistic behavior among sailors, while giving the outward appearance of horseplay or of an archaic rite of passage, actually helps those who initiate and who undergo initiations "to resolve the basic paradoxes of life." On sea this paradox, according to Richardson, is that "landlubber officers" must be incorporated into the society of common sailors who are their inferior in rank, but not in seniority, experience, and the steadiness of their sea legs. Fraternity members have used these findings to say that hazing activities—particularly if they are mild or if no physical injury results—are justified. In spite of laws and prohibitions, historically African American or white fraternities, sororities, athletic clubs, and other organizations will likely think, or perhaps rationalize, that they are merely strengthening their groups when they conduct pre-initiation ordeals. Members excuse their actions philosophically by claiming that hazing makes unworthy initiates worthy of membership, thereby upholding the standards of the group. Social psychologist Elliott Aronson found that, in a sense, such a group justifies its actions with its belief that members are merely providing newcomers with a series of tradition-mandated obstacles to overcome as a way to force bonding with fellow initiates, and to raise the ante, so to speak, with regard to their commitment to a group.[51] After members bring the initiates to the point of rage or tears, they release them into the company of their fellow pledges, who console one another, plot a course of survival, and, frequently, take revenge on active members. This is often successful in terms of bonding, noted Aronson.

The exception occurs when initiates quit the group, but it is common for an entire pledge class to band together to convince one of their number not to let them down by leaving.

Activists such as Stevens retort that concentration camps also helped people bond, and ways exist to assist pledges in achieving unity that do not involve sadistic acts, alcohol overdoses, or demeaning treatment that run counter to the goals of education. Even if the rituals practiced as a part of hazing had caused only a single death, Stevens said, any purpose they may achieve is insignificant in the fact of lost life. And, she pointed out in a 1997 telephone interview, not one but many such deaths have occurred over time.

3

Alcohol Misuse

All current studies of alcohol use among men and women attending institutions of higher education point to binge drinking as *the* major campus social problem, particularly among fraternity and sorority members. In 1998 the Harvard School of Public Health released a report that discouraged many Greek leaders. Four out of five fraternity and sorority members reported themselves to be binge drinkers, admitting that they engaged in risky sexual behaviors, acted irresponsibly at times, and hurt their academic standing. Study director Henry Wechsler said in an interview with the author in January 1999 that binge drinkers are drinking far more than ever. The only positive finding was that about one in five college students abstained from alcohol, a slightly higher percentage than was indicated by a previous Harvard survey. Half of all college students admitted to indulging in heavy drinking. The report tabulated responses from 14,521 students at 116 colleges in 39 states.[1]

Stunned and distressed, the National Interfraternity Conference (NIC) contracted an independent research team from the Center for Advanced Social Research at the University of Missouri, Columbia, to look into Greek drinking patterns to determine the dimensions of the problem. While the team found that the excessive use of alcohol was less prevalent among fraternity and sorority members than it was among the students whose self-reports contributed to the Harvard Study, the Missouri findings were still highly troubling for NIC and National Panhellenic Conference (NPC) leaders.[2]

Campus problems with student alcohol abuse in the United States can be traced back to the nation's first institution of higher learning. In Harvard's early days, "discipline was severe without being just, duty was narrowly defined, [and] individualism was repressed," wrote school historian Arthur Stanwood Pier. Nonetheless, in spite of prohibition and of the quickness with which students were expelled for rowdy behavior, some Harvard students consumed alcohol and terrorized the townspeople of Cambridge by blowing up buildings with gunpowder.[3]

From colonial times to the present, students in the United States have viewed drinking alcohol as a rite of passage, just as many other cultures, both primitive and sophisticated, have done. Arnold Van Gennep, author of *The Rites of Passage*, noted that part of the socialization process for many peoples is the habitual exchange of bottles or the purchasing of drinks.[4] This custom, now ingrained in college fraternal culture, is as old as Harvard itself. During the institution's first years, students shared rum and skins of wine with each other and with townspeople. Although authorities reprimanded students caught with spirits, they could do little to enforce prohibition and were unable to shut down a groggery near the college run by a prominent Cambridge citizen. When two Dutch visitors came to Harvard in 1680, they saw so much evidence of tobacco and wine use in student quarters that they mistakenly believed they had entered a tavern. In the seventeenth century, students not only continued to consume "distilled lyquours" in their chambers; they also began to disrupt solemn activities such as commencement, their boisterousness outraging the legislature.[5] Free-spirited students such as Caleb Cushing said they preferred to celebrate "the bonds of friendship, which always tighten when they are wet."[6] Even future politicians used alcohol to celebrate at Harvard. After his Porcellian initiation on November 2, 1878, Theodore Roosevelt (also claimed as a member by Delta Kappa Epsilon) celebrated until he became uncharacteristically drunk.[7]

Fraternal problems with alcohol go back to the late nineteenth century, as a reading of dusty university histories readily demonstrates. Then, as now, alumni dropped in at fraternity houses for visits bearing bottles of cheer, alternately filling impressionable heads with war stories about the good old wild days and inspiring young students to go out into the world and find success. Right up to his death (from complications caused by appendicitis) in 1902 at age thirty-two, the American author Frank Norris, whose novels include *McTeague*, continued to visit his old Phi Gamma Delta house at the University of California,

Berkeley (from which he failed to graduate), defending the right of his fraternity to haze in order to turn rough cobs into what he called "regular guys."[8] Critic Warren French suggested that "participating in fraternity hazing offered [Norris]—as it has many others—an unconscious anti-intellectual compensation for the 'intellectual hazing' he had to endure in the classroom."[9] French also said,

> What the social fraternity does for its members is rarely understood by self-appointed critics or the members themselves. Upon arriving at college, freshmen are expected to think responsibly for the first time in their lives. Many fall by the wayside simply from paralysis occasioned by the shock of the unprecedented demand. The fraternity accepts the individual apparently as he is and thus offers a refuge where he may maintain his dignity without developing his mind. . . . The 'Greek' attitude of inherent superiority colors much of Norris' work. He was probably not even much aware of much of the racial and class snobbery in his writing. . . . The worst thing about the fraternity attitude is that it may persist long after members graduate, as it does in Norris' writings. Despite their superficial array of officials and rituals, fraternities are anarchical. The group functions to reinforce the members' assumption that they are really right when they insist—as Norris does in his essays—that the school may teach a few technical tricks but has no effect upon the thinking or personality of the individual.[10]

Fraternities also boomed in the Roaring Twenties before the Depression. During this decade, fraternal historians reported a drastic breakdown in values as a result of gambling, drinking to excess, and pledging of athletes. Fraternal historian Frederick D. Kershner noted that early athletes were more like mercenaries than like students.[11] Executive Vice President Robert A. Biggs of Phi Delta Theta headquarters in Oxford, Ohio, has heard older fraternity members talk about the attraction of alcohol for Greeks back in Prohibition times. The writings of William Faulkner (Sigma Alpha Epsilon) and F. Scott Fitzgerald reveal how a generation of younger Americans, like today's collegians, viewed drinking as a glamorous, forbidden activity back then, said Biggs in a 1998 interview for this book.

By 1933, educators at fourteen colleges—including Amherst, Bowdoin, and Williams, all Greek strongholds at the time—signed an agreement to eliminate harmful Greek practices such as hazing. William Hoy, a 1930s fraternity reformer, accused fraternities of practicing "gross hedonism." Hoy demanded that universities pull the plug on houses that sponsored "booze parties and hell-week parties," with unchaperoned women staying at the houses for two or three nights at a time.[12] The author of a 1930 *New York Times* commentary noted that universities needed to contain the party-happy "gay-dog alumnus" who

Biographers of Frank Norris, the author of *McTeague* and other novels, have noted his lifelong devotion to Phi Gamma Delta. As an undergraduate at the University of California, Berkeley, Norris established an annual pig dinner that is a tradition at all Phi Gam chapters today. Norris, reflecting widespread attitudes in the 1890s, defended hazing as a molder of young men. Norris's classmates donated a marble chair to the university in his memory.
Photo courtesy of Ed Gabe, Phi Gamma Delta

came back to visit his fraternity house with the means to procure alcohol in spite of national Prohibition.[13] At about the same time, Delta Chi field representative Albert S. Tousley called liquor in the house a "bugbear" to control, complaining to NIC delegates that undergraduates refused to abstain because visiting alumni brought corn liquor or spiked beer with them on visits. "If you can violate prohibition laws at 40, we can do it at 20," Tousley said he had been told by undergraduates.[14]

In 1940, seven years after Prohibition had ended, a highly publicized fraternal alcohol-overdose death took place while future columnist James Kilpatrick was a student at the University of Missouri. The incident occurred in a drinking-oriented fraternity, Theta Nu Epsilon, that was not recognized by the school or by the NIC. Begun in 1870 at Wesleyan University as a fraternity for males who were already in a fraternity, Theta Nu Epsilon was often condemned by college presidents for its members' dissoluteness. Although the national itself died out officially in 1942, sub-rosa chapters operated in the 1950s, and today some alumni still discuss trying to revive a reformed Theta Nu Epsilon.[15] Kilpatrick became an outspoken critic of hazing.[16]

Alcohol weakened the moral and intellectual underpinnings of fraternities from the 1960s through the early 1990s, said Jonathan Brant. Even a few sororities allowed alcohol in their houses during the "do your own thing" '70s, although those houses quickly became dry again when NPC leaders recognized that allowing alcohol in sorority houses was risky and instituted a ban that continues today, said Syring in a telephone interview. More recently, sororities have experienced problems with alcohol violations, and on some occasions even with sexual assaults, when they co-sponsored parties with fraternities—particularly when these parties were held on fraternity property or off-campus locations.

The rash of alcohol-related deaths in national fraternities goes back to at least 1971, when seventeen-year-old Wayne P. Kennedy drowned as a result of what was termed "horseplay" in Lake Pontchartrain during a Delta Kappa Epsilon rush event at Tulane.[17] In 1974 a drunken Tau Kappa Epsilon ritual at Bluefield State College in West Virginia ended with the shooting death of one member and the wounding of another; the fraternity's graduate adviser was imprisoned for manslaughter. Three drinking deaths claimed young men in local student clubs at the University of Nevada, Reno, the University of Wisconsin–Stevens Point, and Northern Illinois University in 1975. Since then, deaths from alcohol poisoning and as a result of accidents in which alcohol was a factor have claimed the lives of male students belonging to (or visiting) local or national Greek groups at schools of higher education such as Alfred University, Loras College, Rutgers University, Truman State University (formerly Northeast Missouri State University), the University of South Carolina, the University of Texas, Tennessee State University, American International College, the University of Washington, the University of Mississippi, Pennsylvania State University, Bowling Green State University, the University of Arkansas, Kansas State University, Stanford University, the University of Toledo, Colorado State University, Rider College, Dickinson College, Purdue University, Louisiana State University, Carnegie Mellon University, Bloomsburg University, MIT, the University of Pittsburgh, Texas A&M University, the University of Iowa, the University of Vermont, and Indiana University. Students leaving parties or on pledge runs involving alcohol have perished at Trinity University, Hampden-Sydney College, Oregon State University, and the University of Georgia. Deaths of students—many of whom were intoxicated and failed to awaken—in fraternity fires have occurred at the University of North Carolina; Radford University; the University of California, Berkeley; Bloomsburg University; and Ohio Wesleyan University.

The problem of fraternal deaths escalated in the 1980s as fraternity houses hosted more and more parties during which huge amounts of liquor were available, and as off-campus bars began offering discounts. Drinking became an almost daily activity for some students and was a particular temptation for fraternity members, who could find a drink at any hour of the day or night. Some states raised the drinking age to twenty-one, but many students quickly found ways to obtain counterfeit identification cards to get into bars illegally. Reacting to reports of out-of-control drinking by those under twenty-one, the U.S. Congress voted to amend a federal highway funding bill that in effect punished states that failed to raise the drinking age, by depriving them of federal highway dollars. Thus in the '90s college officials found themselves selectively enforcing alcohol prohibition for underage students on campus, even as students aged twenty-one and over continued drinking legally in campus pubs and fraternity houses.

Not only was the law well-intentioned, it was also essential, given the rising number of fatal automobile accidents that involved drinking drivers under twenty-one, said nationally known alcohol expert Lewis Eigen, who is president and chief executive officer of Social & Health Services, Ltd. (SHS) and a former director of the National Clearinghouse for Alcohol and Drug Information and the National School Resource Network. Unless the problem of high student alcohol use is dealt with, even fraternity members who get through college without apparent alcohol-related injury may be headed toward major problems with alcohol later in life, said Eigen. "I think the eighteen-year-old drinking limit was a terrible thing to do," he said in a 1997 interview for this book. "However, the only thing worse would have been not to do it. We can't argue with the [number of] lives saved. The challenge to schools and universities is to come up with other means of moderation. As soon as they work, you will see the eighteen-year-old drinking ban disappear quickly." Eigen said that once young people finally return to moderate drinking, we may see the laws allowing eighteen-year-olds to drink being reinstated.

Fraternity reaction to the law passed by Congress varied dramatically. NIC and NPC leaders such as Brant and Syring urged fraternal compliance with state alcohol laws and advocated a move toward sobriety. On the other side, the headquarters of Delta Kappa Epsilon, a conservative fraternity whose alumni include four U.S. presidents (one honorary) and many powerful politicians, passed a 1998 resolution unanimously condemning the legislation that it considered unfair. "This action of the Congress of the United States is a clear violation of the doctrine of states' rights and separation of powers," said the DKE delegates in a formal proclamation. The politically conservative international DKE fraternity, which has not been an NIC member since 1994, has followed its own path with regard to drinking in contemporary fraternal culture. For example, at the DKE convention in 1998, participants heard a presentation titled "Risk Management & Personal Consequences of Our Actions" and also attended what one conventioneer termed an "amazing" cocktail party at the Bacardi distillery.[18] While several large international fraternities have shut down houses indefinitely in response to behavior problems, and have incurred a financial loss as a result, Delta Kappa Epsilon rarely shuts down a chapter unless a university closes it. For the most part, only when a fatality occurred, or something repugnant—such as a theme party making fun of minorities—took place, has Delta Kappa Epsilon headquarters offered a public apology and publicly rebuked a chapter. By refusing to boot out troubled chapters at Colgate and Tulane, the fraternity has clearly established its attitude that young males, being young males, will occasionally run off course, and if we hang in there with them, all will be well in the long run. In a phone interview with the author, DKE executive director Dave Easlick said he was opposed to reforms that he considered a capitulation to advocates of political correctness.

Thus even as newspapers across the United States were running dozens of articles and editorials supporting Greek efforts to curb drinking and to establish alcohol-free housing, privately national fraternities were as divided on this issue as they had been after World War II, when fraternal reformers butted heads with "right to associate" defenders on the issue of constitutional clauses restricting the membership of Jews and African Americans.

On the side of a return to fraternal values and the substitution of wholesome activities for alcohol-centered events were Brant and his NIC staff, many NPC leaders, and many influential Association of Fraternity Advisors (AFA) members. Opposed to such a movement were executives and influential alumni from Delta Kappa Epsilon, a great many undergraduate fraternity members and influential alumni, and fraternal supporters in executive positions. Partisans in the DKE camp were of the opinion that Congress had been wrong to pass a prohibition law singling out those who were otherwise old enough to vote and join the military. DKE opponents found themselves colliding with fraternal reformers and Greek-affairs educators, and in a telephone interview for this book, Easlick chided the NIC for forgetting its role as a "fraternal trade group." The campaign of DKE headquarters to separate the affairs of Greek headquarters and college Greek advisers received a boost in 1998 when a Grand Council member of Phi Delta Theta—one of the NIC's model fraternities for alcohol-free housing— strongly condemned the NIC's practice of sponsoring joint national meetings with the AFA and asked that such meetings be discontinued.[19] Michael Carlone of Sigma Phi Epsilon said that breaking the relationship would be a mistake, calling the NIC-AFA marriage a progressive step toward achieving reforms in the Greek system. Yet even some supporters of the NIC-AFA efforts to curtail alcohol misuse worry that activities proposed by partnership may be so "milk-and-cookies" wholesome that they turn away young people who are not chronic drinkers but are not candidates for sainthood, either.

On October 7, 1998, the Deke national headquarters claimed that the Greek movement and the American Civil Liberties Union (ACLU) had achieved a victory over what it considered invasive, overprotective college administrators when President Bill Clinton approved legislation with an amendment forbidding schools receiving federal aid (such as Middlebury College, Bowdoin College, and Colby College) from levying sanctions against students belonging to Greek groups after the schools had outlawed fraternal organizations. But several months after its passage, few observers thought the amendment had the power to bring back fraternities where they were not desired by colleges.

As a consequence, Greek-life educators and fraternal leaders found themselves in disagreement over what course fraternities and sororities should take in the twenty-first century. On one side were pro-NIC reformers, who advocated aggressive internal housecleaning, a reduction in the role played by alcohol in socialization, and cooperation with college Greek affairs professionals to punish so-called animal houses. On the other side, the secessionist Dekes and allies wanted each fraternity to educate its own undergraduates about risks such as alcohol misuse and recommended taking a course of aggressive legal action to see if courts would force universities to tolerate Greek organizations under protections offered by the First Amendment of the Constitution.

Clinton's signing of the Higher Education Amendment of 1998 came months after the national executives of Phi Delta Theta, Phi Gamma Delta, Sigma Nu, Theta Chi, and other large fraternities urged their respective undergraduate convention delegates to vote to operate houses that would be free of alcohol and drugs. And even though nine national voting fraternities in the NIC announced plans to institute dry houses in many campus chapters (which voluntarily agreed to this plan or were recolonizing because they had been shut down by the national and/or school), it was also made clear that because of internal disputes, some chapters of Sigma Nu, Theta Chi, and Phi Delta Theta would not be able to make a commitment to alcohol-free houses by 2000. In spite of strong support on the part of fraternity executives such as Theta Chi's Westol, Sigma Nu senior consultant Maurice "Mo" Littlefield, and Phi Gamma Delta's Bill Martin, undergraduates at the trio's annual conventions voted for various time extensions that would make large-scale nationwide compliance with alcohol-free housing measures unlikely (even in these reformist fraternities) before 2003. Nonetheless, the NIC was encouraged by the fact that most of the undergraduate delegates from the three fraternities agreed in principle to support long-term alcohol-free housing, and that Phi Sigma Kappa and Alpha Kappa Lambda delegates voted to ban alcohol entirely in August 2001. In addition, the NIC received NPC backing after the latter endorsed a motion that encouraged twenty-six member sororities to support alcohol- and drug-free fraternities. "The women are totally supportive of the efforts of the nine groups that have made a commitment, and we will give this support where it counts—on the college campus [by attending alcohol-free functions]," said Lissa Bradford of the NPC in an October 1998 interview. "Alcohol-free housing does not mean prohibition, and it is not the total answer to the alcohol crisis on the campus (and in society), but it can be very successful when combined with the right kind of education programming and leadership development. Besides, what other choices are there?"

During the 1998–1999 school year, the NPC put on an alcohol-awareness workshop called "Something of Value" at about twenty campuses, according to Bradford, and the NIC took other substance-free programs to many more colleges. Both initiatives stressed to undergraduates that fraternity houses weren't always synonymous with drinking hangouts, emphasizing that the unremitting pattern of alcohol-related fraternal deaths that had been occurring since the '70s began in the '50s as houses started to install wet bars and to make available ever-flowing kegs.

By 1998, some U.S. colleges had begun to ban alcohol. West Virginia University decided that it would forbid the use of alcohol on campus in the year 2001. Nine other universities (Kentucky, Idaho, Oklahoma State, Iowa, Utah State, Washington State, Colorado, Northern Arizona, and Rhode Island) agreed to make their residence halls and fraternities alcohol-free. MIT announced a campus-wide alcohol ban, but not until it had become the object of nationwide criticism because of policies allowing new freshmen to join fraternities that critics said had contributed to the death in 1997 of eighteen-year-old Scott Krueger, a Phi Gamma Delta pledge from suburban Buffalo, New York.[20]

The decision by these schools to outlaw alcohol indicates that college officials had been unable to persuade fraternal chapters to use alcohol in moderation. Not only have extensive educational programs had limited success, but campus police enforcement of state statutes regarding underage drinking, public intoxication, and driving under the influence has often been hindered by some administrators' concerns about how their institutions will be perceived if the fact that these things are problems on campus is brought to light. But university administrators' reluctance to see students hauled off to jail may be lessening thanks to the criticism of miscellaneous city officials in Boston, Baton Rouge, and Berkeley, who have pointed to administrators for not doing more to prevent student deaths and alcohol misuse. The University of Virginia, Pennsylvania State University, Virginia Commonwealth University, and other schools now occasionally allow outside law-enforcement and liquor-control agencies to conduct sting operations.[21]

ADDICTIVE ORGANIZATIONS

While he was an Indiana University doctoral student, James "Jim" Arnold spent nearly three academic years in a college fraternity culture observing alcohol use by undergraduate members as part of the research he conducted for his dissertation.[22] In this respect he went beyond the boundaries of researchers whose information comes from surveys and statistics. Arnold's research took place at a high-status fraternity in the Midwest that he does not identify because of guarantees of confidentiality he made in return for full access.[23]

Arnold studied what was on the surface a law-abiding fraternity respected by the dean of students. Behind closed doors the group hazed its pledges, abused alcohol, and violated state and university statutes against underage drinking. In the course of the study, Arnold saw how drinking was valued by the group, which then passed on attitudes toward alcohol to new members. Counselors use the terms "addict" and "alcoholic" to refer to an individual or group that is in an *unhealthy* state, meaning that an addicted fraternity has an illness, not that it is inherently "bad." The term "addictive system" was inspired by Anne Wilson Schaef, author of books on addiction. While Schaef focused on work groups in Western society, Arnold applied the concept of the addictive organization to college fraternities, where drinking is part of member socialization.

Characteristics commonly associated with addicts are also associated with addictive social groups. Arnold learned that collegiate rites of passage involving alcohol began even before a student started college. One fraternity member told him that one of the main reasons he'd come to college was to party. Students don't always envision the world they are entering as a sanctum of learning. "I went into the field to study adolescent student drinking in college fraternities and came to believe that I must understand the explicit and implicit messages conveyed to new members . . . ," Arnold wrote in his dissertation, entitled "Alcohol and the Chosen Few."

Arnold, who many years before had personally experienced the negative consequences of drinking, stressed that the insights he arrived at "may not ever occur" to insiders who have "lived" the socialization process as members. Collegians, he concluded, had no wish to denounce the drinking excesses of their peers. "I wouldn't have had the energy to tackle something so rough if it didn't mean so much to me at my core," said Arnold.[24]

Maintaining peace between campus authorities and Greek groups is actually a form of game playing, noted Arnold. His study fraternity presented a responsible image to campus administrators. The office of student affairs played the game as well, engaging in house visits announced in advance and giving higher-echelon college administrators the impression that they too were behaving responsibly. The only real rule that Greek groups observe today is the one dictating that rules are meant to be broken, observed Arnold. College fraternity members frequently dissimulate in the name of protecting the status quo. Advice given delegates at the 1998 Delta Kappa Epsilon convention indicates that some fraternities also clearly communicate to their members that anyone who gets in trouble should contact his national office before speaking to his school administrators.

Even so, as a result of crackdowns on behavior by many national headquarters, where chapter members formerly regarded their Greek leaders at national headquarters as allies, the more rebellious undergrads sometimes now see them as authority figures to be deceived, not as role models to be emulated, according to field representatives from three national headquarters. One field representative said that his once-enjoyable job had become stressful. Dave Westol noted in a 1998 interview for this book that undergraduates plead with him to put off reforms because they insist they are capable of making the older system work, denying such evidence as the alcohol-related deaths of two Theta Chis in two years.

Arnold observed a "monstrous gap" between what was actually happening at the local level and what the nationals said they perceived was happening there. "The [undergraduate] officers of that organization explicitly told me they signed off on forms they were required to sign off on with their nationals that said they did not serve alcohol to minors, that alcohol was not available to under-twenty-one-year olds at their events, and that they did not engage in hazing practices," said Arnold. "But the information they gave me was that they routinely signed off on this and did what they wanted to do anyway."[25]

Arnold found that national fraternities and college administrations are both in effect part of a conspiracy of sorts, having constructed a mutually supportive environment that supports underage drinking, hazing, and other inappropriate behaviors. If nothing drastic happens, the status quo is maintained. But sooner or later something usually goes wrong in an addictive system. Inevitably, overdoses, alcohol-related accidents, sexual assaults, or violent acts will take place in some addicted houses.

Dave Westol of the Theta Chi fraternity central office in Indianapolis visits campuses to put on a mock courtroom drama called "Hazing on Trial." He is one of a handful of Greek leaders with the national clout necessary to influence student affairs advisers, other fraternity executives, and even activists such as Eileen Stevens. However, even Theta undergraduates rebel against strict hazing and anti-alcohol policies, as the 1997 death of Theta Chi pledge Binaya "Bini" Oja, 17, of Clarkson University demonstrates.
Photo courtesy of Theta Chi

The values held by Greek national leaders and Greek affairs administrators (who are themselves Greeks) are often established during their own days in fraternities and sororities. As a result, they may be unlikely to push for sweeping changes unless they have had a negative experience with the consequences of alcohol abuse personally or have had to deal with an alcohol-related death professionally. Unless something dramatic makes these leaders feel that they themselves have "hit bottom," in Arnold's words, or that they have lost the professional respect of college administrators, faculty, and the general public, they'll do enough to satisfy the legal requirements of their job but typically won't conduct the sweeping investigations necessary to uncover hazing, alcohol violations, and pledging infractions. "There is a payoff for them to not be aware," said Arnold. "If they admit there is this terrible stuff going on, they might be obliged to address it. If they view it as a small problem that they can address with small-scale education type programs for their membership, they can say they are doing what they need to be doing."[26]

College authorities commonly try to protect their institutions' reputations as safe havens by thwarting press attempts to get them to disclose information. So do national fraternities. Delta Kappa Epsilon advises its undergraduates to contact the national after the occurrence of a problematic incident to obtain guidance about how to respond to the press. Thus, it has become particularly hard for student newspapers and the media to get accurate information when a hazing incident occurs, and school newspapers in Georgia and California have gone to court in an attempt to learn the details of incidents handled by campus judicial officers. "If hazing or drunkenness occurs, or students and student athletes are acting out of line, other students need to know that as long as the facts are reported clearly and accurately," said Ingelhart in a 1998 interview for this book.

One reason for the silence is that a campus community that supports an addictive organization may be addictive itself, Arnold found. Fraternity and sorority executives often express frustration with the lack of institutional controls on college campuses. Until the mid-1990s, many college presidents turned their heads and crossed their fingers, hoping all would be well in spite of the extent of students' alcohol abuse. "For five years this office has tried to inform the administration of Duke University of the abnormal excesses of the recognized fraternity system," said Durward W. Owen of Pi Kappa Phi headquarters in a 1993 letter to the editor of the *Charlotte Observer*. "All of our efforts have fallen on deaf ears. The Greek system at Duke University and the administrators are so far behind the times as concerns alcohol consumption that it defies description." (Since Owen's letter was published, Duke has introduced extensive alcohol reform plans.)[27]

Self-denial is part of the addictive system. Fraternity members convince themselves that they are responsible about alcohol because they sponsor alcohol-free rush events. Arnold observed that "dry rush" was a term without basis in reality. Prospective members abstained from alcohol during this period, but members did not. All in all, the group's excuses for drinking sound much like those an individual alcoholic might make, Arnold found. The approval the group receives from its national and from the university may reinforce an image in the collective mind of the members that the house uses liquor responsibly. Even if a house does have a dry rush, it shows prospective members slides conveying the message that fraternity members have fun getting intoxicated at formal and informal gatherings. "While, technically, no alcohol is consumed at rush by rushees, the behavior of members is certainly not 'dry' at all as the slide show proceeds," according to Arnold. "Members hoot and cheer as the many pictures of alcohol-laden events are displayed. [Fraternity] members are quite simply being dishonest if they believe that rush is alcohol-free. While they are actively denying that alcohol plays any part in rush, in truth, alcohol use and messages about its use are everywhere."[28]

Arnold reveals dry pledgeship to be a similar sham. "It does not take long to discover that this prohibition is often violated," observed Arnold. "[A member] had told me in an early interview that despite the no-alcohol rule for pledges there were definite times where drinking is sanctioned by the chapter. On one occasion, seniors served as bartenders, and the pledges got "'really . . . butt wasted,'" he learned from a member.

Rita Saucier said that taking alcohol out of the houses is nothing more than a tactic to get public support and to lower insurance costs. She pointed to a recent statement made by Phi Delta Theta members at the University of Alabama, who said there were not going to be any rules about fraternity members stumbling home drunk from bars. "That isn't reform," she said. "It's the national fraternities just covering their butts."[29] Supporting such a contention are examples of students who died after drinking at off-campus bars. Atif Bhatti, a pre-med University of Pittsburgh honors student, died after drinking massive quantities of alcohol while celebrating his birthday with Delta Sigma Phi brothers at an off-campus pub in 1994. At the University of Virginia, a Pi Kappa Phi chapter member died in a car driven by the intoxicated chapter vice president in 1996 after leaving an off-campus rush function held in a mountain cabin. Benjamin Wynne, who is mentioned in an earlier chapter, died in 1997 at the Louisiana State University Sigma Alpha Epsilon house after drinking a lethal amount of alcohol in Baton Rouge pubs. Theta Chi member Jason Greco, twenty, died in a fall down the basement stairs of his house at Rutgers University after drinking at an off-campus tavern in October 1998.

Because many fraternity deaths are low-profile, dismissed as accidents, or occur on campuses that tend to receive minimal national news coverage, there is no single term that covers them. Many of them are mistakenly termed hazing deaths when, rightly or wrongly, college and/ or civil authorities have ruled them non-hazing deaths. From the fraternity perspective, hazing deaths get blown all out of proportion when members of the media estimate deaths. For example, *U.S. News and World Report* erred on the high side when it quoted an anonymous source who said that from 1973 until April 1996, an estimated sixty-five hazing deaths had resulted from beatings and stress.[30]

While hazing is a major societal problem and alcohol abuse is another, in the world of Greek-letter societies these two separate problems become even more troublesome when they are intimately linked. "It's hard to imagine that you could cleanly separate them out," said Arnold. "They are just part and parcel of what goes on in the fraternity world to a large extent."[31] Arnold's fraternity hazed its pledges even as it touted itself as a responsible, non-hazing group. "Anytime you want to indoctrinate somebody, the way you do it is to restrict their food, restrict their sleep, get them run down and then really emotionally play with them," said the president of the group Arnold studied.[32]

One of the most intense nights of pledging in the group Arnold studied was designed to wear the pledges down, he said. More than two dozen pledges came to the house in suits, anticipating having their picture taken for the international fraternity. Instead, members locked the young men in a tiny cell that was as hot as a steam room for an hour or more. Then the members came in to scream at the pledges and to chastise them for real and imagined shortcomings. The pledges were asked to drop their pants, and a photo was taken. The yelling intensified throughout a long, stress-filled night. Fraternity members also blew smoke in the direction of the pledges until the recruits became nauseated, said Arnold. The night of abuse taught pledges the "real" rules of the house, including what their cleaning duties were to be and precisely what "pertinent" information about the international fraternity and the chapter they would be expected to memorize. Instead of sleeping in comfortable rooms as they had anticipated doing, they were assigned floor space just large enough to put down a laundry bag. Pledges also met two members who played "good cop" to the "bad cop" act of the rest of the members, telling the pledges to come to them if there were real problems and serving them unlimited quantities of cold soft drinks. When members thought that hazing had put the pledges under too much stress, they told the recruits it was time they blew off a little steam by drinking and socializing with women.

In the course of his research, Arnold also became immersed in the activities of a second fraternity chapter that had recolonized as a non-traditional, progressive fraternity espousing ideals and rejecting hazing and alcohol. But once the students who had provided the energy behind the reforms had graduated, the chapter became indistinguishable from other fraternities, particularly when it moved from a residence hall into a fraternity house, said Arnold. The new members wanted status, and the quickest way to get that was to throw parties and to condone hazing rituals the reformers would not have approved of. In short, the so-called non-hazing fraternity was still reputed to be progressive, but it was now engaging in lower-end hazing, leaving open the possibility that heavier hazing might start to occur as the group aspired to even higher status.

Arnold's study revealed that some Greek chapters compete to throw the toughest Hell Night and the wildest parties. Given the current absence of a strong truth ethic on campus, too often a "high-status group" is likely to sign statements saying that it doesn't haze or break campus alcohol regulations, when in fact it does. Houses demonstrating the worst addictive behaviors because alcohol is at the center of all group

activities may issue the strongest denials. Ironically, some of the national fraternities that preach about the need for a system of values
have failed to recognize their own value system as fraudulent and in
need of reform. Chapters whose status is low in the eyes of other fraternity members are in this position because their members are good
citizens; hazing fraternities look down on them because of the absence
of hazing and free-flowing kegs at the parties thrown by low-status
fraternities, said Arnold.[33]

Whether dry-house policies in national fraternities will save lives
or merely provide fraternities with a two- or three-year respite from
bad publicity remains to be seen. If Arnold is right, not only is it likely
that in a few years the fact that a fraternity bills itself as "alcohol-free"
will mean nothing in terms of members' total alcohol consumption,
but "progressive" fraternities and fraternities that have done very little
to mandate change will have the press off their backs without significantly reducing the risk of alcohol-related deaths. Judging from past
press coverage, the bad publicity will return if reporters perceive that
the promised reforms were reforms in name only.

If Brant and the NIC are correct, fraternity reforms such as Select
2000 and the expulsion of troublesome chapters will keep backsliding
from occurring. Select 2000, according to Brant, was an attempt by the
NIC to define core values important to the very concept of fraternity
and to then transmit those values to undergraduates who are asked to
adhere to principles such as accountability, leadership, proper ethical
conduct, honesty, integrity, academic scholarship, college/community
service, and freedom from vices and substance abuse. Brant said that
future Greek recruitment efforts will target first-year students who do
not consume alcohol regularly and who would thus prefer fraternity
housing that is safe and conducive to studying.[34]

Brant said alcohol was by far the biggest NIC risk-management
concern. According to the most recent NIC self-disclosures, alcohol was
present in 95 percent of falls from house roofs and other high places,
94 percent of fights, 93 percent of sexual-abuse incidents, 87 percent
of automobile accidents, 67 percent of all falls on fraternity property,
and 49 percent of hazing incidents. Eight out of ten injuries resulting
in paralysis and just under nine out of ten deaths occurred where alcohol use or abuse was a factor. "We are dedicated to having the greatest
risk reduction," said Brant in an interview.[35] "The NIC is here to help
students who believe [fraternity life] is a valuable experience."

The NIC stresses in its literature that most students do not have a
drinking problem. Rather than barraging students with negative statistics on binge drinking in college, the NIC cites a 1994 survey conducted
by the Higher Education Research Institute at UCLA, which found that
the number of first-year students who drank beer and hard liquor was

actually lower than it had been in the 1980s. Brant also praised the results of a Northern Illinois University campaign (which has been imitated at Ball State University and other schools) that tried to get undergraduates to alter their perception of how other students misused alcohol or otherwise misbehaved. According to research conducted by Michael Haines, the campaign stressed that inappropriate behaviors occurred less often than students had assumed.[36] Brant said that many students are opposed to binge drinking but that they need adult and peer encouragement to take a stand on behalf of drinking in moderation or not at all.

Research conducted by Core Institute co-director Philip W. Meilman and Southern Illinois University at Carbondale researchers Cheryl A. Presley and Jeff. R. Cashin and published in the *Journal of Studies on Alcohol* in 1998 notes that during the study period, sorority and fraternity leaders tended to consume more alcohol than did lower-level Greeks.[37] According to the study, which was conducted with government support over a nine-year period, three out of four fraternity leaders and more than half of all sorority leaders had participated in binge drinking within the previous two weeks. The survey was conducted at two- and four-year institution and involved 25,411 Greeks. The research revealed that more Greek leaders than non-Greeks surveyed said that drinking had caused them to botch a school test or end up in trouble with police or school officials.

The survey backed what Greek leaders, having seen college fraternity leaders perish after drinking large amounts of alcohol, already knew. Alpha Delta Omega president Rob Jordan died of drowning after drinking nearly a half gallon of alcohol at Hartwick College during a traditional party in May 1997. An Alpha Tau Omega fraternity leadership conference delegate fell to his death from a high bridge while intoxicated. And president Tristan G. Pinzke of the now-outlawed interfraternal spirit group St. Pat's Board at the University of Missouri, Rolla, died in an off-campus auto collision with another drunk driver's car while he was driving intoxicated. However, on an encouraging note, Michael Carlone of Sigma Phi Epsilon said that leaders in his fraternity who get involved in the reformist Balanced Man Program seem to him, based on strong anecdotal evidence, far less likely to abuse alcohol.

THE ROAD TO RUIN

One frustrating reality for Greek reformers and Greek affairs specialists who combat hazing and fraternal alcohol deaths is that sometimes failure "rewards" their hard work. Each academic year, young people make headlines with their deaths, even after institutions, administrators, and

Greek leaders have pointed out the consequences of bad decisions in pamphlets and educational programs.

Arguments for and against Greek groups have been around since the nineteenth century, and new ones continue to emerge. But the stakes have been raised as a result of the increase in the number of deaths traced to excessive alcohol use, beatings during pledging, and other miscellaneous hazing behaviors that some of these groups practice. In an essay published in the *Chronicle of Higher Education,* alcohol experts George Kuh and Henry Wechsler question whether colleges should retain their association with Greek-letter organizations, pointing to long- and short-term problems associated with alcohol. In a January 1999 interview with the author, Wechsler stated that articles in a number of U.S. newspapers in 1999 that said the worst days of binge drinking might be over were premature, since no substantial surveys exist to back up such claims.

The NIC's Brant and the NPC's Syring have not counterattacked arguments that vilify Greek life, but they have tried to emphasize the positive aspects of Greek groups. Brant points to high college dropout rates as evidence that the Greek system is needed to make students feel at home on campus, and he said that the new dry houses can make that home a safe one. The American College Testing Program reported in 1996 that more students than ever were dropping out before their sophomore year—26.9 percent in four-year colleges. Brant notes that for every Williams, Bowdoin, and Lowell that has ended its long-time campus involvement with fraternities and sororities, there is a Rhodes College, Auburn University, or DePauw promoting the Greek system as a productive adjunct to classroom education. In separate interviews, Brant and Syring maintained that participation in Greek life can enhance a college learning experience, citing a recent NPC/NIC-sponsored study concluding that fraternity and sorority members tend to become more involved in community life later on than do non-Greeks.[38]

Others from the Greek world have similarly shown their concern over criticism of their institutions. Michael Gordon, an outspoken advocate of reform in African American and white Greek groups, said that critics need to get some perspective. "For the first time in the history of education, people are openly addressing the issue of hazing," said Gordon, an Indiana University faculty member and NPHC executive director.[39] Gordon and Michael Carlone of Sigma Phi Epsilon view the closing of chapters, the creation of new anti-hazing programs, and the movement toward dry houses as evidence that the worst days of fraternity excesses may be over. Carlone said his fraternity's closing of prestigious chapters—even Sig Ep's "Alpha" (original) chapter at the

University of Richmond (Virginia) after several pledges were taken to an emergency room for intoxication—was a sign that his group is at least determined to face the future with healthy, nonaddicted members in its ranks.[40] Carlone said he hoped that Sigma Phi Epsilon would attract students looking for a home in the company of serious fellow students who drink in moderation and look to successful alumni as mentors.[41]

Arnold said that he sees good and bad in the Greek system he studied for his dissertation. On the one hand, he concedes that Greeks are significantly involved in public and community service and in raising money for charity. He said,

> At a very young age, people who find themselves in leadership positions of a group like this find themselves running a business or corporation and have to make practical, real-life decisions about how organizations run that certainly I never learned at that particular age. But if you turn the positive side of that leadership argument over, what they learn is that the end justifies the means. They learn how to skirt the rules. They learn how to say one thing and do another. They basically learn how to run an amoral business. That there are lots of ethical calls that have to be made when you are in charge of an organization, and lots of times the ethical calls these organizations are making are outside the ethical bounds of what I would consider right or just. Sometimes the calls they make can do more harm than good for the members.
>
> Whereas you can argue leadership skills on the one hand, you can argue that the leadership development they are undergoing is on the dark side of ethical behavior. It greatly troubles me if you take a look at all the dark side things of fraternities—the secretiveness of them, the playing outside of ethical bounds, the drinking part of them, the destructive behaviors that one can learn. The things that I described in terms of the socialization process, the pledgeship. The group I described in my dissertation showed they learn to do to others what was done to them. And what was done to them was not very pretty. So they engaged in the same kind of hurtful behaviors that were heaped on them as they were in transition coming into the group. So they are taught things which they then pass on. I view that as very dark, as very sinister.
>
> I would say these dark things overshadow the positive things one gets out of these groups. I have leaned more and more in recent years toward the abolishment of these groups even though they've existed on campuses traditionally for a very long period of time and that you can make positive arguments for them.[42]

NIC, NPC, and NPHC leaders Brant, Syring, Carlone, and Gordon counter arguments that favor abolishing Greek groups. The four stress that critics simply fail to notice the large number of chapters that have existed for decades with few or no stains on their records. Former Greek bastions such as Williams College, Colby College, Middlebury College, Amherst College, and Bowdoin College ordered the abolishment of fraternities, but none of them have an alcohol-free climate as a result to make them a model for other schools to emulate. In October 1998 Colby found itself dealing with a public-relations nightmare in the aftermath of critical injuries incurred by a nineteen-year-old student rugby player, Rosamond "Lindsey" Huntoon, who fell from her dormitory window after drinking at an off-campus apartment complex. On the day of the fall, the Colby student newspaper quoted a state liquor inspector's denouncement of what he termed inadequate efforts by school authorities to control students' alcohol consumption. Although a school spokesperson had defended Colby's anti-alcohol efforts, the inspector noted that underage Colby students had been cited more than a dozen times for drinking violations in just the first two weeks of school. Even though it doesn't have a Greek presence, the *Princeton Review*'s 1998 school social rankings placed Colby high on its list of schools where beer flows freely.[43]

What troubles Greek leaders and Greek Affairs staffers is the strong belief that expelling chapters won't stop other chapters from abusing alcohol and from hazing. Too often punishments for hazing, such as suspensions and even expulsions, have little or no effect on Greeks two or three years down the road, said DePauw's Loser, who worked at Rutgers University months after the 1988 alcohol-related death of Lambda Chi Alpha pledge James C. Callahan. Not even a death—not even many deaths—will deter those determined to haze, she said in a 1998 interview at her Greencastle, Indiana, office.

A former Ball State University (BSU) fraternity adviser shared Loser's view. During Richard Harris's tenure at BSU, a student whose blood-alcohol level was 0.38 was hospitalized on a Friday but drank heavily the next weekend. "Rather than this being a wakeup for either the kid or fraternity, it just reinforced the sense of invulnerability," said Harris.[44] Another time a BSU fraternity held a "road to ruin" party at which two first-year males came within five minutes of dying after they consumed eighteen or more drinks. The same fraternity sponsored an "anniversary" road-to-ruin party to celebrate the near-misses, he said.

Arnold's experiences corroborate this anecdotal evidence. He said that college communities mourn a loss intently for about a week and then move on. "Part of the prevailing norm or philosophy of society is that 'we're going to lose a few along the way and I guess that's okay,'" said Arnold. "I don't know what that means about the moral fiber of our society to be totally direct about this. I don't get it myself. . . . Kids go back to drinking just as heavily as they did before even when they've lost a friend last month."[45]

As part of their argument that eliminating Greek groups won't do away with young people's alcohol problems, administrators of fraternal groups often note that the rioting bands armed with bottles, bricks, and rocks who have challenged police in many U.S. cities in the late nineties are made up of students (both Greek and non-Greek) and nonstudents alike.

Alcohol-related disturbances in 1997 and 1998 near the campuses of Ohio University, the University of Colorado, Washington State University, Michigan State University, Pennsylvania State University, and Plymouth State College were reminiscent of soccer riots in Europe. In May 1998 at Miami University of Ohio, some five hundred people were involved in two nights of disturbances in Oxford, resulting in thirty-nine arrests. "It is a sad state of affairs for academia, and I hope we will begin to see some decisive decision making versus more discussion making," said Biggs of Phil Delta Theta, whose Oxford headquarters are near the site of the student clashes with police.[46]

College administrators today might do well to get past their outrage over student alcohol rebellions in the late 1990s and work harder at addressing the underlying causes of rebellion, suggested Rich Zeoli, a former undergraduate president of Phi Delta Theta at the University of Maryland in a 1998 telephone interview for this book. Student riots, alcohol excesses, hazing, and generally uncivil behavior may seem less serious placed against the backdrop of the "naughty '90s," which have been punctuated by such unseemly events as Bill Clinton's sex scandal and the circus-like O. J. Simpson trial, as well as by the stunning revelation that the United States buries 90 percent of all young people murdered in the world each year.[47] The correlation between aggressive student behaviors, substance abuse, and campus unrest in the '60s and '90s during times of national discontent and political upheaval cannot be overlooked.

Rich Zeoli said he thought it was unlikely that student street fighting would simply stop unless students were convinced that they had a hand in self-governance. Alcohol may appear to be the issue, he said, but actually it is empowerment. Zeoli disclosed that he himself was reluctant to accept Phi Delta Theta's new "dry" house movement, but only because the international's headquarters had issued a mandate that students launch it. Zeoli, who said he has no wish to protest violently himself, added that the disturbances also signify that professors and administrators have lost touch with their students. Students should not need to go to graduate school to find a connection with their professors, he said.[48]

Former Delta Gamma sorority national president Maureen Syring had another view of student rioters. "What part of no drinking under twenty-one don't they understand?" she said. She conceded that Zeoli's comments had merit, but countered that in a democracy, students who felt strongly that the state drinking laws were passed in error could take their case to legislators and to the press for an amendment. Those committed to protecting the rights of students must give a little too and consider the rights of their fellow citizens, she said. Collegians who drink to excess often commit crimes or make mischief, drive intoxicated, and assault others, she pointed out in a 1998 interview with the author.

DRINKING GAMES

Tim Higgins, a Navy pilot, reared his son Gabriel (Gabe) on a regime of military discipline before divorcing his wife, Ruth Harten. Tim left Gabe with Ruth in Idaho and moved to Texas, where he remarried. Except in the summers when Gabe visited, Mr. Higgins was unavailable to camp, fish, and race Hobie Cats with Gabe as he had done with his older son, Brian. Gabe referred to himself as a "momma's boy," because his mother was his protector and confidante. "Being a momma's boy ain't all bad, given the momma that done you right," Brian consoled him.[49]

When Gabe was seven, his mother taught him to keep an eye on the sidewalk for pennies, because they brought people good luck. One day he and his mother went to a cafe for curly fries and a burger. As she paid the bill, she gave him four pennies. He slipped one into a gum machine, then flung three pennies onto the sidewalk.

"Why did you do that, Gabe?" asked Mrs. Harten.

"Somebody's got to put the lucky pennies down for people, Mom," he said.

In high school Gabe wrote a first-person short story about a six-year-old with a secret hiding place, a river that comforted him when "things began to get rough" in the house. The river became a caring, soothing father. "The water never yelled at me," wrote Gabe.

His mother remarried too hastily, she said in retrospect. This brief second marriage was hard on her younger son. The new husband demanded obeisance from free-spirited Gabe. Specifically, Gabe clashed with both his father and stepfather over alcohol. They insisted on abstinence without giving him their understandable personal reasons for wanting him to abstain, said Mrs. Harten.[50]

After Gabe graduated with honors from a small high school in Idaho, he chose to attend the University of Texas (UT). After moving to Austin, Gabe became obsessed with good grades. Eager to impress his parents and older brother, a doctoral student at the University of Califor-

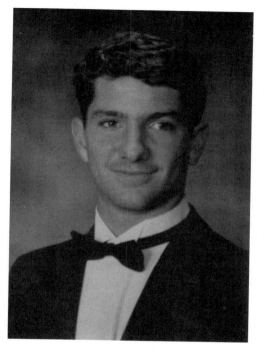

Gabriel "Gabe" Higgins in a formal portrait. He died in an alcohol-related drowning during an all-night Texas Cowboys initiation ceremony at the University of Texas.
Photo courtesy of Ruth Harten

nia, Berkeley, he was always calculating his GPA and worrying about tests in physics and calculus. Although he never earned straight A's, Gabe's academic achievements were above average. His grades and his membership in Kappa Sigma fraternity brought him a bid from the Texas Cowboys, a prestigious UT spirit, service, and social club whose alums include former Texas governors Dolph Briscoe and Allan Shivers, Texas senator Lloyd Bentsen, and ex–Dallas Cowboys coach Tom Landry. Academically and socially, the Cowboys were an elite organization. Members "needed a certain number of hours and a 2.5 [GPA] to become a member," said Sherri Sanders, associate dean of students at UT, in a 1998 correspondence to the author. They had to show leadership potential, noted Ruth Harten. All "Newmen," as the Cowboys called their pledges, submitted to an interview with a selection committee made up of Texas Cowboys officers and alumni, plus a member of the UT Dean of Students office, before being approved for membership. The only dark spot on the group's record was its reputation for engaging in hazing activities such as paddling, branding, abusing young men with a cattle prod, and drinking games.[51]

On January 24, 1995, Gabe wrote to Brian:

> This really means nothing to you, but I'll tell you anyway. I got picked to be a Texas Cowboy. . . . It is an incredible honor. Kids that go to U.T. have dreams about being a Cowboy. I really hope you get excited for me because I really want to do this. It's going to take a lot of time, and I really want to prove myself. I've never really envisioned myself as being a leader and this type of opportunity will give me a chance to demand the respect and honor I deserve. . . . This is really, REALLY, an incredible honor. I have gotten nothing but congratulations from everyone around me who has knowledge of who the Cowboys are. You might know the Cowboys as being the guys dressed up [in] hat, boots, chaps, other random shit, who shot off [Smokey] the [C]annon when U.T. scored their points last season. After I go through [initiation] I'll be able to get on TV and shoot a cannon.

In a letter of January 31, 1995, he also boasted to a female friend, a self-described feminist, that he was getting into the Cowboys. "I am happy for you," she wrote back. "They couldn't have picked a better person—an awesome person, yet still a chauvinistic male."

Sensitive and bright, Gabe did seem a perfect fit for the Cowboys organization, whose members were basically service-minded, upstanding young men who often came from influential families. Gabe not only worked hard to raise money for charity, but he was fun loving and nonjudgmental, and unlikely to criticize a little hell raising. The Oldmen—or initiated Cowboys—were looking for something in a recruit that a social psychologist would call a "core of consistency." They knew they could count on Gabe Higgins to be gung-ho, to wear the Cowboys outfit proudly, and to endure anything thrown his way without quitting or tattling. He also loved being in Kappa Sigma, and living in a house was one of his great pleasures in college.

Also selected by the Cowboys was John Welsh IV, one of Gabe's fellow Kappa Sigs and one of his closest friends. Gabe and Welsh told each other that Cowboy membership would stand out on their resumes. The two agreed to serve as each other's partner for the one-semester apprenticeship as Newmen. Each partnership was supposed to raise $5,000 or $6,000 per semester, according to Ruth Harten. They were to turn in money to the Oldmen every Wednesday at a weekly meeting, said Harten. Gabe became obsessed with fund raising, begging a friend in the dormitories to get her suitemates to purchase a $100 full-page ad in the program the Cowboys printed for a celebrity concert they sponsored. Maintaining his grades and selling ads became stressful for Gabe. Wednesday after Wednesday, he came into the meeting rooms and emptied his pockets of up to $600 at a time. "It seems strange that I bitch about money so much, yet I'm giving an organization thousands of dollars so that I can join," he complained to Brian by the end of March. "That Cowboys deal [is] getting real old, and I'm hating it every day I do it. It's kind of like pledging in the way that I'm really sick and tired of it, but I'll probably enjoy it once I get through it. After all the money, time, and effort I've put into it, I better enjoy it."

Gabe wanted to belong to the Cowboys because he envisioned himself impressing female students, but once recruited he found pleasure doing the required volunteer work. He enjoyed playing his guitar for special-education youngsters at the Rosedale School in Austin. The volunteering seemed to make Gabe more mature. He sent distant friends e-mail that said he was curtailing his partying. During his first year at UT, he often had a beer even before playing basketball, but now he cut down. Too often he met women while he and they were giddy with alcohol, and he didn't like the results. He dated one woman he cared for, but she dumped him for an old flame who "came back with a little wine and strawberries," Gabe confided to a friend. Nonetheless, resolutions to change old drinking habits die young, and he told another friend he planned to get drunk right after final exams.

Lonely, Gabe was loyal to many female pals, keeping one dateless woman company on her birthday. Women with relationship problems sought out "Sigmund Higgins," the self-mocking name he used while giving advice. "Dr. Higgins" was unthreatening, so friends lowered their guard with him, revealing fears, dreams, personal failings. Now, as he went through a sort of pledgeship as one of twenty-nine males who had been "tapped" for membership in the Cowboys, he began dating a woman at UT who was "pretty cool," and the two agreed to enjoy an alcohol-free date. Gabe also wrote to his brother to say that he hoped to know his father better as a person and to make an effort to improve the relationship. He wanted his future children to have a relationship with a loving grandfather, he said. He told Brian he knew his father's military-style "chain pulling" was out of habit, not intentional, and that he "sort of" respected his opinions.

One day a male student walked into one of Gabe's classes with a little girl. "Is that your sister?" Gabe asked.

"My daughter."

Gabe was startled. "It really hit me how old I am now. People around me have all these responsibilities and I'm wondering what kind of liquor I'm going to be drinking when the weekend rolls around," he wrote a friend. Maybe I need to grow up."

On April 26, with the semester and the pledgeship nearing an end, Gabe attended a meeting with other Newmen. Oldmen handed out wristbands that were to allow the Newmen through the gate into the concert the group was sponsoring on the following night. The Cowboys discussed specific work duties, assigning Gabe responsibility for selling souvenirs. The day after the concert there would be a blowout party at a ranch, said an Oldman. Each Newman needed to write a short essay on what he thought being a Cowboy meant.

Gabe realized he was about to be initiated. His only fear of hazing, he wrote to a friend, was that the Oldmen might want him to dip snuff; and he was thinking about grinding up beef jerky to put in a Copenhagen container. The Oldmen announced that each Newman would have to purchase steaks and premium cold beer (for the Oldmen), hot dogs and low-grade warm beer (for the Newmen), and cans of beans, a cooler, charcoal, lighter fluid, cigarettes, Red Man Golden Blend chew, and two dozen bottles of MD 20/20. Gabe, who was broke, hated to hear that he would have to shell out more money. His phone had been disconnected, and he owed a late bill and a reconnection fee. More and more, he had begun to think he had been a fool for joining the Cowboys. "I'm so sick and tired of it I can't tell you," Gabe complained to a friend in an e-mail message. "I've sunk more money into it than I'm willing to tell, and all I know is that so far it hasn't been worth it, but supposedly it gets better after you've gone through."

Gabe was only nineteen, too young to purchase beer in Texas. A Newman used a phony ID card to buy beer at a discount store on April 27, 1995. He bought MD 20/20 at an Austin liquor store that failed to ask for proof of age. In addition, an Oldman contributed two half-gallons of Jim Beam whiskey. The concert, starring Waylon Jennings, made $15,000 for charity, which put the Cowboys in a celebratory mood. On Friday, April 28, Oldmen and Newmen met at the Delta Tau Delta fraternity house at about 4:00 P.M. to receive directions to the party site. The Cowboys wore their recognizable uniform: boots, tan jeans, white shirts. Welsh ate before coming, coating his stomach for a night of drinking. He also brought a change of clothes, figuring that his would get soiled. Some Cowboys downed beers at the fraternity house, then drove off, arriving at the ranch on the Colorado River several hours before sundown.[52]

Welsh rode with four other males in a Ford Explorer. They stopped to help a woman with nine children whose vehicle had broken down.[53]

Gabe and the Newmen gathered dry wood to build a campfire for the Oldmen and a second fire for themselves. A stand of trees on a hill divided the two camps. Some Oldmen and Newmen stood on a high bluff and drove golf balls into the river with clubs. Others flipped a football and a Frisbee.

The purpose of the evening was for the Oldmen to get to know the Newmen. In spite of all the time Gabe had spent on fund raising and other Cowboy activities, few of the senior Cowboys knew much about him. This night of socializing, ending with a formal initiation ceremony, was intended to dissolve any animosities and to ensure that the lines of communication would remain open, keeping the organization strong.

The Newmen split into groups of three. They were told to get together with initiates other than their fund-raising partners. Gabe was paired with Todd Kinsel and an energetic Newman named Cliff Condrey. The Cowboys lit campfires at dusk. The Oldmen selected Gabe and Welsh to cook steaks for them in a barbecue pit, then sent them back to their own campfire.

After eating, the Oldmen used a car horn to summon Newmen by groups to interview them. Some hazing took place. Condrey was swatted with a paddle. Todd D. Shapiro and Scott Newberry were handed hot dogs laced with snuff to eat. All the Newmen were given warm beers. Some drank, some did not. Welsh had stayed out late after the concert. He drank very little this night.[54]

After the interviews, the Oldmen summoned all the Newmen with a prearranged signal, one long car-horn honk. Each Newman read a one-page statement stating his loyalty to the group. Those who hadn't written essays talked extemporaneously.

The Oldmen then praised this year's fund raising and talked about what the organization meant to them. Flickering flames from the campfire illuminated their faces. The vocal patterns of some of the Oldmen changed as the liquor they were drinking took effect. At midnight, as if embarrassed by their display of emotion, the Oldmen started roughhousing, tackling the pledges in the dark. Condrey retaliated, stealing one Oldman's baseball cap and another's felt hat. Soon afterward the Cowboys led the Newmen in drinking games. One group at a time, groups of three Newmen chugged bottles of MD 20/20 while kneeling or sitting on the ground. One recruit, who had earlier consumed twelve to fifteen beers, drank half his bottle and vomited. An Oldman protectively snatched the bottle and poured the rest out.

Gabe's group was one of the last to drink. He forced down most of the sickly sweet liquor, hoping to be declared a "winner" and to show how well he held his booze. The drinking became a competitive event. "It built up more and more and became a big deal," Welsh said.

Some Oldmen passed plates of beans to the Newmen. Gabe Higgins came over to chat with Welsh. "He went from standing to sitting in one motion like drunk people do," Welsh said. Welsh asked Gabe if he was all right.

"Yeah, I'm fine," Gabe replied.

"You don't look fine to me," said Welsh. "You look peaked."

Gabe's eyes were glazed, and Welsh slapped him in the face, hoping to bring him around. "You may say you are fine, but if the wine bites you in the butt thirty minutes from now I don't care whether you are in my group or not. You tell me and I will take care of you."

Gabe didn't seem to hear. Welsh shook him. "Pay attention."

The chugging contests began, and Gabe went over to compete. "It was not said, 'Drink, drink!'" said Newman Sean Nimmo. "But the tradition is to get drunk."[55]

After the game, the Newmen got on their hands and knees to leap-frog over fellow Newmen in a sort of athletic drill. Their reflexes dulled by drinking, to the Oldmen many of the young men looked more comi-cal than athletic.

At about 1:00 A.M. Gabe's group was told to rest. One Newman, recognizing that he was too far gone to do anything else, slept by the fire. Another Newman who had an ulcer and had not consumed alco-hol turned in as well. Condrey left the campfire to try to steal the Oldmen's cold beer, but his derring-do was foiled. Condrey was "a neat but rambunctious guy," said Welsh. He had the leadership qualities Gabe was hoping to develop by joining the Cowboys. Condrey came up with another plan for how he would stick it to the Oldmen.

"Condrey had the idea to go to the river," said Welsh. "Everyone was 'liquored' up so they said, 'Yeah, it's a great idea.' It was the typical college, invincible, fun, great thing to do."[56]

Condrey and Gabe, holding hands for support in the dark, led the way to the Colorado River, which they could hear but couldn't see. Condrey stumbled once. Gabe caught him. The others followed them down the steep and treacherous brushy slope. Some tripped on ex-posed tree roots. A Newman said the trek was too dangerous. Condrey was a cheerleader, encouraging everyone to continue. The leaders found a flatter route next to a creek that led to the river.

"It was pretty neat," said Nimmo. "Everyone was helping each other out, making sure everyone was safe and not hurt and pointing out dangers for each other. It made me feel close to the other guys and was a neat experience I will remember forever."[57]

Gabe and Condrey arrived at a small cove that fed into the Colo-rado River, and then separated. "All of us waded into the river with our boots and jeans on, and I didn't think a thing about it," said Nim-mo.[58] Condrey kept his boots on because of sharp rocks on the cove bottom and on the sandbar.

The Newmen forged through the water to the sandbar. They screamed and whooped and slapped high fives, congratulating one another for their boldness. Nimmo jumped Gabe, and the two tussled in knee-deep water. Gabe then wrestled with Patrick Howard, tearing the shirt off his back.

Gabe and a handful of Newmen elected to swim. Not everyone followed them. It was too dark to see who did and who didn't.

Nimmo hesitated to slip into deeper, faster waters. "I am sure if the entire group had swam to the other side I would have joined in and swam across also," he said. The undercurrent near a bend in the river was strong. Experienced river rafters worry about such conditions even in daylight, knowing that tree limbs, debris, and tree trunks can lurk unseen in a torrent. Shapiro floundered twice in eight to ten feet of water. Patrick Howard helped him to the far bank. Shapiro clutched a tree branch until his strength returned. But when he tried to cross again, the current was still too much for him. Condrey heard a yell, swam over, and pulled Shapiro to the shore.

The Newmen fooled around in the water for maybe twenty minutes. In the darkness and confusion, they lost sight of Gabe.

Two Oldmen with flashlights arrived. They insisted that the Newmen return to their campfire. One Oldman jerked the reluctant Newmen out of the river bodily. They pointed flashlights to help the Newmen get back to the path. The Newmen ran shouting up the hill.

The Oldmen counted heads at the campfire. It was 2:30 A.M. Welsh's stomach dropped. "Gabe's missing," he and another man told the group.

Some Oldmen checked to see if Gabe had fallen on the path. Several others, accompanied by Welsh and Condrey, returned to the river with flashlights. High above them, Oldmen lined their trucks along the rim above the Colorado. Their headlights shone eerily upon the rescuers below. One of the Oldmen and Condrey plunged into the river, looking for Gabe on the opposite shore. Other Cowboys on the bank shouted his name in case he had become disoriented or had passed out in the brush. The trucks had cellular car phones, but Greekthink had set in, and no would-be rescuer called 911.

Between 4:30 A.M. and 5:00 A.M., the weary Oldmen, Condrey, and Welsh returned to camp. At dawn some Oldmen and Newmen again searched the river, which had risen. The sandbars, rocks, tires, trash, and jutting tree limbs visible the previous night were covered by swiftly flowing water. Some Newmen loaded beer cans and MD 20/20 bottles into a truck, and a driver hauled the trash away.

Sometime before 8:00 A.M., an Oldman used his cellular phone to call his father, an attorney. Welsh borrowed a phone to call the Kappa Sig house. He reached an Oldman who had skipped the picnic. "Check Gabe's room," Walsh said. The other did so, and found no evidence that Gabe had come home. Welsh phoned Gabe's new girlfriend, alarming her.

At roughly 11:30 A.M., nine hours after the head count had taken place, an Oldman informed James M. Morgan, who owned the land where the Cowboys had been camping, that the pre-initiation ceremony had gone terribly wrong.[59] Morgan, a businessman whose son was a Cowboy alum, asked hard questions, then called the authorities. Morgan's wife brought food to the beleaguered young men. Some Oldmen who had skipped the picnic drove up. This was the time that blindfolded Newmen were supposed to get their symbolic chaps and paddles.

The attorney that an Oldman had called also arrived at the ranch by noon. Not until 12:31 P.M. did a law officer, Cpl. Earl Pence of the Bastrop County sheriff's department, arrive. Morgan told him that the Cowboys used his property twice a year. "This is the first time anything like this has happened," Morgan said.[60]

Morgan took the officer to the campsites. The officer told everyone to stay put, then took down the names of those who had to leave. In the confusion he failed to interview Welsh. The investigation was joined by Lt. David Campos, a sheriff's department officer, who would later complain to a reporter that he had run into a "wall of silence" when he'd tried to get facts from witnesses.

Some witnesses told the police that Oldmen had given the Newmen two rules to follow during an otherwise ruleless night: don't go down the cliff side, and don't go in the river. Welsh didn't hear the rules, but he said helping the stranded motorist might have prevented his group from doing so. Another pledge didn't hear this directive either but said that he must have been collecting firewood when the orders were given. Newman Cliff Condrey insisted he had heard an Oldman officer advise everyone to stay away from the river.

Cpl. Pence continued to ask questions. "Did anybody hear the victim yell for help?"

No one had.

"How much did he have to drink?"

"About six beers," replied Condrey.

The officer asked Condrey to show him where he had last seen Gabe Higgins. The two walked down a hill to the water. Condrey pointed to a spot on the river past the sandbar.

"What time was that again?" Condrey told him.[61] The officer shook his head. "Why such a big delay in calling 911?" Pence wanted to know.

The Cowboys recited a litany of "not sures." Pence asked again if Gabe had been drunk. Condrey insisted that Gabe's speech had been coherent.

A game warden happened by. Pence enlisted his help and asked to use his boat. Pence also called his own supervisors, requesting that a swift-water rescue team be sent. Two rescue crew members came to help, and Bastrop Chief of Police Ronnie Duncan also arrived to offer assistance. Rescuers dragged the river, keeping an eye out for underground tree limbs and snags that could hang up a body.

An officer phoned Tim Higgins in Galveston. He was out. The officer left a message on his answering machine.

Condrey, Todd Kinsel, and Scott Archer left for Austin. Welsh and several of the Oldmen stayed in spite of their exhaustion. A rescue worker spotted a set of footprints going the wrong way. The rescuers were unsure if the prints were Gabe's, but they worked that area of land and river.

At 4:46 P.M., searchers cast out two draglines, each about 12 to 15 feet long, to scrape the river bottom. Some 150 yards from the sandbar where the young men had celebrated, a rescue worker in the boat hooked a human leg between the knee and ankle. Rescuers brought the body to the bank.

Gabe's corpse was clad in leather boots, a white button-down cotton shirt, and tan denim jeans. His arms were extended outward. Both thumbs were tucked into his palms. Gabe's bottom lip was wedged into his mouth, cinched in place by the top teeth. Someone log-rolled him to one side. Blood gushed from his nostrils.[62] Several Cowboys called their friends in Austin, and the terrible news spread from fraternity to fraternity.

"Until we realized Gabe was gone, it was a great time," Jacob DeLeon later would insist. He called his fellow Newmen "a unified group of guys."[63]

On the day of Gabe's death, Ruth Harten sat up in bed at 6:30 A.M. "I bolted awake in panic and a state of dread," she said.

The night before, she had rented a Sean Connery film, *Darby O'Gill and the Little People.* She rented it to hear the "banshee wail" of the piano for an assignment for a course she was taking at Idaho State University. "When death comes to someone that's the sound they hear, and I wanted to hear it," she said in an interview conducted at her home in Pocatello, Idaho.[64]

The rest of her day was routine. But at 5:30 P.M. the phone rang. It was Brian Thorp, a pal Gabe was always "introducing" to his mother over the phone. "I don't know if you remember me or not, but I'm a good friend of Gabe's?"

"Oh, yes, I remember you." said Mrs. Harten politely.

"I'm sorry to inform you that Gabe's dead," Thorp said. His voice was rehearsed and flat. "They found his body this afternoon. I'm so sorry."

Ruth Harten put up a wall of denial. She tried to reassure him. "It's all right, it's all right."

Some time passed before she called the Bastrop County sheriff's office. A male had drowned in the Colorado River, she learned. His pockets had been empty. He had no driver's license with him.

She got off the phone. Her older son Brian called. Atypically, he had phoned the Kappa house instead of sending his brother e-mail. He had spoken to the house's president, had heard his voice break. "Mom, this is no prank," Brian said.

Mrs. Harten made arrangements to come to Texas. On May 1, authorities took her and Gabe's father to the site of the drowning. Tim Higgins told police that Gabe was an expert swimmer.

Tim Higgins and Ruth Harten went to the funeral parlor. They saw Gabe separately. An attendant had propped his head up on a pillow. His body was discolored, and his handsome features were somewhat swollen. Mrs. Harten found it impossible to maintain her composure. She ran into the hallway. There she saw Tim Higgins, the ex-Navy pilot, mourning the son who had wanted a better relationship with his dad. An autopsy showed that at the time of his death, Gabe's blood-alcohol level had been 0.21.

As the investigation continued, contradictions among members' stories disturbed Mrs. Harten. Some witnesses said that no Newmen were pushed, tied, blindfolded, hit, or paddled. Others said Condrey was paddled. Newman Jacob DeLeon said that whether or not a Newman was paddled was between him and his Oldman. "Your Oldman and you do your own thing, but my Oldman . . . wasn't into that type of thing," said DeLeon. "There's a code. You don't talk about what your Oldman does. You don't say much about it. It's not really a code. It's just not important, so you don't tell many people a whole lot."[65]

One year after the death, a Bastrop County grand jury declined to issue a criminal indictment for hazing against members of the Texas Cowboys. Nor did the Texas Alcoholic Beverage Commission press charges against those who had provided alcohol to a minor or minors. Gabe's estranged parents sued Morgan, six former officers, and the Cowboys. They settled for $1.09 million, according to the *Chronicle of Higher Education*.[66]

After an investigation, UT authorities concluded that the activities on the Morgan Ranch constituted hazing. The Cowboys were suspended for five years. At the time of the suspension, three other fraternities at UT were also suspended for serious infractions. UT President Robert Berdahl told *Austin American-Statesman* reporter Mary Ann Roser that the school was doing all it could to eliminate hazing, but said it was as hard to get rid of permanently as crabgrass is.[67]

Ruth Harten disagreed. The high incidence of deaths and hazing incidents connected with social clubs at UT over the last ninety years has led her to conclude that a long line of college presidents have lost all historical perspective or have been imprisoned by political realities. The sheer number of hazing incidents perpetrated by fraternities should cause the university to shut them down for good, she charged. "It makes you question what the real objectives of higher education are," Mrs. Harten said in 1998.

Unlike several mothers who have worked as activists with fraternal organizations, Ruth Harten wants such groups abolished, saying they have no place on college campuses. In a January 14, 1998, letter to the author she said:

> Since Gabe's death, I have heard more and more horror stories about the terrible things the Greeks have done. Sometimes they haze their pledges all semester long with such cruelty and lack of compassion that the reaction most people have is disgust. These stories come from the institutions of higher learning involving the nation's most promising and intelligent young people. . . .
>
> Are they to teach our young people that their goals in life should be to tell the truth and develop high standards and strong morals, or are they taught just the opposite?

In the same letter she criticized as a facade "the John Wayne image that the Texas Cowboys try so hard to project."

According to Mrs. Harten, such groups may have once emphasized good character and high moral standards, but their founding fathers would close the groups themselves if they knew what went on during pledging today. "While the Greeks argue that it isn't bad and that the friendships and brotherhood shared are very wonderful and fulfilling things, I wonder, At whose cost?" she said.

She gets angry when she talks about hazing in institutions of higher learning that sponsor student organizations. They disgust her, she says flatly. They offered Gabe the family away from home he sought to lean on, and they made him participate in a foolish and dangerous series of activities. She charged that the organization's vaunted alumni should have told the Newmen that what some of them had endured as new Cowboys was wrong and potentially dangerous.

Some of the Cowboys told UT associate dean of students Sherri Sanders that they do not haze, but they define hazing as singling out pledges for prolonged brutality, she said in a 1998 phone conversation for this book. "They don't see intimidation, servitude, and so on as hazing."

Nor do they pay much attention to stories about how pledges and members from UT chapters of Delta Kappa Epsilon, Phi Kappa Sigma, Sigma Nu, Phi Kappa Psi, Delta Tau Delta, and Beta Theta Pi died during hazings, pledging activities, or drinking marathons. Gabe died with his boots on. Phi Kappa Psi pledge Mark Seeberger wore handcuffs while swilling twenty ounces of rum in two hours for the UT chapter in 1986. Seeberger, notes Ruth Harten, didn't officially die during a hazing, either. She asked what kind of incident it would take for a grand jury to rule that a pledge had died as a result of hazing. "The universities and, really, society itself have looked the other direction, therefore condoning [student] activities," she said. There may be laws in place, but the enforcing of those laws is way too lax. . . . How many deaths is it going to take?"[68]

"For those of us who were here at the university and went through Gabe Higgins's death, it's hard to believe it has no effect," Sanders said in a phone conversation. Ironically, while at least seven hazing-, pledging-, and alcohol-related deaths and as many serious injuries have occurred in Greek groups at UT since 1928, for at least twenty years the school's administration has invested many staff, faculty, and administrator hours in the formulation and execution of alcohol- and hazing-prevention programs. Its self-study of hazing was revealing and self-critical. Its publications developed to increase awareness of hazing have been numerous and detailed.

Gabe's death offers many lessons about alcohol misuse on campus today. Too many parents and educators remember their own relatively harmless experimentation with alcohol when they were young and underestimate the amount of alcohol that otherwise responsible students such as Gabe and the other Texas Cowboys actually consume today. Also underestimated is how frequently these students drink to excess.

In addition, because the consumption of staggering amounts of alcohol has become so common, undergraduates themselves underestimate the dangers of drinking. Under the influence of alcohol, they also tend to indulge in risky behavior, as Gabe and his new friends did when they entered the dangerous waters of the Colorado the night he died. For every death of a drunken collegian listed in Appendix A of this book, there are many, many other instances of students cheating death thanks to good luck or to the prompt action of their peers, campus police, or emergency rescue squads. That college students have a cavalier attitude toward drinking is clear. Witnesses to potential destruction laugh off the danger, sign their names on the bodies of comatose friends, or, for their own private amusement, make drunken young people perform exercises, as the Oldmen did in Gabe's case.

It must be pointed out that regular alcohol consumption, particularly when the alcohol is consumed to excess or in conjunction with hazing, tempts collegians to defy death. This is particularly true if a newcomer like Gabe has a tendency to overdo it with alcohol anyway. Perhaps groups such as the Texas Cowboys and universities such as UT that revere their frontier traditions and demonstrations of valor may be a little more prone to experiencing repeated tragedies in spite of attempts by officials to establish education programs.

However, UT staff member Sherri Sanders strongly disagreed with the notion that UT group members may be more inclined to test their mettle than their counterparts elsewhere. In a 1998 e-mail she said that she rejected the notion that a Texas frontier mentality had anything to do with UT's numerous serious incidents. "Young adults believe they are invincible and take greater risks than they should," said Sanders. "I believe this is especially true with college men as they give in to peer pressure and try to prove they are a man. . . . Texas has certainly had its share of problems, but hazing and alcohol abuse exist nationwide."[69]

In November 1998, another University of Texas fraternity member, twenty-three-year-old Jack Ivey of Phi Kappa Sigma, died after downing enough alcohol to raise his blood alcohol level to 0.40. Meanwhile, Ruth Harten's life, like the lives of other parents of hazing victims, goes on, marked by celebrations: the graduation ceremony Gabe missed at UT in 1998, her son Brian's receipt of his doctorate, his marriage, and the marriages of Gabe's friends. "I keep hoping that the Greeks would understand how their flamboyant lifestyle changed mine, or how—in the name of brotherhood?—their partying and disregard for protecting life itself has made such a divot on my life," she said. "Are they so bent on partying and pursuing that lifestyle that they don't care about the consequences? If it were just Gabe, maybe I would swallow my pride and just deal with it. But the death list keeps growing."[70]

Gabe's guitar and cowboy paraphernalia, displayed in Ruth Harten's living room in Pocatello, are a shrine to his memory. Every now and then she scours sidewalks to find a lost penny. She has collected one hundred and five.

4

A Weed in the Garden of Academe

THE ORIGINS OF HAZING

For centuries young men and boys have engaged in activities that would now be known as hazing. The Greek philosopher Plato, who founded the Academy in 387 B.C., likened the savagery of young boys to the acts of ferocious beasts. Scholars writing about the ancient centers of learning in Berytus, Carthage, and Athens occasionally referred to this social problem.[1] Hazing in Athens consisted of practical jokes played by unruly young men that injured the hazed and citizens who got in the way.[2] Similar hazings that involved taunting and bullying occurred during the fourth century at the center of learning in Carthage. The *eversores*—Anglicized as the "Overturners"—attracted and repelled a hedonistic student named Augustine, who later became the Catholic bishop of Hippo Regius. The Overturners' unruly lifestyle and sadistic ways, which had intrigued him as a youth, repulsed him as a mature writer.[3] Like contemporary organizations that haze, the Overturners were fun to be around, except when they were tormenting a newcomer. "There was something very like the action of devils in [the Overturners'] behavior," wrote Augustine. After the newcomers gained acceptance, they became Overturners and abused the next crop of students. Because they too had endured hazing, they denied the wrong-ness of their actions. "[The hazers] were rightly called Overturners, since they had themselves been first overturned and perverted, tricked by those same devils who were secretly mocking them in the very acts by which they amused themselves in mocking and making fools of others," wrote Augustine.[4]

His was not the only voice raised to express indignation over stu-dent hazing. In the sixth century, law students' acts of hazing outraged Justinian I, the Byzantine emperor who codified Roman law. Justinian tried to end the hazing of first-year law students by issuing a decree outlawing the practice. He may have been successful, or perhaps per-petrators hazed in secret. At any rate, not until the twelfth century does history begin to commonly note hazing occurrences.

During the twelfth century and for hundreds of years afterward, hazing was a common scourge that universities failed to eradicate. The problem may have arisen spontaneously, or perhaps, as one medieval-ist has conjectured, a scholar may have come across Justinian's edict and reintroduced the practice. University documents from the Middle Ages contain so many references to hazing and alcohol misuse among students that then, as now, the case can be made that the two practices were among the most serious social problems facing administrators and faculty on university campuses.

During the Middle Ages, hazing was common among young male university students who saw themselves as possessing a culture of honor. William Ian Miller, an expert on everyday life in medieval cultures, has written that "a culture of honor is often perceived by both insiders and outsiders to be a culture of threat and violence."[5] Members in cul-tures of honor feel compelled to "reciprocate" for bad things done to them, to perform acts of kindness in exchange for good deeds.

The term "university" was not used until the thirteenth century. Early centers of education in Paris, Salerno, and Oxford were called "studium generale." Students came from far-flung outposts to study at centers of learning. The growth of these learning centers coincided with the growing political power of towns located on trade routes. At first nearly all power at early centers of learning such as the one at Bologna was in the hands of student guilds; these guilds were called universi-ties. For a long time, until the hierarchy slowly began to reverse in northern France, Germany, and England, the masters at these institu-tions were thrust into a position of servitude by the students who paid them. The power balance began to shift after students started to allow their teachers to determine which teaching candidates were worthy of receiving a license for entrance into the profession. Eventually these educated laymen formed their own guilds, and political power swung their way. Student power dissolved further as schools of higher learning came under church dominance and professorial administration, but for an extended period before that happened, students maintained power in Italy, southern France, and Spain. They set fees and salaries, and fined or expelled incompetent lecturers.

These early universities in western Europe had much in common with today's Greek-letter fraternal groups. They set membership requirements, made rules, and required dues. As the subordinates of master scholars, medieval university pupils eventually came to resemble guild apprentices. Just as today's collegiate secret societies refrain from giving out certain information to outsiders, guilds of the Middle Ages kept out interlopers by hoarding trade secrets available only to members.

Following the rise of universities, medieval centers of learning were revered by the pope, royalty, and rich merchants. Knowledge (or at least the perception that a scholar had knowledge) was power then, just as information is power today. In part to prevent charlatans from passing themselves off as scholars and in part to raise standards, the universities imitated some guild practices, demanding evidence of scholarship from a prospective teacher before deeming him qualified to teach. To receive a teaching license from a chancellor, scholars needed to demonstrate proficiency in Latin, an ability to memorize long passages from books, and an ability to pass examinations. Thus would-be scholars endured a training period that lasted years and was characterized by poverty and many trials. Hazing came to symbolize their ordeals. A newcomer would have to undergo indignities before he was judged worthy by those who imagined themselves his betters by virtue of their one year's seniority. In the thirteenth through fifteenth centuries, it was understood that boys who wished to gain the status afforded by attending a school of learning would have to submit to brutal hazing by older students, just as they had to pay for university fees and to buy books. As older students began routinely hazing newcomers, such practices became ritualized. Scholars moved from school to school and brought their customs with them, so that silly, irritating, and dangerous practices that took place at one university in western Europe resembled those performed at others.

During the Middle Ages, students considered hazing a natural way to teach newcomers precedence. New students served as waiters for the seniors at table and paid them obeisance.[6] In return, hazers engaged in acts of abuse that went far beyond puckish exhibitions of exuberance. Justified by the privileges of precedence, they humiliated the new boys and made them demonstrate animal-like displays of submission. First-year students at Avignon were hit with a wooden object, a practice predating today's paddling custom. Newcomers at the University of Aix were paddled with a book or frying pan up to three times each, although when "noble or honorable ladies" were present the new boy received fewer punishing strokes, according to one school statute of the time. In response to the dropping out and transferring of many new students, the anti-hazing Fraternity of St. Sebastian was begun by twenty-six men at Avignon in 1441. The organization was the first of several anti-hazing fraternities that have formed since then.[7]

In the fourteenth century, universities had prestige, not wealth. Instruction took place in dingy rented rooms with straw for mats. University students were mainly children aged about twelve to fourteen. They paid landlords and innkeepers large sums for dirty, flea-infested garret rooms, bad food, and sour wine.

The newcomers then faced a chattering horde of masters promising to open their minds in exchange for open purses. They endured abusive hazing by older students who regarded them as mere "unfledged birds," the lowliest of the low.[8] Initiating newcomers satisfied three desires in older students. "It gratified alike the bullying instinct, the social instinct, and the desire to find at once the excuse and the means for a carouse," wrote medievalist Hastings Rashdall. At the university in Heidelberg, students had to wear a ridiculous cap with a yellow bill, according to the *Manuale Scholarium*, a 1481 account of student life.[9] Typically, at many European schools, newcomers were derided as *bejauni* (*becs-jaunes* translates to "yellow bills"). In some cases horns and animal ears were attached to the caps and were later pulled or sawed off. This "deposition," as it was known in Germany, was a rite of passage during which a new student was abased by veteran students to make him psychologically turn away from his former life. The hazers accused the trembling newcomer of being either a criminal (the hazing custom in some parts of France) or a loathsome wild beast called a *beanus* (in Germany and elsewhere in Europe) that required a sort of ritualistic exorcism.[10] To be so accused was a frightening prospect in an age during which most people not only feared incubi and succubi but also were afraid of being branded a witch or some other horrible creature, which could result in one's execution. The initiate needed his inner beast—his corruptibility—to be symbolically destroyed, the hazers assured him. Medieval student ruffians overpowered each new student, pretending that an unbearable stench was emanating from every one of his orifices. Like most hazers and exploiters of other people, they awakened fear and self-doubt in the young students, getting them to go along with abominable treatment.[11]

Perpetrators commonly soaped the first-year student's face, clipped his beard and hair (using burnt cork to "replace" it), scraped the skin off his ears with a surgical instrument, and symbolically put his nose to a hand-turned grindstone.[12] To shake the new boy's trust, one student would pretend to be a priest and would hear the "confession" of whatever sins the initiate committed; he would then use the young man's words against him. Stunned, a dozen boys' spittle merging with the tears on his face, the student would invariably turn to one person in the group who had been feigning empathy. The "benefactor" would then hand him a container of liquid. Relieved, the young man would drink, only to find his mouth fouled with urine or a salted beverage. If the boy refused to drink more, the liquid was forced down his throat.[13]

In the Middle Ages, students were willing to take such abuse in order to obtain a license that would admit them into the elevated society of scholars and allow them to assume the title of master, doctor, or professor, depending upon their discipline. Young men born in poverty were particularly vulnerable. Unless they could use their abilities and wits to move into an ecclesiastic position of power, they were doomed to a life of penury, near-starvation, and back-breaking labor. Nor could they expect faculty members to intervene. Until university reforms were enacted, students typically endured mistreatment from their masters, too, and the abuse continued until the chancellor handed the student a license, effectively ending the torment. The young men then went out to teach or perform priestly duties.

Even obtaining a license involved a process that was a type of hazing. The custom then was to endure indignities in silence (just as it is the custom among doctoral students today not to confront committee members who decide to recommend or not to recommend conferring a Ph.D.). Hazed students took comfort in the knowledge that if they successfully passed all the tests of endurance, they too would someday subject would-be licensees to similar hardships. Such hazing was certainly ritualistic. The yellow-billed cap ceremony parodied the granting of a license in which a veteran master symbolically welcomed a successful young student into the world of scholars by placing a biretta on his head.[14]

The ceremony known as an inception, during which a medieval student was named a master or doctor, was originally nothing more formal than a show of "mere jollification or exhibition of good-fellowship," according to Rashdall. Like students that hazed, school authorities made rituals up as they went along, eventually requiring newly recognized masters to deliver a lecture as entertainment for the colleagues whose company they were to join.[15] "The idea that a newcomer should 'pay his footing' seems almost a primitive instinct of human nature. It formed an essential part of inception that the 'inceptor' should entertain at a banquet the whole or a considerable number of his new colleagues," wrote Rashdall in 1895. "Presents of gloves or gowns had also to be made; and gradually contributions in money to the funds of society were exacted in addition to the presents to its individual members—an exaction which has ever since been the inseparable accompaniment of degree-taking even in those universities in which all other formalities are most generously dispensed with. The whole affair was originally nothing but a piece of unauthorized buffoonery—hardly more dignified or important perhaps than those sometimes brutal . . . student initiations."[16]

Extortion of younger students by older ones was also common during the Middle Ages. Older students, dressed in the fashionable gowns or frilled shirts, netherstocks, and round caps of the day, extorted so much money from new boys that one thirteenth-century father grumbled that his son never wrote without pleading that replacement funds be sent him. Traditional hazing ended in a mock trial, at which time the newcomer learned that he was to be ushered into the academy as a "student," but only upon paying for food and drink for all present. The amount of money demanded was significantly larger if the young man's father was a wealthy landowner or a member of the nobility.

Such customs at first were viewed as reprehensible by many university authorities. Prohibitions against ritualized mistreatment of the *bejauni* were passed by several institutions. University of Paris authorities objected to hazing, and in 1340 they enacted an ordinance that prohibited it under possible pain of expulsion. Nonetheless, students continued the practice in broad view of all. On Innocents Day, a religious holiday, older University of Paris students made first-year students parade on donkeys through the streets. Excommunication for hazing was stern punishment. A student who lost the protection of the university would have no one to turn to for protection or retaliation if he were attacked by highwaymen or townspeople. The fact that hazing persisted even in the face of potentially dire consequences for those who participated in it is indicative of its appeal. When statutes proved unable to end hazing, some universities took a pragmatic approach and tried to regulate it. In Germany some institutions sanctioned the practice of paying for one's initiation party. The custom, at least in Germany and Switzerland, spread from universities to secondary schools. *The Autobiography of Thomas Platter*, published in 1576, told of how a new student had to give food and money to an older student.

The establishment of a medieval university inspired pride in trade cities such as Paris, which otherwise were similar to other towns on a trade route. Even the most impecunious new university students experienced a sudden desire for power over others to go with the intellectual awakening they felt. Older students acted superior to new ones and to the town's magistrates, citizens, and young women. Student pride, poor behavior toward women, and the rude treatment of local citizens often led to conflicts with authorities in the towns surrounding the institutions. Townspeople of the Middle Ages had to contend with reprehensible student behaviors such as vandalism, rape, or mistreatment of local citizens. Records at the University of Leipzig in the late fifteenth century note that students were wont to douse townspeople with pans of water, beat the night watch, harass the local hangman, and play outrageous practical jokes. Not only did students at Oxford regularly poach game in the king's forests, but those who left in disgrace sometimes exacted revenge by robbing and beating other students traveling to and from the university.

Time and again a new group of students turned out to be as irresponsible and violent as the one preceding it. Students with nothing more to show for their lives than a year of schooling grabbed the role of quasi-gatekeepers, elevating themselves in their own minds by belittling newcomers before permitting them to pass through those gates. Perhaps one explanation for this behavior is the tendency of the young to view other young people who dominated them as models to emulate. The behaviors of a young medieval scholar who observed his peers misbehaving (or who was praised by his peers for his own misconduct) were likely reinforced. The hooligan-scholars of the Middle Ages acted superior to other mortals in town and superior to newcomers. Their arrogance was bolstered by the support the nobility and the Church gave them.

The bad choices made by students hundreds of years ago were therefore not dissimilar to the bad choices many collegians make today. The former chose to get drunk—often; they behaved vilely on occasion, and they rioted now and then. But then, as now, the general public expected, even demanded, that school officials do things they were not qualified to do—namely eliminate students' reprehensible actions that reflected the presence of social problems. Occasionally student battles with townspeople in the Middle Ages led to the deaths of young men. For example, a riot that started in 1354 after Oxford students threw a vessel of wine at a vintner resulted in the deaths and maimings of numerous students.

It may seem appropriate to try to come up with an intellectual explanation for why students haze in violation of custom or law. Numerous scholars have concluded that hazing in the Middle Ages allowed newcomers to demonstrate that they possessed the stamina and courage necessary to survive symbolic ordeals.

Martin Luther entertained self-serving justifications for hazing. As a scholar at the University of Wittenberg, the center of the Protestant Reformation that took place in the sixteenth century, Luther urged first-year students under his care to bear the temporary cross required by upperclassmen "with equanimity." Luther, who at seventeen underwent a symbolic de-horning and a cleansing pseudo-baptism with wine at the Augustinian school and monastery at Erfurt, maintained throughout his life that hazing strengthened a boy, enabling him to endure more easily the perils and challenges of life as an adult. The son of a manipulative, authoritarian father, Luther alternately hated and submitted to ecclesiastical authority. For example, while he believed that his own faith and reason entitled him to revolt against the Church, he praised the extermination of some thirteen thousand peasants who revolted against authorities in 1525.[17]

In England during medieval days, as it is in the twentieth century, it was common for older males to use younger students for sport. At Merton around Christmas it was the custom for new students to tell a joke or recite a maxim or "some eloquent nonsense" to entertain the older students. If a student refused or failed to entertain, one of his "betters" would scratch the young man's chin with a thumbnail hard enough to cause bleeding. At some English institutions, the hazed student would then be required to drink beer from a salt-rimmed container, according to the Oxford diaries of Anthony Wood.[18]

Medieval universities rejected the authority of town officials, but they all instituted their own statutes in a hopeless effort to end hazing, extortion, and other abuses of newcomers by older students. Some universities, for example, stripped hazers of any honors they had won. Universities also urged the hazed to come forward, ordering new students to report hazing violations to proctors and deans who read such charges aloud in church meetings. Moreover, landlords in some towns who rented to students were obligated under statutes to report hazing and any threats of retaliation made by hazers. In time some universities published lists of specific acts that were considered hazing. For example, in 1846 the University of Heidelberg forbade older students to force first-year students to sing or to submit to being pelted with trash.[19]

Still, many medieval universities tolerated and even encouraged hazing. The so-called "purgation" of the yellow bills at Avignon was conducted as a regular ceremony in the chapel of the Dominican church. Hazers also got away with convening a kangaroo court twice a week to try newcomers for alleged offenses, punishing the unlucky with up to one year's servitude.[20]

Also rampant in finer English schools was a practice called fagging, which flourished into the twentieth century. In essence, an older student was entitled to require a younger boy to act as his servant in the residence hall and on the cricket field. The "fag" fetched tea and food for his young "master," serving as a valet and submitting to a brutal kick or a hard rap if he tarried or failed to obey an order. The system was alternately praised and condemned, depending perhaps on the critic's own experiences as a fag. Many educators and commentators complained that educational institutions should have been able to anticipate that savagery and abuses were the inevitable consequences of fagging.

Fagging flourished in public schools because rigid-minded educators placed obedience first among all the virtues a schoolboy should display. It was believed that the system of maltreatment kept younger boys under thumb and out of mischief. "Before it is possible for a man, much more for a boy, to rule, it is a maxim as venerable as our copybooks, that he must first be taught to obey; and it is this invaluable lesson that our fag-system teaches, better perhaps than any other method of instruction inculcates it," a 1896 article in *The Cornhill Magazine* stated. "There must be no nonsense about it, no evasion—the obedience must be complete and it must be instantaneous. The sanction is very near at hand, in the shape of the boot, the fist, or the wicket; there is no cumbersome process of court-martial or summons in the country court to compel it. It must follow on the command as the flash is followed by the thunder."[21]

HAZING IN EARLY AMERICA

European students or their tutors may have brought the custom of fagging to the New World. The earliest Harvard College students were born abroad, and a former Oxford student was enrolled there in 1641; he may have passed on stories about hazing to his peers. Although the term "hazing" would not be commonly used on college campuses until after the Civil War, acts of servitude similar to European fagging bedeviled new students at Harvard as early as 1657. The 1657 incident, involving acts similar to those now called hazing, resulted in a judgment by the administration in favor of Harvard first-year students John Cotton and John Whiting. The transgressors paid a fine of six shillings, eight pence each for "abuse" inflicted on the two.[22] Because seventeenth-century Harvard authorities only occasionally recorded accounts of misbehavior by students, sadistic pranks and fagging "may have been matters of frequent occurrence," wrote one Harvard historian.[23]

The first Harvard College student punished for hazing was Joseph Webb of the Class of 1684. The president expelled the upperclassman for hitting first-year students and for requiring them to perform acts of servitude. Two months later, having repented, Webb returned to his studies with the permission of Harvard authorities. He graduated with his class.[24] A public confession in front of the student body and a formal petition to return were the usual conditions for returning to Harvard College after a student had been caught committing a serious offense. Unrepentant students such as Daniel Henchman, expelled in 1696 for theft, failed to graduate.[25]

If hazing was a weed in the garden of academe, as one nineteenth-century educator characterized it for an audience at Harvard University during the 1860s, then alcohol was the rain that helped it flourish.[26] The seventeenth-century Puritan clergyman Increase Mather decried local drunkenness, mixed dancing, and the flashing of breasts by "wanton women."[27] Mather inveighed against sin, but Harvard officials were inclined to forgive experimentation with alcohol and sex by Harvard students. A repentant Benjamin Shattuck, a senior caught in the act of intercourse, returned to school after sitting out one year and admitting his crime. John Wade, thrown out for unspecified "lasciviousness," was readmitted thanks to the intercession of two ministers who declared that he had reformed.[28] "This does not mean that the puritans held such offenses of slight consequence—far from it," wrote Harvard historian Samuel Eliot Morison. "But they did believe that no sin was too great for God's grace, after a genuine repentance; and unlike some who profess and call themselves Christians, they followed the example of forgiveness that their Master had enjoined."[29]

During the eighteenth century, personal servitude became an inescapable part of every first-year student's life at Harvard. Student hazing customs were published by the sophomore class and passed out to the first-year males in chapel. New students had to doff hats while speaking to seniors, and he who at first refused to submit was later forced to yield. Those then known as "freshmen" ran errands for seniors except after 9:00 P.M. and during study hours. They also purchased sports equipment for the use of upperclass students. According to one historian, fagging ceased in 1798 after first-year student Joseph Story persuaded an upperclass member that the practice was abhorrent, but it may be equally likely that the practice didn't die out but rather evolved into rougher initiation pranks that gained popularity during the 1800s.[30]

Fagging at Yale University clearly continued into the late nineteenth century. Sophomores used first-year men as "errand boys," and such conduct was regarded not as dangerous or demeaning but as merely "mischievous," according to an educator of the day, Benjamin Silliman.[31] Years before the arrival of the Greek system at Williams College in 1805, after which the school ejected the system for encouraging poor behavior among students, hazing was used there to teach precedence and to minimize student insubordination and effrontery. To maintain "order" and "due subordination," the Williams regulations specified "that the members of an inferior class [must] pay a proper deference and respect to the members of the classes above them." The newcomers had to let upperclassmen enter doors and gates first, were instructed to knock before entering upperclassmen's rooms, and were told to "acknowledge both in language and behavior, their superior rank, and claim to respect."[32]

At Harvard during the nineteenth century, rough practical jokes were especially popular, but they were also all the rage at other campuses, including the University of Virginia, Amherst College, and Miami of Ohio. Harvard students sometimes frustrated the college president by preventing the ringing of a bell that called the college community to morning services at the chapel, which was the center of university activities. Harvard historians have noted how pranksters turned the bell over and filled it with water in winter; the water would freeze, immobilizing the stopper. They taunted the sexton by severing the bell's rope with sulfuric acid or a knife and by plugging the keyhole of the belfry door with wax or nailing it shut.[33]

Occasionally someone was injured as a result of one of these jokes. While the nation was at war with Great Britain in 1812, William Hickling Prescott was blinded in one eye by a fellow student who used a bread crust as a missile. A group of Harvard students in the nineteenth century slipped a concoction used to induce vomiting into the water boilers. Nearly everyone who drank coffee (including the perpetrators, who consumed several cups in the hope of covering their part in the misdeed) became violently ill. All the pranksters were discovered and punished.[34]

During the first quarter of the eighteenth century, before Greek-letter groups had arrived on American campuses, a number of short-lived student organizations existed at Harvard College and at institutions such as the College of William and Mary. What inspired the founding of these organizations, in addition to students' need for camaraderie, was a powerful love for rivalries that in time would lead to the rise of competitive sports on U.S. campuses.

The first student organizations were, at least on the surface, serious ventures, reflecting the tension of the colonies' war with Great Britain. In 1781, around the time soldiers fought at Yorktown, the Alpha of Massachusetts chapter of Phi Beta Kappa began at Harvard, five years after that literary society had been founded at the College of William and Mary.

The educational system tolerated Phi Beta Kappa. Founders convinced school authorities that the organization possessed the same worthy intellectual and moral purposes as did American colleges themselves. Had they been purely social organizations—as fraternities have become—they likely would have been prohibited. The Hasty Pudding Club was born at Harvard in 1795 to give students the opportunity to discuss philosophy, literature, and serious ideas of the day. As such societies evolved, silly stunts and pranks became a part of them. "The first official duty I was called to perform as head of [Harvard] University which considers itself first among American Seminaries, was to administer a private admonition to a Sophomore for pinning the coat-tail of the boy who sat before him to the settee," wrote Edward Everett, who was president of Harvard from 1846 to 1849. "I saw in that one instance that I had made a woeful mistake."[35]

By 1860, the year Abraham Lincoln was elected to the U.S. presidency, Harvard had decided to take a hard line with student miscreants who abused their peers. That year the institution expelled eight individuals for hazing. One of the fraternal groups that caused Harvard administrators the most trouble during the nineteenth century was the Dickey Club, whose members demanded servitude and played pranks worthy of Augustine's Overturners.[36] Kershner and other fraternity historians believe that hazing entered fraternities because Dartmouth, Princeton, Harvard, Columbia, and Yale classes and societies engaged in stunts and horseplay. Another possibility is that dropouts from West Point and other service academies brought them to the colleges they next attended. Still others say that hazing just flares up, like spontaneous combustion, whenever young people form a club that considers itself elite and enforces exclusionary admittance practices. All three theories are certainly plausible.

In 1818, four members of the Harvard Class of 1820 founded a popular organization called The Med. Fac. Society, dedicated to fun and high spirits. Candidates for admission were hazed as a matter of practice. Members referred to themselves as the society's "faculty" and required new members to engage in stunts such as swimming on the floor. If a prospective member refused to comply with an order, "gendarmes" armed with bayonets and muskets offered convincing arguments for his compliance. The administration dissolved the group in 1824, but it remained a sub-rosa secret society for eighty more years and dedicated itself to the sort of merrymaking that alums delight in talking about years later. The society's most famous stunt involved Czar Alexander I of Russia. Members wrote to tell him that the society had awarded him an honorary degree. The duped czar shipped medical instruments to the perpetrators as a demonstration of his gratitude, but these were seized by college authorities when word about the prank leaked out.[37]

Francis Parkman, a high-strung young man who came to Harvard in 1840 and went on academic probation before straightening out his life, sometimes neglected his studies to sip champagne, madeira, and whiskey punch. Parkman, who later became a famous historian, was nabbed in a small room by a dozen seniors, who filled the room with cigar smoke.

Hazing at other colleges during the nineteenth century was regarded as a type of "disorderly conduct" that interfered with the governance of an institution, according to an 1874 letter from the president of the University of Michigan to parents of six students suspended for the practice. Rivalries between first-year and upper-class students evolved from wars of words in debating societies to annual ferocious, often bloody turf wars. During the nineteenth and early twentieth centuries, class hazing between first-year classes and sophomores sent many participants to the infirmary.[38]

Even at coeducational institutions, young men were usually the main participants in skirmishes Women did participate in some aspects of class hazing, particularly at female-only institutions. Female students' involvement consisted mainly of the creation of kangaroo courts, shoving matches over class flags, the wearing of silly costumes, and servitude. No known class-hazing incidents involving female students approach the level of violence of those that collegiate males participated in regularly.

The first known deaths that occurred as a result of class hazings in the United States took place at Franklin Seminary in Kentucky in 1838 and Amherst College in 1847. Documentation is sketchy in both cases. The story of John Butler Groves's death at Franklin Seminary was lost in a fire that destroyed all records, but a family history says that Groves's grieving parents refused to send any more children to college. An account of the death of first-year Amherst [Massachusetts] College student Jonathan D. Torrance, who died of consumption in 1847, is preserved in a memoir written by Amherst president Edward Hitchcock. The account is useful because in it Hitchcock decried hazing as a common "brutal" practice and "a barbarous college custom" practiced during the first half of the nineteenth century. Young Torrance fell prey to one of the upperclassmen's most common pranks—wrapping freshmen in icy cold or wet bed sheets. The practice was said, in jest, to be a form of "hydropathy" for new students with attitude problems. Hitchcock claimed that the dying Torrance told him he thought it was the class hazing prank that had first made him ill, although it is more likely that Torrance's lung disease was merely exacerbated by the wetting of his sheets by hazers. "Whether his murderers still haunt the earth I know not, but I do know that they must meet him at the judgment seat," Hitchcock said years after.[39]

It may seem to us that mid-nineteenth-century students had little in common with students today. But in fact the way older students of that time made "sport" with first-year students is similar to the way some fraternity members have fun at the expense of pledges today. Exuberant nineteenth-century students kidnapped class presidents to keep them from holding class meetings, and they burst into dormitory rooms looking for victims to drag away to mock court trials. In 1863 Hitchcock said that the abuse of first-year students gave birth to enough mean-spiritedness to ensure that personal grudges would remain unresolved up to graduation day. "Even when fun and sport are the professed object, such recklessness and abuse are often witnessed as to result in lasting, and sometimes fatal effects," wrote Hitchcock. "The Scripture hath well described it when the wise man says: 'As a madman who casteth firebrands, arrows and death, so is the man that deceiveth his neighbor and saith, am I not in sport?'"[40]

A class hazing at Cornell University in 1894 led to the death of an African American food server and cook, Mrs. Henrietta Jackson. She died as the consequence of a nasty prank pulled by a sophomore or sophomores to get even with first-year students for besting them in a sporting event, according to a letter written by Kenneth E. Stuart, Cornell Class of 1897.[41] One or more students released chlorine gas into a room filled with students from the rival class who were attending a formal dinner at the Masonic Temple in Ithaca, New York. The perpetrators drilled a hole in the floor above the party and inserted a tube connected to a chlorine generator. The hose failed to enter the main hall, in which students were toasting one another, instead sending chlorine gas into an area in the kitchen near a stove. Stuart surmised that quantities of carbon monoxide, triggered by catalysts, reacted with chlorine to create phosgene, a gas used as a lethal weapon during World War I. Students continued their party until 3:00 A.M. Neither they nor the culprits were aware that Jackson was dead in the kitchen, according to an account published shortly afterwards in the *New York Times.* Cornell turned the case over to authorities. But even though the faculty promised a hefty reward to anyone who turned in the perpetrators, no member of the sophomore class gave a private detective or the coroner useful information, according to Morris Bishop, author of the *History of Cornell.* The culprits were never caught. Jackson's death, along with two other fraternity deaths that took place at Cornell during the late nineteenth century, focused national attention on the school.[42]

Serious injuries and some fatalities occurred on college campuses as a result of long-standing annual class fights, referred to then as "battle royals." "Battle royal" was a term used on the American frontier to describe ferocious gamecock melees. The exact origin of these campus skirmishes is hard to pin down. Perhaps they were inspired by a similarly bloody student fight that took place at Oxford around 1258, when students of Scotch, Welsh, northern English, and southern English backgrounds formed individual divisions, waving banners to distinguish one group from the next. Several students died in the battle as they fought to express their regional pride.

Sometimes first-year and second-year classes (or larger upperclass groups) fought over banners or flags, or over the right to paint a water tank. Students such as those belonging to the University of Kentucky's dreaded Midnight Artillery sheared freshmen heads with clippers that one of their number had taken from a town barber.

University presidents and trustees again and again announced that

Hazing of first-year students was common at many U.S. universities in the nineteenth and early twentieth centuries. Students at Gettysburg College in the early 1900s wore intimidating robes and hoods.
Photo courtesy of Special Collections, Gettysburg College Library

hazing was over on their particular campuses, but it was tenacious. In 1901, when the University of Michigan (UM) had supposedly put an end to hazing on campus, the *Michigan Alumnus* hailed a promise made by first- and second-year classes to stop administering hideous haircuts with scissors or knives.[43] But in March of 1905, engineering students Leon Albert Warren and Harold H. Corson were stabbed (though not fatally) during the annual ritual, which had obviously made a return to UM. The story made the *New York Times,* and sentiment on campus turned against the hazers.[44] But a veteran of the hair-cutting wars wrote the *Michigan Daily* a long letter defending the practice's ability to form "the backbone of . . . class spirit." The fault was not with the hazers, but with those who would not submit and who unfairly hauled out weapons in a wrongheaded display of defense, said the writer.

Retaliation on the part of the hazed also led to fatalities. In 1905, Franklin and Marshall College first-year student Oscar Gingrich shot and wounded Roy Ulsh, a sophomore who the shooter said had abused

FRESHMEN, BEWARE!!!!

To that white-livered aggregation of conceit and ignorance known as the Freshman Class, whose unhealthy presence is a mortification in the vitals of civilization and a disgrace to the century which with shame recognizes their existence, this warning is directed. Filled with pain at the hollow and pretentious mockery which here rears its infamous head, the valiant Sophomores have determined to rid the earth of this brood of insignificant vipers. But with a generosity born of pitying scorn we warn these hapless creature. forehand, hoping that at a revelation of their own pusallinimity they will appreciate their true pos ion in the economic workings of the Universe, and do the one worthy deed of their lives by closing them. However, should these benighted wretches fail to recognize their utter detestability and persist in remaining as an incumbrance to racial development, then, on the 22d of February will it be the pleasurable duty of the Sophomore Class to instill into their opaque skulls so keen a sense of the joys awaiting them on the golden shore that they will see the advisability of an immediate withdrawal from the scene of human action.

Among these infamous wretches are some of surpassingly miserable culpability to whom this warning is especially directed:

Empty Wind-bag Thomas, whose gaseous flatulency has well-nigh reached the stage of explosion.

Chief Charmer Pettijohn, the bunko magician, who endeavored to hoodwink his fellows into thinking he was greater even than the doubting Thomas; a veritable calf-bound satire on humanity.

Howling Eternally Martin, whose valor is more manifest in his words than in his achievements.

Far Soaring Parks, whose elevated intellect permits him to become conscious of only the loftiest peaks in the range of human action.

Jagged Badly DuShane, the human demijohn, whose chief claim to recognition is a meritorious attempt to decrease, by a systematic process, the annual output of Budweiser.

Asinine Loquacity Brenner, the doughty knight of the gridiron, whose infantile helplessness is equalled only by his verdancy.

Real Cute Allen, the jealous preserver of University property and the direct heir of Vanderbilt's financial discrimination. P. S.—A good grip for sale cheap.

Rambunctious Thornton, a veritable fire-eater. One of the chief entertainers, (for the Sophomores), at the Faculty Reception.

Climbin' Johnny Offutt, "standin' on the corner, didn't mean no harm."

From the debased apologies for humanity here pictured, can be judged the horrible nature of the Motley collection in its entirety. The agonized wailings of suffering humanity call for the total obliteration of these unhygienic ignoramuses. On the 22d, the purifying visitation will come.

FRESHMEN, BEWARE!!!!

Gotten out by class 1903: I think

Hazing of first-year students was once practiced at many state schools, as this Indiana University flyer demonstrates. *Photo courtesy of Indiana University Archives, Bloomington, Indiana.*

him during a kangaroo court trial. The decade 1910–1920 was particularly troublesome. A hazer at the University of Texas was seriously wounded, and one at St. John's Military College was killed by an angry freshman.

Newspapers that egged on the hazers were partially to blame for

Schools once published rules regulating annual class "scraps," but these quaint regulations failed to prevent deaths and injuries. Deaths as a result of "freshman–sophomore" rivalries occurred at Purdue, Cornell, Kentucky, North Carolina, Wisconsin, Colgate, St. John's Military College, MIT, Franklin and Marshall College, and Cheyney University of Pennsylvania. Here, Indiana University students fight over a bit of ceremonial cloth and "bragging rights" for the next year.
Photograph courtesy of Indiana University Archives, Bloomington, Indiana

the mayhem caused by recurrent class hazings in the early part of the twentieth century. Blustering commentaries by the presidents of these classes were front-page stories that sold papers. These articles preceded the fights by weeks, indicating that college officials of the time were unwilling or unable to halt confrontations, and that many newspaper editors found such highjinks appealing. Cleveland papers, for example, covered scraps at Case Institute of Technology (before it merged with Western Reserve University to form Case Western University) as if they were covering sporting events. "Won Their Revenge" ran a flamboyant headline in the Cleveland *Leader* of October 3, 1894. And when some one hundred students who were engaged in a scrap fell from a high bluff on campus to the pavement below, the Cleveland *Plain Dealer* called the frosh triumph "a battle to the death."[45]

Nor were faculty or administrators, for the most part, courageous enough to stop class fights except when serious injuries or a death occurred. After chapel services erupted in a brawl between first-year students and sophomores at the University of Kansas, the faculty was relatively lenient, wanting to eliminate the dangers associated with class battles but afraid of dampening school spirit. Whenever conscience-stricken, enlightened, or fearful administrators acted to halt class skirmishes, former alums predictably launched a protest. After the board of regents and administration of the University of Kansas put a stop to dangerous scraps in 1910, a task made easier because some undergraduates had begun regarding these fights as quaint and silly, a Class of 1896 member taunted the younger generation, grumbling:

> What's the matter with K.U.? The May Pole scrap is gone, or emasculated into "Ring Around the Rosy"; the junior prom and the senior reception are as tame as a pink tea in an Old Ladies Home; even our old yell is sung instead of shouted. The student body seems to be composed of the most lady-like and Lord Fauntleroyed individuals in the world. . . . [And] the authorities seem to think that the University is a school for namby-pambies and Lizzie boys, whereas all should know it is the youth of strength and originality, the youth who is full of life, who sometimes gets into mischief or more trouble, who is really worthwhile in this vigorous world. K.U. has not grown as it should; we do not change the fact by shutting our eyes. The chief reason is that young men of talent and energy will not go to a school which bears so close a resemblance to a "female seminary."[46]

The usual policy at the end of the nineteenth century and beginning of the twentieth was for colleges either to forbid class scraps or to permit them within limits. If violence escalated and an unlucky participant ended up in the hospital or morgue, ringleaders were generally rounded up, and the tragedy was used as a prop for a ban of the tradition. Given the black cloud that inevitably hung over campus following a student death or maiming, a campus president or chancellor could expect to receive a subdued response from students who felt guilty over their role in the matter, and to win a good deal of praise from the faculty and from some young people who reminded everyone that they had been against the dangerous tradition all along. Even alumni support was predictable, if begrudging, as the old guard wondered how the current generation could let an innocent tradition get so out of hand.

Nonstudents such as townspeople added to the problem, thronging the athletic fields where these annual fights usually took place. At the University of Kentucky flag rush of 1907, hundreds of citizens from Lexington came to campus "to see the fun," reported the *Lexington Leader* on October 9, 1907. In the excitement, some young women fought among themselves. Thousands of onlookers were present in West Lafayette, Indiana, when Purdue University student Francis W. Obenchain died during a clash between first-year students and sophomores.

Typically the losing class not only sported black eyes but also often had to endure public humiliation as they were led through town, shackled together like a chain gang. (A portion of such a chain can still be viewed in Purdue University's library.) These victory celebrations were wildly exuberant and sometimes dangerous. A first-year University of Kentucky student died in 1915 when a streetcar hit a cable that he and his triumphant classmates were carrying.

Even student kidnappings, which were considered innocent at the time, could be dangerous. When future author Thomas Wolfe was a student at the University of North Carolina in 1912, UNC sophomores took first-year student Isaac Rand from his room to make him dance on a barrel. In a remote wooded area on campus, Rand fell onto a shard of glass from a broken bottle, fatally puncturing his throat. Wolfe scholars have shown how the writer—though he was not involved in it—later fictionalized the incident. The governor of North Carolina issued a public announcement carried by the press that criticized the president of UNC and made it clear that he thought the college had a duty to keep acts of malicious hazing from occurring. Such an announcement typically followed hazing deaths, as they still do today.

Although many college presidents bemoaned deaths that occurred as a result of class hazings, they failed to end them until the period of greatest excess began to fade around 1930. Collegiate newspapers credited the decrease in class hazing violence to influential undergraduates who raised their voices against such practices, and at least one university chancellor at the time attributed the decline in the violence between classes to students' desire for law and order. But although those opinions may have been valid in some instances, according to Griffin it is also possible that, during an age of prosperity and growing hedonism in U.S. society, students simply dismissed fighting with one other under a greased flagpole as terribly arcane.[47] In time student demands that hazing cease gave way to their insistence that they be allowed to use liquor and tobacco without restriction. Trustees who had cheered when the class scraps died out now had other worries, as reports surfaced that venereal disease among students was on the rise.

Even so, class hazing continued to take place on some U.S. campuses. For example, in 1960, first-year Georgetown University students had to wear traditional beanies, crawl through doorways, don ridiculous clothing, and roll up their pant legs. Some hazing was violent. Nine female first-year students were injured in pre-initiation activities at Valparaiso University in Indiana in 1959. A violent initiation ceremony conducted by sophomores at Cheyney University of Pennsylvania (then Cheyney State College) in 1975 ended with the death of Theodore Ben, while horseplay during a traditional class initiation at Oklahoma's Phillips University in 1982 led to the accidental crippling of a student bystander.

Some colleges continue to hold ceremonial initiations, regarding these as a pleasant custom, not as hazing. Even beanies, a holdover from medieval university days, can occasionally be found. New students at Elmira College in New York State wear beanies during an orientation period.

MILITARY EDUCATIONAL INSTITUTIONS

Hazing has long flourished in U.S. military and naval groups. The word "hazing" was in common use during the Civil War. A May 14, 1861, dispatch written by a Camp Cameron (Washington, D.C.) Union soldier in the Seventh (New York) Regiment listed "hazing," reading, and letter writing as a soldier's favorite way of passing time in the evenings. From the context of the letter, it seems likely that "hazing" was used by soldiers as a synonym for horseplay or jokes played on newcomers.[48]

The Navy Seals, the Coast Guard, the Marines, and the regular Navy all have hazing traditions. Hazing occurred among these groups for years, with occasional intervention and court martials for perpetrators on the part of military officials, until *Dateline NBC* and CNN aired videotaped evidence of bloody pinnings of parachute pins to the chests of paratroopers in 1997.[49]

Just as contemporary student hazing has recognizable roots in the educational system of feudal times, so too do sailors' present-day hazing practices resemble sixteenth-century initiation customs. Contemporary newcomers to the equator on Navy vessels might "be shaved and drenched with water either by being dunked into the sea from the yardarm, doused in a barrel of sea water, or soused from cans or buckets," according to folklorist Keith P. Richardson.[50] In 1529, when any sea voyage was harrowing, an established ritual celebrated an equator crossing. When the *Parmentier* from France crossed, sailors prayed, ate a symbolic fish, and paid homage to the gods of the sea by flinging them coins.[51] Before long, the custom had acquired all the characteristics of hazing. Ancient mariners put newcomers through an ordeal to make sure that they could be counted on to endure not only the perils associated with a seafaring life but also the rough humor of rough men at sea, according to Harry Lydenberg, author of the quaint *Crossing the Line*.

From the nineteenth century up until today, the press has revealed the hazing abuses of elite U.S service academies. Some males who dropped out of the academies presumably spread knowledge of hazing practices and perhaps also brought the practices themselves to the state and private colleges they later attended. Highly publicized incidents occurred at West Point in 1881, 1900–1901, 1907, 1917, 1973, 1976, 1979, and 1990. President William McKinley launched a 1900–1901 congressional inquiry into hazing at West Point after a young man who had been driven out of the academy by older cadets died in Pennsylvania. An examination of the testimony reveals the evasiveness of cadets such as Douglas MacArthur and the sons of Ulysses S. Grant and Philip Sheridan, who were torn between maintaining their tremendous loyalty to the U.S. Military Academy and revealing the truth to a committee of inquiry made up of six members of the House of Representatives. In his *Reminiscences* MacArthur said that his mother recommended that he keep silent.[52] He did, however, disclose to the committee of inquiry that he considered hazing to be "cruel treatment" and did "not think it is essential" for the development of a cadet. The committee concluded that the plebe Oscar Booz had been beaten, mercilessly hazed, and forced to swallow large amounts of undiluted pepper sauce, but that a health problem, not mistreatment, was probably the direct cause of his death. The committee uncovered what the plebes had been expected to endure, particularly in the middle of the night and between supper and taps:

◆ While on his feet, a new man had to squat over a bayonet pointed at his groin, sometimes for many hours.

◆ A new man had to do up to 400 exercises similar to knee bends, at one stretch.

◆ While lying on his back, and, with his knees straight, the newcomer had to draw his legs up at right angles with his body and then drop them as often as the hazer required.

◆ New men had to don heavy clothing and bedding in the heat of summer, sometimes remaining at attention until they fainted.

◆ New men slid on a slick floor covered with soapy water that entered their noses and mouths, choking them.

◆ A fourth-class man had to stand on his head while reciting and saluting with his right foot.

◆ A new man had to strip naked and run through a gauntlet of older males who doused him with icy water.[53]

MacArthur returned to West Point as superintendent and outlawed what he considered the worst hazing practices, but he was unable to eliminate all abuses.

Nor was an attempt to end hazing at the Naval Academy in 1920 any more successful. A superintendent's efforts to shame hazers were thwarted by a unified show of peer support by all classes. Middies once dared defy a furious admiral by cheering madly to support expelled hazer Charles Snedaker as he left through the gates in a ceremony meant to signify his dishonor. Earlier hazing scandals that took place from 1905 to 1912 drew media attention to the United States Naval Academy. In addition, in 1912 midshipman William L. Bullock died on the U.S. *Hartford* after he climbed the main mast to "spike" his cap, according to custom. Harsh hazing was uncovered again in 1915, causing President Woodrow Wilson to demand that hazers be punished. Four years later Wilson was dead, but hazing was alive and had been linked to two attempted suicides and to the collapse of a third Naval Academy student.

Some state military institutions or colleges with military programs have been criticized for overzealous hazing practices. Texas A&M has drawn criticism for beatings and brutal tests of endurance in the Corps of Cadets. The university expelled 466 students for hazing in 1913 but took most back after they swore to cease whipping the uncovered flanks of the new men, or "fish." Months later, hazing began anew, and two hazers were sent home. Public attention focused on hazing at Texas A&M was particularly intense in 1984, after first-year student Bruce Goodrich perished following an exercise session, and again in 1991, when female cadets reported harsh abuses. Cadet Travis Alton said that he was taped "like a mummy" about the head and was punched, kicked, and required to cut his own body with a knife in 1996.[54] The next year, newcomers charged that they had been beaten with ax handles, encouraged to drink alcohol even though they were under twenty-one, and forced to perform calisthenics in a steam room—a practice that caused a pledge's death at Ithaca College. The university now spells out what "fish" can and cannot be made to do, limiting the times when physical training is permitted and even calling a halt to calisthenics after a "fish" has performed forty push-ups or sit-ups. Texas A&M Major General M. T. Hopgood Jr., commandant of the corps of cadets, issued a zero-tolerance policy toward hazing in a public statement that termed it the "moral equivalent of rape," because those with power preyed on those without it.[55]

Many hazing incidents have also occurred at Norwich University. Norwich folded its once-prestigious Skull and Swords Society for hazing in 1995, then punished eight students who tried to revive it in 1998—one year after former cadet William C. Brueckner Jr. won $2.2 million in compensation for the twenty days of round-the-clock hazing and punching he said he had endured. Some of the problems at Norwich in the '90s were supposedly caused by a clandestine on-campus group called the Night Riders, which has been blamed for several hazing incidents that took place beginning in the '20s.

Similar clandestine hazing activities at the Citadel inspired a work of fiction, *The Lords of Discipline*, by alumnus Pat Conroy, and were featured in long, lurid nonfiction exposés on school hazing practices in *Sports Illustrated* and the *New Yorker*. Media attention shifted away from the Citadel—but not until the institution stopped harassing African Americans, opened its gates to female cadets, and introduced new policies to curtail hazing in the mid- and late 1990s. In 1997, attention turned to the Virginia Military Institute (VMI) after women began to be admitted to the institution. Although VMI's brass was at first defiant, frequent exposés of hazing practices published in the *Washington Post* and in Richmond and Roanoke newspapers in 1997 and 1998 eventually caused the administration to speak less cavalierly about hazing on the "rat" line. In 1998 VMI's governing board booted out six cadets, not for a belt-and hanger-spanking incident that was criticized as hazing, but because the six lied about the affair in statements, breaking the school's honor code. Attorneys for the cadets argued that they had been put in an impossible situation by VMI's unwritten hazing code. Authorities handed its students a system of abuse that too easily spiraled out of control, then offered them two poor options to choose from. If they had tattled, their peers would have driven them out of VMI.

What does the past teach us about hazing? How can hazing possibly be eradicated or even tempered when it seems to be an almost inherent aspect of student behavior?

Most important, the past offers a challenge to educators, legislators, parents, and students themselves. Throughout time, those who educate and those who seek an education have found value in rituals that symbolically prove that newcomers are willing to submit to their supposed betters, willing to show they have the fortitude to bear whatever difficulties they may face in the future.

History also demonstrates the incredible pervasiveness and strength of the belief—more a prejudice or myth than a belief, actually—that hazing serves a worthwhile purpose.

Thus, in the name of that time-honored, so-called "worthwhile purpose," pledges endure all manner of inanities and depravities to enter a Greek organization. Hazers know they are hazing, and many look askance at hazing abuses when they read about them. The conclusion is unmistakable. Hazers justify their own abusive behavior by telling themselves they are actually fulfilling some sort of noble purpose, and that they are not the sort of brutes who would ever take hazing too far.

Hazers, as Arnold has shown, are nothing more or less than addicts in an addictive system. For hazing to continue to survive within the education system, as it has for thousands of years, requires dependence and tolerance—the two common characteristics of addiction identified by deviant behavior researchers—on the parts not only of hazers and the hazed but also of those who supervise them. So long as educators persist in believing that brutish hazing serves a useful purpose that civilized behavior cannot achieve more effectively, the red stain of hazing will continue to besmirch academe's ivory towers. Once educators and young people who are seeking an education can see hazing for the addiction it really is, they will seek proper treatment to end a barbarous custom that has been more than two thousand years in the making.[56]

5

Greek Traditions
and Tragedies

THE FRONTIER TRADITION

Members of Greek male and female social fraternities clearly esteem tradition. The perpetuation of annual events, the hanging of composites, the archives maintained by alumni historians, the extensive libraries of books by members in many fraternal headquarters, and pledging-related practices that go back decades all point to the importance of tradition to these groups. Fraternities generally trace their origins to Phi Beta Kappa in 1776, but the true granddaddy of social fraternities was the Kappa Alpha Society, founded in New York at Union College in 1825. The enormous task that student fraternal founders tackled in the nineteenth and early twentieth centuries is taken for granted by non-Greek educators, who fail to see how remarkable it is that mere students founded groups that have endured and even thrived, producing many illustrious alums who credit their fraternities for part of their success. Having begun a local fraternity, the founders and their successors traveled by train and stage to persuade students at other colleges to start new chapters that would be characterized by all the myths, symbols, and images that went with membership. The first fraternities were syncretic, yoking diverse beliefs in single organizations. Their rituals borrowed from religious systems, educational systems, adult societies like the Masons, and the frontier culture of the day.

Many fraternities originated on the campuses of distinctly New England and Southern colleges. In the nineteenth century, college fraternal organizations with New England or New York roots included Theta Chi (Norwich University); Alpha Chi Rho (Trinity College in Connecticut); Alpha Delta Phi (Hamilton College); Chi Phi (Princeton); Psi Upsilon, Sigma Phi Society, Delta Phi, Theta Delta Chi, and Chi Psi (Union College); Delta Chi (Cornell); Alpha Sigma Phi, Pi Lambda Phi, and Delta Kappa Epsilon (Yale); Delta Psi/St. Anthony Hall (Columbia); Theta Xi (Rensselaer Polytechnic Institute); Delta Sigma Phi and Zeta Beta Tau (College of the City of New York); Delta Upsilon (Williams), Phi Sigma Kappa (University of Massachusetts); and Zeta Psi (New York University). Nineteenth-century fraternities begun in the South include Sigma Phi Epsilon (University of Richmond), Delta Tau Delta (Bethany College in West Virginia, though its 1848 antecedent was the defunct Rainbow or W. W. W. fraternity from the University of Mississippi chapter), Sigma Alpha Epsilon (University of Alabama), Alpha Tau Omega and Sigma Nu (Virginia Military Institute), Kappa Alpha Order (Washington and Lee), and Kappa Sigma and Pi Kappa Alpha (University of Virginia).

In what was then the western frontier wilderness, three national fraternities (Phi Delta Theta, Beta Theta Pi, and Sigma Chi) began at Miami of Ohio. Many of the preceding fraternities started in a frontier environment during a time when society believed that "great personal courage, unusual physical powers, the ability to drink a quart of whiskey [were] at least as important as possessions, and infinitely more important than heraldic crests," noted American thinker Wilbur J. Cash, author of *The Mind of the South*.[1] In many respects, today's fraternities recall frontier days in that they act as a substitute for families one has left. In frontier days "kindliness and easiness" toward people in your community was regarded as "the very marrow of this tradition of the backcountry," according to Cash.[2] The satisfaction that fraternity members say they feel can be compared to what Americans experienced in a close-knit frontier community. "One simply did not have to get on in this world in order to achieve security, independence, or value in one's own estimation and in that of one's fellows," said Cash.[3] Much as fraternity members do, however, members of frontier communities tended to haze greenhorns and newcomers until they were assimilated. Significantly, in the frontier community of Oxford, Ohio, rough-and-tumble "townies" despised and resented students, and owners of groceries exploited these young men by selling them liquor over the objections of the Old Miami faculty. Rather than trying to gain acceptance, Old Miami students banded together in their own new societies that were reminiscent of the Masonic societies their relatives and neighbors back home belonged to.

Newcomers who had left farms to take work in the cities or large towns on the frontier found that they were more eagerly embraced by townspeople if they joined fraternal groups such as the Masons. In the nineteenth century, many new Masons were displaced men who longed for the company and acceptance of other men. Freemasonry was of English origin and had come to colonial America in the 1730s. In the beginning many members regarded the Masons as a drinking club; ritual was less important than were drinks and a good meal. Eventually the Masons in the United States split into two competing groups. One faction enjoyed consuming whiskey with convivial companions. The other became devoted to community service and spiritual matters. By the early 1800s and for years afterwards, non-Masons often regarded Masonic lodges as disguised taverns, much as some critics today regard fraternity houses as mere drinking establishments. However, just as many fraternity members today are involved in works of charity and drink moderately or not at all, so too were a number of nineteenth-century Masons nondrinkers. Like the reformers in fraternity chapters today, many lodge members worked to help rid the organization of its pejorative "Merry Masons" nickname.[4]

EARLY OPPOSITION TO SECRET SOCIETIES

Nowadays younger Greek leaders tend to be unaware of fraternities' Masonic roots. Membership in secret societies has fallen to an all-time low, and many young people don't know they exist at all. National fraternity leaders today tell rebellious undergraduates that the antecedents of fraternities were literary societies, a reminder calculated to improve the young men's behavior. But while members of literary societies revered philosophy and rhetoric and good books, some also loved unruliness. At the helm of the bloody student revolts at Princeton were the leaders of these societies. Wealthy sons of "genteel temperament" were at the heart of the revolts, wrote Helen Lefkowitz Horowitz, author of *Campus Life*; they "brought to college a love of pleasure, an attention to manners, a restless ambition, and an easy conscience."[5] These students clashed with administrators—particularly administrators who were sons of ministers and had been raised to revere authority. Those college presidents used threats and punishments to impose their will. Wealthy students regarded such authority not only as unreasonable but also as reminiscent of the authoritarian rule that the American Revolution had been fought to depose. When rioting broke out, many "moderates" among the student body tended to fight along-

side the rebellious literary society leaders, rather than choosing to side
with college administrators.[6]

A good number of nineteenth-century college presidents, trustees,
and faculty—particularly the sons of ministers, once again—vehemently
opposed college fraternities. They charged that the societies conducted
secret back-room dealings, played pranks, and sometimes drank. In
1842, the University of Michigan faculty likewise condemned the formation of secret societies on campus. In 1841, the Old Miami trustees
outlawed secret societies on pain of expulsion.[7] In 1857, the president
of Washington College (later to become Washington and Lee) criticized fraternities as "excrescenses," saying that they were uncontrol-
lable and violated school prohibitions against drinking festivals.[8] But
while many colleges banned fraternities, students wanted them enough
to risk maintaining underground chapters.

At first students opposed to fraternities tended to have religious
backgrounds, and wealthy, hedonistic students from more secular backgrounds favored them, wrote Horowitz. Over time, when even the sons
of ministers began joining Greek-letter groups, fraternities continued
to wage political warfare with non-Greeks, then pejoratively called "Barbarians" or "Barbs." In the nineteenth and much of the twentieth century, many class officers were elected not for their qualifications but
because of the number of votes their fraternity brothers were able to
muster for them, Horowitz noted.[9]

Fraternities, with rare, nonsectarian exceptions, discriminated
against men of the "wrong" national origin, religion, and skin color.
The first young men to join fraternities in the 1800s may have been
serious students who were highly competitive when it came to writing
essays and delivering orations, but they also plunged into trouble. For
example, in 1848 at Miami, members of Alpha Delta Phi and Beta Theta
Pi blocked the historic Old Main building with giant snowballs. After
President Erasmus McMaster castigated the perpetrators as if they had
committed some nefarious crime, the pranksters crammed the building with ice and snow, rendering it unusable for three days. An irate
McMaster expelled every Alpha and all but two Betas.[10] Many initiation-related stunts required of pledges during this era were public displays of burlesque. Fraternities at Wabash College made pledges ride
broomstick horses and sent them off on safaris to hunt bumblebees
with a bow and arrow.[11] Yet for all their silliness, the founders and
members of early fraternities during the early days often possessed
admirable virtues. During the nineteenth and part of the twentieth
century, many fraternity members respected truth, literature, and science. Phi Sigma Kappa at the University of Massachusetts (formerly
Massachusetts College) was founded in 1873 to promote brotherhood,

TV comic David Letterman was a member of Sigma Chi at Ball State University. Thousands of celebrities, athletes, politicians, authors, and business leaders belonged to Greek groups in college. Few celebrities have taken a public stand against hazing. Two exceptions are comic Bill Cosby (Omega Psi Phi) and journalist James J. Kilpatrick (Sigma Alpha Epsilon).
Photo courtesy of Ball State University

stimulate scholarship, and develop the character of its members. Phi Kappa Tau was founded in 1906 at Miami of Ohio with the purpose of promoting equality, democracy, and square dealing.[12] Psi Upsilon was begun in 1833 at Union College by young men declaring their desire for "moral, intellectual and social growth."[13]

FRATERNAL HISTORIES AND MYTHS

For all the emphasis fraternity members put on fraternal history, and though most fraternities have published histories (though their quality varies), many undergraduates pass through college with little idea of how their groups have evolved over time. One interpreter of frontier America, Henry Nash Smith, explained the source of this ignorance when he wrote that history is both made and experienced. Smith's belief that history is based on "what people thought they were doing as much as on what they actually had done" is useful to keep in mind when one reads founders' versions of their fraternities' beginnings to see how they viewed the importance of their then-struggling enterprises. For example, the founders of Phi Kappa Psi in 1852 imagined themselves founding an elite society with "higher character and with loftier aims" than those of their alma mater, Jefferson College (now Washington and Jefferson College).[14] Similarly, historian Anne M. Butler has noted that part of the American character is to embrace stories about the handed-down lives of heroes that contain more fable than truth. Americans tend to care about the invented characters they carry in their minds, said Butler; it soothes us to think of the past as being peopled not with flawed individuals but with heroes and heroines who met all challenges, faced hardship with stoicism, cherished principles, and, if necessary, fought for what they believed.[15] Scholarly objections to hyperbolic tales of the past are of no concern to the people the stories comfort. Like many Americans who relish tales about frontier folk heroes because "these myths give foundation to a modern sense of identity," many Greeks have reinvented the tales of their founders to serve their own purposes.[16] Contemporary pledges who are abused take comfort in the fact that their suffering is worthy if it will allow them to gain entrance to a group whose founders they have idealized. This is not to say that there were no authentic heroes among the nineteenth-century fraternity men. A disproportionate number fell in battle during the Civil War. One of the most inspiring true tales told by Sigma Chis commemorates the initiation of a group of Confederate brothers into the fraternity in Atlanta right before the Yankees burned the city.[17]

Most fraternities today celebrate their links to the distant past on Founders Day, though members often do so by drinking instead of by contemplating, as their predecessors mostly did. Undergraduate members sometimes convince themselves that severe hazing must have begun with the founders. "It wasn't so much that the members in the fraternity now went through everything," said one former Omega Psi Phi pledge. "You endured it because the founders were said to go through it."[18]

The only problem with revering larger-than-life historical figures, wrote Butler, is that the "details of their humanity" tend to "blur." Males in fraternities today are misled in thinking that such heroes never had any "tedium, no sense of entrapment," to borrow Butler's words.[19] Thus certain aspects of fraternal history—the pranks, the triumphs over rival fraternities, and the tales of brothers who wore fraternal pins into battle—give today's fraternity males a romantic, distorted picture of what Cardinal John Henry Newman and other educators said that student life in academe is meant to be. All the myths and romantic tales about wild hazing affairs and drinking marathons that have been passed down from alums to members and pledges make it even harder to eradicate objectionable practices. Reformers working at national Greek headquarters today frequently claim that fraternity founders would not have approved of hazing. Frederick Doyle Kershner, a Delta Tau Delta historian, and Dave Westol, Theta Chi executive director, have attributed the rise of hazing in fraternal groups to nineteenth-century fraternities' use of pledging as a way to recruit prep school students even before they enrolled in college. Instead of inducting new members right away, fraternities with pledgeship programs made the waiting period before initiation longer and longer. Gradually, pledges were hazed as part of an ordeal by which they "earned" membership. Pledging supposedly builds pledges' need to belong, but hazing teaches newcomers that members have little respect for their organization's policies, rules, and leaders. Pledging has evolved so that its worst nineteenth-century feature—the side stunts occasionally required for admission—have become synonymous with hazing practiced by Greek groups in our own time. In a 1998 interview for this book, Westol said he tells undergraduates that pledging and hazing have not always been a part of Greek life. It is true that none of today's ultraviolent hazing practices took place in the nineteenth century. However, fraternities have been inventing trumped-up "side degrees" for the purpose of inserting undignified horseplay into the initiation ceremony for more than one hundred years.

Take the example of Pi Kappa Alpha fraternity, which was founded at the University of Virginia in 1868. At first it had neither rush nor pledging. Before too long, members came up with the idea of requiring initiates to endure buffoonish rituals, according to Pi Kappa Alpha historian Jerome Reel.[20] It appears that by 1898 the buffoonery was threatening fraternal decorum. The fraternity unanimously passed a motion to end horseplay, but in spite of the well-meaning gesture, hazing continued and still continues in some chapters.[21]

Defenders of fraternities such as educational historian Frederick Rudolph maintain that fraternities introduced students to sophisticated pleasures and prepared them for the real-world life of business and politics. Rudolph, writing in the 1970s, said that in the long run fraternities were good for colleges, making them less provincial and forcing some authoritarian administrators to consider new viewpoints. Literary societies and social fraternities were successful even though many college presidents were disdainful of extracurricular activities, and thus Greek groups paved the way for other student activities to gain a place on campus, reasoned Rudolph in his *Curriculum: A History of the American Course of Study since 1636*.[22] Other defenders took a more personal approach, contending that colleges had an obligation to make student life as meaningful as it could possibly be. The function of a fraternity "is to replace the homes of our students," said John R. Dyer, men's adviser at the University of Kansas in 1925. The fraternity house offered "affection, encouragement, stimulation, comradeship, food, shelter, refuge, rest, and a thousand other blessings which deny enumeration," said Dyer.[23] Nonetheless, said Dyer, fraternities had faults. He criticized their vulgar regard for wealth and social standing, their hazing excesses, and their acquisition of status symbols. In the late 1940s, University of Kansas chancellor Deane W. Malott predicted that fraternities would eventually self-destruct unless their leaders could significantly alter members' behavior and beliefs.[24] Malott, who eventually left the University of Kansas to become the president of Cornell University, said that if Greek organizations wanted to justify their presence, they needed to give members a means by which to demonstrate loyalty to the university, to strengthen the character of members, and to improve the intellectual prowess of undergraduates. Today the executives of national fraternities are saying the same things that Malott brought up.[25]

"The most important part of that frontier culture [in the fraternity founders] was courage," said Mitchell B. Wilson, executive director of Kappa Sigma Fraternity and president of the Fraternity Executives Association, in a 1998 telephone interview for this book. "We tell our undergraduates one chapter can change the culture on the campus, but they'll need courage and conviction . . . to be an outstanding chapter with character."

Wilson noted that weaker chapters that tend to cause problems buy into what the shallower students on campus consider indicative of high status—the ability to hold liquor, to fight, to party constantly. "We tell them that is the wrong kind of status to achieve," said Wilson. "We get them to articulate what really are their values and the fraternity's values. . . . Independents on campus might not value Greeks, but they can recognize an outstanding chapter with character."

DYING TO BELONG

The first fraternity-related hazing death to make national news took place fifty years after the founding of the first fraternity, although it is certainly possible that other deaths occurred before this point and were dismissed as the unfortunate consequence of male horseplay. In 1873, Charles William Wason and Charles H. Lee, members of the Kappa Alpha Society at Cornell University, blindfolded a pledge in the countryside near the Ithaca school, where they were to meet other Kappas for a ritual ceremony. Unable to get his bearings in the darkness, the newcomer, Mortimer N. Leggett, and the two members tumbled into a gorge near Giles Street. Leggett was killed. The two surviving Kappa Alpha Society males swore that they had taken the blindfold off before the tragedy occurred, although a letter written by Leggett's father indicated that he thought his boy had died while blindfolded. Members met with Leggett's heartbroken father, and in a symbolic gesture offered him the membership his son had sought. Cornell faculty and President Andrew D. White, an active member of one fraternal organization and inactive member of another, said that the only secret societies that would be tolerated at the school had to be "favorable to scholarship, good order, and morality."[26]

The Kappa Alpha Society, then in its fifth year at Cornell, was allowed to continue operating. The organization failed to pass the tragic lesson it had learned as a result of Leggett's death on to future brothers. In 1899, twenty members of the same Cornell fraternity ordered eight pledges to get off a train in a rural area near Geneva, New York, and take a hike to kill time before a formal initiation ritual was to take place. Pledge Edward Fairchild Berkeley, a St. Louis resident, stumbled in the dark and fell into a canal. His drowning was noted on the front page of the *New York Times*.[27]

Fraternity antics escalated during the early part of the twentieth century. In 1909, while addressing the Cambridge, Massachusetts, Phi Beta Kappa chapter, Princeton University President Woodrow Wilson referred to student activities as "the side show that threatens to swallow the main tent."[28] Shortly afterwards, a University of North Carolina (UNC) researcher, citing figures for two academic years (1909/1910 and 1910/1911), discovered that the collective scholastic average of newly initiated sophomores was far below that of nonfraternity men. Some ninety years later, few educators would argue that pledging in hazing fraternities still wrecks the GPAs of many students, but the UNC survey was hot news in 1912, and many educators called for an end to the Greek system.

In 1912 the chancellor of the University of Kansas said he had reservations about fraternities' usefulness, even though he was a member of Psi Upsilon.[29] Stung leaders of the National Interfraternity Conference (NIC) (then the Interfraternity Conference) met at the fourth annual convention in New York City to discuss ways to stimulate scholarship and to improve relations with college administrators. Thus began a press and NIC dance that continues to the present. Each time a new fraternity scandal shocked the public, "bad press" ensued and the NIC met with reporters to announce another resolution banning hazing or this and that. Nonetheless, fraternity-related events were the scene of so few deaths between 1912 and 1944 that they probably could be fairly termed isolated incidents, although the fact that even a small number of deaths resulted from hazing should have been intolerable.

The number of news articles pointing out the risks associated with fraternities soared after 1945. More and more Greek group members and initiates were dying grotesque deaths and incurring severe injuries as a result of hazing. NIC resolutions could no longer deflect exposés. The larger, status-conscious national and international fraternities saw their reputations crumbling but failed to make adequate repairs, although many fraternities—particularly smaller nationals with fewer than thirty chapters—operated then and continue to operate now relatively or fully scandal-free.

THE WRITER AND THE FRATERNITY

Several biographies of writers, in particular, provide insights into some demeaning, silly, and potentially dangerous fraternal practices. Perhaps because these authors-to-be were already lusting for an audience at a young age and found encouragement in fraternities, the Greek world has attracted as pledges or members the likes of George Ade, James Thurber, Thomas Wolfe, Stephen Crane, Robert Frost, Zane Grey, Joyce Kilmer, Thornton Wilder, Stephen Vincent Benet, John Jakes, John D. MacDonald, Archibald MacLeish, Willie Morris, John Nichols, Ernie Pyle, Jack Kerouac, Philip Roth, Irving Stone, Booth Tarkington, E. B. White, Tennessee Williams, and Charles Gilman Norris. Playwright Tennessee Williams, Class of 1930, recalled a brutal paddling he endured as an Alpha Tau Omega pledge at the University of Missouri, Columbia, that he termed "spine-breaking."[30] And the details of fraternity life at Indiana University in the 1930s can be gleaned from the biography of Ross Lockridge Jr., later the best-selling author of *Raintree County* and at that time a brilliant student who deserved the nickname "A+" that his Phi Gamma Delta fraternity brothers gave him. He was a "legacy"—the son of a father who also had been a Phi Gam. Lockridge's biographer (and son), Larry Lockridge, wrote:

> Not to be in a fraternity or sorority was widely regarded as being nothing at all. Bloomington had as yet little in the way of a supportive bohemian culture—so he . . . took the pledge proudly, polished the [house] dance floor on Saturday morning, and endured the rituals. . . . Hell Week in the spring was only a thickening of the field of torture that extended throughout the year. It was easy to accumulate infractions that translated into paddlings, for instance failing to get cigarettes for an upperclassman with sufficient speed. When bending over [to be paddled], pledges *were* permitted to lift their testicles. In the Elephant Drill, they were stripped naked and ordered to follow one another around on all fours, goosing one another and then sucking fingers. They were blindfolded and made to eat peanut-covered bananas floating in johns, and were for routine defecation forced to sit on the john backward. They were confronted with live chickens, blindfolded, and ordered to open their mouths, into which stinky

As a Phi Gamma Delta pledge at Indiana University, Ross Lockridge Jr. was known to members as a "legacy." His father, Hoosier historian Ross Lockridge Sr., had belonged to the same fraternity at the university. Lockridge Jr., photographed autographing his novel *Raintree County*, endured hazing that included group nudity, eating unpleasant food concoctions, and paddling. Larry Lockridge, his father's biographer, was also a Phi Gam pledge but "dropped out . . . . because of cultural differences between my peers and me. I was in spirit more of a [Bloomington] townie, an intellectual, with bohemian friends, and with no interest in sports," he said.
Photo courtesy of Indiana University Archives, Bloomington, Indiana

Reformers in Greek organizations attempting to halt the physical abuse of pledges face an uphill battle. Paddles have become synonymous with Greek life. Yearbooks at many universities contain photos of real or simulated paddlings. In this photograph, brothers at a chapter of Beta Theta Pi administer an unusual punishment.
Photo courtesy of Indiana University Archives, Bloomington, Indiana

cheese was dropped. During Hell Week they were fed nothing but unseasoned beans three times a day and required to keep a Fart Chart on frequency and intensity of blasts. They were administered electric shocks on their buttocks. And they were ordered to sit on the floor naked with their legs spread. An upperclassman read to them from *Nights in a Harem* while the other Phi Gams gathered around to monitor erections. Bets were placed and an incipient erection was cheered and hooted. With his usual concentration, Ross Lockridge warded off any hint of arousal by silently reciting Tennyson. The repressed homoerotic component of all this went unacknowledged. Any mention of homosexuality was pretty much outside the available discourse.[31]

Given that such behavior was hardly confined to colleges in Missouri and Indiana, why have fraternities continued to be a part of college life in the United States? One commonly expressed opinion among educators, which the heads of national Greek organizations often challenge, is that fraternal organizations appeal to undergraduates who desire to play in a spacious "clubhouse" with all the comforts—and few of the restrictions—of their parents' homes. During the '20s, Thomas Arkle Clark, who was then a revered dean at the University of Illinois, maintained that colleges needed to build houses of worship and Greek houses on campus in order to graduate people of good character and high moral purpose. At that time many university officials were predicting that the proliferation of attractive student unions and residence-dining halls would cause fraternities and sororities to die out. But Greek houses remained part of the campus scene even when colleges in the '30s reduced chapters' income by mandating that students had to eat meals in campus dining rooms.

The Greek system endured during World War II as well, even as fraternity members enlisted in large numbers, and periodicals such as *The Magazine of Sigma Chi* printed dozens of tributes to college members who died in combat.[32] Many chapter houses continued to exist only because alumni paid for their upkeep or because the government rented them to house servicemen. Following World War II, returning servicemen, unwilling to accept the indignities that nonveteran undergraduate males would subject them to during pledging, at first showed a disinclination to pledge fraternities. Nonetheless many did join, drawn by the lure of camaraderie, social status events with sororities, or the have-fun, drink-hard-if-you-wish-to environment, which was particularly appealing in contrast to the years of privation and danger they'd endured. Others joined because they had grown used to a pecking order and a chain of command.

POST–WORLD WAR II PRESS COVERAGE

By the late '40s, many fraternities were subjecting pledges to such ordeals as road trips and excessive physical exercises and calisthenics. Three pledges died in the United States between 1950 and 1956. A truck killed Alpha Tau Omega pledge Dean J. Niswonger of Wittenberg University while he slept on a country road. A car struck Swarthmore student Peter Mertz, heir to a publishing fortune, after Delta Upsilon (historically known as a non-hazing fraternity) members dropped him in the Pennsylvania countryside. And Thomas Clark of the Massachusetts Institute of Technology fell into a reservoir and drowned after Delta Kappa Epsilon members abandoned him. Clark's father first disputed accounts that called the death an accident, labeling the drop-off a "criminal" action, but later softened his stance and said the chapter's negligence was probably unintentional.[33]

Hazing meant much press coverage, not only in local publications but in a scathing *Time* magazine account. These deaths coincided with a change in the tone of articles dealing with Greek issues. What happened? Why did the pre–World War II front-page puff pieces that came close to gushing about fraternity and sorority activities give way to highly critical coverage after the war?

First, journalism itself was changing. Reporters began to see old, familiar subjects in a new way. They started monitoring their subjects, in the view of sociologist Herbert J. Gans, labeling people and putting them under moral surveillance.[34] They also found that readers hungered for coverage of disasters and safety risks. Because members at first hazed pledges mercilessly in public, such actions were taken by reporters to be cruel, sadistic, and harsh.

The press also criticized national fraternities and sororities that refused to admit African Americans and Jews as members in the late '40s and early '50s. Many editorial writers urged universities to end their association with Greek groups—even with some that had existed as chapters for more than a century. Much of this press coverage was professional and objective; some reporters covered the Greeks' charitable community service and also exposed the dry rot in fraternal timbers when members misbehaved.

By the mid- to late '50s, however, a great deal of what was printed in newspapers and magazines about Greeks was by any standard disdainful, derogatory, and derisive. In 1959, *Nation* writer Wade Thompson, an ex–University of Chicago fraternity member, poked fun at those who insisted that there was a difference between "frats" and "fraternities." He mocked the pronouncement that "great college fraternities . . . are style-setters under God for the world at large," made by a New York pastor, Ralph W. Sockman, in a speech to representatives of the NIC. "I point out to Dr. Sockman that a frat boy wouldn't know what a moral style-setter was if one came up and goosed him," said Thompson. "'These great college fraternities,' as Dr. Sockman calls them, are the silliest, stupidest institutions invented since the . . . chastity belt. They have no more moral style than a collection of Mafia gangsters, D.A.R. girls, Army generals or ladies of joy. . . . Their demerits are so numerous, their shortcomings so short: they codify snobbery, they pervert values, they corrupt decent instincts. They eat on exclusiveness, they thrive on intolerance, they presume to stratify peoples and beliefs, they gorge on stupidity and inanity, and they disgorge heartache and viciousness."[35]

Writers such as Thompson began to deliver, in Gans's words, "reality judgments" that clearly expressed their loathing for fraternities. Most often the reality judgments came in the form of news stories and were undetectable to the average reader unable to distinguish news from agitprop. "The values in the news are rarely explicit and must be found between the lines—in what actors and activities are reported or ignored, and in how they are described," said Gans. "If a news story deals with activities which are generally considered undesirable and whose descriptions contain negative connotations, then the story explicitly expresses a value about what is desirable." Significantly, even the usually subdued *New York Times* began denigrating the fraternities, a special-interest group that had formerly been the subject of positive editorial coverage. In a *Times* feature of November 11, 1962, called "Showdown on Fraternity Row," about Williams College and its impending decision to abolish fraternities, author David Boroff subtly indicated what he thought the institution should do. He used positive descriptions to label critics of fraternities and not-so-positive or negative labels for those who favored the continued existence of fraternities at Williams. Some examples are as follows:

◆ Boroff wrote that a Bennington undergraduate was "perceptive" because she found fraternities "sad."

◆ A professor of history who said fraternities fail to appeal to Williams men with "broad horizons" was characterized as "an able historian" with "a long-range vision."

◆ In one long section, Boroff abandoned all pretext of writing an objective story about Greeks at Williams: "Fraternity types range from some of the best brains on campus—inevitably, since fraternities encompass 84 percent of all sophomores, juniors and seniors—to beer-swilling Neanderthals who exhibit most of the classical vices of Greek letter societies: stubborn lightheadedness, snobbishness, and occasional nastiness verging on hooliganism." Negative newspaper portrayals of fraternities—targeting in particular behavior such as hazing—contributed to the public's growing antipathy toward fraternities. In addition, Hollywood released a number of movies showing fraternity members in an unfavorable light. These included films of serious intent such as *Fraternity Row,* Spike Lee's *School Daze,* and *The Graduate,* with its one memorable fraternity house scene. Even more one-sided were the B-grade horror and comedy films that depicted Greek males as louts and sexual predators.

Increasingly during the '50s and '60s, angry NIC leaders and fraternity executives began to object to the "Greek bashing" they were being subjected to by the press. People started using the label "animal house" to refer to many fraternity chapters fifteen years before the movie by that name starring John Belushi was filmed, as keg parties proliferated and reports of group debauchery began to surface. As was noted at Williams, the media attacks coincided with college administrators' and trustees' attempts to take control of or abolish fraternities and sororities. One by one, beginning in the East and the Midwest, colleges demanded that fraternities get rid of exclusionary clauses. A number of private schools, including Colby, Amherst, Middlebury, and Bowdoin, threatened to follow the example of Williams and outlaw their ancient Greek systems (and all four eventually did so). The chancellor of the New York state university system succeeded in banning Greek nationals from state universities and colleges until national fraternities mustered enough legal strength in the late '60s to begin returning to campus. The chancellor's decree failed to ban hazing, however, which continued to be problematic.[36]

No sooner did national Greek groups capitulate to outside pressure by rewriting their charters to eliminate their discrimination on the basis of race or religion, than a nationally covered hazing scandal that took place in 1959 incited a fresh spate of criticism on the part of the press and of the public. At the University of Southern California, Kappa Sigma pledge Richard Swanson choked to death on a quarter-pound portion of raw liver. The incident inspired national indignation, not only in response to the repulsiveness of the ritual, but also because of the accusations of the ambulance driver, who said Swanson might have lived if members had divulged the cause of his choking. "I asked if the boy had eaten anything," said rescue worker Nathan Rubin. "They told me no. I got practically no cooperation. If I'd only known he had eaten something, I might possibly have saved him. I was prepared for such an emergency. I had an extractor and could have removed what was in his throat. I was working in the dark and didn't have a chance. Neither did the kid."[37] Fraternity members told police they had tried sticking their fingers down his throat and even holding him upside down to knock the three-fourths-inch piece loose. The then chapter president said the tradition began back in 1925 when the Kappa Sigs started a USC chapter. In 1959 and 1960, underestimating the enormity of the public relations calamity that was in the process of occurring, the NIC responded to the public's disgust with hazing by doing what it had done for the past half century each time a serious incident had taken place—it prepared yet another resolution asking its member fraternities, which at the time numbered fifty-nine, to take a firm stand against hazing "accidents."[38]

Between 1960 and 1969, as undergraduates became politically active during the Vietnam War era, many perceived fraternity members as being pro-establishment and unhip. As a consequence, membership in Greek groups declined. When fewer undergraduates sought bids, pledge classes shrank, and some chapters did away with intense hazing. Following the drop in membership, two pledging-related deaths occurred in social clubs in the 1960s, as compared to the high death total accompanying the fraternity boom and the rise in hazing occurrences after 1976.[39] Still, in the '60s, some stronghold members continued to abuse pledges. Zeta Beta Tau pledges at the University of Southern California passed raw eggs to one another using their mouths. The Delta Tau Delta group at the University of Colorado made pledges run up and down stairs carrying concrete blocks. At the University of California, Berkeley, Pi Kappa Alpha pledges danced in one another's vomit, drank a "goat shake" (molasses, vinegar, Worcestershire sauce, mustard, coffee, and prune juice), sat naked on blocks of ice, raced naked holding marshmallows between the cheeks of their buttocks, put out a fire with mouthfuls of Tabasco sauce, smoked cigars under a rug while actives pounced on top of it, wore Kotex pads, slept in a tiny bathroom, endured the application of analgesic balm to their private parts, and thought they were swallowing a member's urine and eating his feces (in reality, it was vinegar and bananas), according to Larry Colton, author of *Goat Brothers*.[40] Esther Wright, another author, said a male friend confided to her that his hazing ordeal went beyond the boundaries of mental hazing. While naked, on all fours, and in a line with his fellow pledges, Wright's pledge friend had to lick the buttocks of another pledge when the "Hell Master" cracked the whip. The activity was common enough to have earned the name the "dog lick."[41]

ANIMAL HOUSES AND FRATERNITY REFORMS

As the Vietnam War wound down after 1970, the consumption of alcoholic beverages—and Greek groups, too—became trendy again. At first the press noticed no jump in hazing cases. For instance, a newspaper in the Lehigh Valley of Pennsylvania called Lehigh University Delta Phi pledge Mitchell Fishkin's 1973 fatal fall from a moving car "spontaneous horseplay," quoting a district attorney who used the term.

But during the mid-'70s, pledges (and Greek members being punished for "attitude problems") started dying in bizarre rituals, and press coverage of hazing began to increase. Monmouth College members of Zeta Beta Tau took pledges off campus to the Atlantic Ocean and made them dig their own graves, resulting in the suffocation death of an African American pledge when a mound of sand collapsed on top of him. A road trip in which seventeen pledges at a Grove City (Pennsylvania) College local fraternity participated ended tragically when four young males were killed by a car. Other road trips, off-campus scavenger hunts, and calisthenics drills that took place in the '70s resulted in the deaths of Greek newcomers or members at California's Pierce College, Texas Tech University, Washington State University, the University of Maryland, and Louisiana State University. In two of these deaths, the pledge's recent or long-term health history was problematic.

It is significant that in 1975, new members of fraternities began to chug grotesque quantities of beer, wine, and liquor as a pre-initiation ritual. Young men (mostly in local social clubs at first) died as a result of drinking too much at one time at the University of Nevada, Reno, Northern Illinois University, the University of Wisconsin at Stevens Point, Iowa State University, Alfred University, and Loras College. Some others were saved by the good work of emergency-room personnel. All this was a grim prelude to the fraternal deaths that occurred as a result of miscellaneous causes in the '80s and '90s.

According to the author's count—with the benefit of input from other hazing researchers, CHUCK, and Security on Campus—fifty-four fraternity hazing- and pledging-related deaths (that is, deaths that involved activities meeting the FEA definition of hazing, even if hazing was not officially blamed for the death) occurred in the United States from January 1, 1970, to January 1, 1999; two sorority hazing/pledging-related deaths also occurred.

Other hazing/pledging-related deaths that occurred in Canada and the Philippines are not reflected in this total but are listed in Appendix A of this book.

Six additional hazing/pledging-related deaths occurred in collegiate military school organizations, college spirit clubs, and athletic clubs; at least three of those deaths involved participants and/or victims who also belonged to fraternal organizations.

Fourteen males and two females drank themselves to death in fraternities without any clear evidence of hazing.

Five females and thirty males died in falls of all kinds (house, car surfing, cliff falls); many, but not all, were intoxicated or had been drinking when they fell.

Many other deaths of Greeks, guests at Greek houses, and innocent strangers listed in Appendix A occurred as a result of miscellaneous auto accidents involving Greeks or their guests, alcohol-related killings, and fraternity house fires at which the victims were often (but not always) intoxicated or at least had been drinking and/or using drugs. The author loosely refers to these dozens of additional miscellaneous alcohol-related deaths—for want of a more precise term—as deaths resulting from fraternal alcohol syndrome. The above totals are minimum verifiable figures. In particular, it is impossible to know with certainty just how many adolescents and young adults have died in automobile accidents that directly or indirectly involved someone who had been drinking at a fraternity function.

With highway carnage at an all-time high, activist members of Mothers Against Drunk Driving stressed the need for a higher legal drinking age. Once tavern owners across the country began closing doors to the under-twenty-one group for fear of being deemed liable if a minor were to get into a fatal accident after drinking at their estab-

Rookie Nicholas Haben perished during a long night of frenzied drinking in an initiation sponsored by the Lacrosse Club at Western Illinois University. Nicholas's mother, Alice Haben, became an anti-hazing activist and crusaded successfully to strengthen Illinois's hazing law. Athletic hazing incidents plague professional teams such as the New Orleans Saints, and university teams and clubs such as those at Murray State University, Kent State University, Ithaca College, SUNY–Potsdam (women's lacrosse), the University of Washington, and Alfred University.
Photo courtesy of Alice Haben

lishment, not-so-discriminating Greek houses once again became the campus drinking parlors of choice. Not only did alcohol-related deaths rise, but so did the number of fraternity-related sexual assaults and gang rapes. In spite of these problems and of the often-deserved criticism they received at the hands of the press, however, during the '80s and early '90s national fraternity and sorority organizations saw their memberships soar to the highest levels in their history.[42]

The deaths of young males during hazing and initiation activities inspired the arrival on the scene of Eileen Stevens, Alice Haben (the mother of Nicholas Haben, a Western Illinois University student who died during a lacrosse club initiation), and Rita Saucier—activists hoping to have the same effect on hazing as MADD had on drunk driving. Stevens, whose son Chuck Stenzel died in 1978, inspired a number of angry and embarrassed fraternity and sorority leaders to demand that Greek houses make some changes. One such leader was Delta Tau Delta historian Frederick Doyle Kershner, a Butler University alum who in

1977 published an article on the history of hazing and who in the 1980s condemned hazing in an NIC report.[43] Another was Bruce D. Hornbuckle of Sigma Alpha Epsilon, who in 1981 published a pamphlet, "Death By Hazing," that Stevens distributed nationally on U.S. college campuses.

National sororities tended to take care of their problems quietly, and many members refused to return reporters' calls. One early exception was the outspoken Maureen Syring, who worked for Delta Gamma for eight years (and served as national president from 1986 to 1990). Jean W. Scott and Lissa Bradford are two other NPC leaders who have been active in the fight against hazing- and alcohol-related injuries and deaths. Also, a number of sororities instituted strong alcohol- and hazing-awareness programs; these include Alpha Chi Omega, Chi Omega, Delta Delta Delta, Zeta Tau Alpha, Kappa Kappa Gamma, and Delta Zeta.

Among several strong voices of reason in historically African American fraternities during the '80s were Michael Gordon, a member of Kappa Alpha Psi; Charles Wright of Phi Beta Sigma; and John Williams of Alpha Phi Alpha. They were joined in the '90s by Jason DeSousa and Walter Kimbrough, student activities advisers and researchers studying issues affecting African American Greek groups. The publication *Black Issues in Higher Education* also took a stand, televising a nationwide videoconference on hazing in October 1998.

In a speech on chapter values made in the 1990s, NIC fraternal activist Frank J. Ruck Jr. of Sigma Phi Epsilon succinctly summarized the problems facing fraternities and sororities. "The basic motivation and ideals of our collective founders are long gone; we know that much is wrong and sometimes harmful with our Greek System," said Ruck, speaking at a Theta Xi planning session. "Focus on fun and entertainment dominates the culture and many, if not all of us, give shallow lip service to our roots. The reality is that in far too many locations we do harm to our young people. And that realization really hurts."[44]

Also in the '90s, NIC executive vice president Jonathan J. Brant urged national fraternities to adopt reforms to eliminate alcohol from houses, to adopt a statement on fraternal values and ethics, and to end pledging abuses. The NIC and NPC also began authorizing the Center for Advanced Social Research to conduct independent studies to determine whether documented evidence indicating that former Greeks are more active than non-Greeks in community affairs as adults shows that values emphasized in fraternities and sororities eventually take hold in adults, making their members better citizens.

In the mid-'90s, Ruck became NIC president. He won some fraternal friends and ruffled the feathers of others with his unswerving attacks on hazing, sexual harassment, poor academic achievement, high liability insurance costs, lack of adult involvement, dishonest academic behavior, property damage, poor recruitment standards, and the perpetual running of Greek organizations under crisis management. "Many people believe that if the Greek system is to survive in the twenty-first century, massive change is essential," Ruck declared at the aforementioned Theta Xi planning session. "The challenge is to change the culture and the need [is] to reinvent fraternity."[45]

Ruck made his influence felt when in 1991 he became chairman of the Baird's Manual Foundation, the publisher of *Baird's Manual of American College Fraternities*. Long a voice of boosterism in the Greek world, *Baird's Manual* inserted strong editorial commentary into its twentieth edition in 1991, which was edited by Robert F. Marchesani Jr. of Phi Kappa Psi and Jack L. Anson of Phi Kappa Tau. In an emotional essay, writer Kent C. Owen echoed the old Baird's theme when he said that fraternities were emblematic of life's best times—"enduring friendships founded on shared principles and personal affinities; living out good lives, not just having good times; cordial laughter, delightful gaiety, robust merriment; the lively pleasures of good companions; the sustaining loyalty of old comrades through whatever fortune or adversity may appear; the settled conviction that lives are lived to the best effect when firmly secured by mutual bonds of deep affection, administration, and respect." But he also aimed a verbal round of bird shot at critics on college campuses who thought the "permanent extinction" of the Greek system would be the best way to achieve "social justice." Abandoning his ironic tone, Owen pointed out that the unprecedented rise in the numbers of Greeks from 1977 to 1991 had made the Greek world prosperous, but on the other hand, "the wholeness . . . that had once organically connected fraternity life with the greater life of the academic institution, was irretrievably different and strange." He cited signs of havoc that included drunken brawls, gang rapes, drug raids, racial confrontations, dangerous hazings, and vandalism.

By the late '90s, several respected old-guard members such as Anson, Charles Wright, and Ruck had died. Kershner, fighting illness, retired to suburban Buffalo, New York. In October 1998, Eileen Stevens, whose aged parents needed care and who wanted time with her grandchildren, announced her retirement from speaking, although she continued working part-time on behalf of CHUCK. In 1999, the NIC's Jonathan Brant resigned unexpectedly after seventeen years with the conference. He accepted the prestigious position of director of the Beta Theta Pi Foundation. Many national fraternities, university Greek affairs, and the NIC experienced upheaval among their staff, many of whom retired around this time. These included a number of influential executives such as Sigma Nu's Maurice "Mo" Littlefield (though he remained active in the fraternity in another capacity), Lambda Chi

Alpha's Thomas Helmbock, and Zeta Beta Tau's Jim Greer Jr. Several cited weariness after having spent years dealing with what seemed like one scandal after another or having to answer tough questions in court during civil suits. One who left was Zachary C. Tucker, who had served as a University of North Texas Greek affairs administrator for twenty years. "In my opinion, university administrators and alumni of fraternities and sororities lack the character and convictions needed to address and make the tough decisions to change the fraternity movement for the better," said Tucker, who began a career in banking upon his departure from the university. "These people depend on their lawyer for the interpretation of their responsibility. . . . I see none of the leadership organizations—FEA, AFA, NIC, etc.—with any clear sense of what needs to happen to turn this around. The fact that a young man or woman can come out a worse person as a result of joining a fraternity is unacceptable. They come out worse because [they] leave with less integrity and less character because of the environment [to] which they are subjected."[46] Reformers welcomed some of these retirements. Certain veteran board members of national fraternities who had blocked hazing reforms left and were replaced by men who were less inclined to coddle unruly undergraduates.

Jacques L. Vauclain III and Michael Carlone of Sigma Phi Epsilon became strong advocates of cooperation in the mid- to late '90s, inviting Greek advisors to fraternal meetings to talk openly about their fraternities' past problems, current triumphs, and goals of lowering their members' alcohol consumption to levels below that of the average student population. In February 1999, Carlone announced his decision to work for the fraternity in a volunteer capacity, and sought employment outside the Greek world. Dave Westol, a former assistant prosecuting attorney in Michigan, has also become such an advocate; he travels from campus to campus, putting on simulated hazing trials to make members think about their behaviors, their responsibilities as campus citizens, and the impact of the untoward actions of individual members on fraternities as a body. Other Greeks at national headquarters who began voicing public demands for change included Tom Pennington of Phi Kappa Psi, Littlefield of Sigma Nu, Mick Wilson of Kappa Sigma, Mark Timmes of Phi Kappa Phi, Robert A. Biggs of Phi Delta Theta, and Bill Martin of Phi Gamma Delta. Other fraternities that had rarely encountered problems with hazing or alcohol misuse, such as Farmhouse, are now afforded more status by other fraternity executives than they had been previously.

TRADITIONS DIE HARD

But no one in the fraternal world has claimed a victory over alcohol or hazing. In spite of Greek reforms at the executive level, there is a huge discrepancy between what the nationals have decreed and what undergraduates actually do. Field representatives sent to chapter houses often quit after a year or two, frustrated and sometimes a little hurt by the poor reception and constant deception they encounter during inspections. NIC staff has experienced a great deal of turnover, as well, and university student life professionals, many of whom charge that their status is low and that they are paid accordingly, jump to other professions or to the colleges where they say they can find fair pay and respect, said Teresa Loser in a 1998 interview at her office, adding that she is treated well at DePauw. Nonetheless, the *DePauw Online* announced that during a one-year time period, seven key individuals who worked with the dean of students departed from the university.

Even Auburn University's President Muse, who has devoted so many of his working and personal hours to the Phi Delta Theta tragedy and the Kappa Alpha controversy when Auburn's academic, alumni, and athletic affairs also demanded his attention, said in a 1999 interview for this book that he had no choice but to drop the lion's share of his previous time commitment to the international Tau Kappa Epsilon fraternity and the NIC. "I see with sadness what is happening with fraternities," said Muse, adding that alcohol misuse has clearly hindered the long- and short-term ability of young people who "use alcohol as a crutch" to "function as a human being. . . . [Young Greeks] are not saying, 'We're not going to have the preparties and the afterparties or the bottle exchanges, and we're not going to encourage people to get inebriated.' Otherwise sensible young men with all the potential to become outstanding leaders in our society just do not seem able to deal with that dimension in their lives and in their brothers."

Greek groups have not authorized a dispassionate research institute to survey their members in order to obtain a reasonable estimate of what percentage of Greeks perform acts commonly defined as hazing. And many are understandably reluctant to give inexact estimates of the percentage of college fraternity chapters who haze. However, Biggs thinks that about 10 percent do so. Westol estimates that hazers make up about 10 to 15 percent of any fraternal organization. With NIC enrollment at between 320,000 and 325,000 members, those estimates mean that between about 32,000 and 48,000 males a year are making many more young men perform silly or demeaning tasks. A small percentage of members also require the performance of potentially dangerous hazing stunts that may involve excessive alcohol consumption. Hazers, "in the face of education, lawsuits, state law, books, pamphlets, newsletters, speakers, campus regulations and policies, national policies, videotapes, ad infinitum, say 'We didn't consider this to be hazing,'" said Westol in a 1998 e-mail to the author. "I am convinced that they know what is hazing and what isn't—they are attempting to utilize the ignorance defense in order to continue to haze or to justify their actions ex post facto. If they admitted to understanding the definition, that would deprive them of the one 'innocent' defense which they can utilize."

Because the roots of the Greek system run as deep as the roots of the American education system, hazing is unlikely to disappear until both systems work as one to address problems prevalent in fraternities and sororities today.

Although many college presidents and Greek leaders have acknowledged the evils of drinking, hazing, and sexual assault that have turned fraternity houses into virtual icons of depravity in the public's mind, they must somehow find a way to isolate and remove members whose behavior is deviant. Just as genetic researchers try to isolate the chromosomes that cause certain kinds of disorders and illnesses, so too must behavioral psychologists engage in long-term studies of hard-drinking, hazing fraternities to identify dysfunctional characteristics that are common to generations of "brothers." In addition to contributing to the treatment of present problems, such studies may be able to help prevent hazing, alcohol misuse, and mistreatment of women from being passed along like genetic disorders to future generations of fraternity brothers.

6

Sororities

THE STORY OF A PLEDGE

Widener University was founded in 1821. Once a military college, it is now well known for its programs in business, hospitality management, and the human service professions. Amanda Smith enrolled at the university's Pennsylvania campus, taking honors classes that she hoped would prepare her for a career as a doctor. She worked as an assistant director in the campus production of *Crimes of the Heart* and attended sorority rush in 1996. The vitality of the women of Phi Mu impressed her, and she loved the organization's well-kept sorority house.

Phi Mu, an old and prestigious national fraternity for women that has more than 100,000 members, distributed literature calling the organization "proud, principled, progressive." Amanda learned that its international philanthropy project was Project Hope and its national one the Children's Miracle Network. Euphoric after receiving a bid inviting her to become a "provisional member," she attended her first pledge function.

Amanda received a ceremonial ribbon and wore it, as she had been directed, over her heart. She accepted a pledge manual listing the sorority's dos and don'ts, which emphasized that hazing provisional members was forbidden. Widener has written regulations forbidding hazing, according to Craig J. Loundas, dean of student life.[1] Smith's pledge manual stated that initiated members of Phi Mu possessed deep meanings and secrets. Provisional members could not share in this rapture until they earned a Bond of Unity and underwent initiation. The manual emphasized what the fraternity expected of a pledge. She needed to maintain good grades, perform her duties in good spirits, represent Phi Mu properly in dress, and show the Phi sisters her full interest.[2]

Smith soon realized that pledging Phi Mu was going to involve activities that Phi Mu headquarters did not have in mind. The chapter required her to do things that violated the policies of the university and of the national. She got her first clue that this would be the case when members told the pledges to make forbidden pledge books—notebooks with handcrafted, decorative covers. Inside were pages for interviews with fifty-two Phi Mu sisters. The back was reserved for required signatures. The Phi Mu pledge manual stressed that provisional members were to get to know the initiated members through ordinary social discourse. The headquarters and Widener forbade pledges to perform servile tasks to get interviews and signatures. According to the rules of the local chapter, said Smith, pledges were expected to spend two hours most days with Phi Mu sisters in the sorority house, residence halls, and personal apartments.

Although the house was dry by national decree, sisters served pledges small amounts of alcohol from the outset. Members and pledges drank openly, and several took snapshots. Smith said she took a couple of mouthfuls of champagne. All sang "I've Loved These Days" and linked arms. Smith wasn't bothered, but she was surprised that rules were being broken. "As my pledge class and I walked from the house to the library for our first study time, we contemplated the rules and decided that if that was all that we had to do, pledging would not be so bad," Smith said.[3]

Smith's second meeting with the Widener Phi Mus mirrored the first. She drank more champagne, accepted flowers and a pledge pin, and joined the members in song. The pledges visited member after member the first two weeks. Nothing untoward occurred, and the two weeks of pledging were representative of the full pledging term of many sorority chapter programs, which are hazing-free, or at least relatively so. "They treated her like gold," said Judy Smith, Amanda's mother.[4]

But then Amanda Smith began to suspect that she had chosen the wrong Widener sorority to pledge. The Phis dressed up on Wednesdays, and she considered the custom akin to a finishing-school activity. They raised eyebrows at her preppy look; she thought their black outfits funereal. She resented having to put in three hours at a mandatory study hall at the library, saying she could manage her own academic affairs. Meals had to be taken at the Phi Mu table in the Widener cafeteria. Smith also noticed a change in pledging requirements during the third week. The sisters now wanted conformity from members of the pledge class. They told the prospective members to dress alike and to wear their hair in ponytails. Pairs of pledges interviewed members. They sat on the floor while the interviewee talked to them from a couch, as if she were royalty. Pledges had to say hello to every member they encountered, looking away as a sign of deference.

One evening the pledges hurried to the entrance of the sorority house in high spirits. They wore jeans, tee shirts, and tennis shoes.

A member opened the door, shrilly scolded the pledges for being late, and slammed the door in their faces. Uncertain of what to do, the pledges stayed outside. After the pledges had endured a long wait, the "Phi mom" opened the door. A phalanx of members awaited them inside the main room. The members' demeanor had changed. Orders flew. The pledges were told to stand in line, then to stand in line on top of their pledge books.

The yelling grew louder. Members criticized pledges' clothes, shoes, and jewelry. A member stuck her face next to a pledge's nose. She told the pledges they were supposed to be one pledge class, to look, act, dress, and speak as one.

Members barraged pledges with conflicting orders. One member told a pledge to look down, not at her. Another member screamed at the pledge for not meeting her eyes when they talked.

Smith's features began to reveal her stress. Members told the pledges that they were a disgrace and that their pledge class's attitude "sucked." The sisters ordered pledges into a chapter room ordinarily used for house meetings. Anyone who lagged was pushed. The members retreated, leaving pledges in a candlelit room. The pledges complained to each other about this rotten treatment. As they did so, two Phi members popped up from a hiding place behind a couch. They recited a litany of all the transgressions the class had committed collectively and individually. The pledges were cocky, rude, inconsiderate, greedy, disrespectful. They seemed to think they were going to be given their sisterhood on a black and gold platter.

The two demanded that Amanda Smith recite the Greek alphabet. She wondered how they knew she had memorized it. Had a member milked a fellow pledge for information? "Alpha, Gamma, Delta. . . ." Amanda rushed through the alphabet. The sisters ordered the pledge sisters to join her. When they could not, the sisters berated Amanda. She had held out on the class. Upstaged her mates. Been selfish. Hadn't given a rat's tail about whether her sisters learned what they needed.

Next the members noticed that Amanda's pledge pin was missing. She had lost it while visiting her mother. Other sisters came in and led two blindfolded pledges out at a time. They took Amanda and another pledge out the door, across a floor, up many stairs. The pledges were ordered to the floor. The blindfold was yanked from Amanda's eyes, and she found herself in an unlit room. A flashlight beam shone in her face. Sisters fired questions at her. The pledges' answers were wrong, stupid, inane. Smith and her pledge sister were so hopeless, they didn't belong in Phi Mu. Members put the two on their feet and blindfolded them again. People screamed at them to get out. A member led Amanda and her pledge sister to another room that the Phi mom was watching over. Pledges were holding hands and staring at lit candles. The Phi mom asked what the pledges had learned. The pledges spoke in subdued voices. Their arrogant taking for granted of the kindness and courtesy of the members during the first two weeks of pledging had provoked the wrath of the sisterhood, concluded one pledge. Cocky, disrespectful, and disorganized, they had failed to show the commitment needed to become true Phi Mus.

The mom nodded and displayed sympathy, suggesting that the pledges spend the night together and collectively promise to do better. A pledge told her that they would work harder so that the yelling would end and the sisters wouldn't become so angry. At this point, one of Amanda's pledge sisters rebelled. She'd had enough of being yelled at by undergraduate women. She quit.

The Phi Mu mom went to see the pledge. All would be well if she would only wait things out. The mistreatment was not meant as abuse but had meaning she would understand when she became a sister herself. The pledge returned her pledge book, pin, and related paraphernalia. After her departure, some members promised the rest of the pledges that things would be even harder in the future. The pledge class was given more duties, more requirements, and more sorority jargon to memorize. Pledges were to strike "no" from their vocabulary. Instead of "no," or even "know," they were to say "negative."

Every morning pledges brought the day's cafeteria menu and a weather report to the sisters who wanted them. They decorated posters, stayed up late to write the lyrics to songs about pledging, and created portraits of each sister. Mostly, pledges had to clean the members' rooms and living quarters. "We were essentially slaves to the sisters," said Amanda.[5]

Two members used a pledge to play tic-tac-toe. The pledge carried the game sheet back and forth from one sister's apartment to another's room in the sorority house until the game ended. "All of the tasks that the sisters asked of us do not sound bad one by one, but when there are fifty-two sisters and only nine of you, it is impossible to keep everyone happy," said Amanda.[6] Off doing fools' errands, she began missing classes and arriving late to lectures. Her grades dropped. Instead of class material, Amanda memorized minutiae about each sister, another activity forbidden by the school and headquarters. One night the pledge class assembled in formation. Members directed questions at their backs, demanding that pledges name sisters' fiancés, their favorite mixed drinks, and other details.

Even when a pledge answered correctly, the members expressed anger if the class failed to respond in unison. A wrong answer brought a new punishment that meant more sleep deprivation. The ignorant pledge would have to write the correct answer dozens of times by the next morning. A sister asked the pledges to hold hands without letting go, then demanded that they put out a hand to receive drink coasters from her. Unable to do both, the pledges kept holding hands. "She stuck [the coasters] down the back of our pants," said Amanda. "We were told to squeeze our butt cheeks together to keep them up."[7]

The pledges tried to comply, wriggling this way and that. The sister watching demanded that they stop, saying the display was making her sick.

Amanda's phone conversations with her mother began to reflect her strain. Mrs. Smith sensed her daughter becoming reserved and distant. Concerned, Mrs. Smith asked Amanda to come home for a visit. Amanda said the sorority would not let her leave.

Out of self-preservation, Amanda stopped answering her phone. She looked around to make sure no sisters were nearby before leaving a school building. Some nights she grabbed only three or four hours of sleep. "When I finally did get to bed, I was so upset over what had happened that day and so frightened over what tomorrow would bring, I could not sleep soundly," she said.[8]

When Amanda finally came home at spring break, she resembled a cornered rabbit, said Judy Smith, a Baltimore hairdresser. "Who is abusing you?" Mrs. Smith asked Amanda. Mrs. Smith said she was perplexed at first. Her son had pledged a fraternity some years before Amanda and had not been hazed. He still loved attending alumni events.

Amanda refused to quit, telling her mother she was determined to finish pledging. Not long after, Amanda brought some of her pledge-mates home. "They were all exhausted, much more than normal college students would be," said Mrs. Smith.[9]

When Amanda returned, some members said that her clothing, makeup, and trademark preppy barrette were a disgrace to Phi Mu. She drew a line, refusing to wear her hair in the style many sisters preferred. Members retaliated, saying they would never sign the pledge book, even tearing their pages out. Amanda and the pledges found themselves apologizing so often that some sisters forbade them to say "I'm sorry" again. Instead, they were to say they'd had a momentary lapse of reason.

Another rule was introduced. Pledges had to purchase gum and cigarettes for the members. Amanda estimated that the class spent about $150 altogether. Most of the money was earned at pledge pretzel and cookie fund raisers. Sometimes pledges had to use their own money.

One night members were in for another surprise. "We were told how much we sucked and how we would never get it together," said Amanda. "We were then pushed down the stairs into a pitch-dark basement where we were told to stand in our lineup, holding hands and looking at the floor."[10]

When the sisters pushed, a couple of pledges broke the chain and were scolded.

Members holding candles came downstairs, grouped together by pledge class. The first to arrive was the most senior group, followed by the next most senior, and so on. The pledges had to listen for a voice, then name all the women who had been in that person's pledge class. Missing even one name—even if that member had left school—evoked the fury of some sisters. "Just because they aren't here doesn't mean they're not important," said the members.

Some alumnae also came to this event, said Amanda, and they thoroughly confused the captives with their voices, which no pledge could identify. "[Alumnae] told us how disrespectful it was that we did not know who they were, but that we would know them by the end of the night, because they were going to take us on a hell ride that we would never forget."[11]

The last group to arrive was made up of the sorority's youngest members. Many had encouraged women in Amanda's class to pledge. They screamed about how presumptuous the pledges had been to assume that a friendship had existed between them. Nerves sanded raw, the pledge class waited in the basement. Another group arrived. These were the pledges' big sisters. They changed the mood and comforted the pledges. Afterwards members herded the pledges to the nearby house of Phi Mu's unofficial brother fraternity, Alpha Tau Omega. "Cry Little Sister" from the *Lost Boys* soundtrack played as sisters took them into the basement. The Phi pledges approached the ATO pledges, who were already lined up.

A member screamed out a now familiar command: "Nose, tits, and toes!" Amanda's class pressed their bodies against the wall.

Several fraternity members questioned the pledge sisters. A young brother who was a friend of Amanda's encouraged her instead of abusing her.

As if trying to show off their tough demeanor, some sorority women harangued their pledges. Amanda began to cry. The member was disdainful, telling Amanda she wasn't enduring half the abuse that previous pledge classes had survived.

The Phi mom ordered the pledges to turn around. Nine ATO members smiled at them. The pledges now had big brothers. Pairing soror-ity pledges and fraternity men in this way is a custom that has been discontinued at many universities because of past abuses and the pos-sibilities of abuse. Many schools have also dropped the little sister con-cept. In an article published in *Gender & Society*, author Mindy Stombler described a slave sale of little sisters during which fraternity males cheered at women simulating sexual acts onstage. Esther Wright, au-thor of *Torn Togas*, described a rape by male Greeks of three passed-out pledges. The act outraged her as a sorority member, but she failed to report it at the time; as a little sister herself, she narrowly escaped be-ing sexually assaulted by a member of the fraternity that had selected her.[12]

But nothing inappropriate occurred. The rest of the night was pleas-ant, recalled Amanda. Soon afterwards, however, she went to clean a sister's apartment and was asked to name the chapter's executive board members. After Amanda botched one name, the sister called the board member. Amanda apologized over the phone. The director ordered her to drop to the fetal position on the floor and to rock back and forth while singing "Row, Row, Row Your Boat."

Another time a sister forced Amanda to hop up and down and make barnyard sounds. Fed up, she and the others in the pledge class defied the sisters and left campus to go to their respective homes. After Amanda took a sister's phone call and cried, Judy Smith refused to put any more callers through. Mrs. Smith told her daughter she had to quit. Amanda refused, saying that her pledge sisters would suffer.

The pledges returned on Sunday. Instead of punishing the pledges, a member announced that the house rules had been suspended. A field representative from Phi Mu headquarters was about to visit. Pledges were to continue visiting the members' apartments but were to stop groveling at the house. A member made fun of the central office's naiveté, saying that the older women imagined that the prospective members were enjoying "sundae parties" and milk-and-cookies events. Lest the pledges get any bold ideas, a member announced that the price of tattling was expulsion. The representative arrived and found each member acting charming. On her first night in the house, the representative went to bed early. Had she walked through the house in the middle of the night, she would have seen the pledges practicing dance steps and a song for an upcoming Greek Week performance.

Greek Week came. The pledge class performed a timid and stiff rendition of the "Banana Boat Song," failing to win. The members yelled at the pledges, then took them to a social event with other Greeks. Pledges were told to stay until the last member left.

Amanda had a test in chemistry the next day. She took it, knowing there was no chance that she would pass, and at dinnertime went to the cafeteria. A member was waiting. No pledges were to eat. Instead they had to go to the house to take part in skits. Pledges had to act out whatever name the members had given them. Amanda played the role of the fictional character "Punky" Brewster.

Afterwards the pledges went to the Greek Week festivities, where they sold pretzels to raise money. Famished, Amanda ate some broken pretzels. Later that night at the Phi house, she fainted. A pledge put a Reese's Cup between her lips. Another warmed instant noodles. Members asked why Amanda had never informed them about her health problem. "I never had a problem before," she responded.

A pledge retreat was scheduled for the next weekend. Amanda looked forward to sorting things out with fellow pledges while making pledge paddles for the big sisters, a requirement she regarded as a labor of love. But the members announced that the retreat had been canceled. Pledges had to suffer the consequences of not spending enough time with members. The pledges staged a mutiny and spent a quiet weekend together, returning to the house on Sunday night. "All of you are standing there so self-righteously, but you don't understand that everything we have done has a meaning and a purpose," an officer rebuked them. "When you are sisters, you will understand."

The other member began to cry. "You are ruining our sorority," she said to the pledges. "We are the strongest sorority on campus, and the reason we are is because we have all been through what you are going through. The older sisters will not respect you if you do not go through everything they went through."

The pledges conceded defeat. At dinner some members refused to talk to them. The shunning was the last straw for Amanda. She couldn't eat and went back to her room. A roommate found her "shaking and crying," said Judy Smith. On her mother's recommendation, Amanda went to see her doctor, who found her mental state altered for the worse.[13] Blood tests revealed hypoglycemia.

Furious, Judy Smith called the school and the national. She was the second mother to complain that semester. When they arrived at home, the Smiths listened to a woman's voice on Mrs. Smith's answering machine, telling Amanda to watch her back. In an interview, Amanda said she had asked an administrator for protection, but he told her she wouldn't need it. Amanda moved out of the residence hall. Although Judy Smith drove her from Baltimore to school to take final examinations, the semester was a washout. Amanda's grades were abysmal. On at least one occasion, Judy Smith and a Phi Mu member exchanged angry words. Mrs. Smith then called a Phi Mu executive. The woman promised to look into the charges. The executive never phoned back, said Judy Smith. Shortly afterwards, the pledges were initiated without Amanda.

In the fall of 1996, Amanda enrolled at the University of Maryland's Baltimore County (UMB) campus. Unable to focus, becoming upset whenever she saw a UMB woman wearing a Phi Mu sweatshirt, she failed every class. She said she began to suffer flashbacks. "Many nights I have held her when she woke up from night terrors," her mother said.[14]

Just getting out of bed and making it to class became a challenge. Amanda consulted a specialist, who said she was suffering from post-traumatic stress disorder. Unable to press criminal charges against Phi Mu for "only" mental hazing, Amanda retained attorney Douglas Fierberg and launched a civil suit, maintaining, among other things, that published materials by the college and sorority give the impression that Greek groups that haze will be held accountable for their actions. "There is nothing that can compensate [for what] I have lost because of this incident, but I hope that I can stop it from happening to someone else," said Amanda.[15]

During the fall of 1998, Phi Mu headquarters suddenly yanked the charter at Widener after a new pledge class made allegations, said Fierberg in November 1998.[16] Widener and Phi Mu authorities began looking into allegations made by one or more pledges that a new class had been made to fulfill pledging requirements that were out of line with university and national sorority rules.

On May 13, 1999, the attorney representing Amanda Smith confirmed that a verbal agreement had been reached with Phi Mu headquarters, although formal wording of the terms was not yet set in stone, and the agreement was not yet signed. According to Fierberg, if the agreement is signed, the Widener chapter will lose its charter, three Widener chapter members will lose Phi Mu membership for hazing Amanda, and Amanda will receive compensation for medical bills and tuition. Judy Smith, reached by phone, said that her daughter's condition had worsened, which took away some of her joy that a settlement had been reached. Craig Loundas, in an e-mail message of May 13, 1999, confirmed that he no longer worked at Widener. He said "respectfully" that "it would be inappropriate" for him to tell the details behind his sudden departure from the institution until a full settlement is reached. "Although I am no longer employed by Widener University, I support the institution and its policies on not condoning hazing," said Loundas. Likewise, Fierberg was unable to supply information about Loundas's leavetaking, saying that Amanda's agreement with Widener was "confidential." Judy Smith, however, said that she had read Loundas's depositions in the case, and that she and Amanda found the university's initial handling of her daughter's hazing allegations against Phi Mu to be wholly unsatisfactory.

If the agreement is signed, Amanda's civil suit will be studied by fraternal law experts, because it may well be the first significant financial settlement resulting from psychic wounding during mental hazing.

ORIGINS OF SORORITIES

Alpha Delta Pi (formerly the Adelphean Society) claims to be the first secret society for women. It originated in Georgia at Wesleyan Female College (now Wesleyan College) in 1851. Pi Beta Phi (founded 1867) and Kappa Alpha Theta (founded 1870) are also sometimes said to be the first such society because they were closer in structure and philosophy to the male Greek groups. Alpha Delta Pi and its rival female Philomathean Society (later the first chapter of Phi Mu fraternity) operated during an era in which female college students were often between about thirteen and eighteen years old. These teenagers were homesick for their families living far away.

Because few men in the nineteenth century thought their daughters' education important, women who attended college tended to be financially well off. The rise in the popularity of sororities can be traced to protective parents' deduction that sorority-house life provided a better moral atmosphere for the female undergraduate than did the average rooming house. Most female undergraduates were sexually inexperienced, and their professors, who also acted as chaperones, made sure that they would remain that way while they were in school.

Sorority chapters did not spread as rapidly as chapters of the first fraternities. Young female collegians visited other colleges less freely than did their male counterparts. Nor did women recruit other young women for membership during the Civil War, the way fraternity males did. Not until the late nineteenth century did fraternity chapters for women find acceptance on multiple U.S. campuses.

Early female societies served a fairly defined purpose. They provided members with a sense of identity. In each other's company, members could talk and laugh with little restraint, discussing books and poems, reading their own essays and poetry, and building a support group. They shared secrets and ideas. And like other fraternal groups, sororities created elaborate rituals, designed badges, and shared secret phrases.

It appears that women began hazing other women around the time the first sororities were formed, but their behavior was never life-threatening or particularly demeaning. When seven women founded Alpha Chi Omega at DePauw University in 1885, their first initiation "in accordance with the customs then prevalent among college students . . . was composed largely of 'stunts' and a 'courage test,'" according to the fraternity's history. Degrees reminiscent of Masonic degrees became part of initiation during the following year, and gradually the initiation ceremony acquired other serious rituals, but silly requirements remained part of the otherwise solemn initiation for about the next twenty-five years.[17]

Women joining these first Greek-letter societies were reminded not to disgrace themselves, lest they bring shame on their sorority. During the first half of the twentieth century, "conduct unbecoming a member of the fraternity, intoxication, indiscreet conduct with men, and dishonesty" merited expulsion, according to the National Council policies of Alpha Chi Omega.[18]

Researcher J. F. Scott found that sorority activities were designed to keep sorority women away from men whom their parents would have considered undesirable mates. Practices such as float building, special Greek Weeks, and Greek activities during Homecoming minimized the contact sorority women had with nonfraternity males, who tended to be poorer than dues-paying fraternity males, found Scott.[19] And as *Men in Groups* author Lionel Tiger has found, fraternities that threw parties attracting the largest number of physically attractive sorority members were in turn accorded status by other males on campus.[20]

Because women who attended state colleges learned about academic subjects instead of about etiquette, as had nineteenth-century women who attended finishing schools and seminaries, sororities' emphasis on social graces pleased many parents. For much of the twentieth century, female fraternities made sure that their members learned banquet manners, stooped to play to the male ego in a discussion, and (by the 1920s) smoked in what was considered a ladylike fashion. (Pledges were usually forbidden to use even moderate amounts of tobacco or alcohol.)

Sorority members began referring to their sorority by its type—often using superficial terms similar to those that male undergraduates used to describe them. For example, one Ball State University sorority still informally calls itself "the pretty girl sorority," according to a recent alum. When a sorority sees itself as accepting only pledges of a certain type, its membership becomes less diverse. Nonetheless, a 1994 study published in the *Journal of College Student Development* revealed that sorority members choose pledges that best fit the sorority's self-promoted image. This has been a problem since at least the early '30s.[21] During the 1932–1933 school year, 3,231 Ohio State University women signed up for sorority rush, but only 231 (7 percent) were initiated. A poll taken to find out how OSU sorority women chose new members revealed that assertive, bright, no-frills women that excelled at many women's schools had little chance of getting into a sorority. The criteria for selection seemed more in keeping with the entrance requirements of a finishing school than with those of a university. Two-thirds of the members responding to the OSU poll said that whether or not a pledge was accepted or rejected depended primarily on her personality and her family background. Other important determining factors were what a pledge wore, her perceived reliability, and her charm, poise, financial status, and reputation. Less important considerations were her scholastic and social standing.

Colleges for women such as Vassar, Mount Holyoke, Barnard, Radcliffe, and Bryn Mawr banned sororities and social clubs in the 1930s because such clubs were not open to all undergraduates, or they supposedly took away allegiance for one's alma mater. A number of educators also opposed collegiate sororities because they considered them to be counter to the purposes of getting an education. Throughout the 1940s, all it took to put an end to female social clubs on some campuses was the objection of a single powerful president or dean of students. Criticisms leveled against sororities in 1949 by the University of Kansas chancellor attacked their "conformance in dress, in hair styling, in social preparation, in taking the usual easy courses on which adequate notes exist in the chapter house files."[22]

Some academics in the 1940s objected to female fraternities for reasons that sound similar to those voiced by critics of the women's movement in the 1960s and 1970s. That is, they objected to women's forming groups, seeing such women as a strong political unit capable of speaking with one national conservative voice—which they were.

Nonetheless, getting involved in controversial issues could put one's sorority membership in jeopardy. Writer Rita Mae Brown claimed that she received a dismissal letter in a Delta Delta Delta silver, gold, and blue envelope after she immersed herself in the civil rights movement.[23] Today, literature distributed by the National Panhellenic Conference (NPC) and by many national sororities trumpets the advantages of diversity. Some sorority members embrace many of the beliefs associated with the feminist movement. Sororities today are committed to supporting "awareness and education" about societal problems, women's issues, and topics such as bulimia that formerly would have been avoided as taboo, according to Marilyn Bullock, national vice president of Kappa Kappa Gamma.[24]

Not everything has changed, though. While some undergraduate sorority women manage to overcome group pressures and to date males who do not belong to fraternities, many Greek females continue to date Greek males, according to Albert Harrison and Esther Wright.[25] Simply talking to non-Greeks was enough to incite disapproval, Esther Wright recounts, speaking of her experience as a sorority member at the University of Southern California in her book *Torn Togas*. Sororities such as hers pressured members to date Greek males.[26]

Sorority hazing existed before 1970, but no deaths were reported until a member perished that year when pledges tried to abandon her in the countryside. Both sororities and fraternities posed for photographs depicting actions that are today considered hazing. These photos were often published in school yearbooks. They trivialized potentially life-threatening practices and show that college administrators once looked the other way when hazing occurred on and off campus. This photo of Zeta Tau Alpha female fraternity is from an Indiana University yearbook. Real-life physical hazing is rarer in sororities than it is in fraternities, but occasional incidents continue to make headlines and to demonstrate a need for awareness programs on college campuses.
Photo courtesy of Indiana University Archives, Bloomington, Indiana

THE DEATH OF A SORORITY WOMAN

While sororities lag far behind fraternities in terms of the number of hazing incidents for which they are responsible and in terms of the severity of the injuries these incidents cause, hazing cases in the '90s have been numerous enough to make field representatives much more vigilant than they once were when they inspect individual chapter houses. During the first half of the twentieth century, there was more evidence of female hazing taking place and of kangaroo courts being held at all-female colleges than in sororities. Reports of hazing among

Donna Bedinger (*top row, fourth from left*), a member of Alpha Gamma Rho, died tragically when pledges dropped her off in the countryside miles from Eastern Illinois University. No charges were brought by the prosecuting attorney, who, coincidentally, had earlier fought to outlaw hazing in his own fraternity after a pledge suffered a head injury. Those pictured with Bedinger in this photograph are members, not pledges.
Photo courtesy of Eastern Illinois Special Collections Department

sorority members were rare; when complaints did arise, pledges described hazing as consisting mainly of lineups and said that they were required to do errands and housecleaning. Because college administrators and national officers generally considered female fraternities more responsible than male fraternities, it is possible that some hazing was overlooked because deans were not expecting to find out about it, and because it was unlikely to cause injury or death. As of the late 1960s, not a single female sorority member or pledge had lost her life because of hazing.

But in the 1960s some sorority chapters began to haze, and some pledge classes sought mild revenge for hazing occurrences. For example, at the University of Florida, after Rita Mae Brown's Delta Delta Delta pledge class of twenty was taken on a road trip, the pledges pelted members with water balloons and put laxatives into pudding. "Our pledge class quickly gained a reputation for giving as good as we got," noted Brown in her autobiography.

In March 1970, on a back road three miles from Eastern Illinois University, Alpha Gamma Delta pledges dumped Donna Bedinger and a second sister in the countryside. As a pledge began to drive away, Bedinger ran a few steps and tried to launch herself onto the moving car's bumper. She miscalculated. Her skull met the pavement, and she died of her injuries days later.

The Coles County official who investigated called her death an accident, and the pledges were not charged. Coincidentally, that official, Stanton Dotson, said in a 1998 interview that when he was an undergraduate, a member of his fraternity had received a head injury. As a consequence, he and other fraternity members outlawed all hazing in the chapter. Dotson said that he thoroughly interviewed the grief-stricken pledges, and that he concluded that nothing they did showed an intent to harm Bedinger that would have resulted in criminal penalties' being assessed.

Although several women belonging to national female fraternities have died in accidents or while intoxicated, and one local sorority pledge has perished in an initiation, Bedinger remains the only NPC chapter member known to have died while engaged in a forbidden pledging activity. Maureen Syring of the NPC said that sororities now universally condemn so-called "pledge sneaks" as dangerous and inappropriate responses to hazing. The national office of Alpha Gamma Delta failed to respond to mailed and faxed requests for an interview regarding Bedinger and its "Seeing Through the Haze" anti-hazing program, which the NPC's Lissa Bradford regards as an excellent educational tool.

Like Alpha Gamma Delta, some national sororities continue to shy away from media interviews regarding hazing incidents. "Too many sororities still have the attitude that their members are in finishing schools," said Louis Ingelhart, an authority on student press law and the First Amendment, in a 1998 telephone interview for this book. "They don't want anyone thinking their women are capable of doing some of the things they are doing."

Other sorority leaders say they are not naïve; they just have high standards. "We expect our members to join the [female] fraternity with a commitment to upholding our standards throughout their lifetimes," said Marilyn Bullock.[27]

State universities have likewise occasionally shielded the identities of sororities in hazings, citing privacy concerns that Ingelhart said are not legally valid since the public has a right to know about such matters. In 1998 a North Carolina appeals court ruled that the University of North Carolina, Chapel Hill, had a duty to keep its student judiciary hearing results from the *Daily Tar Heel* student newspaper, citing the Family Educational Rights and Privacy Act. In the immediate future, until and unless a federal court ruling on the so-called Buckley Amendment ends state-by-state conflicting interpretations, universities will continue to tell individual newspapers and organizations such as Security on Campus that collegiate judiciary rulings—even at public universities—fall outside the public's right to know.[28]

Computer and library searches for incidents involving sorority hazing in NPC groups indicate that far more such incidents were reported from 1988 to 1998 than from 1977 to 1987. Many national magazines and large newspapers have published articles about the perceived increase in hazing in NPC sororities. However, rather than suggesting that such activities are actually becoming more common, the rise may reflect women's tendency to report all types of harassment more readily than they would have a decade or more ago. For now, media attention usually focuses on the rarity of physical hazing in sororities, although that may change if criminal hazing among women begins to become problematic, as have other reported crimes committed by women that were once almost the exclusive domain of males and which, at least according to reports, are on the increase.

More worrisome are a number of incidents in which sorority women have died or were injured while swilling liquor in alcohol-related falls in fraternity houses, and in alcohol-related automobile accidents. The first reports of alcohol overdoses among sorority members were made in 1982 and involved some women associated with Alpha Delta Phi and Delta Pi at the University of Southern California. Though few such deaths and injuries have occurred to date, the trend is still troubling.

Auburn's President Muse, who occasionally addresses conventions of international sororities, said that his own experiences have led him to conclude that while sororities continue to be an asset on campus, they nonetheless must share the blame for fraternal drinking's exploding out of hand. "The greatest impact on the behavior of the young [fraternity] men on the campus could be had by the young [sorority] women," said Muse. "If they would simply say that these are standards of behavior we will not condone and that we will not have anything to do with fraternities that abuse alcohol or engage in [bad] behavior it would be the most significant thing anybody can do on the campus. By not doing that, by continuing to participate fully, whether they are the ones to abuse alcohol or not, they are enablers. There is no more influence on an eighteen- or nineteen-year-old boy or man than whether the women around think he's cool or not."

In 1997, the *Chronicle of Higher Education* reported that sorority leaders were alarmed by a rash of sorority incidents, including physical and verbal hazing at the University of Georgia and a hazing-related auto accident at Hamilton College.[29] All sororities have educational programs whose purpose is to reduce sorority members' drinking, and all national sororities insist that their chapters maintain dry houses. The NPC's Maureen Syring said that the national organizations work hard to provide hazing- and drug-and-alcohol–awareness programs.

Syring cautioned, however, that hazing researchers needed to separate NPC hazing incidents from those occurring in non-NPC sororities (i.e., local sororities and historically African American sororities that do not belong to the NPC), stressing that NPC leaders cannot control or punish organizations outside their jurisdiction. For example, Hamilton College in New York suspended Phi Beta Chi, a local sorority, after authorities linked an automobile accident with hazing that took place at the sorority in 1997. In spite of national sororities' efforts to curb hazing, some troubling incidents have occurred, including the following:

◆ In 1994, Sigma Delta Tau was booted off the C. W. Post campus in New York for three years after being found guilty of alcohol abuse, severe physical hazing, hog-tying pledges, and threatening pledges who went to authorities.

◆ In the mid- and late 1990s, hazing allegations drew media attention to Eastern Illinois University (Delta Sigma Theta), Northern Arizona University (the coeducational Arnold Air Society), Oakland University (Chi Upsilon), Huston-Tillotson College (Krimson Kourt), and Texas Christian University (Chi Omega).

◆ In 1995, the death of a Bloomsburg University Chi Sigma Rho pledge was narrowly averted after she consumed a potentially lethal amount of liquor.

◆ A Chi Omega pledge at Indiana University broke her wrist after leaving the Sigma Alpha Epsilon house following a traditional drinking night during which Greek pledges were paired up with pledge mothers and fathers.

◆ A Kappa Kappa Gamma pledge at Denison University was hospitalized after consuming too much alcohol.

◆ In 1995, the Texas Cowgirls, a spirit club, ordered five new women to bring a large quantity of alcohol to their initiation.

◆ In 1998, at the State University of New York (SUNY), Albany Alpha Omicron Pi members required a pledge to drink at a mixer being co-sponsored with Sigma Alpha Epsilon. The pledge collapsed and was taken to St. Peter's Hospital.

◆ In 1998, five years after a school crackdown on drinking at the University of Idaho, Gamma Phi Beta sorority strongly encouraged pledges to drink.

◆ In 1998, at Indiana University (IU), Kappa Delta sorority was found to have served pledges small amounts of alcohol during drinking games with members of an IU fraternity, Delta Tau Delta, said Dean Richard McKaig after the incident was exposed on the air by WTHR-TV in Indianapolis.[30]

◆ A number of sorority women have died or been hurt in falls, in many of which alcohol was a factor. In recent years these deaths and injuries have included the paralysis of a University of Idaho student at the Alpha Phi house, the death of a drunk Kappa Alpha Theta sorority pledge at a University of Colorado sorority party, the death of a University of New Hampshire sorority member in her alcohol-impaired sorority sister's car, and the death of a Clemson female student in a fall from a third-floor ledge in the Alpha Tau Omega fraternity house.

Recent studies indicate that women today are accustomed to drinking more alcohol, more frequently, than women used to. After a 1994 survey of alcohol use by students was conducted, Core Institute codirector Philip W. Meilman said that alcohol abuse was a problem for women as well as for men, and that "serious" problem drinking was a worrisome national trend. The survey found that just over half of all college males and nearly four out of ten females had indulged in binge drinking in the two weeks before they responded to the survey questions. In 1994, Indiana University researcher Ruth Engs and SUNY, Potsdam, researcher David Hanson found that heavy drinking on the part of female college students had been rising steadily since the two began examining collegians' drinking habits in 1981. In view of such evidence, and to keep the number of tragedies involving women from shooting up, national sororities have stepped up their efforts to educate female undergraduates about drinking dangers.

Some young women have died because they were vulnerable to peer pressure from male friends who urged them to drink. An eighteen-year-old non-Greek nearly died in 1996 after drinking sixteen shots because two Duquesne University fraternity males urged her to do so. And Radford University student Valerie Cole, age eighteen, died in 1996 with a blood-alcohol level of 0.31 after drinking heavily at the Chi Phi and Pi Kappa Phi fraternity houses.

While there has been no survey conducted to determine whether hazing by sororities has increased in tandem with increased alcohol consumption, the number of incidents being reported by newspapers has certainly jumped. During the decade between 1988 and 1998, female hazing activities in NPC sororities included lineups, brandings, kidnappings, simulated sex acts, and the encouragement of drinking by members.

In separate interviews, Loser and Syring said that anecdotal evidence suggests that mental hazing is the form of hazing most often engaged in by sorority members. In the '90s, however, Loser has seen more reports of physical hazing. She asked, "When it comes to hazing, are women less creative than men? I think not." In a 1998 article she wrote for Pi Beta Phi's magazine *The Arrow,* Jean W. Scott lamented real-life sorority members' practices, for example:

◆ Strapping bottles to pledges' arms until all the liquor is consumed

◆ Visiting pledges at 2:00 A.M. to check to make sure pledges have their pledge pins, ask trivia questions, and make pledges drink shots of alcohol as a penalty for blowing answers

◆ Forcing pledges to wear wet tee shirts while reading pornography to males

◆ Assembling into a panel and asking pledges to reveal their sexual histories

◆ Conducting scavenger hunts that require pledges to visit potentially dangerous locales such as the men's room in an empty stadium.

Such incidents notwithstanding, accepted research suggests that women are less aggressive than men. Researchers Alice H. Eagly and Valerie J. Steffen's psychological comparison of aggression in men and women found no category in which female aggression reached the level of male aggression. Nor were females as likely as males to inflict pain or injury, according to their comparison. Their research may support sorority executives' assertions that hazing deaths are far less likely to occur in local and national female sororities than are hazing deaths in male fraternal and athletic groups. On the other hand, the Carnegie Corporation of New York reported a startling rise in violence among girls in gangs that researchers said were similar to violent acts perpetrated by members of male gangs.

Even though hazing acts perpetrated by women in sororities—or at least reports of those acts—may be on the rise, the fact that no female has died as a result of hazing in the last twenty years should reassure sorority leaders that their education programs may be reaching receptive ears. However, sorority members' increased alcohol use in recent years suggests that complacency on the part of educators and sorority leaders is ill advised. Sorority executives, in particular, need to remind their chapters never to participate in hazing rituals when males are present. They should also continue to discourage sorority members from becoming little sisters to male fraternities, since the hazing of little sisters has long been problematic. Finally, on campuses where some physical hazing involving women has been uncovered, educators and sorority leaders need to take rigorous action lest high-status sororities feel obliged to haze the way fraternity males have done.

7

The Law and Hazing

BURNING TO BELONG

Kappa Kappa Gamma is an international female fraternity with 127 chapters. The national fraternity, which is considered one of the pioneers of sorority life, was founded in 1870 at Monmouth College in Illinois. Kappa has initiated nearly 180,000 members, according to Marilyn Bullock, a national vice president. "Every chapter seeks to nurture individual development reflected in high levels of scholastic achievement, student organization leadership and athletic accomplishments," said Bullock.

In the fall of 1997, the national Kappa Kappa Gamma office considered the DePauw Kappas an exemplary chapter. The 129 members of Kappa at DePauw included the student body president and the campus panhellenic president. The group's GPA had risen recently, and members included three women who had been accepted for membership in Phi Beta Kappa. Twenty DePauw Kappas were on the dean's list, and twelve played varsity sports.

The DePauw chapter's nationally covered hazing controversy began on November 6, 1997, the night some Kappa members who considered themselves a "family" within the chapter planned to carry out

Jessica Zimmerman (*shown in high school graduation photo*) was burned with a cigarette as part of an illicit ritual conducted by some Kappa Kappa Gamma members at DePauw University. Her mother, Cindie Zimmerman (*right*), became a vocal opponent of hazing, and Jessica eventually quit DePauw. Kappa Kappa Gamma chapters long ago prided themselves on being small, close-knit units of about 20 females, but today's chapters frequently have more than 100 members. The DePauw chapter Zimmerman pledged had a number of smaller units that called themselves "families." Ironically, Kappa Kappa Gamma national publications have been vocal about condemning hazing.
Photo courtesy of Cindie Zimmerman

an unorthodox ritual that had taken place each year over the past three years. The pressure on students to belong to a Greek group is probably more intense at a campus such as DePauw, which is 78 percent Greek, than it is at some other campuses, said Fierberg.[1] Some who pledge do so because their parents, grandparents, and other relatives were part of the Greek system. Consciously or unconsciously, these alumni have pressured young family members to continue this tradition as a "legacy." When your grandmother and mother were members of the sorority you are pledging, "dropping out of the house can be devastating," said Mark Freeman, director of DePauw police, in a March 1998 interview.

Early in the evening, some Kappa big sisters hooked up with their little sisters at different meeting paces. Pledge Jessica Zimmerman met her big sister, Sarah McKinney, at a fraternity house near campus. Zimmerman said that McKinney made her a large drink of something that "tasted like pine trees." McKinney urged Zimmerman to finish the drink because a special sorority event was about to take place at Hogate Hall, a DePauw residence hall used by some Kappa women because booming sorority recruitment had made the house too small to serve all members. A self-described light drinker who backed her claim with the assertion that she had been one of the few people on her [residence hall] floor "who hasn't thrown up," Zimmerman was reluctant to finish the drink, she said in an on-campus interview on February 27, 1998.

McKinney seemed wound up, dropping hints or perhaps a warning that the night was to bring something unexpected, said Zimmerman. McKinney told her it was all right to laugh later if events struck her as a little weird. Zimmerman suspected that a pre-initiation bit of buffoonery might be in the works. Perhaps she would have to don silly clothing—maybe wear her bra on top of her shirt. She was prepared to do anything silly that McKinney asked her to do. Zimmerman said that she "trusted" her big sister. During rush, the sisters had assured potential members that their sorority didn't haze.

The two went to Hogate Hall, where six pledges and thirteen active members waited. Some members wore sheets and were humming like spirits. A member squirted pledges with an oversized mechanical squirt gun. *No big deal,* Zimmerman said she thought at the time. *I can get through this.* But three other pledges indicated that they were uncomfortable with the proceedings. Their big sisters led them from the room. Zimmerman, pledge Damara Karamesines, and one other pledge stayed. The sisters encouraged them to take drinks of Hot Damn and other kinds of alcohol. "It was not poured down our throats; it was more like, here, take more," said Zimmerman in an interview that took place on the DePauw campus on February 27, 1998.

Next, two of the three pledges had to kiss a skull decorated with two racquetballs and something resembling pubic hair, then symbolically castrate a member who wore a fake penis.

McKinney then showed Zimmerman a cigarette burn on her hip. The big sister said the burn was the family's sign, said Zimmerman. The burning signified that those burned were to be admitted into a family within the larger Kappa group. Although the ritual was now four years old, no rumors of it had reached DePauw's Teresa Loser, the administrator said in a 1998 interview at her office.[2]

The three big sisters indicated that the pledges should feel special to have been singled out for this distinction. "It's tradition," one big sister explained, Zimmerman said in an interview. "We're proud to have these on our bodies."[3]

The alcohol was affecting the pledges. Things seemed surreal to Zimmerman. In a fog, she watched one member burn her own hip with a cigarette. Zimmerman's big sister pressured her to do the same.

"I don't deal well with pain," said Zimmerman, who has an aversion to tattoos.

The big sister insisted she take the brand for Kappa and the family.

"Fine, get it over with." said Zimmerman. Her big sister applied the brand. It sizzled and made a mark the size of a dime. The odor of burnt flesh hung in the air. The burning took five to ten seconds, "but it felt like thirty," said Zimmerman. Another member grabbed her hand while the cigarette tip pushed into her hip.

Karamesines and the other pledge were burned with lighted butts, too.

That was just the beginning. The pledges were given more alcohol. One or more big sisters encouraged the pledges to take off some of their clothing and to streak across campus. (In 1998, the DePauw University web site identified streaking around a boulder on the lawn of East Campus as a venerable campus tradition.)[4] After doing this, Zimmerman and Damara Karamesines agreed to grovel for cigarettes at a DePauw fraternity house. The fraternity members seemed uncomfortable with the intoxicated women debasing themselves, said Zimmerman.

The next day Zimmerman sought medical treatment for her burn. A doctor mocked her when he heard the story, she charged. That same day a woman who said she was the mother of a pledge called DePauw authorities to complain that her daughter had been burned. Campus police launched an investigation, as did Kappa national headquarters. The DePauw burning incident became notorious, attracting the notice of newspaper columnists and a TV tabloid news show. The incident involved bright, well-spoken, and popular students from well-to-do families at an institution that prides itself on a long roster of distinguished alums such as Dan Quayle and Vernon Jordan, who as undergraduates were both Greeks. At least one member of the board of directors knew the families of the hazed and the hazers. Some of the families whose daughters were present at the pre-initiation ritual were alums and have donated generously to DePauw.

The burning and subsequent bad publicity stunned Kappa headquarters. "Our first reaction was one of disbelief that quickly turned to dismay as the facts became apparent," said Bullock. "In our 127-year history, we have never confronted a hazing incident of this nature. The event, as reported, is repugnant and is absolutely antithetical to the ideals of Kappa Kappa Gamma. . . . While these incidents are reprehensible, the large majority of Greeks are never involved in them. All Greek groups promote high standards of behavior and support and encourage outstanding academic and civic achievement."[5]

This was the second predominantly white Greek branding incident Loser had had to deal with as a university staff member. She had been the Rutgers University dean of fraternity and sorority affairs in 1991, when Delta Upsilon fraternity served a three-year suspension for branding Greek-letter initials on the buttocks of pledges. Nor was this the first sorority to be accused of branding pledges. A University of Maine sorority, Alpha Chi Omega, was suspended in 1988 after members took pledges to a cemetery, blindfolded them, and ritually branded them with the organization's letters.

Sarah McKinney wrote a letter to the DePauw student paper complaining that she was the real victim in the incident, since acts of hazing were widespread, particularly among fraternities at DePauw.[6] Zimmerman, who quit as a pledge, said she disagreed with the letter, maintaining that she had been suckered into being burned and had been given alcohol to reduce her resistance. Loser also took exception to McKinney's viewpoint. Noting that all members had signed an agreement not to haze, she said the Kappas' punishment was deserved.

DePauw and the Kappa Kappa Gamma national headquarters chastised the big sisters who left Hogate Hall with their little sisters for not reporting the brandings. However, one mother of a member who left to protect her unwilling pledge countered that her daughter had thought she was doing the right thing by leaving and was going against peer pressure even by taking that step.[7] Too often, said Loser, parents urge the university to impose strong controls on the Greeks until they learn their child is in trouble for hazing or an alcohol violation. "Now [they] say] we are picking on [the Greeks]," said Loser.[8] Bullock said that hazing is very specifically addressed by Kappa Kappa Gamma and that real-life examples are given to members to guide them. She said the big sisters should have known that they had a duty to report the burnings. "All of our chapters are given extensive materials and information to acquaint them with the expectations for membership in Kappa Kappa Gamma," said Bullock. She said the sorority sends one consistent message to members, namely that hazing is wrong and that violations will be punished. Not only are members told this in person and in writing, but pledges sign and date an entry in a "Kappa Notebook," agreeing to maintain high standards of conduct and to obey university, sorority, and chapter rules. "We expect our members to join the fraternity with a commitment to upholding our standards throughout their lifetimes," she said.[9]

Kalo Heldt, the mother of a Kappa who had been burned as a pledge and who in turn burned Damara Karamesines, said in a March 1998 telephone conversation with the author that everyone connected to the family had somehow convinced themselves that this tradition was "ordinary." Nothing was done to these pledges that hadn't been done to her daughter, she said. Mrs. Heldt and her husband, a former fraternity member who she said had put up with harsh physical hazing as an undergraduate, flew to Indiana from their California home to speak with school officials. Since hazing had been a part of Greek tradition at DePauw for so long, argued Mrs. Heldt, it was the university's duty and opportunity to educate members, not to punish them.

News reports following the branding indicated that the members would face charges of hazing under Indiana's criminal recklessness statute, but those reports were ultimately wrong. The reports indicated that Kappa Kappa Gamma members Amanda Heldt, Sarah McKinney, and Jennifer T. Miller could serve up to six months in jail if they were found guilty of burning Erin Hogan, Damara Karamesines, and Jessica Zimmerman. However, half a year after the incident took place, Matt Headley, the local prosecuting attorney, said in a March 1998 telephone conversation with the author that he was bringing no alcohol charges because proving who had bought the liquor was very difficult. He also allowed the three women who branded pledges to perform community service instead of going to trial. Headley, who had been a fraternity member at the University of Mississippi, said he was confident that DePauw had punished the hazers sufficiently. He said that political considerations had nothing to do with his decision not to pursue a criminal trial, and that as a part-time prosecutor he had a murder case that was taking a great deal of time to research and prepare.

During school judicial proceedings, one Kappa pleaded guilty and was suspended. Twelve members who were present while all or some of the rituals took place denied responsibility and went before an administrative hearing board made up of two faculty members, two students, and an administrator. Three of the five had Greek affiliations. The board recommended the suspension of the student who admitted her involvement, and of one other student, and minor penalties or warnings for eight other Kappas. But the appeals committee rescinded the expulsions and suspensions, giving the offenders one-semester suspensions and social probation. The tough punishment that Damara's father, Chris Karamesines, said that Greek affairs had promised his daughter had been reduced to little more than a short vacation from school, he said in a 1998 telephone conversation.

Two parents of Kappa members who had been present on the night of the branding disagreed with Mr. Karamesines, saying that the trauma of the ordeal was in itself a tremendous punishment for their daughters.

According to Mr. Karamesines, interviewed in February at his place of business in Muncie, Indiana, the fact that he lacked a college degree and was the owner of a small national pizza parlor chain who had made his own way in the world put him at a disadvantage in trying to get the university president to listen to him. Because the Heldts flew from California to Indiana to meet with the president, he concluded that they had powerful fraternal connections and influence that he could not match. Loser, however, said that all the students were treated equally.[10]

The Kappa Kappa Gamma chapter was also punished, although not to the satisfaction of Chris Karamesines. DePauw placed the chapter on social probation until the fall of 1999 and cut its pledge class in half for two years. DePauw president Robert G. Bottoms noted that the chapter voted to retain the thirteen members involved in the hazing, although some members may have been pressured to vote in a certain way.[11] According to Jessica Zimmerman, that "pressure" included the trashing of the room of a member who wanted those who burned pledges expelled.

"One student moved out after having her room and possessions ransacked," said Bottoms.[12]

Kappas angered by the burnings were intimidated, harassed, and shunned by some Kappas who approved of it, said Zimmerman.[13] Julie Egner, a Kappa pledge who was not present at the burning ritual, quit the sorority in response to the hazing. A Kappa Kappa Gamma member retaliated by leaking a confidential letter Egner had written—at the request of two other women—to the DePauw Panhellenic Council that accused a second sorority of engaging in unfair practices to gain an edge in recruiting pledges, said Egner. The leak embarrassed Egner and kept her from getting into the second sorority. "This situation reeks of illegality," said Egner in a November 1998 interview with the author. She said she planned on leaving DePauw.

"The atmosphere in the [Kappa] house is one of divisiveness and turmoil," said Bottoms in a letter he wrote to the DePauw community. In spite of vandalism and a hostile climate, which Mr. Karamesines said seemed to invite a confrontation, the president refused to shut down the house.[14] Nor did the national sorority do so, although it did expel some members, whose names it refused to provide, as a matter of policy.

CRIMINAL AND NONCRIMINAL HAZING OFFENSES

Anyone writing a hazing policy may find it useful to define specific hazing activities as either criminal or noncriminal. A criminal hazing act usually involves an individual or individuals who hurt, harm, or terrorize another individual through actions forbidden by a hazing statute or by a similar law governing a hazing situation. Noncriminal hazing constitutes actions that states consider less demeaning or dangerous but that are nonetheless forbidden by the larger institution or organization with which the group whose members have been accused of hazing is affiliated. For example, verbal abuse during hazing is a rules violation at many state colleges and high schools, but it is lawful in states requiring proof of physical injury for prosecution. Forty-two U.S. states have statutes explicitly or indirectly forbidding hazing, or were actively pursuing a statute's passage in 1999. One such statute was passed in Minnesota in 1997. After a particularly vicious case of high school hazing occurred, state representative Ruth Johnson coauthored a bill that extended the hazing law to every grade from kindergarten through the last year of post-secondary school, acknowledging that high school hazing had become particularly problematic in that state. "Hazing has been around ever since I can remember," said Rep. Johnson.[15]

Predictably, parents whose college-age children were killed or injured in hazing incidents have lobbied for the passage or the tightening of anti-hazing laws. Some such lobbying has occurred in Illinois, Nebraska, New York, South Carolina, Missouri, Alabama, and Massachusetts. In states such as New Hampshire, Maryland, and Minnesota, fraternity and sorority members lobbied on the side of activists, urging legislators to pass statutes instituting penalties for hazing. However, an attempt to pass a hazing law in Colorado failed in 1998, even though members of Colorado fraternities and sororities favored the law's passage. (A Colorado hazing law was nonetheless approved in 1999.) A legislator who had been a fraternity member in college told the *Denver Post* that hazing has some important benefits.[16] Other legislators said that existing laws prohibiting underage drinking, manslaughter, and assault in Colorado are sufficient to cover hazing. In a March 1998 telephone interview, Eileen Stevens said she disagreed, citing the perpetrators of several deaths who went unpunished because of the lack of a specific statute. Harry Randles, an educator who has written on legal controversies in public schools, has theorized that when legislators pass laws that relate to education, they base their actions on their own experiences as students, thereby ensuring that all legislation is already out of date at the time that it is passed. "Legislation will be implemented under conditions which the legislators could not know, probably did not foresee, and might not even be able to imagine," he concluded.[17]

Why have a law that governs hazing? Generally speaking, a school located in a state with a stiff hazing statute has an advantage when it attempts to punish hazers, according to Alice Haben, the mother of Nicholas Haben, who won a court fight in Illinois to uphold the constitutionality of an ancient state hazing statute, and then lobbied for the law to be strengthened so that those who inflicted injuries that occurred as a result of rough hazing would be punished. Ultimately, the young men involved in her son's death (many of whom also had Greek affiliations and had undergone ordeals as pledges) were found guilty, not of criminal hazing, but of giving alcohol to a minor. A local prosecuting attorney, William E. "Bill" Poncin, fought on Haben's behalf to see the case come to court, but he pressed for conviction on a charge that he was more certain would stick. The defendants were sentenced to performing community service, a court decision Haben castigated in a 1997 telephone interview with the author as being too light, particularly after some of the defendants spoke at a northern Illinois high school and were upbraided by audience members who found the remorse they expressed insufficient.

But Mark Molzer, a defendant in the Haben case, insisted that his remorse was sincere. He said he has not stopped "being eaten away from the inside [by] the fact that we destroyed so many lives because of one night of careless drinking."[18]

In part because none of the young men who initiated their sons were found by the courts to have hazed, activists Eileen Stevens, Rita Saucier, and Alice Haben have started a public debate over the effectiveness of existing hazing laws. They complain that acts of hazing slip through the cracks in states with no statutes, weak statutes, and statutes that allow certain types of hazing. For example, activities involving ritualized harassment that occur at military colleges such as the Virginia Military Institute are rarely considered unlawful acts of hazing under Virginia law unless injury occurs. Stevens said in a 1999 telephone conversation that she considers Virginia's law especially weak in view of the large number of college campuses in the state at which hazing incidents have taken place.

A few states have amended their hazing laws so that they now say that the fact that a pledge or any other person consents to all or some acts of hazing is irrelevant. By way of example, Connecticut general statutes 53-23a in 1997 says, with regard to hazing, that "the implied or express consent of the victim shall not be a defense in any action brought under this section." Other states' courts have found it to be problematic when a pledge consents to and perhaps even appears to be enjoying one hazing event but balks or becomes traumatized when a member demands participation in some other activity that the pledge regards as too unpleasant, too demeaning, or perhaps too dangerous to engage in. For that reason, Mark Freeman said in a 1998 telephone interview with the author that he frequently compares hazing to date rape. In many ways the problems associated with hazing mirror those facing activists and professionals fighting sexual assault who were striving to get society's attention in the 1960s and 1970s.

The campaigns of Stevens, Saucier, and Haben have added a human element to hazing deaths, forcing the public, the press, and the Greek world to see the faces and souls behind each death. These activists want the laws made foolproof to save parents the agony of losing a child, and then perhaps losing hope as those who they believe contributed to that child's demise are allowed to resume their lives as they were before. Before that happens, a national movement of some sort will have to take place to update weak state laws, and laws will need to be written in states that lack them. Too often, what is considered criminal hazing in one state is not against the law in another. Whether fines and prison terms are imposed upon conviction varies from state to state and from case to case, depending upon the type and amount of evidence collected; on whether a death, maiming, or physical injury has occurred; and on the attitude of the local prosecutor's office toward hazing offenses.

In Virginia, for example, district attorneys have historically accepted the findings of college administrators, campus police, and judicial groups when deciding whether or not to prosecute an individual or a group for an activity that they suspect may be hazing. Thus, after the 1992 death of Alpha Phi Alpha fraternity pledge Gregory Batipps, aged twenty, in an automobile accident, the University of Virginia decided that there was not enough evidence to press hazing charges, even though Batipps had been sleep-deprived and had been hit by fraternity members. As punishment, the University of Virginia judiciary committee recommended that one Alpha Phi Alpha member's diploma be withheld, and that three other members be suspended until they had performed a sufficient amount of community service.

Similarly, prosecuting attorneys may review all evidence and may refuse to press hazing charges if the person who was hazed (or, if the hazing resulted in death, that individual's family) requests clemency for the hazers. In Mississippi, the family of Leslie Ware, who was killed in a prank that had hazing overtones until pledges altered their stories, pleaded that no charges be filed against anyone in the fraternity. None were.

In many states the bottom line is that without bodily harm, there is no hazing. Law enforcement officers who halted what appeared to be an act of hazing being committed by Roanoke College (Virginia) students later had to drop the charges and even to issue an apology because they could not demonstrate that anyone was bruised or otherwise hurt physically as a result of the incident. Police later said they considered the activities potentially dangerous and wanted to stop them before an injury occurred.

Hazing laws differ considerably across states, although overall there are more and tougher laws than there were in the late '80s. Alice Haben said that the unevenness of the punishments being meted out for the

Michael Davis suffered fatal internal injuries after being beaten and kicked during a Kappa Alpha Psi fraternity pledge session. Fraternity members left him dying in a vehicle while they ate Mexican food at a fast-food restaurant.
Photo courtesy of Edith Davis

same crimes is an issue that legislators, educators, the press, and the public need to discuss.[19] At present it is usually only when an underage initiate dies as a result of a beating or in an alcohol-related incident that a prosecuting attorney will recommend that a case be heard by a grand jury to see if it will go to trial. Rarely do hazers find themselves charged with having committed a crime. Only a minuscule number of students serve three or more months of jail time. Many collegians who commit apparently criminal hazing acts are punished by collegiate judicial groups in the United States, not by the courts. For example, consider the following:

◆ The young men sentenced in the death of Kappa Alpha Psi pledge Michael Davis ended up serving a fraction of the time their sentences called for, in spite of the fact that, according to the coroner, damage to Davis's body included "massive subdural [spinal cord] hemorrhage," fractured ribs, a torn kidney, a bruised thigh, and internal bleeding.

◆ Also in Missouri, involuntary manslaughter charges brought against four males in the wake of twenty-eight-year-old Mike Nisbet's death in an initiation into a University of Missouri, Rolla (UMR), spirit and drinking club were eventually dropped by Phelps County prosecuting attorney John Beger, and no criminal hazing charges were preferred. A judge stated that if Beger wanted to prosecute, he would need to prepare for four trials in four different venues—a situation that one prosecuting attorney in the Davis case complained was comparable to playing Bill Murray's part in *Groundhog Day*. "It was a tough position for the prosecuting attorney," said Joy McMillen, the St. Louis attorney who represented Nisbet's parents in a civil suit, in a May 1998 telephone interview with the author. The former defendants also escaped university sanctions by choosing to leave the institution, and UMR failed to expel them in absentia. "It is important to note that since no court action was ever taken on this case, the criminal act of hazing was never established," said a UMR official.[20]

◆ In 1997, ten men were charged with first-degree hazing, unlawfully dealing with a child, and reckless endangerment after the asphyxiation death of seventeen-year-old Binaya "Bini" Oja, a Theta Chi pledge and a Clarkson University freshman, who died following a long night of drinking. The most severe punishment meted out by a Potsdam village justice was a sixty-day jail term.

A few states, such as Texas, have statutes that have been interpreted to mean that members are guilty of hazing even if they have the consent of the hazed. The essence of such thinking is similar to that adopted by certain universities that decree that instructors in a position of power over students must be held accountable if they initiate a sexual relationship with a student who consents. This issue of consent is important. In many hazing incidents in which a hazer said that consent was given, it turns out that the pledge's will had been eroded by sleep deprivation, fear of being blackballed, pressure, or alcohol, said Eileen Stevens in a 1998 telephone interview with the author. Rita Saucier also said that a pledge's consent should not be a factor in determining the punishment of those who were involved in hazing. Interviewed shortly following the hospitalization of five pledges to the historically African American Kappa Alpha Psi fraternity at the University of Maryland–Eastern Shore (UMES) after they had been brutalized with canes and paddles daily for nearly two months,[21] Saucier criticized UMES president Delores Spikes's announcement that pledges who fail to report hazing will be punished along with the members who haze them. "Oh great," said Mrs. Saucier. "[The pledges are] too scared *now* to report it."[22]

The DePauw incident in which Kappa Kappa Gamma pledges were pressured to burn themselves with cigarettes was unusual in that two

Texas governor George W. Bush is considered presidential material today, but as the president of Delta Kappa Epsilon at Yale University, he narrowly escaped misdemeanor charges after pilfering a Christmas wreath for his house. Bush told the *Austin American-Statesman* that his record shows he learned valuable lessons from past indiscretions. He also quit drinking at age forty. Bush today advocates "tough love" punishment for gang and juvenile crimes. *Photo courtesy of George W. Bush*

of the three pledges who were burned took a personal risk to tell their stories to DePauw police. On campuses where the most desirable events are Greek-sponsored, young people who report a house for hazing and cause it to be punished can be subjected to campus scrutiny and snubbing of a kind that few people under twenty-one are willing to endure. "That's why you rarely hear about [hazing]," Freeman said in a 1998 telephone interview with the author. Damara Karamesines, who had been traumatized by the ritual burning, left DePauw University and enrolled at nearby Ball State University, pledging Alpha Gamma Delta but failing to get in. Jessica Zimmerman left school in the fall of 1998 after a DePauw Kappa threatened her, she said. The parents of the young women said medical examinations indicated that the two showed signs of post-traumatic stress.[23]

Details of hazing incidents often tend to get blurred, distorted, or even whitewashed when those who hazed or were hazed meet with their parents, campus officials, and campus police, said Freeman. Those who were hazed may be reluctant to come forward if they committed a crime, say stealing Christmas decorations during a scavenger hunt, as Texas governor George W. Bush confessed to doing for his Delta Kappa Epsilon chapter. He later said he regretted his actions and asked to be judged on how he had learned from his youthful indiscretions. Likewise, few pledges wish to inform Greek affairs before a hazing crime is committed, said Freeman, because their absence would be noted and they would be blamed for the arrest of members.

Many students want to join a student group, some enough to put their lives or well-being in danger by unwisely consuming large quantities of alcohol or submitting to abuse they would not tolerate under ordinary circumstances. Students sometimes keep quiet out of fear that they may not be believed if they reveal what has been done to them. In 1997, members of a fraternity on an Indiana university campus denounced the accuser as a liar, and campus police could not discredit the alibis of those who had been accused, so the accused were never convicted. Students who have been hazed may fear that, like the person who reported the hazing incident just mentioned, they will be blackballed on campus and will get nothing in return.

Freeman, who has worked at Indiana University, said fraternities and sororities tended to be "close knit" and to stick together when charged with hazing. Stevens said that sometimes they lie outright. After a pledge fell to his death at a house a few years ago, she visited the campus and was told by an insider that the young man had been blindfolded in a hazing incident. Members denied it all, and there was no clear proof that hazing had occurred. Police filed the case away as an unfortunate accident.[24]

It isn't just the hazers who deny and rationalize, according to Stevens. Too often, university representatives and leaders of national Greek associations tolerate untoward behaviors that create a climate in which a hazing death or incident is more likely to occur than it would be in chapters where discipline is maintained by fraternal headquarters, Stevens said. Inevitably, every serious hazing incident pits victims or the families of victims against the institutions that have maintained an uneasy alliance with the group accused of hazing. "No one was responsible for my son Chuck's death," said Stevens, who has received apologies and admissions of mistakes from present Alfred officials. "Not Alfred University, not the fraternity, and so-called investigations by the school and district attorney were done without interviewing important witnesses."[25]

The task of law-enforcement officials on campus today is to convince presidents and trustees that any failure to fully enforce the law can come back to bite the school, since a civil suit challenge could arise later, citing the university for failing to take action, said Freeman.

Only a small number of suits were filed against fraternities or colleges before 1978. Since that year, the number of suits has risen sharply.

Stevens was one of the first to sue, taking some members of Klan Alpine fraternity, the person who was at that time the Alfred University dean of students, and the person who was at that time the Klan adviser to court. She eventually settled the suit without Alfred formally admitting to wrongdoing, banking less than $20,000 after expenses and legal fees were deducted, she said. She said she had taken the defendants to court to get answers, not money, but learned far less about the circumstances of her son Chuck Stenzel's death than she had hoped to. The thick file containing *The Estate of Chuck Stenzel v. Alfred University* was lost or permanently misplaced by Allegany County.

Other parents fared better. Ray and Maisie Ballou received $250,000 in actual and punitive damages from Sigma Nu in the 1980 alcohol-related hazing death of their son Barry at the University of South Carolina. The case was especially newsworthy, and it has been of interest as a test case to parents suing fraternities ever since.

Previously, in another civil suit brought by the parents of deceased twenty-three-year-old social club initiate John Davies at the University of Nevada, Reno, no judgment of money was awarded in spite of the Nevada court's displeasure with the actions of members who had asked five pledges to consume eighteen quarts of hard liquor (including grain alcohol), sixteen gallons of wine, and enormous quantities of beer in sixty-five hours. In 1993, in another important case that had a similar outcome, a South Carolina jury ruled that Shannon Gill, twenty, a visitor to the Clemson Alpha Tau Omega house who had brought her own alcohol and had drunk illegally at a local tavern, was to blame for her own actions when she fell from a third-floor ledge of the ATO house while trying to get into a window after a friend of hers had locked his keys inside. Gill died as a result of the fall.

In 1985, not long after the Ballou victory, the family of David Andres won a suit against the local and national headquarters of Alpha Kappa Lambda after their son died of alcohol poisoning at a party in 1979. A jury awarded the plaintiff $181,000 in spite of the fraternity's position that Andres's decision to drink was a personal choice.

After 1985, courts awarded a number of payments in excess of $300,000 to the families of hazing victims, getting the attention of national fraternities that found their insurance rates skyrocketing and their legal fees escalating. Fraternities were able to send a message to some undergraduate chapters by letting students see what a high percentage of their dues was going for insurance to cover the cost of deaths and injuries that occurred as a result of hazing and automobile accidents, as well as the cost of guest injuries, fires, and miscellaneous risk-related problems. Some examples of payments made in compensation for death or injury are as follows:

◆ After a Kappa Alpha party at the University of Texas ended in an alcohol-related crash caused by a member who was on the floor of a truck fooling with the accelerator, paralyzed member Rusty Combes settled with the fraternity and the offending brother for $21 million, according to news reports.

◆ The family of James Callahan, a Rutgers University pledge who died after being encouraged to drink, won $390,000 in an out-of-court settlement with Lambda Chi Alpha in 1990.

◆ In 1991, the parents of Phi Kappa Psi pledge Mark Seeberger were awarded $1.68 million by the courts in a suit against the national fraternity Phi Kappa Psi and individual members of the University of Texas chapter that handcuffed him and asked him to drink up to twenty ounces of rum in two hours. The suit was won even though a Texas grand jury ruled that the case was not a hazing.

◆ In 1994, Hofstra University settled for $850,000 with a former pledge, Andrew Radcliffe, who had fallen from a fifth-floor residence hall window eleven years earlier, shattering many bones and requiring extensive reconstructive surgery on his face. Hofstra paid but maintained that the school fostered a safe environment. Radcliffe had consumed beer and performed calisthenics for a fraternity before visiting a woman who was then his girlfriend, and falling to the ground. Radcliffe testified that he was not drunk.

◆ The parents of Nicholas Haben, who died of an alcohol overdose (his blood-alcohol level was 0.34 at the time of his death) during an initiation, collected $530,000 in a settlement with eleven of twelve former Western Illinois University lacrosse club members, according to Alice Haben and an attorney for one defendant.

◆ In 1996, Pi Kappa Phi Pledge Matthew Krull died in an automobile accident after consuming alcohol at a fraternity party at Oregon State University. Two men who had given alcohol to minors were fined and given jail sentences, one of thirty days and one of four months. Krull's parents settled for $1 million with the national, according to the *Chronicle of Higher Education*.

◆ In December 1996, after seven fraternity members were convicted of felony manslaughter and eight were convicted of misdemeanor hazing in the death of Southeast Missouri State student Michael Davis, Kappa Alpha Psi agreed to a settlement, paying Edith and Boyd Davis of St. Louis $2.25 million. The family had sued the fraternity, a national officer, and five members of the Southeast Missouri State University chapter, said Mrs. Davis in a 1998 telephone interview with the author.

◆ In 1998, a Kent State University pledge paralyzed in a Delta Upsilon accident accepted a settlement of $1.75 million. Chad W. Johnson had broken his back jumping into a mud pit at the request of a fraternity member.

The aforementioned settlements notwithstanding, the Kappa Kappa Alpha burning incident at DePauw is a classic example of why state hazing laws, though numerous, continue to fail to serve as a deterrent against criminal hazing. For the Zimmerman and Karamesines families, Indiana might as well have had no statute forbidding hazing-like activities, rather than having one that raised their hopes before dashing them. Nor should just the latest hazers be singled out for punishment when their own "burners" were allowed to go unpunished by the law or by public naming in the press, said Heldt, the mother of an accused DePauw hazer. Until all hazing incidents in which a victim partially or fully participates are prosecuted routinely and uniformly, the laws as written will remain inadequate. Until all local prosecutors can be educated to regard hazing as a crime that has real victims and to see that the perpetrators must be confronted in a court of law, injustice must triumph time after time. Thus, while hazing activists have been making a major push toward getting hazing laws passed in all fifty states, the Kappa Kappa Gamma incident illustrates the importance of such statutes' uniformity. States must present a united front in the way they address criminal hazing, which can occur with or without the consent of the hazed. Unless that happens, the same activity that designates a hazer in one state as a criminal and sends him or her to jail is going to result in no criminal liability whatsoever in another state.

8

Violence in Historically African American Greek Groups

GENESIS

Historically black Greek groups are similar to historically white fraternities and sororities in many ways. Many reformers from African American and white groups have come together to share information and perspectives. For example, the 1998 *Black Issues in Higher Education* national videoconference featured black college presidents Earl S. Richardson of Morgan State University and Gloria R. Scott of Bennett College, as well as Fierberg, Syring, Gordon, and other panelists.[1]

Cooperation can go only so far, said John Williams, an authority on African American fraternities. "Serious differences in the governance structures prohibit unilateral policies, [though] most non-hazing policies on campuses are mutually applicable. . . . The problem is what to do with violators. 'Pan-Hell' folks are not going to accept NIC enforcement in Pan-Hell organizations."[2]

And vice versa.

The interest of many black Greeks in African traditions and their African heritage makes the culture of these groups unique. Unfortunately, it also means that they participate in some problematic rituals. During the late '80s and '90s, pledging deaths in historically black fraternities occurred as a result of beatings and physical tests of endurance, while pledging deaths in historically white fraternities were associated with alcohol-related incidents and so-called road trips. But, perhaps as a consequence of the rise in reported high school hazing incidents involving youngsters of all cultures, Michael Gordon of the National Panhellenic Conference (NPHC) noted in a 1998 telephone interview with the author that the line separating black Greek problems from white Greek problems has blurred. Members of white fraternal groups who have been injured in fraternity-related incidents incurred their injuries as a result of violent pledging activities; some black Greeks have misused alcohol during the pledge period.

While universities' open admissions policies, efforts to recruit minorities, and enrollment of foreign students and of students with widely differing ages and backgrounds has made U.S. colleges' student bodies anything but uniform in recent decades, over the past thirty years national Greek-letter organizations have all remained homogeneous— although National Interfraternity Conference (NIC), NPC, and Association of Fraternity Advisors (AFA) leaders have all made pitches advocating diversity in the late '90s. A small number of Caucasian and Hispanic students have pledged predominantly African American fraternities and sororities, and though a larger number of blacks and Hispanics have gained admission into the fraternities and sororities that once intentionally kept them out, there are some chapters that to this day have never inducted an African American pledge, said Gordon in the same telephone interview.

The first fraternity for African American men was Alpha Phi Alpha, which was founded in 1906 by students at Cornell University. The Alphas became integrated by their own choice, although there are few white alumni. The next two fraternities to emerge, Kappa Alpha Psi and Omega Psi Phi, were founded in 1911. The fourth, Phi Beta Sigma, formed in 1914. In 1996 the NPHC admitted Iota Phi Theta as its fifth fraternity. Many other national and local black Greek groups for men exist, but these are the only five black fraternities associated with the main black umbrella group, the National Panhellenic Council (NPHC). Unlike white Greeks, who have separate umbrella groups for men and women, the NPHC also includes as members these sororities: Alpha Kappa Alpha, Delta Sigma Theta, Sigma Gamma Rho, and Zeta Phi Beta.

Historically, NPHC organizations have been instrumental advocates of equality, the importance of education for African American youth, and the value of serving the community and humanity. The first four national black fraternities were founded during a time when state laws barred African Americans from state colleges in the South, Missouri, and Oklahoma. Even at schools that allowed blacks to attend, the color barrier on campus was as thick and impenetrable as the color barrier in baseball—and it lasted many years longer. African American collegians depended on fraternal groups for emotional support. Today historically black Greek groups retain their prestige in spite of hazing scandals, as Paula Giddings, author of *In Search of Sisterhood*, has pointed out.[3] The earliest black fraternity members were seen as having been blessed with a talent for "uplifting the race" with what they would achieve in their lives, said Jason DeSousa. DeSousa, assistant vice president for student affairs at Alabama State University in Montgomery and chair of a task force studying fraternity and sorority effectiveness for the National Association of Student Affairs Professionals, was responding to questions sent to him by the author.

Black Greeks were a minority within a minority. "The first two black Greek-letter organizations [Alpha Phi Alpha at Cornell and Kappa Alpha Psi at Indiana University] were founded out of need for blacks at two separate predominantly white institutions to become better integrated into campus life," said DeSousa. "Not allowed to participate in study groups and campus clubs or to live in residence halls, the founders of both Greek-letter organizations established their own fraternity. Alpha Phi Alpha started with the purpose of bring men together for 'literary' development. Kappa Alpha Psi was interested in recruiting men who were interested in achievement."

The first historically black sororities, Alpha Kappa Alpha, Delta Sigma Theta, and Zeta Phi Beta, were founded at Howard University in 1908 and 1913, respectively. The fourth, Sigma Gamma Rho, was established as a college organization at Butler University in 1929, although it had been founded seven years earlier as an organization for black female teachers in Indianapolis. One of the aims of such female fraternities was to improve the social status of black women, and the movement therefore sought feminist gains as well as race-directed respect. Alpha Kappa Alpha's membership rolls contain not only prestigious female members such as activist Coretta Scott King and author/poet/actress Maya Angelou, but also opera singer Marian Anderson and former first lady Eleanor Roosevelt, both of whom held honorary memberships. Today Charlayne Hunter-Gault is a respected television journalist, but as a freshman at Wayne State during the era of civil rights, she found black Greek organizations to be "a virtual necessity" for black students who wanted a satisfying social life. "It was within those organizations that black students found respect and reinforced identity," wrote Hunter-Gault in her autobiography.[4]

Little hazing took place in black sororities before the 1960s. By the early '70s, however, hazing had become severe enough that at a national board meeting, Lillian Benbow of Delta Sigma Theta denounced an injury that a pledge had suffered. "We have to recognize the old ways," said Benbow. "The old harassment, brutality, we cannot carry along."[5]

In 1975, three Delta Sigma Theta sorority members were suspended for inflicting injuries on four pledges by using paddles; the young women fought the punishment, but a Tennessee court upheld it. A young male and female pledging local Greek social clubs perished together in 1979. Black pledges from two social groups were asked to swim, clad in regular attire, to the center of the Appomattox River. Robert Etheridge, twenty-one, a Wine Psi Phi fraternity pledge, and Norsha Lynn Delk, twenty, a Beta Phi Burgundy sorority pledge, died after they disappeared downstream from a dam at around 1:30 A.M. Fellow students failed to report the disappearances for nearly three hours, as a result of which an organized search did not take place until daylight.[6]

During the 1990s, newspapers occasionally published stories about black sorority pledges who were demeaned or hit, or who reported that they had experienced emotional distress during hazing. For example:

◆ A Portage County (Ohio) court punished Alpha Kappa Alpha sorority members for allegedly paddling, pushing, and slapping around thirteen Kent State University pledges until some bled. The lawyer for one sister argued in court that hazing taught prospective members endurance and helped them gain the strength they would need in life's struggles. "Only those who endure make it," said attorney Lawrence Floyd.[7]

◆ At Jacksonville State, Alpha Kappa Alpha pleaded guilty in a Florida court to severely hazing pledges, both physically and mentally.

◆ On March 5, 1998, a pledge of a predominantly African American sorority at Western Illinois University told campus police that she had been physically hazed by undergraduate and alumni members during one month of pledging. Pledge Litesa E. Wallace refused to sign a complaint that would have led to formal charges, but alleged in a police report, among other things, that her hairpiece had been pulled from her head and put in her mouth, that she was kicked and pushed while she was in a squatting position, and that she was required to eat whole raw onions and hot peppers and then to drink vinegar and an entire bottle of hot sauce until she vomited into her own shirt. Any pledge who spat instead of vomiting was required to scoop up the residue with a cup and swallow it. She also alleged that she had to do exercises, including 1,000 sit-ups on one occasion, until the skin on her back and buttocks cracked open. Members required her to grind her elbows into cornflakes until she bled, and then to eat the red flakes. During pledging lineups, any pledge who incorrectly answered questions about sorority history received a blow to the head with a book.

She also had to kneel and jump over a broom. When she failed to clear the broom, she was struck with it. Deprived of sleep and dehydrated, she visited emergency rooms twice for treatment.[8]

Paula Giddings, author of a history of Delta Sigma Theta, disclosed that the paddling she endured as a pledge at Howard University "cast a shadow over the whole sorority experience," and caused her to halt her involvement for some years in response to what she saw as the sadism of some Deltas.[9] In *In Search of Sisterhood*, Giddings wrote,

> Hazing had always been a part of the initiation period . . . but may have a particular meaning and character among Blacks. For example, there is special emphasis on the line of initiates acting in unison, whether through the dance steps that they perform, dressing alike, or even walking against campus in a kind of lockstep. . . . The stripping away of individuality is achieved through activities that are designed to "humble" a pledgee (some would, accurately, characterize it as humiliation). A "one for all, and all for one" mentality is further developed through the knowledge that if one pledgee does something "wrong" the whole "line" is punished; if one is unable to perform a certain task, someone on the line will have to perform it twice. . . . Also inculcated is the unconditional respect for those who are already in the sisterhood. All of these things—the need for unity, for taking responsibility for another's actions, for understanding that one's own actions will affect the entire group—have a particular resonance in terms of the Black experience.[10]

BLOOD ON THE PADDLE

Prospective fraternity or sorority members make an emotionally charged commitment to joining a group. Sometimes members join because they share the values the national group holds sacred. Gordon, a member of Kappa Alpha Psi, stressed that the black fraternal organization is a "jewel" to many African Americans, who revere its heritage, character, history, and values; he worries that many younger members of black Greek groups are more concerned about the superficial status that membership confers.[11]

For some African American students, choosing a fraternity is a matter of serendipity. Joseph Jeremy Snell pledged Omega Psi Phi at the University of Maryland (UM) because his uncle, a track athlete who had run in the prestigious Penn relays, treasured his Omega membership. After his uncle's death, Snell inherited his old running shoes and an Omega fraternity pin. One day he spontaneously phoned his grandmother to inform her that he was going to surprise his aunt.

Snell had one other reason to pledge besides pleasing his aunt. He thought it was time for him to go through a meaningful rite of passage.

Joseph Snell saw the sinister side of pledging an African American fraternity when he was subjected to intense hazing as an Omega Psi Phi pledge at the University of Maryland. He still has flashbacks to the beatings he endured. Omega Psi Phi and other historically African American Greek groups have traditionally provided black students with a support system at colleges where white students were in the majority—particularly during the '60s.
Photo courtesy of Dawn J. Tessman

"I was at an age to do what men used to do—go and have my time for adventure," said Snell.[12]

Upon arriving at UM, Snell met many other black students. He visited some fraternity members and saw shrines devoted to the display of fraternal memorabilia in their personal apartments. Their cars and the walls of their apartments were often painted in fraternity colors. They dressed in their fraternity colors, as well. Snell kidded a Kappa Alpha Psi, asking if he had anything but crimson and cream in his wardrobe.

A criminal justice major, Snell at first was proud to be one little dot on a line of Omega Psi Phi pledges. Like the other fraternities in the NPHC, Omega had strong alumni chapters. By the time Snell pledged,

Omega had adopted a forcefully worded anti-hazing policy, which it distributed to members.

Snell saw himself joining an organization that would have meaning for him all his life. He was impressed with what Omega represented and with its alums. The fraternity had attracted prominent men such as Jesse Jackson, Vernon Jordan Jr., and Benjamin Hooks (former director of the National Association for the Advancement of Colored People [NAACP]). Roy Wilkins, who first succeeded W. E. B. DuBois as editor of *The Crisis* and then succeeded Walter White as executive director of the NAACP, started an Omega chapter at the University of Minnesota when white Greeks prohibited blacks from joining their chapters. The athleticism and physicality of Omega Psi Phi members such as basketball star Michael Jordan also impressed Snell.

At UM, Omega had a dual reputation as a high-status fraternity and as one whose chapters made its requirements for admission exceptionally physically challenging. Even though hazing was forbidden by the national headquarters, in the UM Omega chapter it began right after pledging started, Snell learned. Each pledge was required to bring a food item for a brother to the apartment where the pledge "training" took place. Other members would try to intercept the pledges, hitting them in an attempt to take the food away. If the food was stolen, the pledge was beaten by the brother who'd been waiting for it. Instead of complaining, pledges consoled themselves by telling one another what they were going to do to pledges when they got in. "Lord help 'em," they said to Snell.[13]

In a letter to the author of May 19, 1998, Jason DeSousa said that today's victim who survives hazing is almost certainly tomorrow's hazer. "Many pledges who get initiated vow they will never haze, but the next semester, there they are in the thick of things," said DeSousa, who was initiated into Kappa Alpha Psi fraternity at Morgan State University in Maryland.

Omega members stepped up the abuse. They required Snell and his six fellow pledges to reside in a single cramped room on campus. Snell had to make frequent visits to an off-campus apartment, where he was beaten with a hammer, a chair leg, and a brush. Some members whipped him, which his attorney would later say reminded him of the beatings of slaves by white plantation owners.[14] Some Omegas considered his complexion too light and tried to make him blacker by putting his face next to a space heater.

Given the barbaric severity of the abuse, some pledges required medical treatment. Word of the injuries reached UM police through the complaint of an anonymous tipster. Unlike Dr. Saucier's anonymous complaint to Auburn University authorities, which was ignored, this one received some attention. Maryland authorities checked into the complaint, a decision applauded by Michael Gordon, who said in a 1998 interview for this book that he took unsigned complaints seriously when he was a dean involved in disciplinary matters at Indiana University. But other national fraternity leaders ignore anonymous complaints because they feel that someone who doesn't sign his name is gutless, said Eileen Stevens in a telephone interview.

Police determined that seven Omega pledges "on line" had visited six medical facilities for treatment. The reason they visited different clinics and hospitals was "to avoid detection of a pattern of injuries," said Major Michael McNair, commander of the Operations Bureau, in a June 8, 1993, memorandum to the UM Office of Judicial Programs. The tip may have prevented a death or a crippling injury. What UM police found was bad enough. Omega injuries included a fractured ankle, a battered cheekbone, a ruptured spleen, a blood clot, a collapsed lung, a ruptured eardrum, a cracked rib, a concussion, a neck injury, a chest bruised by a rock, and a stress-related stomach disorder.

Members subjected pledges to dehumanizing indignities. They dropped hot wax on them and asked them "to eat vomit, drink from toilets, eat dog biscuits," according to McNair. Omega members, according to Snell, expected pledges to participate in unethical classroom practices. They made pledges attend classes and write term papers for brothers, the latter of which is considered a serious offense under UM's academic code of honor.

Police ultimately accused two dozen undergraduate and alumni chapter members of inflicting the hazing injuries. After the police investigation began, the Omegas took their fury out on the pledge class, and six pledges directed their own anger toward Snell, believing him the source of the anonymous complaint. One threatened him with bodily harm. Their collective wrath was indicative of their intense desire to gain admission into the fraternity, and of their frustration with Omega's unmasking, which would certainly lead to university sanctions and to a restricted social calendar that would diminish the chapter's prestige on campus.

Police charged individual members with criminal hazing but dropped the charges after members agreed in Prince George's County District Court to pay Snell's medical expenses and to apologize. Members were also ordered to offer him membership, but he declined, knowing that few would consider him a fully initiated member.

The case would have ended there, but the members failed to pay Snell's medical bills. Snell then engaged attorney Douglas Fierberg, who filed a civil suit. Omega Psi Phi countered that the beatings were administered by members whose actions were not sanctioned by the national organization, but the national ultimately lost in court. Fierberg offered convincing evidence that Omega Psi Phi headquarters, in spite of written prohibitions against hazing, failed to act decisively to punish hazing once it became aware that renegade chapter members had beaten, whipped, and mistreated pledges. Snell received a judgment of $300,000 from Omega Psi Phi.

With the cooperation of UM authorities, Snell was able to graduate, taking courses in criminal justice studies at another campus to avoid possible harassment by Omega sympathizers. There are two ways for ex-pledges to ensure that they will be put through hell until they transfer or drop out of college, said DeSousa in a May 19, 1998, letter to the author. One is to inform authorities that hazing has taken place; the other is to quit pledging. Kappa Alpha Psi, Alpha Phi Alpha, and Alpha Kappa Gamma refer to someone who fails to measure up as "eternal scroller," "eternal sphinxman," and "eternal ivy," respectively, according to DeSousa.

Now a doctoral student at the University of Minnesota, Snell said that having his day in court was therapeutic. He said the suit affirmed that he was right to fight back, but his fraternity experiences continue to trouble him. No longer interested in pursuing a career in police work, he is getting a doctorate in American Indian studies in Minnesota. The incident has scarred him. He has tried to put the beatings behind him but cannot do so. "I'm not quite right," he said simply. "I still have flashbacks of the beatings."[15]

HAZING AND THE CULTURE

Each individual Greek national organization, much like a college or a commercial product such as a magazine, has a birth-to-death life, and dozens of Greek groups have folded or merged with healthier organizations. Some members, hoping to prevent that death, or to keep it from occurring in their own lifetimes, consciously introduce hazing rituals, among other activities, to keep their organization vital. Pledging brings in new members whom the old members see as being culturally like them in many respects. In groups that haze, pledges must be submissive, willing to refrain from rebellious behavior, and accepting of a group identity. But the reality is that organizations are always greatly affected by the culture of the larger society, as Walter Kimbrough, Old Dominion University student activities director and author of scholarly studies on historically black fraternities, has stressed.[16] For example, in black fraternities that place a high value on recruiting postgraduate members as well as undergraduates, there is often dissonance between the values and views held by older alumni and those held by undergraduate students, who may have been brought up differently. For example, older members—including black administrators in higher education who now supervise Greek groups—tend to be appalled by any drug use on the part of undergraduates and younger alumni. Some of the younger members who use drugs, on the other hand, downplay their use, saying that they use only recreational drugs. Such a rift makes adversaries within Greek organizations of those who do and those who don't use drugs. That rift is reminiscent of the gap between so-called freaks and nonfreaks on college campuses in the late '60s and early '70s. Nor is the problem restricted to black fraternities, as illustrated by the highly publicized drug busts of white Greek houses at Pittsburgh (Pi Lambda Phi) and Virginia (Delta Upsilon, Phi Epsilon, Tau Kappa Epsilon), as well as the death from heroin of a Lehigh University white fraternity member.

Beatings, paddlings, and other rough pre-initiation practices remain the primary cause of deaths and injuries in African American fraternal groups today. The percentage of deaths occurring in predominantly white local and national social clubs is higher than the number in black chapters, Gordon said during a 1998 interview for this book, adding that he regards even one death in a black fraternity as unacceptable.

Although alcohol is a problem in some black chapters, Gordon said, it has not been a factor in the majority of deaths of African American fraternity members. Only one death, which occurred during a pledging activity in 1983, has been attributed to alcohol use. Tennessee State University (TSU) student Vann Watts, who was on line for Omega Psi Phi, died after consuming a tremendous amount of alcohol (his blood-alcohol level was 0.52 percent at the time of his death) and enduring a whipping with switches. TSU suspended the fraternity for five years. The Watts family brought an unsuccessful civil suit against Omega Psi Phi.

Several mothers of deceased black pledges have vowed to wage an all-out fight against hazing, but none have succeeded in capturing the ears of reporters the way Eileen Stevens did, said John Williams. "We need to find a black parent who is willing to move forward the way Chuck's mother was and make it a national campaign," said Williams in a 1998 interview for this book. "Unfortunately, I fear that even if we were to find someone like that, the media would never warm up to them. The perception is that blacks are naturally violent (current rap artists don't help dispel that myth), and there's not much sympathy for black kids 'who are lucky enough to be in college' and who violate that opportunity by engaging in foolishness. Looks pretty bleak, doesn't it?"[17]

It is disturbing that the first deaths of African American pledges occurred in so-called outlaw black fraternities that had no ties (or had only tenuous ties) to the fraternities' national headquarters. These out-

John "Tony" Williams wrote
his doctoral dissertation on
hazing and pledging issues
in black fraternities and
sororities. He founded the
Center for the Study of Pan-
Hellenic Issues. He was
hazed as a pledge during his
undergraduate years.
Photo courtesy of John Williams

law groups subjected pledges to horrendous physical hazing and endurance tests under the name of the national that the groups had
fraudulently appropriated. Two black maverick organizations, without
the sanction of the national fraternities, conducted heavy exercise sessions that contributed to the deaths of male pledges at North Carolina
Central University and the University of Pennsylvania in 1977. It was
some years before the headquarters of these black fraternities threatened legal action against these groups for using the national's name
without permission. The last pledging-related death in a chapter operating without a charter occurred at Alcorn State University in Mississippi in 1993. When a pledge died while stealing a chair for his fraternity there, it came to light that the national had kicked this chapter out
a decade earlier. Yet this outlaw group was still functioning and had a
faculty adviser.

In the last twenty years, investigations of hazings in historically African American groups have occurred at schools such as Bradley University, the University of Florida, North Carolina Central University, the University of Georgia, the State University of New York at Old Westbury, North Carolina A&T University, Morehouse College, Seton Hall University, Fort Valley State College, the State University of New York at Stony Brook, the Southern Institute of Technology, Indiana University, Illinois State University, and Northern Illinois University. Some beatings involve members who lose control and strike furiously. Some have sexual overtones. Pledges have been jumped on, kicked, pummeled, slapped, thrown down, and cursed. In 1993, Phi Beta Sigma was suspended by California University of Pennsylvania for physical abuse, for example making pledges do pushups with members on their backs.[18]

Many activities push pledges to the limits of their endurance and strength, as if the initiates were prisoners performing for ancient emperors. Such members play right into the prejudices of certain whites who since frontier times have perpetuated the myths of white mental superiority and animal-like black athletic superiority, according to John Hoberman, author of *Darwin's Athletes*. As author Ralph Ellison also pointed out, hurtful stereotypes and myths about white supermen and black giant athletes have set back the progress of race relations. Such assumptions of superiority lead whites and blacks alike to embrace cultures of violence. Specifically, black fraternities get stuck in this "violent tradition"[19] when they insist upon rituals that involve violent acts or that revolve around pledging activities that push pledges beyond the normal human limits of endurance. In Hoberman's opinion, the hazing rituals in black fraternities may symbolically re-create the violent past that African Americans experienced, endured, and revolted against. Fraternity members sometimes take away pledges' names, identify them with numbers, and, after initiation, brand their chests and arms. Hoberman suggested that the violent practices of the present are meant to "evoke" and "perhaps exorcise" the violent past of slave days. In short, black fraternities, with their code of honor, silence, and tolerance for abuse in the guise of respecting tradition, have bought into racist stereotypes by performing symbolic rituals depicting physicality and survival, concluded Hoberman.[20]

Physical and athletic-related activities such as calisthenics are among the most dangerous forms of hazing, said DeSousa, because members underestimate how dangerous they are. "On one hand fraternity members expect new initiates to bear physical and athletic hazing as a test of manhood and perseverance," he said in a May 19, 1998, interview. "On the other hand, such cruel forms of hazing are conducted as a means for chapter members to 'beat' or 'agonize' prospective new members judged undesirable to make them quit the pledge group before initiation. The latter approach is a weeding-out process."

The litmus test of socialization in many black Greek groups is the ability to accept member dominance, and no resistance on the part of pledges is tolerated. Fraternity members select replacements who are malleable enough to accept whatever vices and values the present group in power holds as important. DeSousa, who has no use for hazing, stressed that no fraternity member or pledge has died as a result of premeditated murder. "I don't believe it is in a young person's realm of consciousness that a series of strikes to the body could cause fatal injuries," he said. "No fraternity member is intentional about striking a person so as to rupture the pledge's kidney or break his rib." Nonetheless, he does see such acts as sadistic. "Chapter pledges intend to inflict pain during physical and athletic hazing activities," he stated in a May 19, 1998, letter to the author.

DeSousa also sees ethical problems arising from hazing, because one way pledges and members show loyalty to the Greek group is by their willingness to lie and say that hazing did not occur during pledging. Fraternity pledges, even those injured during hazing episodes, are fiercely loyal to members. As Ernest L. Harris Jr. lay in the University of Kansas Medical Center—on dialysis after a 1998 beating and caning by Kappa Alpha Psi alumni chapter members in Topeka that had battered his kidneys—he feared not for his life but rather that the brotherhood would think he had ratted on them. In light of such attitudes, internecine conflict between anti-hazing and pro-hazing forces has become inevitable in black Greek organizations.

Older fraternity men and women—while acknowledging that hazing and some drug use went on in the '50s, '60s, and '70s—plead with younger undergrads and alums to stop the practices that they see not only as dangerous and out of control, but, from their viewpoint, also as morally wrong. The young fling equally venomous accusations of hypocrisy back at their elders, and to their peers defend their hazing and vices with the rationalization that "things have always been this way."

HAZING AND SACRED VALUES

Ralph Ellison, during a speaking trip to West Point in 1969, talked about the brutal initiation depicted in his unforgettable opening to *Invisible Man*, in which a group of intoxicated white civic leaders use coercion and a financial payoff to get young black men to fight one another in a battle royal. Ellison's fictionalized ritual reinforces the belief in white supremacy of all the white characters who viewed the shameful display.

Rituals have always played an important role in human existence, however. Rituals "projected and reinforced" social values, said Ellison, reminding plebes in the audience of the initiation rituals they were now enduring at West Point. Ritual is a way to dramatize what deep down is important enough to celebrate. Throwing a hat up in the air means nothing. Throwing white caps in the air at West Point means something very special, he said.

When Ellison visited, the first-year students (in 1969, West Point was still an all-male institution) were reading *Invisible Man* as a required text. "The novel's examination of the depersonalizing pressures of institutional demands and the resultant problem of developing a cogent sense of personal identity made *Invisible Man* a particularly resonant book for cadets and faculty," said Robert H. Moore, a scholar who edited the novelist's remarks for publication. Ellison's appearance was poignant, for his grade school principal had been Johnson Chestnut Whittaker, an ex-slave turned cadet who was beaten and tied to his bed in a brutal 1880 hazing at West Point.[21]

Ellison told the audience how he went to a friend's Vermont farmhouse to write his novel, only vaguely aware of what he wanted to write specifically when he created the initiation scene. In general he wanted to convey the notion that Americans—who are not particularly interested in developing their critical-thinking skills—tended to live their experiences, not to understand them.

Even ridiculous hazing rituals have meaning, whether or not participants are aware that they do, said Ellison. "Many of the rites of passage, those rituals of growing up found in our society[,] are in the form of such comic, practical joking affairs—which we ignore in the belief that they possess no deeper significance," he said. "Yet it is precisely in their being regarded as unimportant that they take on importance. For in them we ritualize and dramatize attitudes which contradict and often embarrass the sacred values which we proclaim through our solemn ceremonies and rituals of nationhood."

Because ideas have to pass from one group to another somehow, Ellison said that he, an artist, gave a "symbolic form" to "deeply held values" and made one black man's society the society of every living person. His speech revealed that he had pondered what the significance of rituals really is, and why many young people feel such a powerful need to act uncivilized in a civilized world. Unable to light out for the Territory like Mark Twain's Huck Finn, or to atone for cowardice on a field of battle like Stephen Crane's Henry Fleming, some of today's young people—black, white, female, and male—are making up rituals as they go along. Some strike their peers. Others are struck down by them.

Doing one or the other for a fraternity or sorority wins a young black collegian prestige. "From my insights, students attempting to join black Greek-letter organizations submit to hazing in order to gain 'status' within the group and among their peers on campus," said DeSousa in a May 19, 1998, letter to the author.

The NPHC's Gordon predicted that, by necessity, sweeping changes will be introduced to end hazing in historically black fraternities and sororities. Gordon, Williams, and DeSousa agree that something must replace hazing, which has become the most important socialization step in some African American fraternities, just as it is in some historically white groups. "Members will, therefore, closely guard against individuals' not being adequately socialized into the group," said DeSousa. "And individuals who aspire to membership will compromise their safety and well-being in order to become a respected member."

In 1990 the NPHC outlawed all pledging, making the practice by black Greek members against the rules. "Each group adopted a 'membership intake program,' whereby a prospective member is interviewed, initiated, and then indoctrinated with the organization's culture," said DeSousa. "The new program sent terrible ripple effects throughout the black Greek-letter system. Moreover, it had unintended and unfavorable consequences." Specifically, many undergraduate and graduate members complained that the outlawing of pledging requirements had diminished all the abuse they had gone through to get into the group. They dismissed as "paper" members anyone who failed to go through a full ordeal before initiation, according to Erikka Bettis, a law student in Ohio who conducted a study of African American Greek groups.[22]

Larry Bolles, a judicial officer at Northern Illinois University who said he expels both hazers and those who shield them, stated,

> When the national offices decided to outlaw and ban all forms of pledging or hazing and institute an initiation program which requires zero pledging, this was a major cultural change. Clearly, you understand the problems that can occur when anyone attempts to create a change of culture that has existed since the early 1900s. [The national Greek organizations] cannot simply write a letter and decree that pledging and hazing no longer exist; just check out what is still occurring at the prestigious military institutes in the country. Any cultural change should be accompanied by a well-designed strategic plan that has representatives from the offices of national fraternities and sororities working closely with college and university officials toward making this cultural change within the Greek system, on a daily basis until this matter is resolved.[23]

Part of members' socialization process is the learning of secret songs and sayings. Snell said that some of these songs and sayings are not taught to new members who take the approved non-hazing route. Consequently, when young men who know the words meet others in their fraternity who do not, the hazed brothers dismiss the non-hazed as inferiors.

Another controversial practice intended to demonstrate pride in the group is the administering of brands during a quasi-scarification ceremony. These fraternal symbols are burned into the flesh of one to a dozen or more parts of the body with heated coat hangers. Branding a person is a test of his or her ability to withstand pain, said Erikka Bettis, saying that some members display their brands openly, while others keep them covered.[24] Black Greeks who are branded say they do not consider the activity to be hazing because they did it voluntarily, but others disagree. "Branding and other forms of body mutilation may be a very troubling practice when the culture of the fraternity or sorority represses free will," said DeSousa. "In other words, a new member may be pressured into getting a brand or other form of body mutilation. The concept of groupthink appears to be the case for several sorority women at a southern institution. In this case, all of the newly initiated women received a pierced tongue with a pearl as a sign supposedly of group identification. The women had previously [as pledges] adopted a 'line name' which included the word 'pearl.'"

Hazing in black Greek organizations is the single determinant of whether a member will gain acceptance, said DeSousa. Prospective members will endure every form of disrespect to gain respect. "It is terribly disappointing that fraternity members do not test an individual's manhood on measures such as intellectualism or spirituality," DeSousa continued. "The society in which we live seems to be placing too much stock in athletic and physical prowess at the exclusion of intellectual acuity and spirituality. Society has created a culture whereby young people would rather be a Michael Jordan–type person than a Professor John Hope Franklin–type person."

Thus, when all black headquarters made membership "intake" programs safe and civilized, their actions were perceived as dismantling a sacred tradition of rituals, said DeSousa, who holds a doctorate in higher education from Indiana University. Some undergraduate chapters have complied with the wishes of fraternal governors; others have resisted and continue to haze off campus.

In a 1998 interview for this book, Gordon said that the decision to end pledging was well intended but not well planned. Undergraduates will not stop pledging just because leaders of national black fraternities have banned the practice. The challenge for black Greek leaders is to create some sort of ritual to replace pledging that will satisfy an apparent undergraduate need for socialization, said John Williams, interviewed in 1998.

After a fraternity hazing death occurs, newspapers and magazines are full of stories about the circumstances surrounding it. Generally speaking, since the mid-'70s the deaths of white pledges have been associated with alcohol. A bottle exchange may have taken place, drinking may have been "encouraged" or mandatory, or there might have been a drunken kidnapping or accident (falls and auto crashes being the most common type). On the other hand, autopsies done on African American pledges usually show that there was little alcohol in their systems at the time of death but that blows to the body were a direct or contributory factor. In the next twenty years, depending upon such factors as general societal changes (such as the increase in the percentage of blacks in positions of power), movements toward greater diversity in Greek groups, alcohol awareness, and the tendency of white and black youths to share certain cultural traits and values, the primary causes of death among black and white pledges who perish as the result of hazing may change. What is unlikely to change is the fact that these initiations themselves will continue to be emotional, unusual, and risky incidents in which newcomers and veteran group members get caught up in the group's identity, igniting a lethal mix of conformity, rebellion, and youthful exuberance. In the meantime, Greek activists and Greek affairs staffers who complain that African American Greeks fail to show up at alcohol-awareness and hazing sessions might do well to understand the not-so-subtle differences in the rituals black and white Greeks employ to bring new members into the group. In other words, requiring black Greeks to attend sessions that aren't really applicable to their needs is at best counterproductive and at worst insensitive.

What is not often mentioned in the press, in spite of its importance, is the fact that both black and white youths in the United States evidently feel that it is valuable to test newcomers' ability to endure wrongful rites of passage before accepting them into their midst. And while the stepped-up efforts of educators and Greek executive officers to eliminate hazing and related binge drinking are a hopeful sign, the proliferation of media accounts of hazing and/or initiation-related stories involving high school students makes it clear that much more must be done (and the education process needs to start when students are in junior high school) before the ability to take a drink or a punch will cease to be the litmus test of choice for groups seeking to demonstrate solidarity. Put another way, educators at the college level need to be aware of high school students' changing initiation rituals and attitudes toward alcohol use, rough initiations (in high school athletic groups, for example), and so on. Since such rituals change and evolve over time, educators must realize that alcohol could someday be a problem in black Greek groups, and that therefore some sort of educational programming that warns black fraternity and sorority members of the dangers of misusing alcohol could be valuable.

Educators and Greek leaders may thus need to be more on guard than ever if pledges, black and white alike, have been led to expect that hazing will be a given when they pledge a fraternal group in college. The challenge for black Greek leaders, in particular, is to create some sort of ritual with which to replace pledging in order to satisfy undergraduates' need for socialization, said Williams in a 1998 interview. Whatever that ritual may be, it must make young African Americans in college student groups feel that—in spite of the fact that they are outnumbered by whites at many schools of higher education—they can be in control of their own lives and environment without resorting to violent acts of hazing.

9

Strategies:
What Can Be Done?

Why do many young people literally die to belong to fraternities, so-rorities, and other college social organizations? The answer is complicated, but here is a starting point: Ever since the medieval universities were founded, young people have done whatever it takes to gain acceptance, to break with their past lives, to achieve a sense of power, to carve out a society of their own that isn't quite what their tutors and teachers had in mind. In the United States, hazing and drinking have been endemic in colleges since colonial days.

Problems with fraternal pre-initiation stunts and drinking spiraled out of control in the 1970s. Reforms tried by fraternities and sororities in the '80s and early '90s were too often merely cosmetic. Because at least one college man or woman has died in a hazing- or pledging-related death every year since 1970, the press and public have questioned colleges' ability to guarantee students safe passage through four years of study.

True, much responsibility lies with the now-deceased young men and women who put a bottle to their lips or followed the ridiculous orders of some negligent fraternity member. For the dead who were hazed there are no more options, and the irony of the price they paid for their actions is that their peers don't seem to have learned from their deadly errors. The dead can neither defend the poor choices they made nor attack the poor choices others made for them. The living who made bad choices for the dead, or who stood silent and failed to prevent a hazing- and/or alcohol-related death, too often fail to show even shame for their actions or for their failure to act. Also too hesitant to act or speak out have been the adult leaders of fraternal groups and of our educational institutions, who have lacked the needed courage or conviction to restore civility and order.

But some educators and fraternal leaders are cautiously optimistic about the future of student social groups in the twenty-first century, particularly as research sponsored by the National Institute on Alcohol Abuse and Alcoholism, National Institutes of Health (NIH), continues to make progress toward profiling the genetic basis of alcoholism, which now claims 20,000 lives annually in the United States.[1] Many national fraternities and sororities have said that they are committed not only to keeping alcohol, drugs, and hazing out of houses, but also to recruiting new campus leaders for whom fraternity membership is but one aspect of a rewarding college educational experience. As undergraduate membership in fraternities declined nationally from an estimated 400,00 members in 1991 to between 320,000 and 325,000 in 1999, a number of major fraternities elected to return to the values espoused by their founders, recognizing that members who joined in the past to gain access to an alcoholic rumpus room weren't worth recruiting. Delta Sigma Phi, Sigma Nu, Phi Gamma Delta, Beta Theta Pi, and Phi Delta Theta have instituted programs to combat alcohol abuse. Sigma Phi Epsilon has taken a revisionist approach; its "Balanced Man Project" emphasizes the idea that a healthy fraternity mentoring experience, community service, and a "spirit healthy, body healthy" existence are essential for a life of integrity.[2] Lambda Chi Alpha has earmarked a half-million dollars for chapters to use in attempting to address their problems with alcohol misuse.

Regarding hazing, at the university level reforms have been introduced at the Massachusetts Institute of Technology (MIT), Alfred University, Auburn University, the University of Texas, and other schools that have weathered scandal and deaths. Institutions such as Miami of Ohio, Kansas State, and Loyola Marymount, whose Greek advisers are actively involved in the Association of Fraternity Advisors (AFA), also tend to have strong anti-hazing programs in place. At fewer universities these days do Greek advisers, at the behest of their colleges, handle individual chapter problems such as hazing or alcohol misuse with little input from national fraternities. No one is saying that the problems of hazing and binge drinking can be solved easily or overnight, but too often problems such as hazing get shoved under other paperwork by college presidents unless watchdog groups, the media, and legislators keep pressure on these officials.

Thus, while hazing is a fraternity and sorority problem, and while the majority of those who have died in hazings since 1930 are fraternity pledges, members, and rushees, it is also a broader problem—made worse by the widespread use of alcohol—that society has failed to confront. What follows are some suggestions for big and small steps that can be or are already being taken to confront collegiate hazing and binge drinking. None of the suggestions below should interfere with anyone's "right" to associate with a group of his or her choice. I have tried to give credit where it is due for the ideas listed here.

WHAT IN GENERAL MUST BE DONE

1. Universities should encourage students to enroll in intervention programs after they have been treated for alcohol overdoses.

According to a September 1998 report in the *Brown University Digest of Addiction Theory*, researchers at the Brown University Medical School Department of Psychiatry and Human Behavior reported that young people who were treated for overconsumption in hospital emergency rooms and who then entered intervention programs that work to change their attitudes about alcohol were affected positively. The study, now in its fourth year, was funded by the National Institute on Alcohol Abuse and Alcoholism (NIAAA). Students who participate in the study are given cash payments.

2. Make sure houses are more heavily supervised by responsible adults.

Many national Greek groups hire adults and responsible graduate students, including some who live on the premises, to oversee the houses. Observers of the Greek scene such as DePauw police officer Mark Freeman said the presence of "more active house directors" helps keep fraternity and sorority houses safe and in compliance with hazing and alcohol laws. "In this age group," said Freeman in a 1998 interview for this book, "it's hard to police themselves." What has not worked is the presence of a so-called house mother who goes to bed early when an out-of-control party takes place. What's needed are adults who hold undergraduates accountable by reporting underage drinking, miscellaneous alcohol violations, sexual assaults, or hazing. Supervisors in turn must be accountable to the university and to the laws of the state in which they reside. When chapter members challenge the authority of a live-in supervisor (and they will), the university has to show full support or the chapter will view the live-in adult as powerless.

3. Increase hazing penalties.

Those caught hazing too often get off easily unless they lose civil suits, and even then it is their parents' homeowner's insurance carrier that usually does the paying. Relatively few hazers have had to serve jail time. Some, instead of bearing a social stigma for life, even receive sympathy for the loss of the friends they've killed or maimed. In order to change the system of hazing, and to put an end to ingrained rituals such as bottle exchanges, stiffer penalties must be imposed when someone dies or is severely injured. How to punish hazers is a real concern. Not even a parent who has lost a child in a hazing wants to see the hazers go to prison with hard-core criminals, where the hazers certainly would be victimized. The answer may be to send criminal hazers to minimum-security prisons where they would be made to take mandatory courses in behavior control. They could then seek an education at a new school, where their bad behavior hasn't made them heroes among their peers.

4. Severely punish adults who haze.

That initiation practices—some silly, some just dangerous—take place among members of professional football, baseball, basketball, and hockey teams has been documented again and again, but transgressors rarely are punished. In 1998 the National Football League refused to punish veteran members of the New Orleans Saints who had savagely beaten a number of rookies, although one hazed player, Jeff Danish, later was awarded a financial settlement, according to the February 1999 *Washington Post*. So too has hazing of medical interns been well documented by researcher Henry K. Silver, M.D., and by others. "Just as fraternity hazing can cross the line, the same can occur during the internship," said Dr. Scott Saucier. Hazing also is problematic in the alumni groups of some historically African American Greek groups.

State law-enforcement authorities need to step in when adults haze adults. It is unlikely that a hospital or a pro sports team will punish hazers. Putting members of the New Orleans Saints or a prominent physician on trial, if there is evidence that these people engaged in hazing, is not only the right thing to do; it sends a message to Greek students that they are not being singled out for punishment.

5. Shut down all chapters with an "Animal House" image that demonstrate a protracted pattern of abuses, injuries, and alcohol abuse.

What's needed are housecleanings, said alcohol expert Lewis Eigen. Any time a fraternity chapter begins throwing wild parties and hazing pledges for status, there is one solution: "I would defrock the officers of the local chapter, get new officers, and, if problems repeat, take the charter away," he said in a 1998 statement for this book. "Why are fraternity officers the only organizational officers in America who are not responsible for their organization?"

6. Legislators need to criticize the portrayal of alcohol in advertisements, TV commercials, movies, and TV programming.

In 1998, after learning that Vermont had one of the highest rates of teen automobile accidents (involving alcohol) in the nation, U.S. senator James M. Jeffords, a Vermont Republican, called for ways to force advertisers and distillers to stop targeting college students. In particular, Jeffords cited Abercrombie & Fitch (a national chain of clothing stores that is popular among college students), whose fall catalogue includes a "Drinking 101" section containing drinking games and recipes for strong alcohol concoctions. Other legislators have criticized the way drinkers are portrayed in print ads, TV commercials, movies, and TV programs such as *The Simpsons*.

7. Communities need to impose minimum standards for multiple-resident dwellings.

Architects, psychologists, and counselors have all pointed to dismal fraternity living conditions as contributing to alcohol use and alcohol-related problems. In addition, the rat-trap conditions of some houses have led to numerous fraternity fires, some of which have resulted in fatalities. Houses that cannot meet minimum safety and health standards need to be closed down until they pass muster.

WHAT UNIVERSITIES CAN DO

1. Adopt a zero-tolerance policy.

Increasingly, many administrators have chosen to banish troublesome Greek chapters instead of overlooking their behavior problems. Julie Joynt, the sister of a fraternity pledge who died at Frostburg State University following a pledging-related wrestling match, points an accusing finger at college presidents and administrators who give fraternal organizations a home and then say that their lawyers have advised them to keep a distant relationship with student clubs lest the university become embroiled in a lawsuit. She also criticizes administrators who shirk what she considers their responsibility to punish chapters and individuals for hazing and other abuses by shrugging off fraternal practices as part of a larger societal problem.[3]

On the plus side, more colleges and fraternities have introduced zero-tolerance policies intended to curtail hazing and alcohol abuse. Northern Illinois University staff member Larry Bolles has kicked out fraternal organizations and made them stay out for as long as ten years.

Anti-hazing activists frequently criticize campus judicial offices for being soft on hazing and for handling criminal matters better left to the courts. Larry Bolles of the Student Judicial Office at Northern Illinois University is an exception. He has declared zero tolerance for all hazing offenses and has expelled several students for hazing.
Photo courtesy of Larry Bolles

He calls his tough stance "playing hard-ball with these groups . . . that continue to have reoccurring problems." Bolles said he understands why universities have been reluctant to take a zero-tolerance position, but the reality of so many deaths each year makes harsh measures not only appropriate but necessary. He continued:

> Resources both financial and human will be given as the reason this is not happening. My one man's position on the issue is how can they not afford to do this, especially in light of what is presently oc-curring across the country today. It is clear that so called "renegade" members are influencing the behavior of all Greeks—both black and white—instead of their national, regional and local representatives. College and university officials too often find themselves in the posi-tion of reacting to what has occurred as opposed to being in a pre-ventive role.[4]

In a 1998 *Black Issues in Higher Education* videoconference, Morgan State University president Earl S. Richardson wondered aloud if per-haps schools could regulate hazing by writing some rules that pertain to it. But history teaches us that this is a well-intentioned but bad idea. Many universities had rules and regulations that set out what was and was not permitted during the class hazings of the nineteenth and early twentieth centuries. The string of deaths resulting from class hazings at schools that had such rules demonstrates that authorities cannot regulate hazing; they can only outlaw it entirely. Even the military, with far more accountability and regulations, has trouble with officers who take traditional ceremonies of rites of passage, such as those performed for crossing the equator, and turn them into abusive hazing sessions.

2. Attack alcohol abuse as a university-wide community problem.

Alfred University and MIT, two universities that have incurred national criticism because of alcohol- and hazing-related scandals that have occurred on their campuses, have taken a leadership role in the fight to end fraternal and athletic hazing/alcohol abuses. In 1998, the two schools independently formed alcohol issues councils to try to change student attitudes about drinking and to reduce risky behaviors associated with the consumption of large amounts of alcohol. These councils established student alcohol abuse as a priority issue for the college to address, and enlisted the cooperation of university administrators and staff to deal with it. Self-monitoring attempts by fraternities, sororities, and other student groups have failed to adequately deal with hazing and alcohol misuse. These two universities' efforts to find solutions to the problem should be applauded, and other institutions should monitor their progress.

3. Colleges must keep accurate records of occurrences of hazing and alcohol misuse.

Before the true damage caused by hazing and fraternal alcohol abuse can be assessed, colleges will need to approach a national foundation that can establish an objective national system for tracking incidents involving hazing, pledging-related violations, alcohol/drug violations, deaths, and near-fatal overdoses among members of student organizations and sports teams. Such a central, nonpartisan office would need to have the personnel and budget to compile accurate statistical information for researchers, the public, and journalists. The office should not be an activist group, lest the total number of incidents be inflated. Nor should it be beholden to any fraternal group or institution lest occurrences be underreported.

4. Institutions need to define a model fraternal system.

College presidents could also help curtail hazing by emulating Miami of Ohio and forming campus-wide commissions on the status of student organizations. These would need to involve not only student-affairs professionals, but also faculty (particularly social scientists and psychology professors), wellness staff members, administrators, counselors, representatives from the community, and advisers of Greek-letter organizations. The object of such commissions would be to get a grasp on what kinds and how many hazing offenses occur on individual campuses. Ideally, such commissions would prevent hazing deaths, maimings, injuries, and psychic woundings, and would not simply clean up the shards after a serious hazing takes place.

5. Campuses need to appoint an ombudsman to hear hazing complaints.

"Safe" offices need to be established on campus where there is an ombudsman to hear complaints against fraternal groups and athletic teams. Creating a new position would not be necessary; an existing compliance office could act as ombudsman. Students who have been hazed or asked to drink alcohol need a place where they can find support, referrals to anti-hazing groups, reading materials, studies, and general help. This office could serve to promote awareness and prevent a hazing- or alcohol-related crisis from escalating.

6. Get faculty more involved with new students from day one.

Critics of education such as Jacques Barzun have said that many professors have become specialists in arcane topics and possess knowledge that the majority of students cannot appreciate. Critics frequently scorn college faculty members for the poor quality of their teaching and for distancing themselves from students. A 1997 Governor's Task Force in Kentucky opined that its state universities operated with "little regard for the greater good of students." Faculty of the University of Virginia (UVA), shaken by a decade-long spate of student deaths, began to involve themselves in new-student orientation. President John T. Casteen III asked faculty to immerse themselves in the current student culture instead of meeting students only in the classroom. He said students now are introduced to college customs and culture through Greek rush activities, which often revolve around alcohol and establish the incorrect perception that all college activities should include drinking.

UVA has been plagued by notorious, hard-to-end traditions such as the so-called "fourth-year fifth," according to which many seniors consume a fifth of alcohol to celebrate the last home football game each year. Sigma Phi Epsilon's Carlone, speaking in a 1999 interview for this book, said he thought it important that critics such as Harvard's Wechsler attend national Greek meetings to see for themselves that some Greek leaders are pouring heart and soul into trying to clear alcohol out of the fraternal bloodstream. Rather than blaming parents, the Greek system, schools, or even society for the alcohol problems in the college culture, Carlone echoes other university leaders who call for collective action, not finger pointing, on the parts of all concerned. In addition, Auburn's President Muse, in an interview for this book in 1999, said that, in particular, college presidents with no Greek experience or whose Greek experience was unpleasant need to investigate Greek life more fully instead of distancing themselves from it or jumping on a bandwagon to eliminate it. "The group of top administrators who have had no Greek experience far outnumbers those that do," said Muse, adding that only about ten presidents responded to his request to discuss Greek life at a national professional meeting. "I had a very beneficial experience, and I would like to see that option available to young men and young women in the future. [But] many presidents have distanced themselves. The system has moved in a direction they could not support and they wanted nothing to do with."

7. Postpone rush to the second semester of a student's first year, or do away with it altogether.

Given the deaths of recently arrived (on campus) students Scott Krueger and Ben Wynne at MIT and Louisiana State University (LSU) respectively, as well as the astoundingly high percentage of U.S. college students who use alcohol, universities must consider postponing rush to the second semester of the freshman year or eliminating rush events altogether in order to create the perception that the purpose of college is learning, not drinking. The new movement toward dry rush activities on campus is commendable, but there is far too much evidence that such events are dry in name only. Until there is convincing proof that student culture has truly changed, postponing rush to students' second semester is preferable to allowing it to take place every quarter or semester. Better still may be suggestions made by several national executives of Sigma Phi Epsilon and other national fraternal organizations to do away with rush entirely. The Sig Ep idea is that chapters need to identify and recruit quality undergraduates who are turned off by the shallow, carnival-like atmosphere of rush, during which chapters try to outdo one another in conveying the impression that they are the "partyingest" group on campus. The deaths of rushees during alcohol-soaked rush events at Tulane University, Stanford University, and the University of Arkansas stand as testament that rush events have been out of control since the late sixties.

8. College presidents need a wakeup call.

Denying that hazing and alcohol abuse take place on campus is not something that only college students do. A survey of 1,320 college presidents (with 99 percent responding) published by *U.S. News & World Report* in 1998 found that college chief executives had little idea of how rampant alcohol use was on their campuses. A mere 3 percent correctly estimated that the number of alcohol abusers on campus was as high as the Harvard University study, in which students reported on themselves, revealed. Clearly, college presidents need to blot from their minds their own college days and acquaint themselves with the new realities. Students today are "inhaling" hard liquor through bongs, pouring potent whole-grain alcohol into punchbowls to make outlandish alcoholic concoctions with exotic names, and deciding ahead of time to drink until they lose consciousness. Whether the 97 percent of college presidents who are unaware of the true extent of the drinking that takes place on their campuses are enablers or are simply naïve is of no consequence. Simply banning alcohol is not enough. College presidents must institute a plan by which to punish students who drink irresponsibly. As part of that plan, they must institute an effective means by which to let students know that the institution values students' lives and safety too highly to tolerate drunkenness.[5]

9. Protect the fraternities that have accepted reforms or that were never a problem.

Fraternity houses that have gone dry need to be protected from members of "wet" houses who throw bottles against the dry fraternity houses and taunt their members. Universities need to devise ways of protecting good-citizen houses and of punishing hooligans who make a mockery of reform on campus.

10. Administrators must insist on equal punishment for crimes committed by white and African American fraternal groups.

In a 1998 interview for this book, Michael Gordon of the National Panhellenic Conference (NPHC) said that he applauds white administrators who take a tough stance on hazing in black groups. Some black Greeks have learned to intimidate and get concessions from administrators, said Gordon, who was formerly a dean in charge of fraternal discipline at Indiana University, and who punished both white and black Greeks.

11. Schools must publish a fraternal "rap sheet" that ranks Greek groups.

Universities should compel Greek chapters on campus to publish a list of infractions before rush. Such a disclosure sheet should reveal each chapter's behavior over the past five years and should list all the members who were suspended for hazing, alcohol violations, sexual assault, and fighting. If school officials and Greeks won't do the right thing, student newspapers should consider publishing such important information before the beginning of rush.

12. Universities must crack down on other groups that haze.

Greek members at universities complain, with some justification, that administrators have failed to crack down on athletic groups, bands, spirit clubs, and other organizations that encourage drinking or hazing. Two initiation deaths in the 1990s involved campus spirit clubs. The decade has also seen the death of Haben and the nonfatal collapse of a rugby club initiate at Ithaca College whose blood-alcohol level was above 0.40. Enforcement cannot be selective. At the same time, however, Greeks who drink and haze should not be allowed to justify their actions by pointing to groups who get away with equally reprehensible behavior.

13. Eliminate addicted fraternity chapters.

Greek national fraternal leaders need to purge campuses of chapters with a long, consistent history of alcohol and behavior problems. From 1993 to 1998, Sigma Phi Epsilon "closed fifty-three chapters that have not met Sig Ep's standards," said executive director Jacques L. Vauclain III.[6] That is the standard other fraternities need to meet. A number of national fraternities close fraternity chapters only after universities force them to do so, and they then recolonize at the first opportunity without eliminating troublesome alumni.

A related problem arose when Sigma Phi Epsilon punished its University of Georgia chapter, and the reprimanded young men contacted Delta Kappa Epsilon to ask if they could become affiliated as a Deke chapter, according to executive director Dave Easlick. DKE agreed. While DKE saw its actions as justifiable, said Easlick, Frank Ruck of Sigma Phi Epsilon was incensed. Michael Carlone of Sigma Phi Epsilon confirmed the story in a late fall 1998 interview, adding that he thought allowing an expelled chapter to simply shop for a new home elsewhere sent a poor message.

Another problem occurs when expelled chapters stay together as a local fraternity, whether or not they are authorized by the school. In 1996, a tragic fire occurred at the house of Radford University's Delta Tau Chi—a local that had reorganized after being kicked out by the Sig Eps. Christopher Mirch, whose blood-alcohol level was well over twice the legal limit, died in the fire.

14. Universities should consider forming faculty and student partnerships.

Miami of Ohio was one of the first universities to work with faculty, students, and others in the campus community to assess perceptions toward fraternities and sororities. As a result, the "Model for Greek Excellence" report was published by a Miami task force in 1996. The intent of the report was to ensure that the university would find ways to develop a "preeminent" Greek system befitting the institution's quest for "excellence in undergraduate education." The university also made the decision to work toward implementing extensive reforms in order to reduce the destructive influence of alcohol on Greek programs and on students in general. The Miami study is thorough, self-critical, and informative, and, though it is not perfect, it can serve as a model of what can happen when a dialogue between faculty and students is initiated.[7]

15. Schools should survey Greeks and compare their attitudes with those of the student population as a whole.

Too few schools attempt to track student values, beliefs, and behaviors in order to get a grasp of what student culture is like. The University of Minnesota first conducted a "Greek Experience" survey in 1986, comparing the responses of fraternity and sorority members to those of the general student population. Roger Harrold, author of the Minnesota report, said,

> Since it is administered to the entire membership of fraternities with very high participation rates, what you get in the way of data is not a sampling of responses but a full reporting of how the (nearly) entire Greek membership feels about the issues covered in the survey. We believe it reflects a thorough and very accurate reflection of Greek views, both collectively and by individual chapters. What you get from the data is one, an extensive analysis of the total Greek System, two, separate analyses of the fraternity system and sorority system, and three, separate analyses of individual chapters (i.e., a statistical comparison of Fraternity A vs. all other fraternities). The data is used for strategic planning by the University (administrators, Greek adviser) and is perhaps most useful to individual chapters to see how they stack up against all other chapters as a group. I think it is noteworthy that 88 percent of all Greeks participated in the 1986 survey, and 89 percent participated in the 1996 survey.[8]

The survey, which was modestly funded by the Center for the Study of the Fraternity based at Indiana University, most recently disclosed these findings about Greek drinking patterns at the University of Minnesota:

◆ Fraternity members consumed an average of 12.36 drinks per week. Nonfraternity males had 4.83 drinks per week.

◆ Sorority members consumed 5.42 drinks per week. Nonsorority females had 2.86 drinks.

Although the survey could be easily duplicated by any university, only about twelve schools had followed Minnesota's example by 1998, according to Harrold. Many more would benefit by doing so.

16. Offer healthy social-life alternatives to drinking every weekend.

Given student culture, colleges cannot simply eliminate alcohol-sodden activities without offering enjoyable alternatives. An example of one of the more successful programs is the University of Massachusetts' "Something Every Friday" program. "Our series was developed because many students felt that there was not anything to do on campus, so they would stay in their rooms and drink," said University of Massachusetts spokesman Joseph L. Tolson. "After surveying a number of activity programmers on the campus, as well as some student groups, we decided that there would need to be a number of things in place to make the program a success. One, the events had to be free. Two, there should be refreshments offered. Three, the events should be fun. Four, any movies [shown] should be recent. Five, the events should be multicultural and representative of our student population—[with] a balance between male and female performers or movie themes. [Six], all events [for the most part needed to be held] in one predictable space (with the exception of field events offered off campus)." The series has featured comedians, a ventriloquist, hypnotists, magicians, blues and jazz bands, a cappella singers, African musicians and dancers, and poetry slams and readings. "There are a number of student groups on the campus who offer rock bands and dances so we usually stay away from that," said Tolson. He continued:

> Students want to laugh and have a good time without having to always resort to alcohol. Student activities directors should survey what is *not* happening on their campus and begin to offer those [events]. Often there is no real assessment of the needs on the campus. . . . Finally . . . all of the students on the campus should feel that they are welcome at this event. Many times an event that is sponsored by a particular group will tend to exclude people who are not in the organization or feel uncomfortable in that kind of setting. . . . I cannot say that my program has curbed alcohol use of any students. I can only say that we have tried to get to some of the reasons that students are drinking and offer them alternatives.[9]

17. College presidents need to share information regarding campus and fraternal reforms.

In 1997, a presidents' leadership group was formed to create a plan to address alcohol and substance problems on campus. The group is working in conjunction with the Higher Education Center for Alcohol and Other Drug Prevention, a resource center created by the U.S. Department of Education. The first leadership group was made up of the presidents of the University of Iowa, the University of Rhode Island, Tennessee Wesleyan College, Ohio State University, Prairie View A&M University, and the University of Missouri. The focus of the commission is "environmental management," with an emphasis on "education and intervention strategies."

A nationwide coalition of college presidents who will devote the necessary time and effort to addressing the problems of hazing and substance abuse on campus is needed. The presidents' leadership group is a good first step. Other helpful state-level programs that involve college presidents and alcohol experts in activist forums exist in Indiana and Pennsylvania.

18. Administrators need to identify national programs that work to address problems with current student culture.

A number of excellent national programs attempt to deal specifically with current problems with college culture. One of the best-known is the annual U.S. Department of Education's National Meeting on Alcohol, Other Drugs, and Violence Prevention in Higher Education. This program educates administrators and school representatives, helping them learn about antisubstance programs that seem to be working at other schools. Administrators can also benefit by obtaining and filling out the Core Institute's "Alcohol and Drug Survey," a questionnaire the Core Institute then evaluates for colleges. (For a questionnaire, contact the institute at its web site:

http://www.siu.edu/~coreinst/

This feedback can help administrators assess the effectiveness of their campus prevention programs.

19. Administrators must make it clear that sub-rosa drinking clubs and renegade fraternities will be severely punished for transgressions.

All members belonging to a group that emphasizes drinking as an important activity need to be informed that all involved parties will be punished and prosecuted should anyone be injured or killed while drinking with their group or as a result of drunken behavior by any of their members. Administrators also need to shut down fraudulent chapters that claim to be affiliated with a national group but are not.

20. Criminal hazing, fraternity sexual assaults, and alcohol injury cases should not be tried by schools.

Educators make lousy law-enforcement officers and judges. Serious offenses that violate state law should not be tried by university judicial groups in place of state courts, said Louis Ingelhart, an Indiana-based press law expert. When illegal acts have been committed, law-enforcement authorities must take over and try the cases in state courts. Nor should university judicial courts try cases in order to guard the privacy of students. "If you commit a criminal act, you have no more privacy," Ingelhart said in a 1998 telephone interview for this book. "You destroy privacy by being involved in a criminal situation. The courts have distinguished facts in a criminal matter from 'private facts' papers are not entitled to know. . . . If hazing or drunkenness occurs, or students and student athletes are acting out of line, other students need to know that as long as the facts are reported clearly and accurately." From the point of view of the fraternity and school, Ingelhart said that it is far less damaging for the facts to come out than for the campus rumor mill to begin circulating untruthful versions in the community.

Similarly, campus judicial groups simply cannot duplicate the criminal justice system's custom of due process. The political views of faculty and students influence too many verdicts. High administrative officers make clear how they hope the judicial group will vote, and prejudicial information is printed in campus newspapers that judicial board members read. Accusers are sometimes not present. Defendants and accusers often lack legal counsel. Judicial members' views on jurisprudence may be based solely on John Grisham novels.

21. Evaluate all campus customs.

The University of Missouri, Rolla (UMR), a school nationally known for its engineering program, provides an intriguing example of how a student culture changes over time. The students of UMR turned a feast day originally meant to honor a saint into a holiday marked by drinking, partying, and an initiation death. In 1908, UMR students adopted a custom of facetiously celebrating the feast day of St. Patrick from University of Missouri, Columbia, students, who had honored St. Pat by making him the patron of engineers. Over time, the event evolved into an excuse for week-long parties, and in 1930 it resulted in the creation of the St. Pat's Board, a spirit group made up of fraternity and dormitory representatives whose essential mission was to ensure that a good time was had by all students.

In the late 1980s and early 1990s, student excesses marred the annual St. Pat's celebration. Anthony J. Busalaki, twenty, drank himself to death at a board party in 1988. New member Mike Nisbet, twenty-eight, died during a hazing ritual involving drinking. In October 1991, the university withdrew official recognition of the St. Pat's Board, and John T. Park, who at the time was acting chancellor and who is now chancellor, put the festival under the control of the UMR student council. That council founded the St. Pat's Celebration Committee, according to UMR representative Andrew Careaga. A lawyer for the Nisbet family called the change a name-only alteration. The Nisbets' case against the four males blamed by the plaintiff (but never convicted of wrongdoing in criminal courts) was ultimately settled in 1998, but details of the settlement were not made public. Although UMR is the most prominent business in Rolla, it is legally immune to suits brought by parents. Asked if justice was served, Nisbet lawyer Joy McMillen said in a 1998 interview for this book, "You can't replace the life of a man with money. . . . No one in Rolla really held the interfraternal organization accountable." Although one St. Pat's Board was kicked off campus, its clone now plans the annual extended party, said McMillen. She said she hoped that the suit would be a deterrent for other organizations, but she was not sure fraternity members would let it stop them from hazing or drinking to excess. Clearly, such groups continue to please alumni, but the fact that within a short period two people died during events sponsored by the group indicates that it is dysfunctional and should be shut down. Presidents need to make the hard decisions to evaluate groups after the occurrence of a student hazing or alcohol death. Although they should be, groups are rarely permanently closed down after a death occurs.

22. Ban rooftop beaches.

Deadly falls from rooftops became common when college students began using housetops for beaches some thirty years ago. Steven Butterworth fell to his death after consuming eight to ten drinks at a ceremony welcoming him to pledgeship at Alpha Chi Rho at Dickinson College in Pennsylvania. Paul Walsh died after a bout of heavy drinking at Pennsylvania State University in a fall from the roof of Delta Sigma Phi. A York College of Pennsylvania Sigma Pi fraternity member who had been drinking alcohol fell from the roof of an apartment building in which members of the fraternity maintained a residence in 1990. And the list goes on and on. Rooftop beaches must be banned by colleges and community authorities. Violators should be ticketed. Drunk violators should be arrested. Rooftop beaches are a common nuisance; when drunken fraternity members visit them, the consequences are uncommonly deadly.

23. Studies of hazing behavior are needed.

Researchers need to begin studying hazing in colleges, military groups, and other organizations worldwide. Newsworthy hazing incidents have occurred on college campuses in Canada, Thailand, the Philippines, France, the Netherlands, and Germany. Bullying in Japanese secondary schools and mobbing in Sweden are also serious problems.

Military hazing in the former Soviet Union has resulted in numerous deaths, and though Russian reforms have reduced the number of reported incidents, they have not eradicated the problem. Hazing in the Canadian Airborne Regiment led to a public outcry in 1995 after videotapes showed members of the regiment administering electric shocks to members of the new group. Families in Bulgaria and China have begged the government to do more to end dangerous and humiliating hazings. Since 1997, scandals have tarnished the reputation of the U.S. Coast Guard and the U.S. Marines. The *Dateline NBC* and CNN broadcasts of so-called "blood pinnings," during which jump-wing medals are pinned to paratroopers' chests, made a particularly strong impression. Participants videotaped the ritual in 1991 and 1993.

But the number of serious studies that have been conducted on hazing that occurs in organizations other than U.S. collegiate groups is comparatively small. The subject requires study by graduate students in psychology, higher education, sociology, and military science.

Educators such as Charles Eberly, an Eastern Illinois University professor who works closely with Greek groups, contend that studies focusing on student organizations are too often dismissed by administrators and scholars as lacking in academic seriousness.

24. More faculty and staff need to interact positively with Greek groups.

Universities have a moral responsibility to learn all they can about the fraternities and sororities that operate on their campuses. A few college presidents and administrators shrug off these deaths and injuries as a societal problem or say they need to keep their legal distance lest they find themselves embroiled in civil suits as the result of a fraternal death or serious injury, said Julie Joynt, the sister of a Frostburg State pledge who died suddenly after exerting himself in a pledging activity. "Whenever there is a tragedy, it's not the university's fault," said Joynt. "To me, when we send our kids off to campus, the university is responsible. To me, the fraternities are a part of the university."[10]

Before 1970, many faculty and respected alumni came to fraternity houses regularly to join the members in a communal meal. Today non-Greek faculty without Greek affiliations could be recruited to attend fraternal events if these events weren't controlled by immature young people still stuck in adolescence. "Another reason for getting rid of the alcohol is that faculty and advisers don't wish to get involved because they fear being liable," said Bob Biggs of Phi Delta Theta in a 1998 statement for this book. Of course, the faculty member who drinks with Greeks is doing even more harm than do those who stay away from Greek functions altogether.

The bottom line here? If a house isn't fit for respectable adults to visit, it isn't fit to be connected with a university. Eberly, a faculty member who has made a lifelong commitment to fraternity and sorority members at his college, says:

> Often, students do not come to the well, and we must take the water to them. An ultimate purpose of higher education is to change lives, else the college experience is relatively valueless. If our purpose as faculty is to fulfill that ultimate purpose, failing to try to change lives is not an excuse for the present condition. While we may never reach the ideal, we continue to have the moral obligation to work toward the ideal. Among those ideals is that, some how, some way, young people can be brought to a realization that "there is a purpose and meaning to life," and that its greatest expression is spiritual. I work with a campus fraternity chapter (Sigma Phi Epsilon) to do just that.[11]

25. Punish faculty and staff who fail to report hazing.

Some injuries and deaths could have been prevented if responsible individuals had only reported what they knew, or if they had intervened. A faculty member running on the school track at a university in south Texas stopped to question a black male who was ordering a pledge to run mile after mile, but he did not call the police. The pledge collapsed and died. Texas state law now says that a $1,000 fine and 180-day jail sentence may be imposed on someone who fails to report criminal hazing. Similar laws in all states could compel outsiders to report hazing. But whether or not such laws are put into place, faculty and staff members need to confront hazers, and to report them to campus authorities or police in cases involving criminal hazing.

26. More public and university support is needed for activist programs.

Since the late 1970s, public awareness of hazing and alcohol abuse has increased as a result of on- and off-campus awareness programs sponsored by groups such as BACCHUS (Boost Alcohol Consciousness Concerning the Health of University Students), the Gamma Peer Education Network, MADD, CHUCK, and CHAD. Greek advisers and universities have done a great deal to combat unhealthy attitudes toward drinking by bringing in experts on substance abuse and hazing. In addition, the Gamma Peer Education Network has done a good job of selecting student leaders to work with their peers to bring about awareness through positive peer influences.

Although all institutions have anti-hazing policies and most put out anti-hazing brochures, administrators put stock in their own educational programs aimed at Greeks and first-year students. The hope is that such courses and programs, taught by leadership experts, student-

Eileen Stevens gave hundreds of anti-hazing lectures following the 1978 death of her son Chuck Stenzel in an alcohol-related hazing incident at Alfred University. After her retirement in November 1998, Alfred offered Mrs. Stevens, the founder of the Committee to Halt Useless College Killings (CHUCK), an honorary doctorate. After an alcohol-related hazing of Alfred football team rookies in the fall of 1998, the university also put together a national survey of hazing practices among college athletes.
Photograph courtesy of Eileen Stevens and CHUCK

affairs staffers, or faculty members with a specialization in human behavior, may eventually build up some mental muscle in students so that they will become less likely to succumb to group pressures or to make unwise choices. "The Auburn Experience," a course developed at Auburn University, guides first-year students in areas such as lifestyle, student services, academic issues, time-management and personal skills, and leadership opportunities.

Educator James "Jim" Arnold said in a 1997 statement for this book that such groups plant seeds "that could lead to massive social change."

27. Educators must find a way to educate college students who had hazing experiences before leaving high school.

Although no national stories about a high school student dying in a hazing incident have surfaced in the United States since 1905, there have been several close calls, including a 1997 incident at Santa Fe High School in New Mexico, where a fourteen-year-old first-year student was pressured to drink until he passed out with a blood-alcohol level of nearly 0.40. High school incidents include athletic team hazing, band hazing, cheerleader and pom-pom squad hazing, and club hazing (in clubs such as the Future Farmers of America, for example). Gang beatings of high school students who wish to join the gang administering the beating are also a problem in some areas of the country. Other states in which high school incidents have occurred since 1988 include New Hampshire, Kansas, Massachusetts, Vermont, New York, Connecticut, Pennsylvania, South Carolina, Alabama, Mississippi, California, Texas, Oregon, Washington, Utah, Minnesota, Colorado, Hawaii, Maryland, Kentucky, Missouri, Illinois, Indiana, Florida, Wisconsin, Idaho, North Carolina, and Ohio.

The number of vicious high school hazing incidents across the country makes it likely that people with hazing experiences will be entering colleges expecting more of the same when they join a student group or athletic team, said Maurice "Mo" Littlefield, a senior consultant with the national Sigma Nu office, in a 1997 interview for this book. Educators must make it clear in freshman orientation programs that initiations have no place on the college campus. After a hazing incident occurs, administrators must determine whether newcomers were victimized by predatory peers, or whether they participated because they saw doing so as a quick way to earn the esteem of a group they admired. The many examples of reprehensible hazings at the high school level make it clear that reforms need to be put in place before there is a rash of deaths similar to those that took place in fraternities during the mid-1970s.

Why are these deaths occurring? Perhaps life is imitating Hollywood. Many of today's hazings in secondary schools resemble alcohol-laced scenes from *Dazed and Confused,* a high school rites-of-passage film available in video stores. At a time in their lives when youngsters are confused enough about sexuality, some hazing incidents demean them sexually and/or debase their bodies. First-year high school students and new varsity athletes have been subjected to initiations in which urine, excrement, and disgusting foods played a part.

28. Stress that hazing is wrong, semester after semester.

Some colleges attempt to fight hazing through education programs. William Paterson is one of a handful of colleges that require pledges to attend an anti-hazing workshop. In an attempt to change the perception that drinking is a part of Greek life, William Paterson also discourages its students from wearing fraternity and sorority colors while drinking. Dozens of other colleges regularly sponsor education seminars on hazing, frequently opening these sessions to the campus and the public. Some colleges, such as Edinboro and Rochester Institute of Technology, issue invitations to athletes, coaches, band members, and other student groups, making them aware that while hazing is a Greek problem, it is a societal one, as well.

29. The right way or the highway.

College presidents must order a campus-wide self-study to get a picture of how alcohol is being used on and off campus by undergraduates, graduate students, faculty, and visiting alumni. Presidents have an obligation to point out that it is safest to abstain from drinking altogether; second safest is to use alcohol in moderation. Any campus activities at which alcohol is abused, such as tailgate parties, open pubs, fraternity parties, and alumni functions, must cease. Trustees must hold college presidents accountable if potentially dangerous activities continue. "[Alcohol] is such a part of who we are as a society," Arnold said in a 1997 statement for this book. "My stand has been to not drink and to take a stand against those who abuse it."

30. The tough love approach.

A few schools have adopted a tough love approach to their students with problems. For example, Northern Illinois University has informed Greek-letter society members, pledges, and club athletes that if they criminally haze, the penalty for such negligence may be suspension or expulsion. Issuing such a warning before any unfortunate incidents occur may be extreme, but it is necessary.

31. Designate a specific office on campus as a place that hazing victims or those who are "encouraged" to drink can come to for counseling.

Many educational institutions now fund offices and staff to assist people who believe they have suffered what is legally defined as sexual abuse. Hazing victims have no similar offices on campus to visit when they are feeling stunned, bewildered, lost, psychologically distressed, defiled, and betrayed after a hazing, unless the hazing was somehow sexual in nature. Many such victims call the anti-hazing organizations staffed by parents who have lost their children in hazing incidents, but although the empathy and understanding these mothers offer presumably benefits those who are hazed (or, when someone has died, the survivors), none of the activists who work for these organizations claim to be licensed counselors.

32. Get students to come up with their own innovative programs and connect them with creative faculty and staff who genuinely care about students.

Whether or not they belong to Greek groups, students across the country have come up with innovative ways to combat alcohol deaths among their peers. On so-called Whiteface Day at Gettysburg College, a student dressed in black and painted on a white tear every seven minutes, signifying the fact that someone dies every seven minutes in an alcohol-related incident. The students then go to their classes, according to the *Chronicle of Higher Education*.[12] Such programs benefit students who take an active role in shaping awareness programs on campus.

33. Point out the good, and emphasize it.

Over time, thousands of ordinary and distinguished U.S. citizens have said that fraternities and sororities touched their very center during their undergraduate years. Some members of historically white groups and many more members of historically black groups make a life commitment to their Greek organizations even after graduation, scanning their organizational magazines for news, attending meetings and commemorative dinners, and taking vacations with other members who enrich their lives with shared memories. Some of these Greeks stand up at each other's weddings, serve as godparents to one another's children, and deliver the eulogy when the first among them dies. Unknown to most, Greeks meet at national conclaves every year to plan strategies for recruiting members, sponsor charitable events, put time into volunteer community activities, and fill out grant applications. Delta Gamma sorority has raised hundreds of thousands of dollars for the blind since 1936. Omega Psi Phi is involved in a social action program for civil rights and sponsors a high school essay contest. Five Greek organizations are jointly involved in the American Council on Human Rights. Theta Xi fraternity has adopted the National Multiple Sclerosis Society. Pi Kappa Alpha is known for its leadership programs, Lambda Chi Alpha for its food drives, and Chi Omega for its gift of a Greek theater to its founding institution, the University of Arkansas.

Rarely does a fraternity or sorority deserve no recognition. The challenge is to get these groups to outlaw their objectionable deeds while remaining involved in the constructive ones.

WHAT FRATERNITIES MUST DO

1. Undergraduate reformers must stay the course.

As a result of a heightened awareness of hazing, undergraduate reformers are becoming increasingly common within the ranks of fraternity members. At the risk of seeming disloyal, these reformers object to hazing and may even take the chance of arousing the wrath and indignation of the membership by reporting hazing abuses to the group's headquarters, a school administrator, or an anti-hazing activist. Sometimes reformers do not report the abuse but speak out against hazing during official group meetings or in private conversations with group members who they think may be won over.

2. National Greek groups must remove alcohol entirely from the socialization process.

Reform cannot occur when hazing and alcohol use are seen by a fraternal group as important components of its identity. Students in groups at many schools tend to drink and drink often; they may also encourage—or actually coerce—peers and pledges to drink. College subcultures such as fraternities use alcohol in ceremonial ways to influence the behaviors of one another and of the new members they let into their groups. The drinking—part and parcel of other socialization activities such as pre-initiation ordeals, initiation rituals, and written and unwritten (though *understood* by all members) membership requirements—works to preserve the national fraternal organization in a negative fashion, according to Arnold, who spoke during a 1997 interview for this book.

3. Join the rest of the world in developing a positive attitude toward women.

As Peggy Reeves Sanday, author of *Fraternity Gang Rape,* has noted, too many times fraternity members have "worked a yes" out of female visitors.[13] These instances include unsavory episodes during which members take turns having sexual intercourse with a cornered, often inebriated female student. One member of the fraternity that Arnold studied made a comment that says as much about his feelings for women as it does about the real place of the fraternity in his life: "We always say here, you get out of the fraternity what you put into it," the young man told Arnold. "Use it like a whore."[14] The bottom line is that fraternity members who just don't get it need to just get out.

Advertising pop-culture expert James B. Twitchell, author of *Adcult USA,* notes how shared cultures eventually develop a shared sense of humor.[15] Women are often the butt of fraternity men's jokes, and brothers sometimes spy on other brothers having sex with women who are unaware that they are the object of a group's entertainment. If new members who despise women and minorities make up the majority in a chapter, the chapter becomes increasingly unlikely to change or to welcome change, and will be more apt to block the efforts of the many reformers trying to alter the fraternal gestalt. At the same time, though fraternity members such as those of the Delta Kappa Epsilon chapter at Hamilton College may have a point when they complain of being held to a higher standard of conduct than are the rest of the students on campus, the DKE national office should itself insist that its members behave better than other students do, instead of simply blasting Hamilton officials for political correctness, as it has done. Frederick Doyle Kershner of Delta Tau Delta fraternity has argued that if Greeks cannot be elite in terms of values and conduct, there is nothing elite about Greek groups.[16]

4. Stop making ridiculous tests the litmus test of Greek superiority or of manhood.

The ability to take a drink and to withstand a paddling has meaning for many fraternity members. Deaths occur when members turn the drinking games and beatings into tests of male endurance. Fraternities lose pledges appallingly frequently because they subject them to extreme pressure all year, and then end the pledgeship with an intense night of drinking, during which they order pledges to slug shots as if the liquor were milk.

At some universities, young men celebrate their twenty-first birthday by downing twenty-one shots of liquor. "They call it the Twenty-One Club," Captain Ron Fosnaugh of the Purdue University Police said in a 1998 telephone interview. In recent years he and some of his associates have found young people to be highly responsive to peer pressure, and absolutely fearless about consuming a potentially highly toxic substance, alcohol.

Peer pressure has to be harnessed to stop these dangerous games before they start.

5. Stop feeding alcohol to women.

Activist organizations such as Security on Campus track all campus crimes, including incidents of violence toward women in fraternity houses and residences in which Greek males reside. Alcohol is a factor in almost all such cases, said the group's co-founder, Connie Clery, in a 1997 interview for this book. The point is clear for all members in Greek houses. If you get a woman who is intoxicated to consent to have sexual relations, you do not have consent at all.

6. Encourage chapters to recruit a wide variety of members.

In the late 1990s, as membership in Greek groups has fallen, national leaders of Greek organizations have increasingly urged chapters to recruit students other than those who fit stereotypical and superficial criteria. Jonathan Brant, Maureen Syring, and other leaders have urged Greek groups to recruit men and women whose scholastic record and participation in prestigious student activities make them less likely to accept hazing and alcohol abuse. In other words, the challenge for national fraternities and sororities—given the apparent lack of character of some members now living in Greek houses—is to get individual chapters to recruit individuals who join because the organization has merit, not because they have dependent personalities.

Since it is unlikely that misbehaving Greeks will recruit students who will end up criticizing them, national leaders need to take the radical step of expelling all counterproductive members, even if that means getting rid of a third to half of their dues-paying undergraduate members.

After many years during which the membership of Greek organizations swelled with those who looked at fraternities as round-the-clock happy-hour clubs, in the 1990s the Greek system began experiencing big membership drops nationally. An executive at one national fraternity said that he laughs when the media charge the Greek system with elitism. He said that today's fraternities are drawing from the dregs of undergraduates, and that his own national would be better off if it were to drop 20 percent of its membership to get rid of the worst problem cases.

7. Greeks need to perform academically and to be punished when they interfere with a pledge's studies.

Too often, students who pledge are harassed if they refuse to attend pledge activities because academic commitments take precedence for them. In a 1998 column, *Indianapolis Monthly* editor in chief Deborah Paul said that her son refused to take part in a Hell Week activity because he had to study. When he emerged, he found the words "Paul is a pussy" painted on his door.[17]

Any chapter whose GPA dips under the all-college average ought to be forbidden by its national from recruiting new students, to send a clear message that its first priority is academics.

8. Every Greek group needs to examine its group history in order to assess whether members have strayed from the values of the founders over the years—and if they have, to determine what must be done to put their organizations back on course.

One of the difficulties facing educators, national Greek-letter group leaders, and anti-hazing activists is that many college administrators, faculty, and members of the general public have a cartoonish, stereotypical idea of what fraternities and sororities represent. That stereotype is unlikely to disappear as long as Greek-letter organizations behave in a way that reinforces it. Fraternity leaders must be business leaders too; they must deconstruct their groups before they can begin to reconstruct them, must take stock of the organization's original mission and find out how the current group measures up or fails to measure up to what it was originally meant to be.

9. Put an end to racist, homophobic, and barbaric practices.

In attitude, many Greeks resemble stereotypical nineteenth-century Southerners and frontiersmen such as Mike Fink, who saw themselves as superior to blacks and greenhorns. Long ago, a poor white might have been an out-and-out loser, but he could nonetheless comfort himself with his sense of superiority over plantation blacks, wrote Wilbur Cash, author of *The Mind of the South*.

Such self-deluding arrogance also characterized the members of Indiana University's Zeta Beta Tau chapter who in 1990 sent pledges to snap pictures of "a funny-looking Mexican," and the brothers of Rider College's Phi Kappa Psi who ordered pledges to don costumes demeaning to blacks for a racist "Dress Like a Nigger Night." After they were exposed as lampooning minorities, treating them with disrespect, or excluding them from membership, the Greek members argued that their "joke" had been blown out of proportion.[18]

Some fraternal racism is clearly a holdover from pre-1960s exclusionary clauses in the constitutions of national and local fraternities that kept out blacks, Asians, and Jews. While these clauses are clear examples of the fraternities' bias against nonwhites, they appear to have been kept in fraternal constitutions for so long because members perceived that letting in outsiders would threaten the quasi-superiority they felt over non-Greek "barbarians."

Fraternities must stop throwing racist theme parties and being disrespectful toward racial minorities. Such activities clearly go against all that has been gained in U.S. society since the days of civil rights. One positive outcome of the Zeta Beta Tau scandal at Indiana University is that the young men involved were ordered to work with a black faculty member. In addition to working with them to increase their racial sensitivity, Michael Gordon encouraged Jewish members to explore their families' Jewish heritage and the Jewish heritage of their national fraternity.[19]

In October 1998, eleven Colorado State University (CSU) fraternity and sorority members carried a scarecrow bearing anti-gay slogans in the school's homecoming parade. Seven of the young men were members of Pi Kappa Alpha, and the national issued a statement condemning their actions. Alpha Chi Omega sorority's national office also condemned the incident, in which pledges from its CSU chapter had participated, and it yanked the sorority's charter.

10. Cure institutions first, then their members.

National and international fraternities and sororities must recognize the extent to which their own former exclusionary clauses and current unwritten recruiting practices have contributed to the problems caused by racism, hazing, and alcohol addiction. Greek leaders today must admit to their organizational wrongdoings and then exhibit zero tolerance for students who haze, throw racist theme parties, or assault others.

Greek-letter national organizations and educational institutions in particular have to muster the moral courage to conduct self-examinations in order to understand what it is about their makeup that may reinforce negative behaviors in their members.

11. National groups must expel all members who require pledges to participate in acts of hazing or submission before they are initiated.

At least half of all national fraternities and sororities, both African American and white, have launched changes in pledging procedures and alcohol policy reforms since 1990 and are now separating what has worked from what has not. Some universities have conducted self-studies and appointed task forces to gain a better understanding of their own student groups. Leaders in the Greek anti-hazing movement today say that social groups have no place on campus unless they stress companionship, lifelong friendships, and a strong system of values. But the bottom line is that undergraduate members in many national organizations have created a caste system in order to freeze out "paper" members who were not hazed before being initiated. The self-perpetuating system of hazing has to end somewhere. If Greek national leaders truly believe what they say they believe, they will fold a corrupt chapter before they will hand it over to corrupt members.

12. Fraternities must recruit people with values, not set out to teach values.

Greek groups can teach members that values are to be respected, but they probably cannot teach values per se. Jacques Barzun and other educators have maintained that values cannot be taught. In *The American University,* Barzun wrote:

> The wish [to teach values] is not so laudable as it sounds, being only the wish to have one's perplexities removed by someone else. . . . Even if this were feasible and good, the practical question of what brand of values (i.e., what philosophy, religion, or politics) should prevail would be insoluble. It is a sufficient miracle if a college education, made up of many parts and many contacts with divergent minds, removes a little ignorance. Values (so-called) are not taught; they are breathed in or imitated. And here is the pity of the sophistication that no longer allows the undergraduate to admire some of his elders and fellows: he deprives himself of models and is left with a task beyond the powers of most men, that of fashioning a self unaided.[20]

13. Fraternal reformers need to clean up nationals that refuse to comply with requests that they eliminate hazing and alcohol abuse.

Sigma Nu senior consultant Maurice "Mo" Littlefield said in a telephone interview for this book that he and other Greek leaders are considering whether to openly criticize the few national fraternities that have done too little to institute reforms, thereby threatening the survival of all fraternal organizations. *Do it.* This is a first step toward changing "Greek thinking" into great thinking.

14. More alumni need to take a positive stand.

Entertainer Bill Cosby, a member of a historically black fraternity, said publicly in 1998 that fraternities that engage in violent hazing reminded him of the Ku Klux Klan. He also praised African American fraternal groups for their charitable good deeds. Kentucky senator Mitchell McConnell, a former Greek, has actively campaigned against hazing. Fraternal leaders need to recruit more celebrities, athletes, and politicians with Greek backgrounds to speak out against hazing and alcohol abuse. If people like Paul Newman, Jesse Jackson, Michael Jordan, John Elway, Mike Wallace, Dr. Joyce Brothers, Walter Cronkite, Governor George W. Bush, and Deborah Norville would speak, undergraduates might listen.

15. Stop pinning and engagement ceremonies and put an end to branding.

At some point in the past, sororities and fraternities instituted a pre-engagement tradition. In a custom known as "pinning" a fraternity man gave his beloved an ornamental pin bearing his Greek letters. Women who were so "pinned" were expected to reject the proposals of non-Greek males. House etiquette demanded that fraternity brothers not make sexual overtures to a woman who wore a brother's pin. Members were required to pay heavily for taking an important step that would in effect sever their ties with the chapter. Many chapters covered such brothers with objectionable substances or threw them into ponds. Many still do so today. A number of members have drowned or been injured as a result of this foolish ritual. The practice ought to be made a hazing offense leading to suspension or expulsion.

A number of African American and white Greek groups brand pledges and members. Unless those who participate in brandings truly believe, as many have claimed to, that they are taking part in an ancient scarification ritual, the act of branding is barbaric and has no place in the higher-educational system. However, it is important for educators to recognize that branding has become widespread within the larger community, which also regards body piercing and tattooing as normal. While it may not be possible to put an end to branding altogether, college administrators and fraternity members must make it clear that coercing new members into branding themselves with Greek letters is hazing under all school and fraternal definitions.

16. Send undergraduates for hands-on training to work with alcoholics to make sobriety the norm in chapter houses.

Following the death of Scott Krueger at its now-abolished MIT chapter, the headquarters of Phi Gamma Delta fraternity entered into a relationship with the Betty Ford Center in order to educate alumni and undergraduates on addiction and on the wise use of alcoholic beverages. Undergraduate Phi Gams from the University of Montana and other campuses attended the four-day professional-in-residence program in 1998. Although it is too early to determine whether the attempt to increase members' awareness of alcohol's addictive power will be effective in the long term, Phi Gam national executives and undergraduates were moved by stories of patients who said that their drinking had begun or had escalated in college social clubs. The undergraduates returned to their houses to tell their peers what they had observed, and they will be able to pass along what they have learned about the heartaches of alcoholics who have decided to seek help for their illness. The cost of funding such a program, as several foundations do nationally, is low compared to the cost of a death or lawsuit.

17. The NIC, the NPC, and the NPHC should require individual organizations to conduct alcohol and hazing surveys.

Since 1990, the major fraternal umbrella organizations have devoted a great deal of time and personal commitment to launching programs designed to eliminate hazing and alcohol, as well as to change members' inappropriate or potentially dangerous behavior. In addition, many national Greek executives have made it clear that they will neither condone nor cover up fraternal bad behavior. What the NIC, NPC, and NPHC still must do is order all houses to undergo a review by their Greek headquarters every three years. Greek executives at headquarters must step in to end their association with all dangerous and risky chapters. Moreover, the fact that a chapter has recolonized is no guarantee that it is going to be hazing- or alcohol-free three years down the road. National headquarters not only must be vigilant, they must also be ruthless. They must remove chapter presidents when objectionable practices creep back into the fraternity's culture. Similarly, college administrators must relentlessly investigate Greek groups known as campus outlaws and animal houses. Otherwise these houses will inevitably be the scene of deaths and disasters.

18. Replace anecdotal evidence with hard data.

Greek leaders cannot solve the problem of hazing until they know precisely what percentage of undergraduates haze. But national and international Greek organizations have conducted few surveys to determine this figure. In 1925, worried about the possibility of death or injury occurring because of hazing, Lambda Chi Alpha enlisted the assistance of professors from Ohio University and the University of South Dakota to conduct a survey that asked questions about Lamda Chi Alpha members' attitudes toward hazing. Of those responding, 71 percent advocated retaining rough initiation practices, and each of the forty-one chapters responding listed the type of hazing its members performed. Nonetheless, Lambda Chi Alpha's national leaders were opposed to hazing, and they added their voices to those of other NIC fraternity leaders who condemned hazing in 1928.

Fortunately, one good model exists for Greek leaders to emulate. On January 27, 1999, Alfred University announced that it was conducting a national survey, "Initiation Rites and Athletics," to poll National Collegiate Athletic Association (NCAA) institutions about hazing practices among men's and women's athletic teams. The survey was conducted on the recommendation of the Alfred University Presidential Commission on Athletics. A preliminary report before the formal release of the findings said researchers "found that hazing for athletic teams appears to be more prevalent, dangerous, and degrading than Alfred University had realized. . . ." The survey was broken down further into one for senior administrators and coaches and one for student athletes; research was conducted with financial assistance from Reidman Insurance, one trustee of Alfred University, and the NCAA. For information on the survey, contact any of the following Alfred University Advisory Group members: Mike Hyde, vice president for university relations; Sue Strong, vice president for enrollment management; or Sue Goetschius, director of communications and university relations.[21]

It is impossible to deal with a problem when its magnitude is not known. Surveys ordered by national Greek umbrella groups would go a long way toward determining how widespread hazing is.

19. End stockpiling and deception.

Far too often, university rules meant to keep parties safe and problem-free are circumvented. Fraternity houses that are supposedly dry stockpile enormous quantities of alcohol outside the house with every intention of drinking it *in* the house later. Police caught the Indiana University chapter of Theta Chi fraternity, which is located about an hour's drive away from its national headquarters in Indianapolis, with a stockpile of 4,300 containers of beer and 30 large bottles of vodka. Another Indiana fraternity, Sigma Phi Epsilon, was suspended after members brought more than 2,400 containers of beer into the house.

Jim Arnold's doctoral study showed that deception is common at fraternity houses at a large midwestern university. If you're an unattached underage female without an invitation to a Greek house that is throwing a restricted party, you link arms with the nearest fraternity member and waltz inside for a beer. If you're male, you talk fast at the door until you're motioned into the inner sanctum. All the while, individuals with walkie talkies keep a "dean watch" to alert the others if the dean should show up at the party to see whether alcohol is being misused.

These and other juvenile games must cease. A university that tolerates underage drinking is a university that has buried or will one day bury an underage drinker. University police must stop the games by taking away the game pieces—the kegs and the bottles—and by slapping offenders with the heaviest possible penalties for underage drinking, terrorizing neighbors, and brawling.

20. Accountability begins when alcohol consumption ends.

The NIC and some national fraternities will be unable to effect alcohol reforms unless hazers and alcohol abusers are removed from contact with their peers. Members who see hazing and alcohol-related activities as vital to group cohesiveness and unity must be warned that they will have to change if they are to retain their group affiliation. Addicts and addictive groups "rely heavily on control in the form of rigid conformity," according to Arnold.[22] Only if members give up alcohol abuse and hazing will they be demonstrating a good-faith effort to give up control. Fraternities need to interview members and get rid of those who refuse to swerve from their conviction that only those willing to pay a high price to belong deserve admittance into a group.

Phi Delta Theta executive director Bob Biggs said that "alcohol" and "accountability" are the keys that determine what goes right or wrong in a house. A house that revolves around alcohol is never accountable. A house with members who want to be accountable does not permit alcohol abuse. Members who binge drink or must have one more for the road need to be told to hit that road for good. Getting rid of 5 or 10 percent of the bad influences has little effect on a house's behavior. If true reform means expelling 80 percent of a fraternity house's members, then the nationals must expel them, taking a hard "There's your bottle, here's your hat" stance.

21. Make pledges accountable—to a point.

While most anti-hazing advocates and Greek leaders do not want pledges punished if they have been injured because of hazing, they do concur that pledges must somehow be held accountable for their actions. Pledges who ask to be hazed should be reprimanded by fraternity national executives and school authorities. Those who haze members (particularly if a death results), steal property, and injure nonmembers should also be punished. On the other hand, the fact that pledges are unlikely to report hazing needs to be taken into consideration by administrators. Because hazing often begins gradually or subtly, pledges are like frogs placed in water that is slowly brought to a boil; their instinct to jump to safety is duller than it would have been had they been placed in water that was already hot. The pledge who fails to go through hazing is seen as outside a group that hazes—even if he or she manages to become a member.

My recommendation is that all pledges caught in some misdeed or in an act of underage drinking be made to attend counseling sessions at their own or the university's expense. A pledge who gets into trouble a second time should be as accountable as a member would be.

22. Keep drinkers, hazers, and risk-takers from joining fraternities.

Many Greek national leaders view themselves less as reformers than as business leaders trying to run their Greek groups the way the best corporations operate. Alcohol has fallen out of favor among most businesspeople today, and few deals are closed over drinks any longer. Sigma Phi Epsilon, for example, has stressed the importance of being perceived as a visionary organization by those within and outside the group, according to Michael Carlone, head of the Balanced Man Project at Sig Ep headquarters in Richmond, Virginia.

Other fraternal groups at national headquarters advise their members to pay more attention to character than to what kind of car a rushee drives. During the selection process, members need to identify and exclude those rushees who aren't looking for a good house, but rather are seeking a well-stocked tavern that serves underage drinkers, said Maurice "Mo" Littlefield of Sigma Nu in Virginia in a 1997 interview for this book. In spite of its good intentions, however, Sigma Nu has found it difficult to overcome its members' ingrained attitudes about alcohol. In September 1996, an Indiana State University Sigma Nu pledge was seriously injured after he drank to excess, went back to his dormitory, and fell through a sixth-floor window.

Jonathan Brant has stressed to the NIC's member fraternities that they need to spurn rushees who demonstrate impulsive, risk-taking behavior, noting that in addition to tragic incidents such as Chad Saucier's death, which took place partly as a result of a bottle-swapping tradition, other unfortunate incidents occur because of momentary lapses of good judgment. Studies in abnormal and social psychology have shown that delinquents and criminals are highly impulsive, preferring small rewards available here and now to larger rewards they could have in the future if they delayed gratification. Those who are not troublemakers tend to pass up short-term gain in anticipation of greater gain later. However, such behaviors are not set in concrete. Researchers have shown that delinquents and inmates can be induced to change shortsighted impulsive behaviors under certain conditions. Thus, perhaps there is hope that those who haze can be educated to change their behavior. Nevertheless, the difficulty and uncertainty that would accompany an attempt to do this suggests that it is more practical to simply keep potential hazers out of fraternities altogether.

23. Abolish road trips.

Before and since 1970, deaths at Kenyon College, New Mexico Military Institute, Colgate University, Wittenberg University, Swarthmore College, MIT, Grove City College, LSU, Pierce College, and the University of Texas have occurred as a result of kidnappings and other unauthorized outings and "rides." The number of maimings, injuries, and arrests occurring during kidnappings has been much higher.

The myth exists that there is such a thing as safe hazing. The number of dead pledges demonstrates that road trips and scavenger hunts are unsafe. Members who involve pledges in such activities should get a one-semester suspension. Members who leave dead-drunk pledges on the road deserve expulsion; on their next road trip, they may abandon a pledge who ends up dead.

24. Get rid of troublemaking alumni, and authorize undergraduates to kick them out.

Even a fraternity member who has drunk his way through school is still a brother. He can come back to his fraternity house on Homecoming, bring an illicit bottle, and be someone special when he tells tales to a rapt audience of pledges or visiting women. Fraternities have been so preoccupied with trying to educate undergraduate members that they have not been able to devote enough attention to alumni who return and cause problems.

By 1998, however, major theme issues devoted to hazing and heavy drinking began to appear in alumni publications put out by Sigma Nu, Kappa Alpha, Sigma Chi, Sigma Phi Epsilon, Phi Gamma Delta, Delta Sigma Phi, and many other NIC fraternal organizations. Greek executives have found that they must educate their alumni lest these alums go back to their old houses and goad undergraduates into keeping bad behavior alive in the name of tradition. Sigma Nu and Phi Kappa Tau reformers have been looking for ways to more effectively convince alumni to reduce their alcohol intake.

Alums who recount exaggerated tales about past Hell Weeks and drinking marathons make it even harder on reformers trying to eradicate the practice. The tales perpetuate the myth that risk-taking is part of a satisfying fraternal experience. The problem is intensified by film versions of Greek life such as *Animal House,* which perpetuate the image that there is something thrilling, even noble, in drinking death-defying amounts of alcohol, regarding women as prey, and performing dangerous stunts for kicks and attention.

In 1998, a group of undergraduates at the University of Illinois asked an alumnus to leave because of his untoward behavior. Fraternity members coast to coast should follow in their footsteps.

25. Fraternities need to warn members not to engage in cult-like behavior.

Cult expert Robert Jay Lifton said that the best alternative to cults is "a more open and flexible self that can be in tune with the larger uncertainties that surround us." Such an alternative seems to apply to cult-like Greek groups as well, which hope to reinvent themselves. Reforms instituted in the mid- and late 1990s by national fraternities stress self-awareness and self-growth, helping individuals get in tune with themselves so that they can resist coercive group pressures.

In short, reform strategies such as Sigma Phi Epsilon's Balanced Man Project uphold the notion that members should be intellectual explorers with not only the right, but also the obligation, to pursue the life of the mind. A student organization that impedes an individual's reasoning and growth and also damages that individual's mind or body has no place on a college campus. Even if an organization has a long history, lofty-sounding ideals, and the imprimatur of the college, it still must demonstrate itself to be accountable and at least benign if it wishes to continue to exist. Too many fraternities, sororities, and other student groups have evolved into organizations that are more sociopathic than social, and whose professed values are part of the outer shell they show to the world, not part of their core. What seems astounding to contemplate is that so many universities, administrators, and faculty have for so long tolerated Greek groups whose very existence depends on the ability to coerce, manipulate, and damage the pledges petitioning them for admittance.

26. Fight drug use as hard as you do alcohol use.

Executives of national fraternities have begun addressing the problems of drug use in fraternities, a problem that some say is on the rise. There have been some troubling drug seizures and arrests of fraternity members at the University of Virginia, and a 1997 police raid at the Phi Gamma Delta house near Ohio University turned up marijuana and hallucinogenic drugs. At Lehigh University, a fraternity member who used cocaine in the house died of a heroin overdose while he was away from the university. And in 1998, administrators of historically African American Greek groups and presidents of historically African American colleges began speaking out openly against what they feel is increasing drug use on the parts of black Greeks.

27. Get rid of the stereotypical symbols.

When University of Richmond members of Pi Kappa Alpha wanted to raise money for charity in 1998, their alumni suggested that they cultivate one-dollar-per-mile sponsors and roll a beer keg fifty miles. Bad ideas such as this need to be nixed outright by fraternity headquarters and by chapter advisers. The paddles lining the walls of many universities and university hangouts also ought to be taken down, just as rebel flags should not be present on campus.

28. Give no third chances.

Many college administrators, when considering competing national and international fraternities for new chapters, view Greek-letter groups who have gone alcohol-free more favorably than they do those who refuse to go dry, according to Jonathan Brant of the NIC. That's a good start, and it's a good incentive for undergraduates to maintain alcohol-free houses.

In the future, all new chapters of national fraternities must run substance-free houses. Otherwise reform-minded fraternities are penalized for their forward thinking because they lose recruits to chapters that drink and carouse at will. In addition, all suspended and expelled chapters that are allowed to recolonize must stay alcohol-free or face expulsion. Host universities and the NIC need to make it known that unrepentant houses and bad-actor national fraternities are no longer welcome on campus. Jim Arnold said that while he finds it encouraging that Sigma Nu, Phi Gamma Delta, Phi Delta Theta, and other national fraternities have opted to go dry, the experiment may have limited success because undergraduates often feel they have been coerced into going dry. Individual chapters that have banned alcohol because they felt they had to, not because they saw that change was called for, are less likely to fully comply, said Arnold. "There's no passion there," he said.

Student Rich Zeoli of Phi Delta Theta likewise said that chapters with a history of problems with alcohol and hazing may need watching to make sure they don't relapse. The solution, therefore, is for universities to allow a bad-actor chapter to recolonize only once. Even chapters that have been around for a hundred years or more must be closed for good if they come back and fail to reform. Executive vice president Bob Biggs of Phi Delta Theta said that while he is looking for improvement and not perfection in a chapter, there will be no third chances for chapters that let down the Phi Delt fraternity. "Make one mistake, and I'll give you that one," said Biggs in a 1998 interview for this book. "But don't make a second."

29. Be prepared to wait out the siege of drinking and hazing.

Fraternal executives can hardly be blamed for being a little too eager for good news and immediate results after they've instituted reforms. The reality is that every important national survey and study conducted since 1990 has demonstrated that many members of Greek groups routinely get drunk when they socialize. Arnold doesn't expect to see much change in student drinking habits for many years to come. He said,

> I would like to be the optimist here. The idealistic part of me would really like to believe there is a group of committed people in this country—in which I would include myself—who would like to believe that by zeal and commitment and communication skills we can be influential enough to end this destructive binge and underage drinking in student life. [Therefore,] I would like to say things will be cleaned up ten years from now, [but] I don't really believe that. The bottom line is that students drink. Just as a lot of people know what a fraternity is, a lot of people "know" a traditional college experience is "supposed" to [include drinking]. Whether it is a fraternity house, a dormitory, or off-campus apartment it is going to continue to happen, and people in that age group are going to drink abusively a lot of the time.

30. Fraternities must reform the way they monitor chapters.

Historically African American Greek national groups must find a way to hire and train field representatives to visit campuses. All national historically white fraternities must evaluate how well their field representatives are performing when it comes to reporting on a house's physical condition, pledging procedures, and overall behavior. The national is responsible when it allows itself to become disconnected from what is really happening at the various chapters, as Arnold and other researchers have pointed out.

31. Leave time for a smooth transition.

After new officers are elected, leave the old officers in charge for at least two weeks. Before new officers take their positions, many fraternities such as Sigma Nu designate a two-week period for the outgoing officers to mentor the new officers in such areas as alcohol use, risk reduction, and anti-hazing education programs.

32. Take a few TIPS.

TIPS (Training for Intervention Procedures) is an organization that since 1982 been training fraternities such as Sigma Phi Epsilon and Theta Chi (among other clients) in how to get members to use alcohol safely and responsibly. Members learn how to intervene when their peers are misusing alcohol in a social setting. For information, phone 1 (800) GET TIPS.

33. Start a hazing hotline.

A small number of Greek groups, including Pi Beta Phi, have established an 800 number for collegians, alumni, parents, or administrators to call if they wish to report hazing in their organizations.

34. Contact the parents of pledges who have died.

Maisie Ballou, whose son died in 1980 in an alcohol-related hazing involving the Sigma Nu chapter at the University of South Carolina, said that she feels Sigma Nu's leadership programs and anti-alcohol policies will have little effect, because the national fraternities have shown a lack of respect for her and her son. "Mo Littlefield [former national head of Sigma Nu] has never contacted me about reform movements, nor has any other Sigma Nu leader," said Ballou in a letter to the author of February 14, 1998. "No one ever wanted to tell us about any details surrounding Barry's death. I expect that they would have no interest in keeping me informed of the latest anti-hazing reform movements. There was a [Sigma Nu] scholarship given in Barry's name until we brought the suit against Sigma Nu. We would be informed by the University of South Carolina that someone had been given a scholarship. After the [South Carolina anti-hazing] law was passed, we never heard anything more about the scholarship." Ballou's point is clear. National fraternities should at least make an honest attempt to heal painful wounds by involving parents of victims in reforms.

WHAT PARENTS CAN DO

1. Combat high school hazing.

Foolish initiations and alcohol problems now trouble U.S. high schools. The recent near-death of a Santa Fe High School student in an alcohol-related initiation suggests that students need to be enlightened long before they enter college. If parents cannot convince youngsters living at home that hazing and alcohol abuse are wrong and dangerous, what chance do they have of communicating that message when their children are away at college, under the influence of fraternity members and other peers?

2. Learn about your child's attitudes toward Greek life.

Parents who put money and time into seeing that their children are academically prepared for college—preferably the "right" college, according to one media giant or another—and too little time discussing the social atmosphere their child will face in college are at fault. Parents need to begin talking to their children about Greek groups a year or two before they graduate from high school. Once the pledge process starts, children are so eager to gain acceptance that they often refuse to listen to their parents' advice at all. "Parents [should] talk to their children *before* they leave for college," said Maisie Ballou. "I wish we had been warned about fraternities so we could have talked to Barry about them."[23]

3. Learn about college activities.

Explore the membership possibilities offered by the College Parents of America (CPA). Among other things, the organization serves as a clearinghouse for information about alcohol and substance abuse on campus. Write College Parents of America, 700 Thirteenth Street, N.W., Suite 950, Washington, D.C. 20005. Or visit the CPA web site:

http://www.collegeparents.org/

4. When you visit campus, ask personnel at the student affairs office hard questions about Greek life at the university.

Parents can learn a hard lesson from a bereaved mother who asked too few questions.

"There are parents of boys at Auburn you just want to grab," said Mrs. Saucier. "You want to say to them, 'Did you check the fraternity out? Did you talk to them?' Parents have the same thought the pledges have—that tragedy won't happen to them."[24]

5. Check the web pages of fraternities and sororities.

Don't just look at the pages of national headquarters; look also at pages of individual chapters, some of which disparage minorities or women and glorify alcohol use. A good link to the web pages of fraternities and sororities is put out by Snow & Associates (http://www.arch.org/alphaweb.htm). You can easily find chapters at specific colleges by doing a simple web site search. Do an Internet search to read topics discussed by fraternity members in chat rooms loosely watched over by their respective headquarters. Some fraternities now actively solicit parental contributions, suggestions, and involvement. Some discourage input.

WHAT POLICE MUST DO

1. Don't destroy evidence of hazing, however repugnant this evidence may be.

Some fraternity members instruct pledges to do illegal or repugnant things, putting down these requests in pledge books that are outlawed by all Greek groups. After J. B. Joynt died following a Phi Sigma Kappa pledge sneak and intensive exercise session at Frostburg State University, police determined that his death was not caused by hazing and was accidental, because they thought he should have walked away of his own volition. An officer told the Joynts that he destroyed J. B.'s pledge book because the contents were too vile "for a mother" to read, according to J. B.'s sister, Julie Joynt. Ms. Joynt said she was disappointed by the destruction of the book, which she considered a destruction of potential evidence, even if police did not.[25] She wondered whether the book contained descriptions of anything that Frostburg State University and national headquarters might have interpreted as hazing.

The bottom line is that all evidence must be preserved.

2. Campus police need to compile a record of fraternal arrests made on and off campus so that administrators can study such records.

Why isn't this being done routinely?

"[College presidents] don't want anyone to know there are any problems on campus," said Louis Ingelhart, an expert in student press law, during a 1998 interview for this book.

Campus police must be allowed to do their jobs. While it is not possible to predict with certainty which fraternities or sororities are going to lose a pledge or member to hazing or to an alcohol overdose, it is possible to identify and to eliminate all groups that have reckless pasts and whose behavior does not indicate that they have changed for the better.

3. Campus police need to become certified as emergency medical technicians (EMTs).

Chad Saucier, Chuck Stenzel, and others who died as a result of alcohol-related hazing incidents received help from campus police, who could do only so much until paramedics arrived. Anderson University in Indiana recommends that officers become certified as EMTs, which enables them to be of far more service to students during emergencies. There is a remote possibility that campus police might have saved Chad's life if the officers that came to his aid had been certified EMTs with the authority to keep proper emergency equipment in their patrol cars. A

When they are summoned to deal with emergencies, such as the alcohol-related incidents that culminated in the deaths of Chuck Stenzel and Chad Saucier, campus police often arrive minutes ahead of professional rescue units. Surprisingly, only a handful of colleges send security officers who are certified Emergency Medical Technicians (EMTs). Anderson University (Indiana) officers John Moberly (*back turned*) and Frank Burrows (*right*) completed the 130-hour EMT certification program in five months, according to Walt Smith, Anderson University director of security. Smith said he thought EMT training might save lives, not only in alcohol crises but in many types of emergencies.
Photo simulation of emergency provided by Anderson University Publications

typical EMT certification course takes an officer about five or six months, Anderson University director of security Walt Smith said in a 1997 interview for this book. The school that has at least one officer trained as an EMT on duty every night might be able to prevent a death from occurring.

4. Punish students who have false ID cards and those who peddle the cards.

Students who purchase false ID cards are breaking the law, and some of them are dying or putting themselves in a position to harm themselves or others. In the wake of Scott Krueger's death, Boston police announced their intention to arrest students who use a false ID to purchase liquor. This is a needed deterrent. Scofflaws who make IDs should be prosecuted to the full extent of the law.

5. Take photographs of students participating in riots and arrest them after order has been restored.

During the '90s, tensions on campus began building as a result of alcohol-fueled frustrations over changes in the drinking age, the elimination of alcohol at tailgate parties, and the closure of open fraternity parties. The 1997–1998 riots at about a dozen schools, including the University of Connecticut, Michigan State University, Ohio University, Miami of Ohio, and the University of Oregon, have forced college presidents to admit that students on U.S. campuses *do* have a drinking problem. Yet the number of arrests was far lower than the number of people who created disturbances. Police need to formulate a plan with which to arrest perpetrators after the fact as a way to discourage outlaw acts.

6. Bust 'em.

Four out of five fraternity members are binge drinkers, according to the latest Harvard Study figures, released in 1998.[26] The time for drastic action has arrived. An example of an appropriate response to unacceptable alcohol use is the raid of a midweek Theta Delta Chi party at Virginia Commonwealth University. During the raid, an Alcoholic Beverage Control task force, along with city and campus police, discovered seven beer kegs and two cases of liquor. As a result, fifty-two fraternity males and one female were charged with crimes ranging from underage drinking to maintaining a common nuisance. Prior to the party, the house had been in trouble often for fighting and hosting loud parties.

Is such extreme action necessary? Yes, it is.

It has been known for more than twenty years that several students associated with certain notorious fraternity houses have died, and that many more have come close to dying. While it would be appalling to randomly select houses to be targeted in raids, particularly because there are houses whose behavior is exemplary, it makes perfect sense for task forces to single out houses with a long record of alcohol arrests and complaints from neighbors.

Here is the formula: Bust 'em, close 'em, help 'em back up.

7. Put undercover police in liquor stores.

In the wake of the death of Scott Krueger at MIT, police began working undercover in liquor stores to catch underage students attempting to purchase liquor. Since computer access to drivers' licenses is now readily available, the police are better able than liquor store clerks to catch underage drinkers with phony ID cards. If the idea is implemented nationally, it may reduce the number of students who try to purchase liquor illegally.

8. Police should act as role models for students.

At Purdue University, some campus police officers have joined faculty and staff members in trying to initiate relationships with undergraduates, taking them on field trips and stopping by their residence halls to chat, said Ron Fosnaugh, a captain of special services in the Purdue University police department. In an attempt to dispel the impression that they come over only when a complaint comes in, he and other officers make a point of visiting fraternity houses to talk with members. "We want the students to know someone cares," said Fosnaugh.[27]

9. Interview pledges and members immediately after a death or hazing occurs.

The number of times pledges or members changed their stories after a hazing incident occurs would fill a thick file. Police quite naturally empathize with young people who have just experienced the death of a friend. But to get a more accurate picture of what happened, police must conduct interviews with witnesses as early as possible.

10. View people made to endure hazing in much the same way you would people made to endure rape or sexual assault.

After J. B. Joynt died following a traditional strenuous wrestling match, one law-enforcement official ended the investigation by saying that the pledging-related event wasn't hazing because Joynt had participated in it voluntarily. "Your brother was a big boy," Julie Joynt said she was told by an investigator. "He could have stopped if he wanted to."[28] Admittedly, figuring out exactly what was on the mind of a pledge who became involved in a hazing is difficult. Some fear hazing, others embrace it; and some, often at the urging of members, hold pledge sneaks to haze members themselves. A ruling by a South Carolina court following the death of Sigma Nu pledge Barry Ballou, who had apparently willingly entered into alcohol-related activities required for admission to the University of South Carolina chapter, may help guide us here. The court said that even though Ballou had participated in a drinking ceremony, he did not "freely and voluntarily with full knowledge of its nature and extent incur the risks of dangers created by the fraternity's action[s]."[29]

In February 1998, Barry Ballou's mother said that she very much agreed with the court's opinion. "I am afraid that fraternities still expect young men to drink in order to be accepted. I know that our son, Barry, did everything (washing cars, cleaning the fraternity house) he was told to do in order to belong. He just *didn't* know what that last night of Hell Week would bring. I think that until there are stiff laws and definite consequences for those responsible, fraternity initiations will probably remain much the same."[30]

"Depart therefore from the classrooms, ye inept and unfit

who have your brains in your heels."

—Steno Bielke, 1609

APPENDIX A

A Chronology of Deaths among College Students as a Result of Hazing, Fraternal Alchohol Syndrome, Pledging, Fraternity-Related Accidents, and Other Miscellaneous Occurrences

In this book I have tried to reserve the term "hazing" for those incidents that have been so identified by state or institutional authorities. If a state hazing law has not been invoked, or if a school has said that an incident did not involve hazing even though it apparently should qualify according to the institution's own definition of the term, I have referred to the death as "pledging-related." One of the main items on the agenda of anti-hazing activists is to find a way to prevent college authorities or judicial groups from determining whether a pledging-related death is or is not a hazing. Their argument is that colleges have a vested interest in protecting their institution's reputation, and that local prosecuting attorneys too often use the discretionary powers of their office to refuse to prosecute students who may have been involved in hazing if the school rules that hazing did not occur. Because school safety is a hot-button issue, a school that develops a reputation for hazing possibly could suffer a reduction in the number of applications for admission that it receives. Thus, even the most scrupulous administrators may be reluctant to tag a case as hazing, particularly if they may subsequently become embroiled in a civil suit brought against them by a victim or by a victim's survivors.

An asterisk (*) following an item on this list indicates that at the time it occurred, the death being described was attributed to hazing activities by the victim's family or by authorities. However, either it is impossible to definitively identify the death as one that took place as the result of hazing, or the *direct* cause of death may have been or likely was illness. Readers who wish to offer additional information or to correct any inaccuracy may e-mail the author at Nuwer@IBM.net.

1838
Franklin Seminary (Kentucky)
Class hazing*
John Butler Groves (born October 31, 1819) died in a hazing incident, according to a family history.

1847
Amherst College (Massachusetts)
Class hazing*

First-year student Jonathan D. Torrance left school that fall because of a severe illness he said was caused by upperclass students soaking his sheets. He eventually died as a result of the illness. Amherst president Edward Hitchcock attributed Torrance's death to hazing. The hazing custom was called "freshman visitation."

1873
Cornell University (New York)
Kappa Alpha Society
Road trip

Having been made by KAS brothers to find his way back home through the woods in the night, first-year student Mortimer N. Leggett fell into a gorge and died. "The miserable hocus-pocus heathenish custom of such a night ramble is the sin and disgrace of the society, but this mummery was invented and inaugurated long before any of these young men were born," said U.S. Commissioner of Internal Revenue M. D. Leggett, Mortimer's father, in a letter to his surviving sons.[1]

1892
Yale University (Connecticut)
Delta Kappa Epsilon
Accidental death during pledging activity*

A blindfolded student accidentally injured himself with a sharp object on a carriage while carrying out a command to run down a street. Peritonitis set in, and he died five days later. "The time has certainly come when criminal recklessness and 'childish frivolity' in initiations should be forever relegated to the barbaric past," said a Delta Kappa Epsilon member following the death.

1894
Cornell University (New York)
Class hazing

A female cook/server died when undergraduates who were attempting to play a class prank during a banquet misdirected chlorine gas into a kitchen stove area.

1899
Cornell University (New York)
Kappa Alpha Society
Pledge errand

Pledge Edward Fairchild Berkeley of St. Louis, Missouri, died of accidental drowning when he fell into the Oswego and Seneca Canal near Geneva, New York, while attempting to pin a piece of paper to a tree or bridge (accounts differ) at the request of a fraternity member. The member insisted that the act was not hazing but was rather an attempt to keep Berkeley occupied until his formal initiation, scheduled later that evening at the Hobart College Kappa Alpha Society house. A coroner concluded that KAS was not to blame.

1900
Massachusetts Institute of Technology
Class scrap
During a nonsensical traditional event known as the "cane rush," in which first- and second-year students fought mightily to get the most hands on a four-foot cane, Hugh C. Moore died of a snapped neck, and two first-year males were knocked out cold.

1900
United States Military Academy (New York)
Illness (revealed hazing abuses)*
A House of Representatives committee conducted an inquiry after plebe Oscar Booz died of an illness. The committee was able to demonstrate that Booz had been maliciously hazed, but was unable to prove that his death was caused by anything other than illness.

1903
University of Maryland (Baltimore campus)
Phi Psi Chi (local dental fraternity)
Mystery death*
Inadequate forensic techniques of the day were unable to determine an exact cause beyond "congestion of the lungs" of the death of dental student Martin Loew. The death made front-page headlines when authorities first revealed that a few days earlier Loew and his roommate, Ephraim Stone, had been bruised slightly while performing hazing stunts required for admission.

1905
Kenyon College (Ohio)
Delta Kappa Epsilon
Mystery death
Stuart L. Pierson was struck by a train after DKE brothers left him on a bridge. Kenyon historian George Franklin Smythe termed the death "a mystery."

1912
University of North Carolina
Freshman Isaac Rand bled to death during a stunt.

1913
Purdue University (Indiana)
Class hazing
Frances W. Obenchain died while participating in the annual scrap that pitted classes against one another.

1914
St. John's Military College (Maryland)
Class hazing
William R. Bowlus was shot and killed while hazing a first-year student.

1915
University of Kentucky
Class hazing
Eldridge Griffith, a freshman celebrating a victory over the sophomores in a tug of war, was killed by a streetcar that hit the cable he was holding, throwing him violently.

1915
New Mexico Military Institute
Class hazing*
After being dunked in a horse tank and abandoned far from campus, Ludwig Von Gerichten Jr. died from pneumonia. His family blamed the death on hazing.

1917
College of the City of New York
Phi Sigma Kappa
Death from illness (possibly hazing-related)*
William Ashcom Bullock died of spinal meningitis after members rolled him on the ground in a wet blanket. He had been in ill health before members hazed him. His mother blamed the fraternity for his death.

1919
Colgate University (New York)
Class hazing
First-year student Frank McCullough drowned when he tried to swim to shore after sophomores left him on an island.

1921
Northwestern University (Illinois)
Class hazing (cause of death unknown)
Leighton Mount disappeared after the annual class rush. His body was found beneath a pier two years later. It is not known how he died. His death is classified as a mystery.

1922
Hamilton College (New York)
Class hazing or horseplay
Duncan Saunders, 15, died of a skull fracture and ruptured aorta when he was roughly flung from his bed, according to Hamilton spokesman Frank Lorenz, curator of special collections. Since then a number of stories have surfaced and been published, making it difficult to ascertain whether the incident was hazing or horseplay.

1923
University of Alabama
Sigma Nu
Illness*
Glenn Kersh, who had a faulty heart, died "from psychic effects of excitement" following his initiation, according to a coroner's report.

1923
Franklin and Marshall College (Pennsylvania)
Class hazing
Injuries in class battle
Sophomore Ainsworth Brown died after being injured when first-year students tangled with upper-class students.

1923
Northwestern University (Illinois)
Class hazing
Road trip
First-year student Louis Aubere was killed while on the running board of a car that was searching for other freshmen who had been kidnapped by sophomores to keep them from attending a class event. Another car ran into the vehicle, killing Aubere and injuring a second student, according to a letter written by Northwestern archivist Patrick Quinn to hazing researcher Mike Moskos.

1928
University of Texas
Delta Kappa Epsilon
Fraternity hazing (electrocution ritual)
Pledge Nolte McElroy died from electrical shock when he had to crawl through mattresses charged with electrical current.

1929
Indiana University, Bloomington
Delta Chi
Hazing (illness-related)*
George Steinmetz Jr. died from lung disease after being physically hazed.

1940
University of Missouri, Columbia
Theta Nu Epsilon (unrecognized fraternity)
Required drinking
Hubert L. Spake Jr. died of an alcohol overdose following a required drinking session.

1945
St. Louis University (Missouri)
Phi Beta Pi
Initiation ritual
Robert Perry was burned to death after members coated his naked body with flammable substances and then began to administer electrical shocks to his skin. A spark ignited, turning him into a human torch.

1949
Brown University (Rhode Island)
Fall from stairs (rush night)
During a pre-pledging tour of a fraternity house, 19-year-old H. T. Gehl fell down the stairs. He died of a brain injury two days later.

1950
University of California, Berkeley
Sigma Pi
Road trip
Pledge Gerald L. Foletta, 18, was killed, and Theodore Glassnow, 25, was severely injured, when they were hit by an automobile after members dropped them off in the country.

1950
Wittenberg University (Ohio)
Alpha Tau Omega
Road trip
Dean J. Niswonger, a pledge, was hit and killed by a truck while he slept on a road. Members had taken him and another pledge (who suffered a broken arm) on a road trip.

1954
Swarthmore College (Pennsylvania)
Delta Upsilon
Road trip
Peter Mertz was struck by a car and killed after fraternity members dumped him in the countryside.

1956
Massachusetts Institute of Technology
Delta Kappa Epsilon
Road trip
Thomas Clark, 18, drowned in a reservoir after members took him on a "one-way ride."

1957
University of California, Santa Barbara
Delta Tau Delta
"Pinning" pseudo-initiation
Max B. Caulk, 22, drowned when members threw him into a harbor in a ritual following his pinning to a Kappa Alpha Theta sorority member. Alcohol was not a factor.

1959
University of Southern California
Kappa Sigma
Physical hazing
Pledge Richard Swanson choked to death while trying to swallow a slab of liver at the request of members.

1965
Georgetown College
Pi Kappa Alpha
Death of hazer
Richard Winder drowned in a freak accident while he was hazing a fellow member who had been pinned. He and the other man were swept over a dam. The other person survived. There were more than twenty members present at the ceremony, which took place around midnight.

1967
Baylor University (Texas)
Baylor Chamber of Commerce
Physical hazing (eating ritual)
John E. Clifton choked to death after trying to swallow a foul concoction. The state called the death accidental, but the pre-initiation ceremony included many practices that national fraternities consider hazing.

1970
Eastern Illinois University
Alpha Gamma Delta sorority
Death of member during abduction by pledges
Member Donna Bedinger fell from the bumper of a moving car. The car contained pledges who had dumped her and a sorority sister in the countryside south of Charleston, Illinois. She died from her injuries in a Terre Haute, Indiana, hospital. The death was ruled accidental by authorities.

1971
Tulane University (Louisiana)
Delta Kappa Epsilon
Rush-related horseplay*
Wayne P. Kennedy, 17, died of drowning after being thrown into Lake Pontchartrain during a rush party. Although this incident was ruled horseplay and non-hazing by authorities at the time, this chapter found itself in trouble for serious hazing infractions in 1977.[2]

1972
Pierce College (California)
Chi Chi Chi
Road trip
Fred Bronner, 20, was taken on a road trip without his eyeglasses and fell into a gorge. He died as a result of the fall. He was being punished by fellow members John Berges, Gordon Gillespie, and John Morgan for allegedly having a bad attitude.

1972
University of Maryland, College Park
Sigma Alpha Mu
Physical hazing
Brian Cursack, a large young man, collapsed and died after performing calisthenics.

1973
Lehigh University (Pennsylvania)
Delta Phi
Kidnap attempt (pledge leaped from car)
A 19-year-old pledge, Mitchell Fishkin, died after he jumped from an automobile to keep from being taken to a location far from campus. Although kidnapping is listed as hazing by all national fraternities, the university and national fraternity called this incident "horseplay."

1974
Grove City College (Pennsylvania)
Adelphikos
Road trip
Seventeen pledges who had been dropped off in the country were headed back to campus when a driver who had fallen asleep at the wheel drove his car into the group. Killed were Thomas M. Elliot, John Curtin, Rudolph Mion, and Gary Gilliland, all 18.

1974
Monmouth College (New Jersey)
Zeta Beta Tau
Physical hazing (grave-digging ritual)
Seven members made William Edward Flowers, 19, dig his own grave on a sandy beach. It caved in. A grand jury ruled that Flowers died accidentally of suffocation.

1974
Bluefield State College (West Virginia)
Tau Kappa Epsilon
Pre-initiation shooting death (involuntary manslaughter)
During an odd pre-initiation ceremony in which a can was put on the head of a pledge and knocked off with a stick while a pistol shot rang out, graduate adviser Edwin Taylor began shooting at those present. He killed Michael Bishop, 20, a member. He was convicted of involuntary manslaughter.

1975
Northern Illinois University
Wine Psi Phi social club (not affiliated with university)
Alcohol-related death
Richard A. Gowins, 23, died from drinking a mixture of gin, tequila, and wine given to pledges of a local social club.

1975
University of Wisconsin, Stevens Point
Siasefi fraternity
Annual drinking custom
Newcomer David Hoffman died in his sleep after finishing a so-called "Death March" during which students drank heavily at area taverns.

1975
University of Nevada, Reno
Sundowners (drinking fraternity)
Initiation-related drinking marathon
Pledge John Davies, 22, died, and Gary Faulstich went into cardiac arrest but survived after three days of marathon drinking.

1975
Washington State University
Tau Kappa Epsilon
Hell Week death caused by pneumonia*
Jon Asher, who was sleep-deprived and who voluntarily performed calisthenics though he was very ill, died in a hospital bed following Hell Week activities.

Pershing Rifles pledges at Indiana University endured silly but not life-threatening hazing. In 1976, while on a so-called training exercise (similar to a pledging initiation), Queens College junior Thomas Fitzgerald, 19, died. Fitzgerald had been trying to get into the elite Pershing Rifles connected with St. John's University Reserve Officers Training Corps. The death occurred after cadet officer James Savino accidentally plunged a knife into Fitzgerald's heart during an interrogation. Savino had meant to put the knife into a makeshift sign that read "P.O.W." *Photograph courtesy of Indiana University Archives, Bloomington, Indiana*

1975
Cheyney State College (now Cheyney University of Pennsylvania)
Freshman-sophomore class hazing
Brutal physical hazing
Following a long, intense session of physical hazing, Theodore Ben, 19, was slammed into a wall. His skull was injured, and he went into a coma. He died later in a hospital. The college president then denied all responsibility.

1976
Texas Tech University
Pi Kappa Alpha
Scavenger hunt: member death
Members and pledges lost track of member Samuel Mark Click on a scavenger hunt during which a letter was put under a railroad tie. Members later went to search for him. He had been hit by a train and killed, suffering numerous injuries to his head and body. No hazing charges were filed.

1976
Iowa State University
Phi Delta Theta
Alcohol-related death
Dennis Redenbeck died in the fraternity house after drinking massive quantities of different liquors and beer.

1976
St. John's University (New York)
Pershing Rifles
Bayonet stabbing death
Following a kidnapping, ROTC pledge Thomas Fitzgerald, a student at another school who had applied for admission into the Pershing Rifles, was being intimidated with a bayonet when the blade accidentally entered his chest.

1977
North Carolina Central University
Unrecognized and unofficial local chapter
Calisthenics-related pledging fatality
A pledge died after performing calisthenics. The outlaw chapter was not officially connected with the Omega Psi Phi national fraternity, but members had appropriated the national's name. No hazing charges were filed.

1977
University of Pennsylvania
Unrecognized and unofficial local chapter
Heart attack following extreme exertion
Robert Bazile, 19, died after weeks of heavy hazing that included beatings and paddlings, acts of servitude, and sleep deprivation. He died after being paddled and forced to run long distances. Omega Psi Phi denied that hazing had been a factor in the death, according to the *Washington Star*.[3] Omega Psi Phi also said it had not sanctioned the chapter.

1977
Oklahoma State University
Fraternity accident
Electrocution
Three young men working on a castle that was part of a fraternity float were accidentally electrocuted. The dead men were pledge Merle George, pledge Randall Logan, and member Kevin Wilson. Hazing was not a factor.

1977
University of Missouri, Rolla
Kappa Alpha Order, and Daughters of Lee
Initiation accident
A cannon that misfired during a Daughters of Lee little sisters' initiation was incorrectly reloaded and blew up when it fired, injuring an initiate and killing Randall Crustals, 21.

1978
Loras College (Iowa)
Gamma Psi
Drinking death
Stephen J. McNamara, 22, died of acute alcohol intoxication after barhopping on a Sunday with brothers from this underground local drinking fraternity. McNamara had already blacked out once when members put him to bed in his dormitory room.

1978
Case Western Reserve University (Ohio)
Zeta Psi
Roof death
Michael Quaintance, a member, accidentally fell to his death after going to the top of the roof alone. He had been attending a "Welcome Back" party.

1978
Alfred University
Klan Alpine fraternity
Alcohol-related hazing death
Pledge Chuck Stenzel, 20, died and two others were in critical condition for many hours after they participated in the intense drinking required as part of Tapping Night, Alfred's traditional first night of pledging.

1979
Louisiana State University
Theta Xi
Road trip (ritual march)
Bruce Wiseman was one of twenty blindfolded pledges marching in a group along a dark road en route to a fraternity ritual. A driver plowed into the group, killing Wiseman and injuring five other pledges.

1979
Virginia Polytechnic Institute and State University
Phi Delta Theta
Fall while drinking
Paul Hayward, a 20-year-old party guest, fell down the stairs into the house basement. He died from head injuries a few days later.

1979
University of South Carolina
Kappa Alpha Psi
Shooting spree
A student from another school who was visiting the university opened fire during a party, killing Terrel Johnson and Patrick McGinty, both 18.

1979
Northeast Missouri State University (now Truman State)
Alpha Kappa Lambda
Alcohol-related death
David Andres, 19, drank himself to death at a party his fraternity co-sponsored with a sorority. His blood-alcohol level was 0.43 percent at the time of his death.

1979
Valparaiso University (Indiana)
Phi Delta Theta fraternity
Alcohol-related stabbing death
Mike Spagoletti, 18, died of multiple stab wounds in a fight after fraternity members asked him to leave following a quarrel between him and another partygoer.

1979
Rutgers University (New Jersey)
Delta Phi
Death of pledge in alcohol-related incident
A drinking ritual at a tavern at dawn was considered a voluntary, non-hazing activity by university officials. Richard C. Fuhs Jr., 20, who partici-pated in the activity after having been rousted out of bed, was killed when the car he was in following the session hit a telephone pole. Three others survived the crash with minor injuries.

1979
Virginia State College
Beta Phi Burgundy female social club, Wine Psi Phi male social club
Double drowning (during quasi-baptismal pledging ritual)
Two students in predominantly African American social clubs drowned near the campus in a joint "going-over" ceremonial party. Because the event was held in darkness, the students were not missed immediately. Pledge Norsha Lynn Delk, 20, of Beta Phi Burgundy, and pledge Robert Etheridge, 21, died in the mishap, which occurred when currents apparently swept Delk away as she took part in a "cleansing" ceremony. Etheridge was apparently trying to rescue Delk but could not make it back to the shore of the fast-running Appomattox River. Alcohol was present during the ceremony.

1979
University of North Dakota
Sigma Nu
Member stabbed by member
A member was going to be slapped on the stomach and given a "cherry belly" by fellow members who believed he wasn't carrying his share of the fraternity's workload. He pulled out a knife to frighten away several attack-ers and inadvertently jammed the blade into the chest of Kingsley Davidson, 19, who died from the stab wound. Although the university called the inci-dent hazing, the member was tried for involuntary manslaughter but was found not guilty.

1980
Clarkson College (New York)
Alpha Epsilon Pi
Late-night road jogging
Pledge David Masciantonio, 19, and three other young men were hit by a car while pledges and members were jogging at 3:00 A.M. Masciantonio died. In spite of the hour at which the incident occurred, the school insisted that there had been no hazing, but at least one anti-hazing activist disputed that judgment.

1980
Virginia Polytechnic Institute and State University
Fraternity party
Alcohol-related auto accident
Michelle Greenleaf, 19, died while she was a passenger in a car driven by a young man who had attended a dance sponsored by a Tech fraternity.

1980
Mississippi State University
Pi Kappa Alpha
Pledging-related accident
Pledges were driving a member to a mudhole traditionally used for dunkings when the member apparently leaped from the car. Curtis Huntley, 20, had celebrated his birthday the day before, and that may have been why pledges wanted to capture him. He went into a coma and died.

1980
University of Missouri, Columbia
Phi Kappa Psi
Fraternity-related horseplay
Pledge Lex Dean Batson fell to his death from a bluff following a prank during which pledges and members were asked to urinate on a statue.

1980
Ithaca College
Delta Kappa
Calisthenics-related hazing
A long-standing tradition of forcing pledges to perform calisthenics in a steamroom with the heat turned up high finally claimed a victim, Joseph Parrella, 18.

1980
University of Lowell (Massachusetts)
Delta Kappa Phi
Calisthenics-related fatality
A pledge, 19, died after having been in a coma for a week. Steve Call had become ill after he was required to perform extensive calisthenics.

1980
University of South Carolina
Sigma Nu
Alcohol-related choking death
Pledge Barry Ballou, 20, choked to death after he passed out. Members had urged him to consume massive quantities of alcohol in a drinking ritual.

1981
University of Wisconsin, Platteville
Phi Sigma Epsilon
Roof death
Billy Benes, the chapter president, fell to his death from the roof of the fraternity house.

1981
California State University, Long Beach
Sigma Pi
Alcohol-related accident

Robert Harris Jr. died hours after a beer keg accidentally exploded at a Sigma Pi party, slamming into him.

1981
Creighton University (Nebraska)
Phi Delta Theta and other fraternities
Party-related deaths

Three students died when a car struck them while they were leaving a fraternity party. Alcohol was a factor in the tragedy.

1981
University of Wisconsin, Superior
FEX (local fraternity)
Physical hazing

Rick Cerra, 21, collapsed and died during calisthenics. He had been made to wear winter clothing on a warm day.

1981
Pittsburg State University (Kansas)
Sigma Tau Gamma
Alcohol-related accident

Drunk on pure grain alcohol, member Robert "Brad" Wohltman, 20, of Independence, Kansas, died when a police car rode over him while he was lying on a city street.

1982
University of Texas at Austin
Sigma Nu
Drinking death

Member John Calkins, 20, drank himself to death at a party.

1982
Towson State University
Alpha Omega Lambda
Sleep deprivation, servitude, auto accident

Fraternity members frequently encourage or require pledges to wear demeaning costumes. A sleep-deprived pledge, Victor "Ricky" M. Siegel, was wearing a Playboy bunny costume when he rolled his car, killing himself and injuring two fellow pledges. The three men were on a mission to get signatures from alumni of this local fraternity.

1982
University of Virginia
Sigma Chi
Alcohol-related accident

Two young men died and sixty-three were hurt when a rental van en route to a party collided with another vehicle. The driver of the van had been drinking. The two killed were Brian McKittrick, 17, and Chris Meigs, 18.

1983
Tennessee State University
Omega Psi Phi
Pledging-related drinking marathon
The fraternity was suspended for five years after pledge Vann Watts died of an alcohol overdose. A surviving pledge said he had been hazed and beaten with switches, but the rest of the pledge class said no hazing had occurred. Watts's blood-alcohol level was 0.52 percent at the time of his death. His head had been shaved.

1984
Hampden-Sydney College (Virginia)
Theta Chi
Accident
Alcohol was a factor in the death of a member, although at the time of his death he was not legally drunk according to the state's definition.

1984
Indiana University
Zeta Beta Tau
Arson
A nonstudent set a fire that killed Israel D. Edelman, a student at the Richmond, Indiana, branch campus, and injured thirty-four people.

1984
University of California, Davis
Kappa Alpha Order
Drunk driving
A truck filled with pledges and members heading toward a traditional graffiti rock to write a message and paint their Greek letters crashed on Interstate 80, killing Brad Bing, 21, and injuring seven young men.

1984
Texas A&M University
Corps of Cadets
Hazing (calisthenics)
Heatstroke killed Bruce Ward Goodrich, 20, a second-year member of the Corps of Cadets who had been participating in a strenuous workout that started at 2:30 A.M. One student was found guilty of destroying evidence in the form of a company exercise schedule; three others pleaded guilty to hazing.

1984
American International College
Zeta Chi (local fraternity)
Pledging-related drinking ritual
Jay Lenaghan, 19, died in his sleep in a bathtub following a drinking ritual in which he and others consumed small plates of spaghetti washed down with enormous quantities of wine. Members had placed him in a tub to clean him up after he experienced bowel failure. Members failed to understand that Lenaghan's bowel failure was a sign that he was dying. His blood-alcohol level was 0.48 at the time of his death.

1984
California State University, Chico
Tau Gamma Theta
Pledging-related drag race, drinking

Ten pledges were encouraged to consume two gallons of wine the night pledge Jeffrey Franklin Long, 23, was killed by another pledge's speeding automobile in a pledging-related drag race. Some pledges and members of the local fraternity were charged with concealing facts related to the fraternity's treatment of Long that evening. To keep the details of the drag race from being made public, they claimed that he had been taken on a ride and left in the country. Members still maintain that the press overreacted to the death.

1984
University of Toledo (Ohio)
Alpha Sigma Phi
Drinking death

Michael Leffler, 17, attended a fraternity party and scuffled inside with other partygoers. He died of an alcohol overdose on the porch of the house.

1985
University of Georgia
Theta Chi
Alcohol-related accident

Fraternity member Ronald Edward Wells, 21, fell off the hood of a moving car near the fraternity house. He had consumed about two sixpacks of beer. He died the next day.

1985
University of Kansas
Alpha Phi
Fall from third-floor window

Witnesses said Jeanna M. Carkoski, a sophomore member, voluntarily climbed onto a ledge outside her sorority house to wash windows. She fell to her death while washing a window of her room. Alcohol and hazing were not factors, according to Alpha Phi spokeswoman Joyce Shumway.

1985
University of Colorado
Kappa Alpha Theta
Alcohol overdose and fall

Pledge Sherri Ann Clark's blood-alcohol level was three times the legal limit when she fell to her death at a party sponsored by two sororities.

1985
University of Missouri, Columbia
Lambda Chi Alpha
Alcohol-related auto accident

A rushee being driven home from a rush party by a member was killed in a car accident.

1986
Ferris State College (Michigan)
Tau Kappa Epsilon
Alcohol-related accident
First-year student Keith Colangelo died, and two others were injured, when two cars returning from a TKE party struck them as they walked back to their residence after having been at the same party.

1986
Lamar University (Texas)
Omega Psi Phi
Death following stringent exercise session*
A man whose grades were too low to permit him to pledge tried to pledge anyway, and chapter members made little or no effort to discourage him. A male in an Omega shirt who was no longer a student at Lamar University strongly urged him to run laps on a school track. Initiated members did little or nothing to intervene or to prevent a nonmember from getting involved in fraternity business. Pledge Harold Thomas, 25, died because of a hemorrhaging heart. A university panel and the national fraternity ruled that hazing was not involved. The Thomas family disagreed. Cases such as this have caused historically African American fraternities to take strong measures against illegal or so-called "renegade" members and chapters.[4]

1986
University of Texas at Austin
Phi Kappa Psi
Alcohol-related hazing
Mark Seeberger, 18, died in 1986 after members handcuffed him, drove him around in a car, and fed him large quantities of rum and beer. He was left in his dormitory room, and he died in his sleep. His blood-alcohol level was 0.43 percent at the time of his death. A Travis County grand jury refused to indict anyone.

1986
Bowling Green State University (Ohio)
Phi Kappa Psi
Drowning
Scott Davis, 22, drowned in a river after leaving a fraternity formal.

1986
University of Washington
Alpha Delta Phi
Fall from window
Thomas John White Jr. fell to his death while drinking at a house party.

1987
University of Washington
Beta Theta Pi
Roof death (not alcohol- or hazing-related)
Brian P. Lopez, 18, died in a fall from the house roof three days after he arrived at college from his home in Spokane, Washington.

1987
Carnegie Mellon University
Delta Tau Delta
Stabbing of guest
Jeanne Goldberg, 20, a visitor from Robert Morris College, was stabbed to death at a fraternity party. The mother of the dead student charged that drugs and alcohol at the party created an atmosphere that led to the killing.

1987
University of Virginia
Sigma Phi Epsilon
Fall
James Christopher Haughay, 21, a former student from Spartanburg, South Carolina, died when he fell from a ledge while trying to get into a locked room. His blood-alcohol level was over 0.30.

1987
University of Western Ontario (Canada)
Alpha Epsilon Pi (international fraternity)
Pledging-related auto death
Samuel Zahavy, 19, and Joel Swirsky, 18, were passengers in a car filled with pledges taking a long trip. There was an accident, and the two were killed. Three others pledges in the vehicle were hurt, but pledges in three other cars were not injured. Zahavy had quit pledging just before the accident, but a friend had talked him into coming back, said Yehezkel Zahavy, the boy's father.

1987
University of Mississippi
Kappa Alpha Order
Alcohol-related fall
Although the death of Harry "Skip" Cline Jr., 18, in a fall was ruled accidental by university officials, it occurred after an annual drinking-related party at the fraternity house at which big brothers encouraged pledges to drink.

1987
SUNY Plattsburgh
Sigma Pi
Alcohol-related accident
A truck driven by a 21-year-old fraternity member plowed into a group of college students walking on an icy street. Toni Bloom, also 21, died of head and chest injuries after her body was swept under the truck and dragged five hundred feet. The driver was convicted of criminally negligent homicide. He said he had not been aware that he had hit a person, and he apologized to Bloom's family for not stopping. He denied being drunk, but he was never given a test to determine his blood-alcohol level.

1987
University of Arkansas
Pi Kappa Alpha
Alcohol-related accident
Rushee Todd Prince, an underage drinker, was killed by a passing vehicle after he was given alcohol by members at a fraternity hayride. He was struck while other hayriders used a restroom.

1987
Kansas State University
Phi Delta Theta
Roof death
Member Jeffrey Nolting fell to his death while participating in a foolish annual ritual that involved throwing televisions and appliances off the house roof.

1987
Stanford University
Zeta Psi
Drowning
Rushee David Dunshee, 20, died during a fraternity party held on a lake. His blood-alcohol level was 0.25 when he died.

1987
Pennsylvania State University
Delta Sigma Phi
Roof death
Paul Walsh was drunk when he fell to his death.

1988
Rutgers University
Lambda Chi Alpha
Alcohol-related pledging ritual
James Callahan died after members set up more than two hundred mixed drinks for the pledges to consume.

1988
SUNY Albany
Tau Kappa Epsilon
Electrocution during pre-initiation "cleansing" ceremony
A pledge died in a quasi-baptismal ceremony meant to symbolically wash away pre-pledging characteristics; members and pledges agreed to step into a lake that, unknown to them, had an electrical current running through it. Pledge Bryan Higgins, 20, of Mahopac, New York, died after an underwater cable malfunctioned, turning Indian Lake into a high-voltage death trap. Hazing did not occur, said school and law-enforcement officials.

1988
University of Richmond (Virginia)
Pi Kappa Alpha
Automobile accident
Matthew S. McCoy, 18, died in an automobile accident, having fallen asleep at the wheel after he and other pledges volunteered to do some projects. A school official ruled that the incident did not qualify as hazing.

1988
University of Texas
Delta Tau Delta
Chase
Member Gregg Scott Phillips, 21, perished in 1988 when he fell from a cliff while trying to escape from pledges intent on throwing him into a swimming pool.

1988
University of Tennessee
Phi Kappa Tau
Altercation outside fraternity house
Thomas H. "Tommy" Baer, a fraternity member, was armed with a bat and handcuffs when he tried to detain an intoxicated Jeffrey R. Underwood at the request of other members. Underwood killed Baer (who was sober). Underwood received a fifteen-year prison term.

1988
Rider College (New Jersey)
Theta Chi
Pledging-related death
A car carrying three intoxicated pledges who were getting alcohol for a party for pledges and a kidnapped fraternity member hit a parked pickup truck, killing pledge Sean Hickey, 19. The 19-year-old driver, John Delesandro III, was speeding at the time of the accident and received a one-year sentence.

1988
University of Arizona
Delta Tau Delta
Alcohol-related vehicle accident
An inebriated 20-year-old pledge leaving a fraternity beer party during the first week of school hit the car of Rueben A. Hernandez. The accident left Hernandez blind, paralyzed, and brain-damaged. He died nearly two years later as a result of his injuries.

1988
University of Missouri, Rolla
St. Pat's Board
Binge-drinking death
Anthony J. Busalaki, 20, died after consuming lethal amounts of alcohol at a party put on by a group whose main function was to boost school spirit by sponsoring an annual St. Patrick's Day celebration.

1988
University of Florida
Sigma Alpha Epsilon
Fall
Visitor Jason T. Miller, 21, fell to his death from a balcony of the fraternity house.

1989
Morehouse College (Georgia)
Alpha Phi Alpha
Physical hazing
Pledge Joel Harris, 18, had an enlarged heart. He died in a case of rough physical hazing. His mother, Adrienne Harris, began a brief campaign to fight hazing in fraternities. Nonetheless, she said in a 1990 interview with the author that she sympathized with the Alpha Phi Alpha chapter members who demonstrated remorse for Joel's death. "I almost came out on the lighter side, the easier side," said Harris. "These poor kids have to live with that [horrific] memory. I only have happy memories. We forget what the fraternity world was organized for. It was for community work, for community service and for brotherhood, not for death and pain." Subsequently, *School Daze* movie director Spike Lee visited Morehouse College, his alma mater, and urged the school to ban fraternities. They remain on campus.

1989
Cornell University (New York)
Alpha Epsilon Pi
Fight
Cornell's Alpha Epsilon Pi chapter served alcohol to minor Todd M. Crane, who got into an alcohol-related fistfight with an ex–Ithaca College student. The fight, which took place in an Ithaca College parking lot, ended in Crane's death. The ex-student who killed him, Alexander P. Lesburt, had also been served alcohol. Cornell's Theta Chi was also cited for serving Crane.

1989
Clemson University (South Carolina)
Alpha Tau Omega
Fall of guest
A young woman died in a fall from a ledge at the fraternity house after she tried unsuccessfully to climb through a friend's window. Shannon Gill's blood-alcohol level was 0.17 at the time of her death, which indicates that she was intoxicated. The school later installed security devices on windows.

1989
University of New Hampshire
Pi Kappa Alpha Fraternity/Alpha Chi Omega sorority picnic
Alcohol-related auto accident
Laura J. Dexter, 23, a University of New Hampshire student, was found guilty of driving under the influence following the death of her sorority sister in an automobile accident. After drinking at a picnic, Dexter crashed a 1985 Honda, killing sorority sister Christine L. Duplessis, 22. She was fined $500, and her driver's license was revoked for ninety days. The university imposed sanctions against the Greek groups.

1990
Drexel University (Pennsylvania)
Alpha Pi Lambda
Fall, alcohol-related death
Rosario Pagnotti, 20, apparently fell to his death while attending a party. His body landed in an alley and was not discovered until the following day.

1990
Dickinson College (Pennsylvania)
Alpha Chi Rho
Fall from roof
After drinking about ten drinks at a rush party, Steven Butterworth fell out a window to his death. The death was ruled accidental, but the fraternity had violated school rules governing alcohol use.

1990
York College of Pennsylvania
Sigma Pi
Roof death
Brian C. Lefever, 20, died in a fall from the roof of the apartment building that served as home to several members of Sigma Pi. Lefever was legally intoxicated at the time of his death.

1990
University of Rhode Island
Tau Kappa Epsilon
Suicide
Pledge David Lallemand, 19, accused of having taken part in a gang rape, committed suicide after the victim said she had been drunk and could not recall all the details.

1990
University of California, Berkeley
Phi Kappa Sigma; Kappa Kappa Gamma
House fire
An early-morning fraternity house fire killed Kappa Kappa Gamma member Natalia Avril James, 19, and Phi Kappa Sigma members Robert Douglas Sciutto, 21, and Ryan Hamilton, 19. Hamilton and James were cousins. Brian Hilton, 23, a nonstudent guest who had set a couch on fire as a prank and had failed to put it out, was convicted of manslaughter.

1990
University of Vermont
Kappa Sigma
Roof death
Brett Klein, 21, was intoxicated when he fell outside his fraternity house and landed on a pipe that pierced his body. He was attempting to enter a locked room and fell ten feet.

1990
University of Texas, Austin
Beta Theta Pi
Roof death
A former University of Texas student, Byron Gauntt, continued to live in the Beta Theta Pi house even after he began attending Austin Community College. Gauntt fell from the roof after returning with friends from a nightclub. He died of massive head injuries.

1990
Jacksonville, Florida
Alpha Tau Omega national conference
Alcohol-related fall
A student delegate plunged from a bridge to his death after he had been drinking.

1990
Western Illinois University
Lacrosse club
Alcohol-related hazing death
Nick Haben, who was underage and who was ordinarily a nondrinker, died of an alcohol overdose while participating in drinking games required for admission into the lacrosse club. "I do not feel there is one particular person to blame for Nick Haben's death," said lacrosse club veteran Rian Sanders. "I hold myself personally responsible along with other lacrosse players, alcohol, and peer pressure. Nick was in a difficult situation. He was young and just starting out in college, He, along with the rest of us, wanted to fit in with his peers."[5]

1991
University of Missouri, Rolla
St. Pat's Board
Alcohol-related hazing
Mike Nisbet, 28, choked to death on his own vomit during a drinking ritual required of new members being initiated into an organization which at the time was considered elite on campus. Its purpose was to raise money for an annual St. Patrick's Day party. Nisbet was present as his residence hall's representative to the board.

1991
University of Missouri, Rolla
St. Pat's Board
Alcohol-related death
Member Tristan G. Pinzke, 20, died at the wheel of his car while he was intoxicated.

1991
University of California, Berkeley
Phi Gamma Delta
Alcohol-related fall
Pledge John Moncello, 18, was told twice by fraternity members to visit the house even though he protested that he had been drinking. He came and fell to his death from a fire escape in the middle of the night.

1991
Ateneo University (Philippines)
Aquila Legis legal fraternity
Physical hazing
Leonard Villa, 22, a first-year law student, was kicked, mauled, and beaten to death in a hazing incident.

1991
University of Vermont
Sigma Alpha Epsilon
Fall
John Andrews, 23, died after falling out of a window. He was attending a party at his fraternity house.

1991
Georgia Tech
Sigma Alpha Epsilon
Alcohol-related death
The body of Michael Adams, 20, was pulled out of an Atlanta lake after he had been permitted to drink a tremendous amount of alcohol at his fraternity house, a local restaurant, and a nightclub. Although police were not able to piece together all the events of his last hours, they learned that his fraternity brothers had left him in an inebriated state at a nightclub, where he spurned the efforts of rival fraternity members who tried to take him home.

1991
Trinity University (Texas)
Triniteers
Alcohol-related pledging accident
Pledge Rolland Christopher Pederson died when he was hit by a vehicle while running back to a car filled with members and pledges headed to a pledge retreat. The car stopped so that pledges could urinate and vomit. The pledges had consumed wine given to them by a member and had drunk beer at a keg party co-sponsored by the Triniteers and the Spurs sorority. The school ruled that the accident was a violation of alcohol policy, and was not hazing.

1992
University of Vermont
Sigma Phi Society
Rush party death
Jonathan S. McNamara, 17, fell from a cliff after a campfire-side chat with members of the fraternity he hoped to join. At the time of his death,

Jon McNamara (*right, in striped shirt*), 17, fell to his death during a Sigma Phi Society pledging event at the University of Vermont. The fraternity denied that hazing had occurred, but McNamara's twin brother, Dylan, said that his brother had phoned him before the event and admitted that certain pledging rituals were taking place that members forbade him to talk about. Since the mid-'70s, at least thirty fraternity and sorority members have died in alcohol-related falls.
Photo Courtesy of Rob McNamara

McNamara's blood-alcohol level was 0.125. Members of the fraternity said he lost his balance while putting out a campfire. His twin brother, Dylan McNamara, said that he was unsatisfied with the chapter's explanation, saying he received conflicting reports from members about the use of alcohol in pledging rituals.

1992
University of Virginia
Alpha Phi Alpha
Pledging-related automobile accident
Gregory Batipps, an Alpha Phi Alpha pledge, had slept little or not at all for the four days prior to his fatal auto accident. The university refused a *Washington Times* reporter's request that it discuss the link between hazing and the death. Albemarle County Commonwealth Attorney James L. Camblos III called the death accidental.

1993
Auburn University (Alabama)
Phi Delta Theta
Alcohol-related death following bottle exchange
Chad Saucier, who was a pledge even though he was not an Auburn University student, died following the chapter's traditional bottle exchange.

1993
Alcorn State University (Mississippi)
Alpha Phi Omega (banned chapter)
Claimed prank
At first a group of fraternity pledges said they were stealing a nearly worthless chair because a member had asked them to do so. Then they said they had taken it on their own, to play a prank on members. Whatever their story, they could not change the fact that pledge Leslie Ware, 18, was shot and killed by the boyfriend of the woman who owned the chair as Ware and his pledge brothers tried to take it at about one A.M. on a school night.

1993
Mississippi State University
Pi Kappa Alpha
Roof death
Stanford W. "Wes" Smythe, 20, fell sometime in the night and died on the concrete patio of the Pi Kappa Alpha house. He had either been on the roof or was on the ladder and had been leaving or coming to the roof.

1993
Cornell University (New York)
Sigma Alpha Mu
Chimney death
The body of Terrence Ward Quinn, 21, was found wedged into the chimney of a rival fraternity, Psi Upsilon. Quinn, an honors student praised by friends for his sense of humor, was a senior from Malden, Massachusetts. He had once been refused admission to a Psi Upsilon party because he had been drinking. Police and school authorities did not determine with certainty his reason for climbing into the chimney.

1993
University of Kentucky
Kappa Sigma and Sigma Pi
Alcohol-related vehicle accident
A drunken Gregory Cooney, 19, died in a car accident after attending two University of Kentucky parties.

1993
Brandeis University
Zeta Beta Tau
Automobile accident (high speed a possible factor)
Zeta Beta Tau pledge Jeremy Abcug, 19, of Morris Plains, New Jersey, was killed in a car accident. His death was ruled accidental and was not pledging-related.

1993
Rider College (New Jersey)
Phi Beta Sigma
Shooting death
A fraternity party ended with the death of Bernard McBride, 21. A high school student was charged with murder. Although alcohol was not allowed at the party at the Student Center, many people consumed beer in the parking lot.

1994
University of Colorado
Vehicular horseplay after a fraternity party
Amanda MacDonald of Portola Valley, California, died in a vehicle accident while "surfing" atop a Toyota 4-Runner after drinking at a fraternity party. Darrell Gschwendtner, 19, crashed the Toyota while she was surfing; he was convicted of drunk driving and now speaks at alcohol-awareness seminars (occasionally with Amanda's father) as part of his sentencing.

1994
Johnson & Wales University (Rhode Island)
Tau Kappa Epsilon
Criminal alcohol-related accident
Five members of Tau Kappa Epsilon were flung from a speeding automobile during a night of barhopping while they were on spring break in Florida. The dead were Aaron B. Ebbert, 24, of Amherst, New Hampshire; James J. Smith, 23, of Lindenhurst, New York; and Peter D. Scott, 22, of West Islip, New York. The injured were Darren Moll, 22, of Farmington, New York; and the driver, Mark S. Sterner, 22, of Quakertown, Pennsylvania. Sterner pleaded guilty to three DUI counts and served three years in a Florida prison.

1994
University of Oklahoma
Phi Kappa Psi
Accidental death during a celebration
Members celebrating a house accomplishment were giving a fraternity cheer near their house when they shook a flagpole—a house ritual that members spontaneously took part in on occasion. The pole snapped, and a large piece struck and killed member Jason Henry Wittrock, 20. Alcohol was not a factor, and hazing was not involved.

1994
Bloomsburg University (Pennsylvania)
Delta Chi
Alcohol poisoning
Terry Linn, 21, a member who drank a great deal of alcohol at a pledge Hell Night, died. His blood-alcohol level was 0.40.

1994
Bloomsburg University (Pennsylvania)
Beta Sigma Delta
Fire
Five Beta Sigma Delta fraternity brothers perished when their off-campus house burned down.

1994
University of Pittsburgh
Delta Sigma Phi
Alcohol-related death
Atif Bhatti, a pre-med honors student, drank a considerable amount of beer and sixteen shots while celebrating his twenty-first birthday with Delta Sigma Phi brothers off campus in November 1994. He subsequently died.

1994
Southeast Missouri State
Kappa Alpha Psi
Physical hazing death
Fraternity "candidate for initiation" Michael Davis died after the Kappa chapter had put pledges through an ordeal on an athletic field, making them run to seven locations known as stations. The members pummeled the pledges and struck their bare feet with a cane like the kind used in the fraternity's step dances. They also hurt the pledges in other ways. Members beat Davis mercilessly. He never regained consciousness.

1994
Carnegie-Mellon University (Pennsylvania)
Pi Lambda Phi
Alcohol-related death at house party
Former Carnegie-Mellon University student Justin Chambers, 19, died of alcohol poisoning. While attending a party with fellow members at his former fraternity house, he drank about a fifth and a half of whiskey. His blood-alcohol level was 0.54 when he died. Paramedics had visited the house before Justin died to treat another student who had hurt himself in a fall. They saw Justin lying on a couch but assumed he was sleeping.

1994
University of North Carolina
Chi Psi
Alcohol-related shooting accident
Christopher Todd Stewart, 20, died of a gunshot wound to the chest while he and another partygoer were playing with a loaded semi-automatic pistol. Stewart's blood-alcohol content was twice the legal limit when he died.

1995
University of Texas
Texas Cowboys
Alcohol-related drowning death
Gabriel "Gabe" Higgins drowned in the Colorado River after participating in initiation drinking games.

1995
University of North Carolina
Fraternity party
Fall following fraternity party/bar drinking
A young woman died in a fall after she drank heavily at a fraternity house and off-campus bar. Jamie Cyndra McGee, 18, from Wilmington, North Carolina, fell from a ladder outside the Phillips Hall Annex building. She and a male friend were trying to get onto a roof. Her blood-alcohol level was 0.19 at the time of her death.

1995
Wittenberg University (Ohio)
Phi Gamma Delta
Alcohol-related automobile accident following party
Driver David Creager, 19, and passenger Eric Devine, 20, were drunk when they got into David's Honda Accord to go buy more alcohol. The two perished when the car hit a tree at sixty-seven miles per hour. The *Dayton Daily News* cited a source that said David was in possession of false ID, and that the two had attended a Phi Gamma Delta party earlier that night.[6]

1995
University of Nebraska
Lambda Chi Alpha
Alcohol-related wreck
John Miller, 19, a member of Lambda Chi Alpha, was a passenger killed in the crash of a Mazda driven by a high school friend. Police blamed the accident on alcohol and high speed.

1995
Lehigh University (Pennsylvania)
Lambda Chi Alpha
Heroin overdose
Bradley Taylor died at his father's house after snorting heroin with a boyhood friend, a non–fraternity member. A fraternity brother admitted that he had seen Taylor using cocaine at the house.

1995
Northern Illinois University
Sigma Chi
Alcohol-related automobile accident
Michael G. Simkins, 19, of Wheaton, Illinois, was killed when he was thrown from a car that had rolled over. The driver of the vehicle and three other passengers survived the wreck, sustaining numerous injuries. They were headed to an unauthorized pledging activity that was being held at an off-campus park. The driver had been drinking.

1995
University of North Carolina, Chapel Hill
Phi Gamma Delta
Fire after a party
Five students perished in the Phi Gamma Delta house during a tragic fire. Four had been drinking heavily—perhaps enough to have affected their chances of getting out safely. Joanna Howell, one of the students who died,

had not been drinking. The four were Mark Strickland, Ben Woodruff, Josh Weaver, and Anne Smith. Several other fraternity members and guests were injured.

1995
University of Iowa
Lambda Chi Alpha
Alcohol-related death
Michael Garofalo choked to death in his sleep at the Lambda Chi Alpha house. His blood-alcohol level was 0.19 when he died, and a coroner estimated that it may have reached as high as 0.30.

1995
Lafayette College (Pennsylvania)
Kappa Delta Rho
Suicide
Brian Scott Arena, 20, of Staatsburg, New York, hanged himself on campus.

1995
University of Iowa
Tau Kappa Epsilon
Suicide
Bradley Swanson, 21, from Rockford, Illinois, died of a self-inflicted gunshot wound in the fraternity house. Swanson was the president of Tau Kappa Epsilon.

1996
Tulane University (Louisiana)
Pi Kappa Alpha
Vehicle accident
A 20-year-old pledge in a Jeep Cherokee accidentally killed Sgt. Gilbert Mast, a Tulane campus police officer, shortly before dawn. The student admitted that he had gone barhopping as part of a fraternity-sponsored event but said he had not been drinking.

1996
University of New Hampshire
Acacia
Roof death
Todd Cruikshank, 18, was intoxicated (his blood-alcohol level was 0.18) when he fell to his death from the house roof on August 30.

1996
Elmhurst College (Illinois)
Fraternity party
Vehicle accident
Jon Partipilo, 21, and Ryan Schrader, 20, were killed in an auto accident on their way back from a fraternity party. A third youth was injured. The car, which was traveling at high speed, took out a street light and utility pole.

1996
Frostburg State University (Maryland)
Kappa Beta Zeta
Alcohol-related death
John Eric Stinner, 20, died after drinking to excess at a party at a sub-rosa fraternity. His blood-alcohol level was 0.34 percent at the time of his death. After plea bargaining, penalties for eight young men involved in the death were reduced to community service and fines.

1996
University of South Florida
Alpha Delta Pi
Suicide
A series of setbacks apparently caused Brenda D. Goben, 23, to jump from the roof of the Tampa International Airport parking garage. Goben had quarreled with a boyfriend and had lost her bid to become the sorority chapter president.

1996
Bowdoin College (Maine)
Chi Delta Phi, Alpha Kappa Sigma
Roof death
A visitor fell to his death during a party while attempting to get onto the roof of the Chi Delta Phi house. The college closed two houses that were believed to have served alcohol to Cameron Brett, 20, a University of Maine sophomore.

1996
Oregon State University
Pi Kappa Phi
Alcohol-related accident
Pledge Matthew Krull died in an automobile accident after consuming alcohol at a fraternity party. Two men who had given alcohol to minors were fined and given jail sentences, one of thirty days and one of four months. The driver of the van carrying Matthew and others had not been drinking, but he had yanked the wheel to startle the occupants.

1996
Louisiana Tech University
Delta Chi and Delta Kappa Epsilon
Shooting during prank
John Lars Elfervig of Delta Chi died after he was shot in the head by an irate member of Delta Kappa Epsilon. Elfervig and two friends were pilfering DKE wooden letters as a prank.

1996
University of Virginia
Pi Kappa Phi
Alcohol-related fatality
A chapter member from Billings, Montana, died in a car accident after leaving a rush function held away from campus in a mountain cabin. Brian N.

Cook, 21, chairman of the rush event, died of head injuries. Driver John Duncan, chapter vice president, was charged with driving under the influence of alcohol.

1996
Radford University (Virginia)
Chi Phi and Pi Kappa Phi
Alcohol-related death

Valerie Cole, 18, died of alcohol poisoning in the early morning hours after drinking heavily at two fraternity parties. At the time of her death, her blood-alcohol content was 0.31, according to a medical examiner. The university and national fraternities suspended both chapters for serving a person under 21 years of age and for possessing kegs, which was a violation of university policy.

1996
Radford University (Virginia)
Delta Tau Chi
Alcohol-related death in house fire

A house used by Delta Tau Chi, a fraternity that was not recognized by the university, burned in the night. Christopher Mirch, 21, died in the fire. His high blood-alcohol content may have impeded his ability to respond to the emergency.

1996
Ohio Wesleyan University
Phi Delta Theta
House fire

Casey William Polatsek, 20, died in a house fire. His blood-alcohol level was slightly over the legal limit and may have hampered his efforts to escape.

1997
Virginia Polytechnic Institute and State University
Fraternity party
Alcohol-related accident

Virginia Polytechnic student Matthew West, 18, and Jonathan Levy, 20, died in a car crash shortly after drinking beer from a keg spout. They were headed to a party that was being given by West's fraternity. A Radford professor who was in an oncoming car was also killed in the accident. West's blood-alcohol level was eight times the state limit for his age.

1997
Bloomsburg University (Pennsylvania)
Delta Pi
Fall behind house

Matthew Miller climbed a fence behind the Delta Pi fraternity house, falling ninety feet to his death.

1997
Texas A&M
Phi Gamma Delta
Asthma attack*
A Brazos County grand jury decided that no charges should be brought against members of the Phi Gamma Delta chapter who had sprayed a pledge with water on a chilly January day. William "Trey" Walker died of an asthma attack six hours after being soaked. Phi Gamma Delta received a two-year suspension for hazing. Nonetheless, members of the fraternity house denied allegations that hazing had led to Walker's death. Walker was cleaning and redecorating the house at the time of his death, and members insisted that dust and paint fumes, not hazing, led to his demise.[7]

1997
UCLA
Lambda Chi Alpha
Accidental drowning
Pledge Brian Toshio Sanders, 19, and Brian Pearce, 22, drowned during a fraternity outing at Lake Mead. Alcohol was present.

1997
Lehigh University (Pennsylvania)
Phi Gamma Delta
Suicide
Edward Tyler Morris, 21, died of asphyxiation after hanging himself.

1997
Indiana University of Pennsylvania
Alpha Chi Rho
Alcohol-related suicide following shooting
A tragedy took place at a fraternity in which there were at least eight guns. Tim Foreman, 21, came home from a night of drinking and used a nine-millimeter pistol to shoot at a wall silhouette. The bullet went through the wall, seriously wounding a fraternity brother. Tim, horrified, then used the weapon to kill himself.

1997
Purdue University
Sigma Phi Epsilon
Fall while sleepwalking
Nathan Frank, 20, a student who had a problem with sleepwalking, died in a fall from his third-floor bedroom window. Although Nathan had been drinking, his grief-stricken father said that his son had been sleepwalking all his life.

1997
North Carolina State
Tau Kappa Epsilon
Drowning following initiation
Steven Velazquez, 19, of Goldsboro, died when he and other TKE members dove into a lake for a semitraditional swim following the initiation of

pledges. Steven's absence was not noted until all the rest had returned to the fraternity house. The death was ruled an accidental drowning. Hazing was not a factor, police said, although the fraternity member who called 911 said they had been "roughing around" when Steven disappeared.

1997
Hartwick College (New York)
Alpha Delta Omega
Alcohol-related drowning

Chapter president Rob Jordan, 22, and many of his fraternity brothers had been in the process of drinking up to a half-gallon of liquor each at an annual party when Jordan fell into a river and drowned.

1997
Louisiana State University
Sigma Alpha Epsilon
Pledging-related alcohol poisoning

Benjamin Wynne, 20, died just after midnight on August 26. He had been celebrating his bid as a fraternity pledge. His blood-alcohol level was nearly six times the legal limit at the time of his death. Three other students were also taken from the SAE house and hospitalized.

1997
Clarkson University (New York)
Theta Chi
Alcohol-related hazing death

The object of the Theta Chi "bid night" was to get the twenty-one pledges sick and drunk. Members provided at least twenty bottles of an alcoholic concoction made from scotch, whiskey, bourbon, vodka, and schnapps. "The members and the other pledges cheered when a pledge got sick," Brian Simmon, a pledge, told the *Watertown Daily Times*. "When it was over, we jumped around and hugged people."[8] The next morning members found the lifeless body of Binaya "Bini" Oja, 17, with his head next to a garbage pail.

1997
Washington and Lee University (Virginia)
Beta Theta Pi
Fall

Freshman John Joseph "Jack" Bowden of Darien, Connecticut, suffered fatal head injuries after falling from his dormitory window while wearing only undershorts.

1997
Massachusetts Institute of Technology
Phi Gamma Delta
Pledging activity involving alcohol

Scott Krueger, 18, of Orchard Park, New York, went into a coma and died after a pledge event at which he ingested enough alcohol to raise his blood-alcohol level to 0.410. His case gained national attention when prosecutors took the unusual step of filing charges against the chapter instead of against Phi Gam members; they ended up dropping the case when no members from the chapter or from fraternity headquarters showed up. Educator Michael Gordon, a longtime opponent of hazing, blasted the decision to prosecute a defunct organization, believing it sent a message that culpable individuals can go unpunished.[9]

1998
University of Washington
Delta Kappa Epsilon
Suicide

A suicide occurred at the University of Washington during the 1997–1998 academic year, according to John Rhoades, University of Washington Interfraternity Council executive director. While Rhoades said he could not determine specifically why John Laduca, 18, a newly initiated member of Delta Kappa Epsilon, killed himself, Laduca had endured stress from hazing and had been deprived of sleep the previous semester. "The experience could have contributed to a diminished mental capacity," Rhoades said.[10] Laduca also was experiencing problems with a girlfriend and was said to be severely depressed when he killed himself in the fraternity house, according to Rhoades.

1998
University of Washington
Zeta Psi
Suicide

Drew Robinson, a Zeta Psi member who lived outside the house, committed suicide by hanging himself with a rope. University of Washington Interfraternity Council executive director John Rhoades said the death appeared to be unrelated to fraternity activities. However, he said he could not rule out the possibility that press coverage of a suicide by another Greek member weeks earlier could have been a factor, if Robinson was a suggestible person.

1998
Virginia Polytechnic and State University
Delta Gamma
Fall, slashed wrists

First-year student and pledge Paige Payne Miller, 19, slashed her wrists, then fell to her death from a high perch in the Virginia Polytechnic football stadium.

1998
University of the Philippines
Alpha Phi Beta
Physical hazing

The death of pledge Alexander Miguel Icasiano, 19, is being looked into by authorities following allegations that he had been subjected to a brutal hazing.

1998
Southwestern University (Texas)
Pi Kappa Alpha
Drowning
George Rocha, 21, drowned in the San Gabriel River at 3 A.M. after jumping from a cliff in a local park. He was fully dressed. He was a legislative aide at the Texas capitol and was well liked by fraternity members and capitol staff.

1998
Rollins University (Florida)
Tau Kappa Epsilon
Alcohol- and drug-related death
Jennifer Kairis died after a fraternity party. She had a large amount of prescription drugs in her system and was legally intoxicated.

1998
University of Michigan
Phi Delta Theta and Chi Omega
Fall
Courtney Cantor died when she fell out of her dormitory window after drinking a small amount of alcohol that had been given to her by the fraternity. Cantor's blood-alcohol level of .059 was below the Michigan standard for intoxication, and her father, who said he was aware that his underage daughter occasionally drank alcohol, put the blame on window placement instead of on the fraternity and sorority. "These are not bad kids. These are not kids that I have any great depth of hatred for," George Cantor told the *Detroit News*. "What they did was wrong. At the same time, I recognize that this goes on in every (Greek) house on every campus across the United States."[11] An autopsy later turned up a trace of a date-rape drug in Courtney's system.

1998
Rutgers University (New Jersey)
Theta Chi
Alcohol-related house fall
After drinking at an off-campus tavern, Jason Greco, 20, died of head injuries following a fall down the basement steps of his fraternity house.

1998
Murray State University (Kentucky)
Rugby club
Hazing and fire
After Michael Minger, 19, died in a fire in Hester Hall, local authorities found evidence of rugby hazing that had taken place that night.[12] A parent of one accused young man admitted that hazing had kept the rookies awake all night, but denied that hazing had anything to do with the blaze.

1998
University of Mississippi
Sigma Chi
Suicide
Dudley R. Moore IV died after hanging himself. Investigators said he had been despondent prior to his death. They found he had also recently been hazed as part of his gaining admission to the fraternity. "Students join fraternities and sororities . . . seeking friendship—brotherhood and sisterhood, a family away from home," said Debra G. Bonaminio, a former Ole Miss staff member. "[But] Dudley feared [some members]. The fraternity house was not a home or refuge for him—it was a place to avoid. If Dudley Moore did come with emotional baggage, and if he was troubled, the very individuals who should have been there to help him through the rough times drove him away."[13] The family of the dead youth "indicated" to the Memphis *Commercial Appeal* that they did not fault the fraternity chapter for Moore's death. "Is Sigma Chi solely to blame? Probably not," said Bonaminio.

1998
University of Texas
Phi Kappa Sigma
Alcohol-related death
Jack L. Ivey Jr., a 23-year-old member, died off campus after drinking heavily. At the time of his death, his blood-alcohol level was 0.40.

1998
Indiana University
Pi Kappa Alpha
Alcohol-related death
Joseph Bisanz, 19, suffocated to death when he inhaled his own vomit after a night of drinking. According to the coroner, the amount he drank would not have been enough to cause his death under other circumstances.

1998
University of South Florida
Phi Beta Sigma
Murder
James E. Walker, 21, was found murdered in his car.

1998
College of New Jersey
Theta Chi
Shooting death
Jamal Lane, a nonstudent, was shot during an illegal keg party while trying to pursue robbers armed with a rifle.

1998
University of Arkansas, Pine Bluff
Omega Psi Phi
Shooting deaths
Charles Gilbert, 20, and Gabriel Walker, 20, died during a shooting incident at a fraternity-sponsored party.

1998
University of Michigan
Zeta Psi
Substance-related death
A member died at a friend's home in an incident away from his fraternity. The fraternity issued a statement stressing that the death of Christopher Giacherio was unrelated to the chapter, and that it regularly holds educational programs on substance abuse.

1998
Delta Zeta
Ferris State University
Alcohol poisoning of guest
Allan Montero Hewer, a 24-year-old nonstudent, had been drinking heavily the night he entered a sorority house where a party was in progress. He passed out and died in his sleep with a blood-alcohol level of 0.40. Hewer's family did not blame the sorority, saying that he had been an alcoholic for many years.

1999
University of Missouri, Rolla
Pi Kappa Alpha
Fire death
Jered Adams, 21, a resident of the Pi Kappa Alpha fraternity house, died of smoke inhalation in an early-morning fire.

1999
Southwest Texas State University
Tau Kappa Epsilon
Alcohol-related manslaughter
A pledge who had passed out after drinking in the TKE house was slammed in the head with a weapon. The blow killed him. The dead youth was Nicholas George Armstrong, 21, a pledge who had been drinking. The assailant, a former student at the school, killed himself after police impounded his van for examination of physical evidence.

1999
University of Pennsylvania
Phi Gamma Delta
Fall
Michael E. Tobin, 26, a Penn alum, fractured his skull and died while drunk at a fraternity house party.

APPENDIX B

Where to Find Help and Information

1. Perhaps the most comprehensive look at what is happening in the United States with regard to alcohol education is the Education Center for Alcohol and Other Drug Prevention:

55 Chapel Street
Newton, MA 02158-1060
(800) 676-1730
E-mail: HigherEdCtr@edc.org
http://www.edc.org/hec

2. The Center for All-Collegiate Information provides links to a wide variety of collegiate information sources, including many anti–substance abuse organizations:

http://www.collegiate.net/infof.html

3. Parents: Consider joining the College Parents of America. In addition to providing many valuable tips on saving for college, the organization is now educating parents on alcohol and substance abuse on campus.

College Parents of America
700 Thirteenth Street, N.W., Suite 950
Washington, D.C. 20005
http://www.collegeparents.org/

4. Keep up to date on alcohol research by visiting the web site of the Project Cork Institute at Dartmouth Medical School. In addition to the other health-care services it offers, the institute has a terrific online database that makes available substance-abuse information and teaching materials.

http://www.dartmouth.edu/~cork/

5. Check out the Core Institute, a federally funded program that provides up-to-date information that will be useful for institutions of higher educa-

tion that are developing drug-and-alcohol-prevention programs. For particulars, see:

http://www.siu.edu/~coreinst/

6. Keep informed about young people's drinking by visiting the Harvard School of Public Health's College Alcohol Study:

http://www.hsph.harvard.edu/cas/

7. Get a worldwide perspective on drug- and alcohol-related deaths from the International Council on Alcohol, Drugs, and Traffic Safety (ICADTS), a nonprofit organization that puts on valuable conferences and shares information provided by concerned professionals in a variety of fields:

http://raru.adelaide.edu.au/icadts/

8. The National Institute on Alcohol Abuse and Alcoholism (NIAAA) supports and helps fund biomedical and behavioral research on alcoholism and alcohol-related problems. NIAAA also provides valuable educational information and direction to institutions attempting to combat these problems.

National Institute on Alcohol Abuse and Alcoholism (NIAAA)
6000 Executive Boulevard, Willco Building
Bethesda, MD 20892-7003
http://www.niaaa.nih.gov/

9. The Robert Wood Johnson Foundation is dedicated to, among other things, funding programs that "reduce the personal, social and economic harm caused by substance abuse—tobacco, alcohol, and illicit drugs."

The Robert Wood Johnson Foundation
P.O. Box 2316
Princeton, NJ 08543-2316
http://www.rwjf.org/main.html

10. Keep up with hazing and alcohol-related problems reported each day on the Hazing e-mail list. To join the hazing list, which provides information on hazing for educators, journalists, and organization leaders, type the words "subscribe Hazing" (without quotation marks) to:

LISTSERV@LISTSERV.IUPUI.EDU

Note: The author is co-owner of this free e-mail list. He receives no payment for his services.

11. College students, both Greeks and non-Greeks, who consider themselves campus leaders can participate in COOL, a national organization dedicated to ridding America's colleges of alcohol and drug problems.

COOL
1101 15th Street, NW, Suite 203
Washington, D.C. 20005
http://www.ncl.org/anr/partners/cool.htm

12. The BACCHUS and GAMMA Peer Education Network describes itself as "an international association of college and university based peer education programs focusing on alcohol abuse prevention and other related student health and safety issues." The organization combats peer pressure by substituting peer-run education and wellness programs, among other activities.

The BACCHUS & GAMMA Peer Education Network
P.O. Box 100430
Denver, Colorado 80250-0430
(303) 871-0901
http://www.bacchusgamma.org/

13. The Substance Abuse and Mental Health Services Association (SAMSA) tracks alcohol information and makes databases available to the public, in addition to providing many other valuable services in drug and alcohol education:

http://www.health.org/

14. The Center for Science in the Public Interest "Alcohol Policies Project" is a nonprofit education and advocacy organization that, among other concerns, educates the public on alcohol. In particular, it provides up-to-date information on alcohol studies and news articles concerning alcohol advertising:

http://www.cspinet.org/booze/index.html

15. For a comprehensive list of both private and government-sector sources from which to obtain alcohol and drug information, check out the Education Center for Alcohol and Other Drug Prevention's updated list of web sites:

http://www2.edc.org/hec/track/list.asp

16. To contact the Committee to Halt Useless College Killings (CHUCK), write:

Eileen Stevens
P.O. Box 188
Sayville, NY 11782

Enclose a stamped, self-addressed envelope for reply. Stevens has retired from speaking but still expresses her opinion on hazing issues.

17. To contact the Cease Hazing Activities and Deaths (CHAD) organization, write:

Rita Saucier
P.O. Box 850955
Mobile, AL 36685

Enclose a stamped, self-addressed envelope for reply.

18. "Alcohol 101," a CD-ROM program developed by William L. Riley and Janet S. Reis of the University of Illinois to help young people make responsible choices about alcohol, is available from the NIC, the NPC, and the Bacchus & Gamma Peer Education Network. Alcohol 101 is free to colleges and universities. Funding was provided by the Century Council, an organization of U.S. distillers. The Century Council can be reached at:

http://www.centurycouncil.org

19. The Multi-Jurisdictional Task Force (MJTF) is a group of concerned students, educators, parents, and colleges that supports anti-hazing legislation and activism. The MJTF has members in New Hampshire, Vermont, Georgia, Massachusetts, and Ohio. You can visit its web site at:

http://www.stophazing.org/

Note: In February 1999, the author agreed to write a journalistic column on hazing for the stophazing.org web site. He will receive no compensation for his work.

20. The National Fraternity Conference (NIC), the national umbrella group of fraternities, sells videos on hazing and other topics to members and non-members alike (discounts are available for members only). Write the NIC for particulars:

3901 West 86th Street
Suite 390
Indianapolis, IN 46268

21. The National Panhellenic Conference (NPC) is the umbrella group of historically white sororities. To contact the NPC, write:

NPC
3901 West 86th Street, Suite 380
Indianapolis, IN 46268

22. The National Panhellenic Council (NPHC) is the umbrella group of affiliated African American fraternities and sororities. Write the NPHC at:

NPHC
Memorial Hall W108
Bloomington, IN 47405

23. Security on Campus tracks campus deaths and crimes and serves as an effective legislative lobbyist group to require colleges to divulge crime-related information and statistics. For information, write:

Connie and Howard Clery
Security on Campus, Inc.
215 West Church Road, Suite 200
King of Prussia, PA 19406-3207

24. The longest-running periodical devoted to a discussion of fast-moving changes in fraternal law and risk-management issues such as hazing and

alcohol misuse is *Fraternal Law*, published by the law firm of Manley, Burke, Lipton & Cook, 225 West Court Street, Cincinnati, Ohio 45202. For current subscription prices and back-issue information, phone (513) 721-5525. The firm publishes four issues annually.

25. The NIC functions as a resource for schools, fraternities, and sororities that wish to participate in Adopt-a-School, a program that puts college students into the classroom to form relationships with elementary school children that make a difference in the lives of both the helped and helper. For information, contact:

NIC
3901 W. 86th St., Suite 390
Indianapolis, IN 46268
(317) 872-1112

26. The Emory University Health Sciences Central Library maintains a web page with links to many valuable sources of information on alcohol and drug addiction:

http://www.gen.emory.edu/MEDWEB/alphakey/substance_dependence/a.html

27. Attorney Douglas Fierberg maintains a web site devoted to legal issues in hazing:

http://www.smcalaw.com/hazing/default.htm

28. Anti-hazing activist Alice Haben is interested in all issues related to hazing, but particularly in athletic hazing, high school hazing, and anti-hazing legislation at the state level, especially in Illinois. Contact Haben at:

P.O. Box 143
Oswego, IL 60543

NOTES

GLOSSARY

1. See Irving L. Janis, *Victims of Groupthink* (Boston: Houghton Mifflin, 1974).

I. THE TRADITION

1. Rita Saucier, letter to author, January 18, 1998.
2. Rita Saucier, telephone interview with author, June 7, 1998.
3. K. Scott Saucier, e-mail to author, May 1998.
4. Information on AU's fraternal programs and its publications was provided by Jim Hardin, AU assistant director of student life. Information on AU athletics was provided by David Housel, AU athletic director. Information on AU's definition of hazing was provided by Hardin, and by C. Grant Davis Jr. Davis also provided a great deal of information about AU hazing and alcohol-misuse prevention programs. I also refer to information on hazing in AU literature written by Deborah Shaw Conner, director of the AU Greek Affairs staff.
5. My knowledge of AU sports and its history comes in part from multiple visits I made to the campus as an *Inside Sports* magazine contributing writer before writing this book.
6. Information attributed to sociologist Richard Sigal comes from Sigal's letters to the author.
7. Joseph Dale Strada, deposition, April 12, 1995, in *K. Scott Saucier v. Phi Delta Theta*, Circuit Court of Mobile County, Alabama, CV-94-003060.
8. Rita Saucier, letter to author, January 18, 1998.
9. K. Scott Saucier, e-mail to author, May 1998.
10. Rita Saucier, telephone interview with author, December 10, 1997.
11. Noted in CV-94-003060-EBM.
12. Ibid.
13. This quotation is a paraphrase of Lambert's court testimony (CV-94-003060-EBM).
14. Testimony by Hays Waller and Timothy DeLong (CV-94-003060-EBM).

15. Noted in Strada deposition, CV-94-003060-EBM.

16. See court records, CV-94-003060-EBM.

17. See court records, CV-94-003060-EBM. See also the Auburn police department's written accounts of the evening, including accounts of witnesses.

18. Stories about the early days of Phi Delta Theta can be found in the following publications: Walter Benjamin Palmer, *History of the Phi Delta Theta Fraternity* (Menasha, Wis.: George Banta, 1906); Walter Havighurst, *From Six at First: A History of Phi Delta Theta, 1848–1973* (Menasha, Wis.: George Banta, 1975). I am indebted to the entire staff of the Special Collections Department, Miami of Ohio, for providing me with access to many documents and diaries pertaining to student life at Old Miami. I also learned a great deal about Old Miami by interviewing Charles T. Ball, a Phi Kappa Tau historian, and by reading his book *From Old Main to a New Century: A History of Phi Kappa Tau* (Phoenix, Ariz.: Heritage, 1996). See also Walter Havighurst, *The Miami Years, 1809–1984* (New York: Putnam's, 1984).

19. Strada deposition, CV-94-003060-EBM.

20. "Death stuns campus," *Mobile Register*, December 11, 1993.

21. Rita Saucier, telephone interview with author, December 10, 1997, and letter to author, January 18, 1998.

22. Rita Saucier, telephone interview with author, December 10, 1997.

23. Ibid.

24. K. Scott Saucier, e-mail to author, May 16, 1998.

25. Ibid.

26. Ibid.

27. Deposition by John H. Bowen III, June 20, 1995, CV-94-003060.

28. *Friendly Fire: Friends Hazing Friends* is an educational video available in a fraternity and a sorority version. To obtain a copy, write to the National Intrafraternity Conference, 3901 East 86th Street, Suite 390, Indianapolis, IN 46268. Those interviewed about hazing problems in the video include Conner, Lionel Tiger, Eileen Stevens, and the author of this book (who was not compensated for participating in the project).

29. A limited number of guides are available upon request to parents, educators, and interested parties. Although there is no charge for the guides, AU officials request that individuals send money to cover postage. Write to Jim Hardin, Auburn University Assistant Director of Student Life, 228 Foy Union, Auburn, AL 36849.

30. Deborah Shaw Conner, e-mail to author, January 31, 1999.

31. Then AU president James Martin to Robert Biggs, then Phi Delta Theta director of chapter services, October 30, 1986.

32. AU Committee on Fraternities and Sororities (an appointed advisory committee made up of faculty, staff, and students) to then AU president James Martin, quoted in Martin, letter to Biggs of Phi Delta Theta, October 30, 1986.

33. "Death stuns campus."

34. Rita Saucier, telephone interview with author, December 10, 1997.

35. Rita Saucier, letter to author, January 18, 1998.

36. I am grateful to Jim Hardin, AU assistant director of student life, for providing me with this and other AU publications.

37. "Loras settles students' lawsuit," *Des Moines Register*, January 2, 1999.

38. See Hank Nuwer, *Broken Pledges: The Deadly Rite of Hazing* (Atlanta, Ga.: Longstreet, 1990), p. 315.

39. Cantor was not intoxicated at the time of her fall. In addition to some alcohol, she had traces of gammahydroxbutyrate, a so-called "date rape" drug, in her system. "Charges near for U-M frat: They're accused of serving alcohol

to student who died," *The Detroit News,* January 13, 1999; "U-M fraternity shut down," *The Detroit News,* October 21, 1998.

40. Deborah Shaw Conner, e-mail to author, January 31, 1999.

2. GREEKTHINK

1. Tom F. Driver, *The Magic Ritual: Our Need for Liberating Rites That Transform Our Lives and Our Communities* (New York: HarperSanFrancisco, 1991). My own research in this area goes back to 1978, when I interviewed Yale University psychology professor Irving L. Janis; Nathan Azrin, director of research at Ann (Illinois) State Hospital's Behavior Research Laboratory; sociologist Milton Glenn Walker; University of San Diego counselor Robert Kavanaugh; and others. See Hank Nuwer, "Dead Souls of Hell Week," *Human Behavior* 7, no. 10 (October 1978), pp. 52–56.

2. Nuwer, "Dead Souls," pp. 53–56.

3. Two spirit-club deaths occurred at the University of Missouri, Rolla; one occurred at the University of Texas at Austin. The lacrosse-club death occurred at Western Illinois University (WIU). My interviews with members of the WIU lacrosse club came about in an unusual way. Illinois circuit court judge Larry Heiser's sentencing of twelve defendants for unlawful delivery of alcohol to a minor included an order that they contact me to tell the story behind the events that had led to the death of Nicholas Haben, age eighteen, of Oswego, New York. Judge Heiser did not consult me before issuing this order. I did, however, meet separately with him and with McDonough County state attorney William E. "Bill" Poncin, and I agreed to do the interviews with the understanding that I would make this disclosure here and in future books and articles I write about high school hazing, athletic hazing, military hazing, and hazing in international military and educational communities. For coverage of the sentencing, see wire and newspaper stories, for example: Stacey Creasy, "Students involved in WIU hazing death sentenced," *Macomb Journal,* December 20, 1992. For additional information on roof deaths, see Hank Nuwer, *Broken Pledges,* and Hank Nuwer, "Ivied Halls, Rooftop Falls," *Harper's Magazine* (November 1995), pp. 17–18.

4. For the source of this quotation and for a larger discussion of educators and the justice system, see Neil Postman, *The End of Education: Redefining the Value of School* (New York: Vintage), 1996.

5. Brian A. Bippus and Paul R. Rutowski, notice sent by e-mail to the Gallaudet University community at large. The two conceded that changing social values might signify a need for a change in attitudes toward paddling.

6. J. W. Thibaut and H. H. Kelley, *The Social Psychology of Groups* (New York: Wiley, 1959).

7. James A. Aho, *This Thing of Darkness: A Sociology of the Enemy* (Seattle: University of Washington Press, 1995).

8. Albert A. Harrison, *Individuals and Groups* (Monterey, Calif.: Brooks/ Cole, 1976), pp. 288 and 469.

9. Rosalind Miles, *Love, Sex, Death, and the Making of the Male* (New York: Summit Books, 1991), p. 138.

10. For widely varying points of view on group identity, see, for example, Erik H. Erikson, *Identity: Youth and Crisis* (New York: Norton, 1968); Peggy Reeves Sanday, *Fraternity Gang Rape* (New York: New York University Press, 1990); Tiger, *Men in Groups* (New York: Random House, 1969); Jules Henry, *Culture against Man* (New York: Vintage, 1965).

11. Robert Egan, *From Here to Fraternity* (Toronto and New York: Bantam, 1985).

12. James "Jim" Arnold, telephone interview with author, October 29, 1997.

13. "Annual Reports of the Intrafraternity Conference," p. 1. I gratefully acknowledge receiving a copy of the report from NIC headquarters, Indianapolis.

14. For observations on police in groups, see August Vollmer, *The Police* (Berkeley: University of California Press, 1936).

15. William Westley, *Violence and the Police* (Cambridge, Mass.: MIT Press, 1970).

16. Alvin Gouldner, *Patterns of Industrial Bureaucracy* (Glencoe, Ill.: Free Press, 1954).

17. For comparison with police recruits, see Paul Chevigny, *Police Power* (New York: Vintage, 1969).

18. C. Grant Davis, telephone interview with author, May 4, 1998.

19. Rita Saucier, telephone interview with author, May 4, 1998.

20. I gratefully acknowledge the receipt of a copy of this document from Julie Joynt.

21. Bill Smith, "Three Rolla students face charges in drinking death," *St. Louis Post-Dispatch*, October 26, 1991.

22. James C. Collins and Jerry I. Porras, *Built to Last: Successful Habits of Visionary Companies* (New York: HarperBusiness, 1997).

23. Margaret Thaler Singer with Janja Lalich, *Cults in Our Midst* (San Francisco: Jossey-Bass, 1995), p. 5.

24. The following nine characteristics were taken from Singer, *Cults in Our Midst*.

25. In addition to Singer, see also Kay Marie Porterfield, *Straight Talk about Cults* (New York: Facts on File, 1995), pp. 9–11.

26. In addition to Singer, see also Richard Sigal's comments in Nuwer, *Broken Pledges*, pp. 47–54.

27. Robert Jay Lifton, foreword to Singer, *Cults in Our Midst*, p. xii.

28. Singer, *Cults in Our Midst*.

29. Ibid., pp. xxi, 15–17.

30. Lionel Tiger made this observation about "moral qualms" when I interviewed him in 1990 for my book *Broken Pledges*.

31. Rupert Wilkinson, *The Broken Rebel: A Study in Culture, Politics, and Authoritarian Character* (New York: Harper and Row, 1972), p. 21.

32. Both incidents are taken from Helen Lefkowitz Horowitz, *Campus Life: Undergraduate Cultures from the End of the Eighteenth Century to the Present* (Chicago: University of Chicago Press, 1987).

33. My conclusions in this section are drawn from interviews with Janis and Kavanaugh in Nuwer, "Dead Souls."

34. Nuwer, "Dead Souls"; Harrison, *Individuals and Groups*, pp. 203, 236, 238, 239, 473–475; Janis, *Victims of Groupthink*.

35. See court records, Missouri Circuit Court, Twenty-second Judicial Circuit (St. Louis), *Edith and Boyd Davis v. Kappa Alpha Psi Fraternity, Inc., and others*.

36. Anne O'Reilly, "New stories dispute ATO accounts," *Indiana Daily Student*, February 10, 1992, pp. 1, 4.

37. See Singer, *Cults in Our Midst*; see also Hank Nuwer, "What Do We Do about Hazing?" *The Laurel of Phi Kappa Tau* (Spring 1991), pp. 7–9.

38. Singer, *Cults in Our Midst*, p. 62.

39. Jim Killackey, "UCO puts fraternity on probation," *The Daily Oklahoman*, May 6, 1998.

40. Jacques Barzun, *The American University: How It Runs, Where It Is Going* (New York: Harper and Row, 1968), p. 65.

41. See ibid., p. 65.

42. Driver, *Magic Ritual*, pp. 4, 46, 101, 115–116.

43. Ibid., pp. 155–160.

44. Michael Olmert, "Points of Origin," *Smithsonian* (September 1983), pp. 150–154.

45. Gary Schwartz and Don Merten, "Social Identity and Expressive Symbols: The Meaning of an Initiation Ritual," *American Anthropologist* 70 (1968), pp. 1117–1131.

46. Thomas A. Leemon, *The Rites of Passage in a Student Culture: A Study of the Dynamics of Tradition* (New York: Teachers College Press, 1972).

47. Singer, *Cults in Our Midst*.

48. For an extended treatment of the three stages, see Arnold Van Gennep, *The Rites of Passage*, trans. Monika B. Vizedom and Gabrielle L. Caffee (1908; reprint, Chicago: University of Chicago Press, 1960).

49. Keith P. Richardson, "Polliwogs and Shellbacks: An Analysis of the Equator Crossing Ritual," *Western Folklore* 26, no. 2 (April 1977), pp. 154–155.

50. Tiger, *Men in Groups*, pp. 143–155; Richardson, "Pollywogs and Shellbacks," pp. 154–159; Elliot Aronson and Judson Mills, "The Effects of Severity of Initiation on Liking for a Group," *Journal of Abnormal and Social Psychology* 59 (September 1959) pp. 177–181. Aronson and Mills failed to respond to phone and e-mail requests to be interviewed for this book. Lionel Tiger, telephone interview with author, January 29, 1999.

51. Aronson and Mills, "The Effect of Severity of Initiation."

3. ALCOHOL MISUSE

1. Henry Wechsler et al., "Changes in Binge Drinking and Related Problems among American College Students between 1993 and 1997," *Journal of American College Health* 47, no. 2 (September 1998), pp. 57–68. See also Henry Wechsler et al., "Binge Drinking: The Five/Four [Drink] Measure," *Journal of Studies on Alcohol* 59 (January 1998), pp. 122–124.

2. Esther Thorson, "The Impact of Greek Affiliation on the College Experience: Findings from Graduates of 1965, 1975, 1985 and 1994," Center for Advanced Social Research, University of Missouri–Columbia School of Journalism (Funded by the National Interfraternity Conference and the National Panhellenic Conference).

3. Arthur Stanwood Pier, *The Story of Harvard* (Boston: Little, Brown, 1913), pp. 128–129.

4. Van Gennep, *Rites of Passage*.

5. Pier, *Story of Harvard*, pp. 142–143.

6. Quoted in Pier, *Story of Harvard*, p. 124.

7. See extended treatment of Roosevelt's Harvard career in Edmund Morris, *The Rise of Theodore Roosevelt* (New York: Ballantine, 1988).

8. Wallace W. Everett, "Frank Norris in His Chapter," *Phi Gamma Delta* 52 (April 1930), pp. 561–566. See also Warren French, *Frank Norris* (New York: Twayne, 1962), pp. 19–24, 26–32.

9. French, *Frank Norris*, p. 19.

10. Ibid., p. 21.

11. Frederick Doyle Kershner Jr., "Hazing: A Throwback to the Middle Ages," Delta Tau Delta *Rainbow Magazine* (Summer 1977), pp. 3–42.

12. *New York Times*, June 11, 1933, sec. 2, p. 1:7.

13. "Student drinking in fraternities," *New York Times*, October 30, 1930, p. 24:5.

14. "Fraternity men resist dry bans," *New York Times*, November 30, 1930, p. 32:1.

15. Jack L. Anson and Robert F. Marchesani Jr., eds., *Baird's Manual of American College Fraternities* (Indianapolis: Baird's, 1991), p. VIII-26-27.

16. Nuwer, *Broken Pledges,* p. 295.

17. Ibid., p. 11.

18. "154th DKE Convention, Nassau, Bahamas: August 5–9, 1998," on Delta Kappa Epsilon web page:

http://dke.org/

19. In a 1998 letter addressed to the NIC and circulated to many or all national fraternities, Phi Delta Theta berated the fraternal umbrella group for allowing (in Phi Delta Theta's opinion) the AFA—nearly all of whose members held positions similar to Grant Davis's—to "overshadow" the work of NIC delegates by proposing procedures and policies that Phi Delt executives insisted ought to be left to representatives of fraternal national headquarters. Thanks in part to AFA and NPC input, the NIC had transformed itself from an essentially bureaucratic public-relations machine for national fraternities into a proactive organization stressing academics, brotherhood-building exercises, pledging reforms, positive social programming, and renewed emphasis on fraternal values. But Phi Delta Theta wanted the NIC to go back to being a trade group. In a shot aimed above the NIC's bow, M. Scott Mietchen, a Salt Lake City–based member at large of the Phi Delt General Council, said:

> We feel strongly that the NIC annual meeting has lost its focus over the past ten or more years. Phi Delta Theta is a charter member of the NIC but more often than not we believe the NIC is not meeting the needs of its member fraternities. . . . We believe the NIC should focus its attention on the needs and issues of its sixty-six member organizations and leave undergraduate and other miscellaneous programming to individual member fraternities. The NIC is our trade association and as such should sharply focus its annual meeting on the needs of our member groups. We feel that the annual meeting's affiliation with the AFA is no longer necessary, is unwise, and is not a valuable use of our time. . . .

Mietchen concluded:

> We believe the NIC is capable of taking a leadership role on such items as legal issues, federal and state legislative laws and regulations (constitutional rights, tax law, etc.), initiating, developing and coordinating media and public relations efforts, long range strategic planning, association governance issues and volunteer and board development. The NIC should also play a much more aggressive role in facilitating interaction with university presidents and senior student

affairs officials on issues concerning Greek life such as membership recruitment, housing, recognition and academic development.

20. Fraternity and sorority houses that are owned by colleges are easier to police than are privately owned Greek houses. At the latter, the loss of recognition and the suspension of parties are the main weapons administrators can use to enforce compliance with school and state statutes. Also, after Krueger saw the movie *Animal House*, some members asked him to drink enough beer, whiskey, and rum to put him in a coma from which he never awoke. Enforcement of state laws regarding drinking varies from college to college. Annual college disclosures of alcohol-related arrests on school property reveal that many schools place a low priority on arresting students who have broken state laws governing alcohol use.

21. For particulars on one police operation directed against underage drinking, see, for example, *The [Penn State] Digital Collegian*, September 16, 1997.

22. James "Jim" Arnold, "Alcohol and the Chosen Few: Organizational Reproduction in an Addictive System" (Ph.D. diss., Indiana University, 1995). See also Anne Wilson Schaef, *When Society Becomes an Addict* (San Francisco: Harper and Row, 1987), and James "Jim" Arnold and George D. Kuh, *Brotherhood and the Bottle: A Cultural Analysis of the Role of Alcohol in Fraternities* (Bloomington, Ind.: Center for the Study of the College Fraternity, 1992).

23. Arnold was not asked to violate his confidentiality agreement for the purposes of this book.

24. James "Jim" Arnold, telephone interview with author, October 29, 1997.

25. Ibid.

26. Ibid.

27. "Duke debating steps to erase party school image," *Atlanta Journal and Constitution*, October 18, 1994.

28. James "Jim" Arnold, telephone interview with author, October 29, 1997.

29. Rita Saucier, telephone interview with author, June 7, 1998.

30. "Greek Tragedies," *U.S. News and World Report* (April 29, 1996).

31. James "Jim" Arnold, telephone interview with author, October 29, 1997.

32. The quotation is from an interview with a fraternity member whose name was protected. Arnold, "Alcohol and the Chosen Few," p. 193.

33. James "Jim" Arnold, telephone interview with author, October 29, 1997.

34. Jonathan Brant, interview with author, January 6, 1998.

35. Ibid.

36. Michael P. Haines, "A Social Norms Approach to Preventing Binge Drinking at Colleges and Universities" (The Higher Education Center for Alcohol and Drug Prevention, 1996), funded by the U.S. Department of Education.

37. Cheryl A. Presley, Jeffrey R. Cashin, and Philip Meilman, *Journal of Studies on Alcohol* 59, no. 1 (January 1998), pp. 63–70.

38. Thorson, "Impact of Greek Affiliation."

39. Michael V. W. Gordon, conversation with author, Washington, D.C., October 6, 1998.

40. I was a University of Richmond professor when the incident described here occurred. One of the young pledges in the expelled Alpha chapter of Sigma Phi Epsilon was a student of mine. In my mass media class, about a week before the incident that sent pledges to an emergency room, we had discussed how organizations try to send home messages about alcohol and hazing. The student in my class was not one of those sent to the hospital, but he was disciplined by Sigma Phi Epsilon.

41. Michael Carlone, interview with author, Richmond, Virginia, May 23, 1997.

42. James "Jim" Arnold, interview with author, October 29, 1997.

43. "Colby drinking worries state," *Central [Waterville] Maine Morning Sentinel,* October 17, 1998, and November 8, 1998; Susan Young, "Experts clash on 'epidemic' of drinking," *Bangor Daily News,* October 23 and 24, 1998.

44. Richard Harris, statement to author, Muncie, Indiana, October 22, 1997.

45. James "Jim" Arnold, interview with author, October 29, 1997.

46. Robert Biggs, telephone interview with author, October 29, 1997.

47. Carl Jensen, "The Ten Best Censored Stories of 1993," in *Project Censored* (Rohnert Park, Calif.: Sonoma State University, 1994).

48. Zeoli's comments about the college disturbances of the late '90s recall what Lewis S. Feuer, author of *The Conflict of Generations* (New York: Basic Books, 1968), said about student uprisings. "Student movements are born of vague, undefined emotions which seek for some issue, some cause, in which to attach themselves," wrote Feuer. "A complex of urges—altruism, idealism, revolt, self-sacrifice, and self-destruction—searches the social order for a strategic avenue of expression . . . . If 'exploitation' is the master term for defining class conflict, then 'alienation' does similar service for the conflict of generations."

49. Brian Higgins, note to Gabriel "Gabe" Higgins, December 20, 1994.

50. Ruth Harten sent Gabriel "Gabe" Higgins's school documents, e-mail, official documents, and some letters to the author on October 7, 1997; author visit to the University of Texas, July 24, 1998.

51. Ruth Harten, interview with author, Pocatello, Idaho, October 19, 1997; Sherri L. Sanders, e-mail to author, June 28, 1998; "What cattle prod?" *[The University of Texas] Daily Texan,* September 17, 1976.

52. Texas state court records, sworn statement by John Welsh, May 12, 1995.

53. Ibid.

54. The Cowboys' initiation has been re-created using information contained in sworn statements made by Welsh, Cliff Condrey, Jacob DeLeon, Patrick Howard, Marc D. Sachs, Todd Kinsel, Todd D. Shapiro, and Sean Nimmo. Police record and notes (1995) were also consulted. For another interpretation of events, rconstructed from court records, see Mary Ann Roser, "Deadly games: Files shed light on UT's pledge's drowning," *Austin American-Statesman,* March 3, 1996. Roser's article said that Condrey twice showed "deception" after taking a lie-detector test. According to a statement he made to Roser, Condrey said that he told the truth. He blamed problems with the lie detector test on his nervousness.

55. Texas state court records, sworn statements by Sean Nimmo, May 11, 1995, and John Welsh, May 12, 1995.

56. Texas state court records, sworn statement by John Welsh, May 12, 1995.

57. Texas state court records, sworn statement by Sean Nimmo, May 11, 1995.

58. Ibid.

59. Bastrop County, Texas, Sheriff's Department Offense/Incident Reports, Case no. 95-3267, April 29, 1995–May 1, 1995.

60. James Morgan, statement to Cpl. Earl Pence, Bastrop County Sheriff's Department, April 29, 1995.

61. Cliff H. Condrey, statement to Cpl. Earl Pence, April 29, 1995.

62. Photographs of death scene and of Gabe's body supplied to author by

Ruth Harten. Medical examiner's report, Gabriel Higgins, PA-95-0202, Roberto Bayaroo, chief medical examiner, Travis County, Texas, May 2, 1995.

63. Texas state court records, sworn statement, May 16, 1995.

64. Ruth Harten, interview with author, October 19, 1997. Copy of Ruth Harten's unpublished diary of events following Gabriel "Gabe" Higgins's death given to author, October 7, 1997.

65. Texas state court records, sworn statement by Jacob DeLeon, May 16, 1995.

66. Ben Gose, "Efforts to End Fraternity Hazing Said to Have Largely Failed," *Chronicle of Higher Education* (April 18, 1997), A37.

67. Mary Ann Roser, "UT president says he's working to stop hazing," *Austin American-Statesman*, February 9, 1996.

68. Ruth Harten, interview with author, Pocatello, Idaho, October 19, 1997.

69. Sherri L. Sanders, e-mail to author, June 28, 1998.

70. Ruth Harten, letter to author, January 14, 1998.

4. A WEED IN THE GARDEN OF ACADEME

1. Frederic Henry Hedge, "University Reform," *Atlantic Monthly* (September 1866), pp. 296f. See also Kershner, "Hazing: A Throwback," pp. 3–42. I credit Kershner for giving me the idea to look for medieval university documents referring to hazing. For insights into humiliation practices, see William Ian Miller, *Humiliation and Other Essays on Honor, Social Discomfort, and Violence* (Ithaca, N.Y.: Cornell University Press, 1995).

2. Will Durant, *Caesar and Christ: A History of Roman Civilization and of Christianity from their Beginnings to A.D. 325.* (New York: Simon and Schuster, 1944), p. 488.

3. Augustine, *Confessions, Books I–XIII*, trans. F. J. Sheed (Indianapolis: Hackett, 1993). Sheed translated the term "Eversores" as "Overturners."

4. Ibid., pp. 37–38.

5. Miller, *Humiliation and Other Essays*, pp. 5–8.

6. Hastings Rashdall, *The Universities of Europe in the Middle Ages.* 2 vols., ed. F. M. Powicke and A. B. Emden (1895; reprint, Oxford: Oxford University Press, 1936). Rashdall describes the following tradition at Avignon: "The freshmen are to serve the seniors at table, not to stand between them and the fire in the hall, to give place to them on all occasions, not to sit at the (head) table in the hall, and not to call one another 'sir.'" In a note, Powicke and Emden speculate about the possible connection between Justinian's edict and the rise in medieval hazing that took place later.

7. Note that Sebastian, martyred for his faith, was said to have offered sympathy and understanding to Christians persecuted for their religious beliefs by the Roman conquerors; this is why he was named a patron saint of the anti-hazing society. To read the text of university statutes issued by medieval universities, consult Lynn Thorndike, *University Records and Life in the Middle Ages* (New York: Columbia University Press, 1944).

8. See Rashdall, *The Universities of Europe.* See also Nathan Schachner, *The Mediaeval Universities* (New York: Stokes, 1938); Joseph R. Strayer and Dana C. Munro, *The Middle Ages, 395–1500,* rev. ed. (New York: Appleton-Century-Crofts, 1959). And see Arthur Gray, *Cambridge University: An Episodical History* (Boston: Houghton Mifflin, 1927).

9. Robert F Seybolt, trans., *The Manuale Scholarium* (Cambridge, Mass.: Harvard University Press, 1921).

10. Schachner, *The Mediaeval Universities*, p. 315.

11. Erik H. Erikson, *Young Man Luther: A Study in Psychoanalysis and History* (New York: Norton, 1958); and Rupert Wilkinson, *The Broken Rebel*. See also Olmert, "Points of Origin," pp. 150–154.

12. Olmert, "Points of Origin," pp. 150–154. See also Thorndike, *University Records;* Rashdall, *The Universities of Europe;* Schachner, *The Mediaeval Universities;* and Gray, *Cambridge University.*

13. Olmert, "Points of Origin," pp. 150–154. See also Thorndike, *University Records;* Rashdall, *The Universities of Europe;* Schachner, *The Mediaeval Universities;* and Gray, *Cambridge University.*

14. An alternate explanation offered by scholars F. M. Powicke and A. B. Emden was that the biretta ceremony might have been inspired by the yellow-billed caps worn by new students. Rashdall, *The Universities of Europe*, notes on pp. 286–287.

15. Rashdall, *The Universities of Europe.*

16. Ibid.

17. Erikson, *Young Man Luther;* Wilkinson, *The Broken Rebel*. See also Olmert, pp. 150–154.

18. See the reference to Anthony Wood in Michael Olmert, "Points of Origin," *Smithsonian* (September 1983), p. 53.

19. Jan Morris, ed., *The Oxford Book of Oxford* (Oxford: Oxford University Press, 1978), pp. 23, 93, 116–119.

20. Rashdall, *The Universities of Europe;* Thorndike, *University Records.*

21. "Fags and Fagging," *The Cornhill Magazine* 1 (1896), pp. 237–245.

22. Samuel Eliot Morison, *Harvard College in the Seventeenth Century*, pts. 1 and 2 (Cambridge, Mass.: Harvard University Press, 1936), 1:82.

23. Morison, *Harvard College*, 1:83.

24. Ibid., 1:463.

25. Ibid.

26. Hedge, "University Reform," p. 296.

27. Morison, *Harvard College*, 1:458.

28. Morrison, *Harvard College*, 1:463.

29. Ibid.

30. Pier, *Story of Harvard*, pp. 74–75.

31. George Frederick Gundelfinger, *Ten Years at Yale* (Sewickley, Pa., 1915), pp. 95–101; Frederick Doyle Kershner Jr., "Report on Hazing, Pledging and Fraternity Education in the American Social Fraternity System" (Indianapolis: National Interfraternity Conference Task Force on Alternatives to Pledging, 1989).

32. Kershner, "Report on Hazing."

33. Pier, *Story of Harvard*, pp. 105–158.

34. Ibid., p. 105.

35. Muriel Beadle, *Where Has All the Ivy Gone* (Garden City, N.Y.: Doubleday, 1972), p. 390.

36. Pier, *Story of Harvard*, p. 215.

37. Ibid., pp. 123–124.

38. For example, at Wabash College in Indiana, sophomores standing at upper dormitory windows doused first-year students with pails of water, dunked them under a pump, or worked in pairs to knock them down, a practice called "turning" in the 1880s. On February 22 of each year, first- and second-year students clashed, fighting to gain possession of the rivals' class banner. In 1890 a brutal donnybrook took place at Wabash, which was an all-male college then, as it is today. See James Insley Osborne and Theodore Gre-

gory Gronert, *Wabash College: The First Hundred Years, 1832–1932* (Crawfordsville, Ind.: R. E. Banta, 1932).

39. Edward Hitchcock, *Reminiscences of Amherst College* (Northampton, Mass.: Bridgman and Childs, 1863), pp. 332–337. Tales of pranks played on new students were spread by students visiting other schools and by student publications that talked about pranks such as bed-sheet wetting in their columns. For a note on a hazing incident at Middlebury College that was similar to the one the deceased Torrance endured at Amherst College, see *[Yale] University Quarterly* (April 1860), p. 377.

40. Hitchcock, *Reminiscences*, pp. 332–337.

41. Kenneth E. Stuart, *[Cornell University] Alumni News*, September 1946, Letters to the Editor section.

42. I am indebted to Elaine Engst of Cornell University for providing me with the text of a letter that Kenneth E. Stuart, Class of 1897, wrote in September 1946 describing the event for a Cornell alumni publication. See also extensive *New York Times* coverage of the event and its aftermath. Also see Morris Bishop, *A History of Cornell* (Ithaca, N.Y.: Cornell University Press, 1962).

43. "Hair Cutting," *The Michigan Alumnus* 8 (May 1901), pp. 340–341.

44. "Hazers in knife affray," *New York Times*, March 8, 1905.

45. *Cleveland Plain Dealer*, October 3, 1984. Cited in C. H. Cramer, *Case Western Reserve* (Boston: Little, Brown, 1976), pp. 369–370.

46. Clifford S. Griffin, *The University of Kansas: A History* (Lawrence: University Press of Kansas, 1974).

47. Ibid.

48. I am indebted to Thomas Hayes, publisher of an Internet web page collecting Civil War letters published in newspapers, for permission to take a passage from a letter written by an "M. H." to the *North Bridgewater [Massachusetts] Gazette*, published on May 28, 1861.

49. Dana Priest, "Cohen 'disgusted' by hazing," *Washington Post*, February 1, 1997.

50. Richardson, "Polliwogs and Shellbacks," pp. 154–155.

51. Harry Miller Lydenberg, *Crossing the Line: Tales of the Ceremony during Four Centuries* (New York: New York Public Library Press, 1957), pp. 15, 173–181.

52. Douglas MacArthur, *Reminiscences* (New York: McGraw-Hill, 1964), pp. 24–25.

53. U.S. Congress Committee of the House of Representatives, *Testimony Taken by the Select Committee of the House of Representatives*. 56th Cong., 2nd. sess., 1901.

54. "Former cadets plead guilty in hazing death," *New York Times*, February 26, 1985; "Former A&M student files $25 million hazing suit," *Austin American-Statesman*, July 19, 1997.

55. Those desiring to read these articles can visit archives of the newspapers on the Internet.

56. Ronald L. Akers, *Deviant Behavior: A Social Learning Approach* (Belmont, Calif.: Wadsworth, 1985). pp. 97–98.

5. GREEK TRADITIONS AND TRAGEDIES

1. Wilbur J. Cash, *The Mind of the South* (Garden City, N.Y.: Doubleday Anchor, 1954), p. 51.

2. Ibid., p. 53.

3. Ibid., p. 52.

4. Mark. C. Carnes, *Secret Ritual and Manhood in Victorian America* (New Haven, Conn.: Yale University Press, 1989).

5. Horowitz, *Campus Life*, pp. 27–29.

6. Horowitz, *Campus Life*.

7. Havighurst, *The Miami Years*, p. 90.

8. Olliger Grenshaw, *General Lee's College: Rise and Fall of Washington and Lee University* (New York: Random House, 1969), p. 104.

9. Horowitz, *Campus Life*, pp. 30–31.

10. Havighurst, *The Miami Years*, pp. 85–94.

11. Osborne and Gronert, *Wabash College*, pp. 169–170.

12. Ball, *From Old Main to a New Century*.

13. Anson and Marchesani Jr., *Baird's Manual of American College Fraternities*.

14. Henry Nash Smith, *Virgin Land: The American West as Symbol and Myth* (Cambridge, Mass.: Harvard University Press, 1950).

15. Clyde A. Milner et al., *The Oxford History of the American West* (New York: Oxford University Press, 1994), pp. 771–802.

16. Ibid.

17. Sigma Chi calls this "the Constantine Chapter."

18. Joseph Snell, telephone interview with author.

19. Anne M. Butler, "Selling the Popular Myth," in *The Oxford History of the American West*, ed. Clyde A. Milner II, Carol A. O'Connor, and Martha A. Sandweiss (New York: Oxford University Press, 1994), p. 774.

20. Jerome Reel, historian of Pi Kappa Alpha (and a Clemson University administrator in Clemson, South Carolina), December 3, 1998, interview with author by phone.

21. Freeman H. Hart, *The History of Pi Kappa Alpha* (Richmond, Va.: Whittet, 1939).

22. Frederick Rudolph, *Curriculum: A History of the American Course of Study since 1636* (San Francisco: Jossey-Bass, 1993).

23. Griffin, *The University of Kansas*.

24. Ibid., pp. 642–643.

25. Griffin, *The University of Kansas*.

26. Bishop, *A History of Cornell*.

27. See issues of the *New York Times* for October 29–30, 1998, and November 2, 6, and 11, 1998, for coverage of the death.

28. Elvin Abeles, *The Student and the University* (New York: Parents' Magazine Press, 1969), p. 102.

29. Griffin, *The University of Kansas*, pp. 642–643.

30. Sororities also attracted undergraduates who became notable authors; these women include Joan Didion, Pearl Buck, Harper Lee, Rita Mae Brown, Maya Angelou, Gail Sheehy, and Sara Davidson. For the Williams reference see Miles, *Love, Sex, Death*, pp. 139–140.

31. I am grateful to Larry Lockridge Jr. for giving me permission to reprint a passage from his *Shade of the Raintree* (New York: Viking, 1994), pp. 98–99.

32. See, for example, the numerous Sigma Chi deaths noted in "Back from Hell," by Robert Butterwick; see also "All Honor to Their Names" and "With the Colors," *The Magazine of Sigma Chi* (February/March 1944), pp. 4–41.

33. "'No malice,' says father at hazing death inquest," *[Boston] Morning Globe*, March 24, 1956; "One-way ride," *Time* 67, no. 9 (February 27, 1956), p. 68.

34. Herbert J. Gans, *The War against the Poor* (New York: BasicBooks, 1995), pp. 1–17.

35. Wade Thompson, "My Crusade against the Fraternities," *The Nation* (September 26, 1959), p. 69.

36. In *Broken Pledges* I disclosed that I had been hazed and had hazed others in what was then a local college fraternity at the State University College of New York at Buffalo. I repeat that disclosure here. See also "Buffalo U. ordered by a court to let fraternities alone," *New York Times*, September 10, 1964.

37. "Youth in hazing chokes to death," *New York Times*, September 18, 1959.

38. See "Fraternity group again bans hazing," *New York Times*, November 26, 1960; "Fraternity ban by state upheld," *New York Times*, June 10, 1996.

39. From 1976 to 1980, eight Greek men (pledges or members) and Greek women died during pledging events, though not all the deaths were called hazing deaths by the schools where they occurred. One other male died while participating in a dangerous activity required by a college ROTC group.

40. Larry Colton, *Goat Brothers* (New York: Doubleday, 1993), pp. 38–40 and note at bottom of p. 451. I am grateful to Mr. Colton for taking time away from his own writing to talk to me by telephone in November 1998 about the initiation, which he recalls as "a bunch of crap."

41. Esther Wright, *Torn Togas: The Dark Side of Greek Life* (Minneapolis: Fairvew, 1996), p. 13.

42. *Baird's Manual*, I-27.

43. Kershner, "Report on Hazing." See also Kershner, "Hazing: A Throwback," pp. 3–54.

44. Frank Ruck, undated letter to author (circa December 1, 1996), with attached copy of his May 1997 speech, "Theta Xi: Recap of Closing Remarks to Chapter Values Session." I discussed the speech with Ruck at a Sigma Phi Epsilon training and informal session held in Dallas, Texas, in July 1998, a few days before Ruck's death.

45. Ibid.

46. Zachary Z. Tucker, e-mail to author, December 8, 1997.

6. SORORITIES

1. Loundas said that he regretted being unable to speak to me for the book, because Amanda Smith was filing a lawsuit.

2. "Phi Mu Fraternity," May 1994, Phi Mu Fraternity headquarters, Tucker, Georgia.

3. Information about Amanda Smith comes from an essay she wrote about her ordeal for me, at my request, in 1998; I then followed up on this information by interviewing her by telephone in 1998. I gratefully acknowledge her written contribution to the book. The Phi Mu headquarters did not follow up on a December 19, 1997, telephone call from me, during which I requested that the sorority's side of the Widener incident be included in the book; nor did the sorority provide information of any kind.

4. Judy Smith, telephone interviews with author, December 11, 1997, and December 14, 1997.

5. Amanda Smith essay.

6. Ibid.

7. Ibid.

8. Ibid.

9. Judy Smith, telephone interview, December 11, 1997.

10. Amanda Smith essay.

11. Ibid.

12. Mindy Stombler, "'Buddies' or 'Slutties': The Collective Sexual Reputation of Fraternity Little Sisters," *Gender and Society* 8, no. 3 (September 1994), pp. 31–33, 49–50.; Wright, *Torn Togas*, p. 3.

13. Henry Marcus Scagliola, M.D., to Craig J. Loundas, April 18, 1996; diagnoses of post-traumatic stress disorder and depression; Ann Lehwald, director, Renewal Counseling Center. Both letters courtesy of Amanda Smith and Judy Smith, in package of documents sent to the author.

14. Judy Smith, telephone interviews with author, December 11, 1997, and December 14, 1997.

15. Amanda Smith, telephone interview with author, December 1997.

16. Douglas Fierberg, e-mail to author, November 4, 1998.

17. Elizabeth R. Dailgiesh, *The History of Alpha Chi Omega, 1885–1948* (Menasha, Wis.: Alpha Chi Omega, 1948), p. 153.

18. Dailgiesh, *The History of Alpha Chi Omega*.

19. J. P. Scott, "The American College Sorority: Its Role in Class and Ethnic Endogamy," *American Sociological Review* 30 (1965), pp. 514–527.

20. Tiger, *Men in Groups*.

21. Gordon Atlas and Dean Morier, "The Sorority Rush Process: Self-Selection, Acceptance Criteria and the Effect of Rejection," *Journal of College Student Development* (September 1994), pp. 351–352.

22. Griffin, *The University of Kansas*, pp. 642–643.

23. Rita Mae Brown, *Rita Will* (New York: Bantam, 1997).

24. Marilyn Bullock, letter to author, March 31, 1998.

25. Harrison, *Individuals in Groups*, p. 288; Wright, *Torn Togas*, pp. 125–140.

26. Wright, *Torn Togas*.

27. Marilyn Bullock, letter to author, March 31, 1998.

28. Kit Lively, "North Carolina Court Lets Colleges Close Judicial Hearings," *The Chronicle of Higher Education* (February 27, 1998).

29. Mary Geraghty, "Rise in Hazing Incidents at Sororities Alarms Colleges," *Chronicle of Higher Education* (June 20, 1997).

30. Barb Alpert, "IU sorority, fraternity face hazing charges," *Indianapolis Star*, February 6, 1998.

7. THE LAW AND HAZING

1. Douglas Fierberg, personal interview with author, Muncie, Indiana, March 19, 1998.

2. Teresa Loser and Jessica Zimmerman, separate personal interviews with author, Greencastle, Indiana, February 27, 1998.

3. Teresa Loser, personal interview with author, Greencastle, Indiana, February 27, 1998.

4. Jessica Zimmerman, personal interview with author, Greencastle, Indiana, February 27, 1998.

5. Marilyn Bullock, letter to author, March 31, 1998.

6. Sarah H. McKinney, "Suspended Kappa says she is the real victim," letter published in *The DePauw Online*, February 24, 1998.

7. Nancy Hayes, telephone conversation with and letter to author, April 23, 1998. Mrs. Hayes was calling me, the author of a previous book about hazing, as a concerned parent. She provided information, she said, because she was certain that most parents lack a full understanding of today's hazing practices. She also provided some recent articles on hazing, which I gratefully acknowledge.

8. Teresa Loser, personal interview with author, Greencastle, Indiana, February 27, 1998.

9. Marilyn Bullock, letter to author, March 31, 1998.

10. Teresa Loser and Jessica Zimmerman, separate personal interviews with author, Greencastle, Indiana, February 27, 1998.

11. Robert G. Bottoms, letter to Friends of DePauw University, "Resolution of the Kappa Kappa Gamma Fraternity Proceedings," February 3, 1998.

12. Ibid.

13. Teresa Loser and Jessica Zimmerman, separate personal interviews with author, Greencastle, Indiana, February 27, 1998.

14. Chris Karamesines, conversation with author at Ball State University, Muncie, Indiana, March 19, 1998. I was teaching a class at Ball State as an adjunct professor at the time of the conversation.

15. Ruth Johnson, state representative, Minnesota, letter to author, December 17, 1997.

16. Nevada and Vermont had laws pending in May 1999. For the quotation, see Dave Curtin, "Push to outlaw hazing reaches Colorado," *The Denver Post*, March 15, 1998.

17. Harry Randles, "Archaic Legislation and the Learning Process," in *Controversies in Education*, ed. Dwight W. Allen and Jeffrey C. Hecht (Philadelphia: W. B. Saunders, 1974), pp. 110–111.

18. Molzer, as part of his court-ordered community service, met with me in May 1993 in Macomb, Illinois. He and most of the other defendants helped me reenact Haben's death and talked about what was on their minds at the time of the initiation. Molzer's quotation came to me in the form of an essay he wrote in the fall and early winter of 1993. I am grateful to the defendants, the attorneys for the defendants, the prosecuting attorney, the court, the probation department, and the family of Nicholas Haben for their cooperation.

19. Dale Haben and Alice Haben, personal interview with author conducted at their Illinois home over the course of several days in May 1993.

20. University of Missouri, Rolla, Public Relations Manager Andrew P. Careaga, to author, March 21, 1998.

21. A Maryland judge in 1998 dismissed felony assault charges against four of eleven members charged in this incident, saying the fact that the Kappa Alpha Psi pledges stuck around for beatings was evidence of their complicity in what was happening. Charges of assault against the other members, plus hazing and reckless endangerment charges, were still pending as this book went to press. "Assault charges dismissed in hazing," *The Des Moines Register*, June 12, 1998.

22. Rita Saucier, telephone interview with author, May 8, 1998.

23. Cindie Zimmerman, interview with author, Greencastle, Indiana, February 27, 1998; Chris Karamesines mentioned the diagnosis of post-traumatic stress during in-person and telephone conversations with me from February 25, 1998, through March 13, 1998.

24. Eileen Stevens, interview with author, October 24, 1998.

25. Ibid.

8. VIOLENCE IN HISTORICALLY AFRICAN AMERICAN GREEK GROUPS

1. I was on this panel, too. "Broken Pledges: Fraternities and Sororities at the Crossroads," a *Black Issues in Higher Education* videoconference held in Washington, D.C., on October 7, 1998, is available for sale as a video from *Black Issues in Higher Education*, 10520 Warwick Avenue, Suite B-8,

Fairfax, VA 22030-3136; (703) 385-2981. I was not paid for my participation.

2. Williams, letter to author, May 11, 1998.

3. Paula Giddings, *In Search of Sisterhood* (New York: William Morrow, 1998), pp. 8–9, 18, 243, 284.

4. Charlayne Hunter-Gault, *In My Place* (New York: Farrar Strauss Giroux, 1992), pp. 138, 146–150.

5. Giddings, *In Search of Sisterhood*, p. 284.

6. *The Richmond News Leader*, March 26, 1979.

7. United Press International, April 22, 1992.

8. Police report, Western Illinois University. (Wallace did not press charges.)

9. Giddings, *In Search of Sisterhood*, pp. 8–9, 18, 243, 284.

10. Ibid., p. 284.

11. "Broken Pledges."

12. Joseph Jeremy Snell, telephone interview with author, May 20, 1998.

13. Ibid.

14. Douglas Fierberg, personal interview with author, Muncie, Indiana, March 19, 1998.

15. Joseph Jeremy Snell, telephone interview with author, May 20, 1998.

16. Michael Gordon, conversation with author, Washington, D.C., October 7, 1998. He later stressed the same point in the *Black Issues in Higher Education* videoconference held that day.

17. Mrs. Edith Davis has begun an anti-hazing organization following the death of her son Michael. In a 1998 telephone interview, she told me that the trauma of the incident and some physical ailments have prevented her from doing as much with the organization as she had envisioned.

18. Allentown *[Pennsylvania] Morning Call*, April 11, 1993.

19. John Hoberman, *Darwin's Athletes* (Boston: Houghton Mifflin, 1997), p. 23.

20. Ibid.

21. Note: Whittaker was court-martialed and unjustly found guilty of staging a phony attack. Eventually he was vindicated, although not in his lifetime. John F. Marszalek Jr., "A Black Cadet at West Point," *American Heritage* 22, no. 5 (August 1971), pp. 30–37. See also Hoberman, *Darwin's Athletes*.

22. Erikka Bettis, e-mail to author, May 6, 1998.

23. Larry Bolles, e-mail to author, March 25, 1996.

24. Erikka Bettis, e-mail to author, May 6, 1998.

9. STRATEGIES: WHAT CAN BE DONE?

1. "Profiling Alcoholism: A Research Update," *Indiana University Medicine* (Winter 1998), p. 2.

2. Michael Carlone, interview with author, Richmond, Virginia, May 23, 1997.

3. Julie Joynt, telephone interview with author, December 11, 1997.

4. Larry Bolles, e-mail to author, March 25, 1996.

5. President's Leadership Group (Robert L. Carothers, Mary Sue Coleman, B. James Dawson, E. Gordon Gee, Charles A. Hines, Manuel T. Pacheco; advisers William DeLong and Catherine Meikle), "Recommendations for College and University Presidents on Alcohol and Other Drug Prevention" (The Higher Education Center for Alcohol and Other Drug Prevention, 1997), pp. 1–58.

6. Jacques L. Vauclain III, interview with author, Richmond, Virginia, May 23, 1997.

7. I am indebted to Miami of Ohio director of Greek affairs Brian Breittholz and to former Miami interfraternity council officer Mark Fiddes for giving me a copy of "The Miami Model for Excellence," a report published by the Miami University Greek Community Commission, June 10, 1996. Fiddes, letter to the author, November 18, 1996.

8. I am indebted to Roger Harrold of the University of Minnesota for supplying copies of the 1986 and 1996 "Greek Experience Survey." Readers wishing additional information may contact Harrold at the University of Minnesota or by sending him e-mail at <Harrold@umn.edu>.

9. Joseph L. Tolson, e-mail to author, April 27, 1998.

10. Julie Joynt, telephone interview with author, December 11, 1997.

11. Charles Eberly, message to discussion group on the Hazing Information for Journalists and Educators <HAZING@LISTSERV.IUPUI.EDU> e-mail list, September 30, 1998. Permission to quote was kindly given by Eberly. James Brown of Indiana University–Purdue University, Indianapolis, and I operate the site. Readers who wish to subscribe to the free list should write SUBSCRIBE HAZING in the body of an e-mail message and send it to the following address: LISTSERV@LISTSERV.IUPUI.EDU

12. "Gettysburg College Simulates Alcohol Deaths," *Chronicle of Higher Education* (November 28, 1997).

13. Peggy Reeves Sanday, *Fraternity Gang Rape*, pp. 113–117.

14. Quotation taken from interview with fraternity member whose name was protected in Arnold, "Alcohol and the Chosen Few," p. 192.

15. James B. Twitchell, *Adcult USA* (New York: Columbia University Press, 1996), pp. 21–23.

16. Dr. Kershner stressed his point to me during a dinner interview in Zionsville, Indiana, while I was conducting research for my book *Broken Pledges*.

17. Deborah Paul, "Join the Club," *Indianapolis Monthly* (January 1998), pp. 10–14.

18. "Animal house," *New York Daily News*, January 22, 1993; Deborah Paul, "Join the Club."

19. I spoke, without a fee, to the Zeta Beta Tau brothers of Indiana University as part of their rehabilitation on November 7, 1998, at the request of Michael V. W. Gordon.

20. Barzun, *American University*, p. 72.

21. I was an unpaid adviser on the Alfred University survey and appreciated the university's invitation to participate in the project.

22. James "Jim" Arnold, telephone interview with author, May 11, 1998.

23. Maisie Ballou, letter to author, February 14, 1998.

24. Rita Saucier, telephone interview with author, June 7, 1998.

25. In support of her charge that the book was destroyed, Julie Joynt supplied a copy of a letter documenting the action taken by the police. The letter, from Det./Sgt. R. C. Resh, administrative supervisor, Combined County Criminal Investigation Unit of the Maryland State Police, said that the "pledge book seized as evidence during the death of John B. Joynt" was destroyed "due to the obscene content" on September 28, 1993. Det./Sgt. Resh said, "I regret that this may have caused you distress."

26. Henry Wechsler et al. "Changes in Binge Drinking and Related Problems among College Students between 1993 and 1997," *Journal of American College Health* 47, no. 2 (September 1998), pp. 57–68.

27. Ron Fosnaugh, interview with author, May 5, 1998. Fosnaugh was also helpful in explaining matters of evidence and other campus police questions during 1997 and 1998 conversations with the author.

28. Julie Joynt, interview with author, December 11, 1970.

29. *Sanford Ray Ballou, respondent, v. Sigma Nu General Fraternity and Maurice Littlefield, defendants,* of whom Sigma Nu is the appellant, no. 0824, Court of Appeals, South Carolina. Heard October 13, 1986; decided December 1, 1986.

30. Maisie Ballou, letter to author, February 14, 1998.

APPENDIX A: A CHRONOLOGY OF DEATHS

1. Letter quoted in Bishop, *A History of Cornell.*

2. Rep. Bob Livingston, R-Louisiana, was a member of this chapter as an undergraduate until he graduated in 1968. Livingston was named honorary president of Delta Kappa Epsilon's international fraternity on August 8, 1998.

3. Ned Scharff, "District student at Penn dies after frat hazing," *Washington Star,* April 26, 1977.

4. I served as an expert witness for the plaintiff in this case, before proposing this book to the publisher. The case was settled by both parties in 1993 without a trial, and the results of the settlement were not revealed to me. My fee was fifty dollars per hour, and I billed for twenty-nine and a half hours, which included travel to New York City. Since then I have declined all requests to serve as an expert witness in cases involving hazing; nor will I serve in this capacity again in the future.

5. Rian Sanders, letter to author, sent on March 2, 1993. Sanders was one of twelve defendants ordered to speak to me, as a hazing expert, by Judge Larry Heiser of the Circuit Court of the Ninth Judicial District, McDonough County, Illinois.

6. "Wittenberg students killed in wreck, drunk," *Dayton Daily News,* September 5, 1995.

7. "No action in death probe," *Houston Chronicle,* February 15, 1997.

8. "Frat brothers charged in death," *Watertown [New York] Daily Times,* February 13, 1997.

9. Michael Gordon, conversation with author, Bloomington, Indiana, November 8, 1998.

10. Rhoades is not a University of Washington employee, though he works with Greeks.

11. "U-M fraternity shut down," *Detroit News,* October 21, 1998.

12. "Seven cleared in dorm fire," *[Louisville] Courier-Journal,* January 12, 1998.

13. Debra G. Bonaminio, e-mail to author, October 28, 1998; "Ole Miss reveals little about pledge's suicide," *[Memphis] Commercial Appeal,* October 31, 1998.

WORKS CITED

Abeles, Elvin. *The Student and the University*. New York: Parents' Magazine Press, 1969.

"Age Law: A Survey of College Administrators and Security Chiefs." Washington, D.C.: U.S. Department of Education (Higher Education Center for Alcohol and Other Drug Prevention), 1995.

Aho, James A. *This Thing of Darkness: A Sociology of the Enemy*. Seattle: University of Washington Press, 1995.

Akers, Ronald L. *Deviant Behavior: A Social Learning Approach*. Belmont, Calif.: Wadsworth, 1985.

Allen, Dwight W., and Jeffrey C. Hecht. *Controversies in Higher Education*. Philadelphia: W. B. Saunders, 1974.

Alterman, A. I., et al. "Heavy Drinking and Its Correlates in Young Men." *Addictive Behaviors* 15, no. 1 (1990), pp. 95–103.

Anson, Jack L., and Robert F. Marchesani Jr., eds. *Baird's Manual of American College Fraternities*. Indianapolis: Baird's, 1991.

Arnold, James. "Alcohol and the Chosen Few: Organizational Reproduction in an Addictive System." Ph.D. diss., Indiana University, 1995.

Arnold, James, and George D. Kuh. *Brotherhood and the Bottle: A Cultural Analysis of the Role of Alcohol in Fraternities*. Bloomington, Ind.: Center for the Study of the Fraternity, 1992.

Aronson, Elliott, and Judson Mills. "The Effect of Severity of Initiation on Liking for a Group." *Journal of Abnormal and Social Psychology* 59 (September 1959), pp. 177–181.

Atlas, Gordon, and Dean Morier. "The Sorority Rush Process: Self-Selection, Acceptance Criteria and the Effect of Rejection." *Journal of College Student Development* (September 1994), pp. 346–353.

Augustine. *Confessions*, Books I-XIII. Trans. F. J. Sheed. Indianapolis: Hackett, 1993.

Baer, J. S., and M. M. Carney. "Biases in the Perception of the Consequences of Alcohol Use among College Students." *Journal of Studies on Alcohol* 54, no. 1 (January 1993), pp. 54–60.

Baer, J. S., et al. "High Risk Drinking across the Transition from High School to College." *Alcoholism: Clinical and Experimental Research* 19, no. 1 (February 1995), pp. 54–61.

Ball, Charles T. *From Old Main to a New Century: A History of Phi Kappa Tau.* Phoenix, Ariz.: Heritage, 1996.

Bandura, Albert. *Social Learning Theory.* Englewood Cliffs, N.J.: Prentice Hall, 1977.

Bandura, Albert, et al. "Transmission of Aggression through Imitation of Aggressive Models." *Journal of Abnormal and Social Psychology* 63 (1961), pp. 575–582.

Barnard, Eunice Fuller. "The College Fraternity Faces a Rival." *New York Times Magazine* (February 17, 1935), pp. 11–18.

Barzun, Jacques. *The American University: How It Runs, Where It Is Going.* Chicago: University of Chicago Press, 1993.

Beadle, Muriel. *Where Has All the Ivy Gone.* Garden City, N.Y.: Doubleday, 1972.

Beery, George S. "Relationship of the College Administration with Fraternities and Sororities." *Educational and Psychological Measurement* (pt. 2) 7, no. 3 (1947), pp. 594–602.

Bettelheim, Bruno. "Individual and Mass Behavior in Extreme Situations." *Journal of Abnormal and Social Psychology* 38 (1943), pp. 417–452.

———. *The Informed Heart.* United Kingdom: Penguin, 1988.

Bishop, Morris. *A History of Cornell.* Ithaca, N.Y.: Cornell University Press, 1962.

Bloch, H. A., and A. Niederhoffer. *The Gang: A Study in Adolescent Behavior.* New York: Philosophical Library, 1958.

Bogardus, E. S. "The Fraternity as a Primary Group." *Sociology and Sociological Research* 24 (May/June 1940), pp. 456–460.

Boroff, David. "Showdown on Fraternity Row." *New York Times Magazine* (November 11, 1962), pp. 32–33, 148.

Brown, Rita Mae. *Rita Will.* New York: Bantam, 1997.

Butler, Anne M. "Selling the Popular Myth." In *The Oxford History of The American West,* ed. Clyde A Milner II, Carol A. O'Connor, and Martha A. Sandweiss. New York: Oxford University Press, 1994.

Carlone, Michael V., Juli N. Finnell, and David S. Anderson. "The Balanced Man Project: An Evaluation Report Prepared by The Center for the Advancement of Public Health (George Mason University)." Final Report: Grant Award No. P183B45000, March 28, 1997.

Carnes, Mark. C. *Secret Ritual and Manhood in Victorian America.* New Haven, Conn.: Yale University Press, 1989.

Cash, Wilbur J. *The Mind of the South.* Garden City, N.Y.: Doubleday Anchor, 1941.

Cashin, Jeff R., et al. "Alcohol Use in the Greek System: Follow the Leader?" *Journal of Studies on Alcohol* 59, no. 1 (January 1998), pp. 63–70.

Chevigny, Paul. *Police Power.* New York: Vintage, 1969.

Clark, Thomas Arkle. *The Fraternity and the College.* Menasha, Wis.: George Banta, 1931.

Collins, James C., and Jerry I. Porras. *Built to Last: Successful Habits of Visionary Companies.* New York: HarperBusiness, 1997.

Colton, Larry. *Goat Brothers,* New York: Doubleday, 1993.

Cramer, C. H. *Western Reserve: A History of the University, 1826–1976.* Boston: Little, Brown, and Company, 1976.

Cronbach, Lee J. "Stereotypes and College Sororities." *Journal of Higher Education* 15 (April 1944), pp. 214–216.

Dailgiesh, Elizabeth R. *The History of Alpha Chi Omega, 1885–1948.* Menasha, Wis.: Alpha Chi Omega, 1948.

Driver, Tom F. *The Magic Ritual: Our Need for Liberating Rites That Transform Our Lives and Our Communities.* New York: HarperSanFrancisco, 1991.

Durant, Will. *Caesar and Christ: A History of Roman Civilization and of Christianity from their Beginnings to* A.D. *325.* New York: Simon and Schuster, 1944.

Durkheim, Emile. *The Division of Labor in Society.* Trans. George Simpson. Glencoe, Ill.: The Free Press, 1933.

Egan, Robert. *From Here to Fraternity.* Toronto and New York: Bantam, 1985.

Erikson, Erik H. *Identity: Youth and Crisis.* New York: Norton, 1968.

———. *Young Man Luther: A Study in Psychoanalysis and History.* New York: Norton, 1958.

Everett, Wallace W. "Frank Norris in His Chapter." *Phi Gamma Delta* 52 (April 1930), pp. 561–566.

"Fags and Fagging." *The Cornhill Magazine* 1 (1896), pp. 237–245.

Ferruolo, Stephen C. *The Origins of the University: The Schools of Paris and Their Critics, 1100–1215.* Stanford, Calif.: Stanford University Press, 1985.

Festa, Roger R. "The Entropy Trap: Resistance, Self-Esteem, and the Integrity of Greek Systems." *The Fraternity Newsletter* 18, no. 5 (April 1991), pp. 1, 6–7.

Feuer, Lewis S. *The Conflict of Generations.* New York: Basic Books, 1968.

French, Warren. *Frank Norris.* New York: Twayne, 1962.

Friedenberg, Edgar Z. *Coming of Age in America: Growth and Acquiescence.* New York: Vintage, 1965.

Furedi, Frank. *Culture of Fear.* London: Cassell, 1997.

Gans, Herbert J. *The War against the Poor.* New York: BasicBooks, 1995.

Garofalo, Robert, et al. "The Association between Health Risk Behaviors and Sexual Orientation among a School-Based Sample of Adolescents." *Pediatrics* 101 (1998), pp. 895–902.

Geller, E. S., et al. "Beer Versus Mixed-Drink Consumption at Fraternity Parties: A Time and Place for Low-Alcohol Alternatives." *Journal of Studies on Alcohol* 52, no. 3 (May 1991), pp. 197–204.

Geller, E. S., et al. "Estimating Alcohol Impairment in the Field: Implications for Drunken Driving." *Journal of Studies on Alcohol* 47, no. 3 (May 1986), pp. 237–240.

Giddings, Paula. *In Search of Sisterhood.* New York: William Morrow, 1988.

Gordon, Milton M. *Human Nature, Class, and Ethnicity.* New York: Oxford University Press, 1978.

Gouldner, Alvin. *Patterns of Industrial Bureaucracy.* Glencoe, Ill.: Free Press, 1954.

Gray, Arthur. *Cambridge University: An Episodical History.* Boston: Houghton Mifflin, 1927.

Grenshaw, Olliger. *General Lee's College: Rise and Fall of Washington and Lee University.* New York: Random House, 1969.

Griffin, Clifford S. *The University of Kansas: A History.* Lawrence: The University Press of Kansas, 1974.

Gundelfinger, George Frederick. *Ten Years at Yale.* Sewickley, Pa., 1915.

Haines, Michael, and A. F. Spear. "Changing the Perception of the Norm: A Strategy to Decrease Binge Drinking among College Students." *Journal of American College Health* 45 (1996), pp. 134–140.

Harrington, Grant, et al. "Difference in Alcohol Use and Alcohol-Related Problems among Fraternity and Sorority Members." *Drug and Alcohol Dependency* 47, no. 3 (September 25, 1997), pp. 237–246.

Harrison, Albert A. *Individuals and Groups.* Monterey, Calif.: Brooks/Cole, 1976.

Harrold, Roger. "The Greek Experience: A Study of Fraternities and Sororities at the University of Minnesota." Center for the Study of the College Fraternity (Indiana University), September 1997.

Hart, Freeman H. *The History of Pi Kappa Alpha.* Richmond, Va.: Whittet, 1939.

Havighurst, Walter. *From Six at First: A History of Phi Delta Theta, 1848–1973.* Menasha, Wis.: George Banta, 1975.

———. *The Miami Years, 1809–1984.* New York: Putnam's, 1984.

Haworth-Hoeppner, S., et al. "The Quantity and Frequency of Drinking among Undergraduates at a Southern University." *The International Journal of Addictions* 24, no. 9 (September 1989), pp. 829–857.

Hedge, Frederic Henry. "University Reform." *Atlantic Monthly* (September 1866), pp. 296f.

Henry, Jules. *Culture against Man.* New York: Vintage, 1965.

Higham, John. "The Reorientation of American Culture in the 1890s." In *The Origins of Modern Consciousness,* ed. John Weiss, pp. 25–48. Detroit, Mich.: Wayne State University Press, 1965.

Hitchcock, Edward. *Reminiscences of Amherst College.* Northampton, Mass.: Bridgman and Childs, 1863.

Hoberman, John. *Darwin's Athletes.* New York: Houghton Mifflin, 1997.

Hopkins, James F. *The University of Kentucky.* Lexington: University of Kentucky Press, 1951.

Hornbuckle, Bruce D. *Death by Hazing.* Sigma Alpha Epsilon, 1981.

Horowitz, Helen Lefkowitz. *Campus Life: Undergraduate Cultures from the End of the Eighteenth Century to the Present.* Chicago: University of Chicago Press, 1987.

Hunter-Gault, Charlayne. *In My Place.* New York: Farrar Straus Giroux, 1992.

James, Henry. *Charles W. Eliot, President of Harvard University, 1869–1909.* Vol. 1. Boston: Houghton Mifflin, 1930.

Janis, Irving L. "Groupthink." *Psychology Today* 5, no. 6 (1971), pp. 43–46.

———. *Victims of Groupthink.* Boston: Houghton Mifflin, 1974.

Jensen, Carl. "The Ten Best Censored Stories of 1993." In *Project Censored.* Rohnert Park, Calif.: Sonoma State University, 1994.

Johnson, Clyde S. *Fraternities in Our Colleges.* New York: National Interfraternity Foundation, 1972.

Kershner, Frederick Doyle Jr. "Hazing: A Throwback to the Middle Ages." Delta Tau Delta *Rainbow Magazine* 140 (Summer 1977), pp. 3–42.

———. "Report on Hazing, Pledging and Fraternity Education in the American Social Fraternity System." Indianapolis: National Interfraternity Conference Task Force on Alternatives to Pledging, 1989.

Kimbrough, Walter Mark. "A Comparison of Involvement, Leadership Skills and Experiences for Black Students Based on Membership in a Black Greek-Lettered Organization and Institutional Type." Ph.D. diss., Georgia State University, 1996.

Kuh, George D., Ernest Pascarella, and Henry Wechsler. "The Questionable Value of Fraternities." *Chronicle of Higher Education* (April 19, 1996), p. A68.

Landre, Rick, Mike Miller, and Dee Porter. *Gangs: A Handbook for Community Awareness.* New York: Facts on File, 1997.

Latané, Bibb, and J. Rodin. "A Lady in Distress: Inhibiting Effects of Friends and Strangers on Bystander Intervention." *Journal of Experimental Social Psychology* 5 (1969), pp. 189–202.

Lee, Alfred McClung. *Fraternities without Brotherhood.* Boston: Beacon, 1955.

Leemon, Thomas A. *The Rites of Passage in a Student Culture: A Study of the Dynamics of Tradition.* New York: Teachers College Press, 1972.

Lehman, Harvey C. "Motivation: College Marks and the Fraternity Pledge." *Journal of Applied Psychology* 19 (February 1935), pp. 9–28.

Lively, Kit. "North Carolina Court Lets Colleges Close Judicial Hearings." *The Chronicle of Higher Education* (February 27, 1998).

Lockridge, Larry. *Shade of the Raintree*. New York: Viking, 1994.

Loeb, Paul Rogat. *Generation at the Crossroads*. New Brunswick, N.J.: Rutgers University Press, 1994.

Lydenberg, Harry Miller. *Crossing the Line: Tales of the Ceremony during Four Centuries*. New York: New York Public Library Press, 1957.

MacArthur, Douglas. *Reminiscences*. New York: McGraw-Hill, 1964.

Marszalek, John F. Jr. "A Black Cadet at West Point." *American Heritage* 22, no. 5 (August 1971), pp. 30–37.

McCabe, Donald, and William J. Bowers. "The Relationship between Student Cheating and College Fraternity or Sorority Membership." *NASPA* (National Association of Student Personnel Administrators) *Journal* 28 (1996), p. 33.

McCreery, Otis C., and George Fox Mott. "Seeing Fraternities in a Larger Frame." *Journal of Higher Education* 9 (June 1938), pp. 331–334.

"The Miami Model for Greek Excellence." Report of the Miami University Greek Community Commission, June 10, 1996.

Miles, Rosalind. *Love, Sex, Death, and the Making of the Male*. New York: Summit Books, 1991.

Miller, William Ian. *Humiliation and Other Essays on Honor, Social Discomfort, and Violence*. Ithaca, N.Y.: Cornell University Press, 1993.

Moore, Robert H. "On Initiation Rites and Power: Ralph Ellison Speaks at West Point." *Contemporary Literature* 15 (1974), pp. 165–186.

Morison, Samuel Eliot. *Harvard College in the Seventeenth Century*. Pts. 1 and 2. Cambridge, Mass.: Harvard University Press, 1936.

Morris, Edmund. *The Rise of Theodore Roosevelt*. New York: Ballantine, 1980.

Morris, Jan, ed. *The Oxford Book of Oxford*. Oxford: Oxford University Press, 1978.

Muelder, Hermann R. *Missionaries and Muckrakers*. Urbana: University of Illinois Press, 1984.

Newman, John Henry. *The Idea of a University*. New Haven, Conn.: Yale University Press, 1996.

Nuwer, Hank. *Broken Pledges: The Deadly Rite of Hazing*. Atlanta, Ga.: Longstreet, 1990.

———. "Dead Souls of Hell Week." *Human Behavior* 7, no. 10 (October 1978), pp. 50–56.

———. "Ivied Halls, Rooftop Falls." *Harper's Magazine* (November 1995), pp. 17–18.

———. "What Do We Do about Hazing?" *The Laurel of Phi Kappa Tau* (Spring 1991), pp. 7–8.

Nuwer, Hank, et al. "Norman Mailer." *Brushfire* (University of Nevada, Reno) 23, no. 1 (1973), pp. 6–20.

Olmert, Michael. "Points of Origin." *Smithsonian* (September 1983), pp. 150–154.

Osborne, James Insley, and Theodore Gregory Gronert. *Wabash College: The First Hundred Years, 1832–1932*. Crawfordsville, Ind.: R. E. Banta, 1932.

Palmer, Walter Benjamin. *History of the Phi Delta Theta Fraternity*. Menasha, Wis.: George Banta, 1906.

Paul, Deborah. "Join the Club." *Indianapolis Monthly* (January 1998), pp. 10–14.

Pier, Arthur Stanwood. *The Story of Harvard*. Boston: Little, Brown, 1913.

Porterfield, Kay Marie. *Straight Talk about Cults*. New York: Facts on File, 1995.

Postman, Neil. *The End of Education: Redefining the Value of School*. New York: Vintage, 1996.

Presley, Cheryl A., Jeffrey R. Cashin, and Philip Meilman. *Journal of Studies on Alcohol* 59, no. 1 (January 1998), pp. 63–70.

"Profiling Alcoholism: A Research Update." *Indiana University Medicine* (Winter 1998), pp. 2–6, 16.

Randles, Harry. "Archaic Legislation and the Learning Process." In *Controversies in Education*, ed. Dwight W. Allen and Jeffrey C. Hecht, pp. 110–117. Philadelphia: W. B. Saunders, 1974.

Rashdall, Hastings. *The Universities of Europe in the Middle Ages*. 2 vols. Ed. F. M. Powicke and A. B. Emden. 1895; reprint, Oxford: Oxford University Press, 1936.

Read, Orville H. *Challenge, Conflict and Change*. Fulton, Mo.: Delta Upsilon Fraternity. 1983.

Richardson, Keith P. "Polliwogs and Shellbacks: An Analysis of the Equator Crossing Ritual." *Western Folklore* 26, no. 2 (April 1977), pp. 154–155.

Ridgeway, James. *The Closed Corporation: American Universities in Crisis*. New York: Random House, 1968.

Ross, Edward Alsworth. *Social Control*. Cleveland, Ohio: The Press of Western Reserve University, 1969.

Rudolph, Frederick. *Curriculum: A History of the American Undergraduate Course of Study since 1636*. San Francisco: Jossey-Bass, 1993.

Sanday, Peggy Reeves. *Fraternity Gang Rape*. New York: New York University Press, 1990.

Schachner, Nathan. *The Mediaeval Universities*. New York: Stokes, 1938.

Schaef, Anne Wilson. *The Addictive Organization*. San Francisco: Harper and Row, 1988.

———. *When Society Becomes an Addict*. San Francisco: Harper and Row, 1987.

Schein, Edgar H. *Organizational Culture and Leadership*. San Francisco: Jossey-Bass, 1992.

———. *Organizational Psychology*. Englewood Cliffs, N.J.: Prentice-Hall, 1980.

Schwartz, Gary, and Don Merten. "Social Identity and Expressive Symbols: The Meaning of an Initiation Ritual." *American Anthropologist* 70 (1968), pp. 1117–1131.

Scott, J. P. "The American College Sorority: Its Role in Class and Ethnic Endogamy." *American Sociological Review* 30 (1965), pp. 514–527.

Singer, Margaret Thaler, with Janja Lalich. *Cults in Our Midst*. With a foreword by Robert Jay Lifton. San Francisco: Jossey-Bass, 1995.

Smeaton, G. L., et al. "College Students' Binge Drinking at a Beach-Front Destination during Spring Break." *Journal of American College Health* 46, no. 6 (May 1998), pp. 247–254.

Smith, Henry Nash. *Virgin Land: The American West as Symbol and Myth*. Cambridge, Mass.: Harvard University Press, 1950.

Stombler, Mindy. "'Buddies' or 'Slutties': The Collective Sexual Reputation of Fraternity Little Sisters." *Gender and Society* 8, no. 3 (September 1994), pp. 303–308.

Strayer, Joseph R., and Dana C. Munro. *The Middle Ages, 395–1500*. Rev. ed. New York: Appleton-Century-Crofts, 1959.

Svaan, John. "The Effect of Fraternity Hazing on College Socialization." Ph.D. diss., University of Texas, 1965.

Thibaut, J. W., and H. H. Kelley. *The Social Psychology of Groups*. New York: Wiley, 1959.

Thompson, Wade. "My Crusade against the Fraternities." *The Nation* (September 26, 1959), pp. 169–172.

Thorndike, Lynn. *University Records and Life in the Middle Ages.* New York: Columbia University Press, 1944.

Thorson, Esther. "The Impact of Greek Affiliation on the College Experience: Findings from Graduates of 1965, 1975, 1985 and 1994." Center for Advanced Social Research, University of Missouri–Columbia School of Journalism (Funded by the National Interfraternity Conference and the National Panhellenic Conference).

Tiger, Lionel. *Men in Groups.* New York: Random House, 1969.

Twitchell, James B. *Adcult USA.* New York: Columbia University Press, 1996.

Van Cleve, Charles Ligget. *The History of Phi Kappa Psi Fraternity, 1852–1902.* Philadelphia: Franklin, 1902.

Van Gennep, Arnold. *The Rites of Passage.* Trans. Monika B. Vizedom and Gabrielle L. Caffee. 1908; reprint, Chicago: University of Chicago Press, 1960.

Vollmer, August. *The Police.* Berkeley: University of California Press, 1936.

Walker, Milton Glenn. "Organizational Type, Rites of Incorporation, and Group Solidarity: A Study of Fraternity Hell Week." Ph.D. diss., University of Washington, 1967.

Wechsler, Henry. "Getting Serious about Eradicating Binge Drinking." *Chronicle of Higher Education* (November 20, 1998).

Wechsler, Henry, et al. "The Adverse Impact of Heavy Episodic Drinkers on Other College Students." *Journal of Studies of Alcohol* 56 (November 1995), pp. 628–634.

———. "Binge Drinking: The Five/Four [Drink] Measure." *Journal of Studies on Alcohol* 59 (January 1998), pp. 122–124.

———. "Binge Drinking among College Students: A Comparison of California with Other States." *Journal of American College Health* 45 (May 1997), pp. 273–277.

———. "Binge Drinking, Tobacco, and Illicit Drug Use and Involvement in College Athletics." *Journal of American College Health* 45 (March 1997), pp. 195–200.

———. "Changes in Binge Drinking and Related Problems among American College Students between 1993 and 1997." *Journal of American College Health* 47, no. 2 (September 1998), pp. 57–68.

———. "Community Solutions to Community Problems (Preventing Adolescent Alcohol Use)." *American Journal of Public Health* 86 (July 1996), pp. 923–924.

———. "Correlates of College Student Binge Drinking." *American Journal of Public Health* 85, no. 7 (July 1995), pp. 921–926.

———. "Fraternities, Sororities and Binge Drinking: Results from a National Study of American Colleges." *NASPA* (National Association of Student Personnel Administrators) *Journal* 33, no. 4, (1996).

———. "A Gender-Specific Measure of Binge Drinking among College Students." *American Journal of Public Health* 85, no. 7 (July 1995), pp. 982–985.

———. "Health and Behavioral Consequences of Binge Drinking in College: A National Survey of Students at 140 Campuses." *Journal of the American Medical Association* 272, no. 21 (1994), pp. 1672–1677.

———. "Predictors of Smoking among U.S. College Students." *American Journal of Public Health* 88, no. 1 (January 1998), pp. 104–107.

Werner, M. J., et al. "Problem Drinking among College Freshmen." *Journal of Adolescent Health* 13, no. 6 (September 1992), pp. 487–492.

Westley, William. *Violence and the Police*. Cambridge, Mass.: MIT Press, 1970.

Wilkinson, Rupert. *The Broken Rebel: A Study in Culture, Politics, and Authoritarian Character*. New York: Harper and Row, 1972.

Williams, John A. "Perceptions of the No-Pledge Policy for New Member Intake by Undergraduate Members of Predominantly Black Fraternities and Sororities." Center for the Study of Pan-Hellenic Issues, Tennessee State University, 1992.

Willis, Jim, with Albert Adelowo Okunade. *Reporting on Risks*. Westport, Conn.: Praeger, 1997.

Wolf, Naomi. *Promiscuities: The Secret Struggle for Womanhood*. New York: Random House, 1997.

Wright, Esther. *Torn Togas: The Dark Side of Greek Life*. Minneapolis: Fairview, 1996.

INDEX

academics and Greek life, 40, 55, 59–60, 124–125, 135, 146–147, 151, 177–178, 184, 218

activists, xi–xx, 13–14, 56, 59–60, 62, 68, 74–75, 89–90, 134–137, 160, 166–168, 195–196, 211, 217. *See also* individuals by name

African American Greek groups, xiv–xvi, xxi, xxiii, 34–35, 51, 63, 74, 129, 257, 264. *See also* National Pan-Hellenic Council

Aix, University of, 94

Akron, University of (Ohio), 17

Alabama, University of, 70, 117, 240

Alcoholic beverages, abuse and misuse of, xv–xviii, 7–13, 16, 20, 22–23, 24, 64–66, 72, 259–264, 265, 266, 267; reforms by fraternities, xii–xxiii, xxiv, xxvii, 3–4, 13–14, 24, 27–30, 63–65, 72, 74–75, 77; binge drinking, xiv, xx, xxiii–xxiv, 23–26, 57, 74; responsible drinking, 23, 63–66, 69–70, 72; underage drinking, 2, 18, 23, 61–68, 70, 77–78, 83–91, 256–259, 263, 267, 268, 270, 273; sold near colleges, 3–4, 58, 62, 70, 117, 133–134, 264–265; deaths related to alcohol, xvii, xviii, 15, 32, 60, 61, 76, 83–91, 247–261, 263–273; blood-alcohol level, 16, 76, 88, 247, 251, 253, 254, 257, 261, 263–268, 270, 273, 274; college response, xiv, 22–26, 61–69, 72, 73; rituals and drinking, 31–32,

51, 90, 259, 260–261, 264; surveys, 57–58, 72–73; laws, 59–60, 62

Alcorn State University (Miss.), 168, 186, 262

Alfred University (N.Y.), xi, xx, 8–9, 43, 61, 133, 134, 172, 195, 200, 212, 223, 247

Allegany County, N.Y., 173

Alpha Phi Omega (sub-rosa chapter), 186, 262

alumni, influence of, 5, 22–23, 27, 34, 35, 53, 58, 75, 109, 116–117, 184–185, 226–227, 274; prominent fraternity males: Neil Armstrong, 14; Lloyd Bentsen, 79; Dolph Briscoe, 79; Bill Cosby, 120; Walter Cronkite, 221; Roger Ebert, 14; William Faulkner, 59; Lou Gehrig, 14; Benjamin Harrison, 13–14; Benjamin Hooks, 182; Jesse Jackson, 182, 221; John Jakes, 125; Michael Jordan, 182, 221; Vernon Jordan, 162, 182; James Kilpatrick, 60, 120; David Letterman, 120; Ross Lockridge Jr., 125–127; Paul Newman, 221; Frank Norris, xviii, 58–60; Dan Quayle, 162; Theodore Roosevelt, 58, 62, 113; Booth Tarkington, 125; Mike Wallace, 221; Roy Wilkins, 182; Tennessee Williams, 125, 292*n*30; Thomas Wolfe, 125; prominent sorority females: Marian Anderson, 178; Maya Angelou, 178; Joyce